AFTER *THE HISTORY OF SEXUALITY*

SPEKTRUM: *Publications of the German Studies Association*

Series editor: David M. Luebke, University of Oregon

Published under the auspices of the German Studies Association, *Spektrum* offers current perspectives on culture, society, and political life in the German-speaking lands of central Europe—Austria, Switzerland, and the Federal Republic—from the late Middle Ages to the present day. Its titles and themes reflect the composition of the GSA and the work of its members within and across the disciplines to which they belong—literary criticism, history, cultural studies, political science, and anthropology.

After The History of Sexuality

German Genealogies With and Beyond Foucault

∾:∾

Edited by

SCOTT SPECTOR, HELMUT PUFF,
and DAGMAR HERZOG

Berghahn Books
New York • Oxford

Published in 2012 by

Berghahn Books

www.berghahnbooks.com

© 2012 Scott Spector, Helmut Puff, and Dagmar Herzog

Library of Congress Cataloging-in-Publication Data

After *the history of sexuality* : German genealogies with and beyond Foucault / edited by
Scott Spector, Helmut Puff, and Dagmar Herzog.
   p. cm.
   Includes bibliographical references and index.
   ISBN 978-0-85745-373-0 (hbk.) — ISBN 978-0-85745-937-4 (pbk.)
   1. Homosexuality—Germany—History—20th century. 2. Gay men—Germany—
History—20th century. 3. Lesbians—Germany—History—20th century. 4. Sex—
History—20th century. I. Spector, Scott, 1959– II. Puff, Helmut. III. Herzog, Dagmar,
1961–
   HQ76.3.G4A38 2012
   306.76'609430904—dc23

                                                                2011040620

British Library Cataloguing in Publication Data

A catalogue record for this book is available from the British Library

Printed in the United States on acid-free paper.

ISBN 978-0-85745-373-0 (hardback)
ISBN 978-0-85745-937-4 (paperbook)

~: CONTENTS :~

∽: FIGURES :∽

~:~

After *The History of Sexuality?*
Periodicities, Subjectivities, Ethics

SCOTT SPECTOR

> *Among the numerous effects the organization of this domain
> ["sexuality"] has undoubtedly had, one is that of having
> provided historians with a category so "self-evident" that they
> believe they can write a history of sexuality and its repression.*
> —Michel Foucault (1978)[1]

What comes after the history of sexuality? More a provocation than a
question, the title of this volume points to a growing body of historical
literature on sexuality in German-speaking lands that gets beyond a certain
impasse its editors and authors have recognized in previous historical work on
sexuality. In the same year that Foucault suggested that historians had engaged
the category of sexuality in an uncritically self-evident way, his landmark *La
volonté de savoir* (*Will to Knowledge*), published in French two years earlier,
appeared in English translation as *The History of Sexuality*, volume 1: *An Introduction*. That work made way for a historiography that would move beyond a
sociocultural history of sexual organization and regulation to one that would
take the historian's understanding of sexuality as one of its objects of analysis.
Yet, as frustrated readers may have noted early on, Foucault's volume offers
everything but a road map of how to embark on histories of sexuality "after"
this sociocultural historical model.[2] There remains hence the question of where
histories of sexuality are after the *History of Sexuality*, and particularly after its
decades-long reception by historians.

The notion entertained by each of the contributions in this collection is that,
in many very different ways, Foucault's intervention has governed the formation of questions in the field, as well as assumptions about how some of these
questions should be answered. On the one hand, some of his revolutionary
insights can be said to have ossified into dogmas or truisms within the field of

the history of sexuality. Yet, as the contributions in this anthology variously reveal, these very truisms can cover up further and very different insights into the history of sexuality that may be derived from a return to and reinterpretation of Foucault's richly complex work, or by turning to other theorists of sexuality in relation to his original work.

The irony of these developments is that Foucault, after Nietzsche, invoked "genealogy" as an alternative to "history" precisely to avoid the hardening of categories, the fetishization of origins, and the telos and presentism of what they each identified as conventional traps of most history writing in their respective centuries.[3] Many citing Foucault have agreed with his skepticism of origins even as they have sought the origins of paradigm shifts; the insights that words do not keep their meanings, desires point in no single direction, and ideas betray their logic have too often incited us to recover the continuous tracks from one set of conceptions to another.[4] The authors of this volume do not reject "history" as such any more than Foucault or Nietzsche did. Most cannot be said to be crusading against linear narrative as much as they are providing intensive archaeologies of particular relations at particular moments. Such work offers something vital to the ways of thinking opened up by the theoretical work of Foucault and others, and there is much more work along these lines to be done.

A second question raised by our title is, why *German* genealogies? Clearly, the state of the historiography of sexuality as introduced here is similar in recognizable ways to that of other Western European and North American histories of sexuality, as well as of those in other parts of the world. We do not intend to make a case for the German example as a unique instance. Yet Foucault's own treatment of the history of sexuality did at once privilege, and at the same time set aside, the particular case of the German cultural realm. The most discussed moment of the first volume of his *History* (and indeed of all three volumes) is surely the passage where the author seems to argue for a specific periodic shift from acts to identities (as the historiography most often has it). It is here that he almost casually declares an alarmingly precise birthdate of the medical category of the homosexual: "Westphal's famous article of 1870 on 'contrary sexual sensations' can stand as its date of birth."[5] But this category also had a specific place of birth, as its author and the journal in which it first appeared both hailed from Berlin.[6] That journal's editors held chairs in Zurich, Göttingen, Königsberg, and Berlin, later Munich and Vienna. From the start the Austrian presence in sexual science was central—not only, if not least due to the University of Vienna's role as host institution of the German-born Richard von Krafft-Ebing. The term "homosexual" was actually the coinage of another Habsburg subject, the sometime Hungarian Karl-Maria Benkert/Károly-Mária Kertbeny, whose influence on Krafft-Ebing came through the mediation of naturalist Gustav Jäger, a Swabian seated in a chair of zoology at

Vienna. In all events, while the emergent science of sexuality naturally had a wider European context, it found and would continue to find especially fertile ground in German-speaking central Europe.

Rather more starkly than was the case for sexual science, the emergence of homosexual self-consciousness and political activism was a largely German-language affair. Before Kertbeny's pamphlets arguing for decriminalization of homosexual acts, an even more outspoken proponent of homosexual emancipation was the Hanoverian Karl-Heinrich Ulrichs. It was Ulrichs who identified himself as one among a class of persons with a particular sexual nature (the formulation and conception of which admittedly shifted in the course of his writings), and who linked this quasi-medical model of sexuality to an emancipation agenda. One can identify a precursor in the person of Heinrich Hössli, whose 650-page, two-volume work *Eros* (1836–38) already constituted a defense of male-male love. Voices like these were not to be found in other cultures so long in advance of the fin de siècle. Later in the century this tradition continued, with the first lesbian activist Anna Rüling, the combination of research and activism in the person of Magnus Hirschfeld and the Institute for Sexual Science, and the first gay journals, both literary-cultural (*Der Eigene*) and scholarly (*Jahrbuch für sexuelle Zwischenstufen*). The women's movement was certainly international, yet the particular contributions of German and Austrian women, many trained in Swiss universities, intersect with this intense engagement with sexual issues (or "the sexual question," as some of them began to call it). As contributors to this volume will argue, this particular feminist engagement with sexuality offered the potential for a unique integration of ethics and sexuality in practice and analysis.

In light of all of this prodigious investment in the deployment of sexuality in its various forms, it is curious that Foucault wrote so little about it directly. The contributions in this volume step into the breach, but it is not just the nineteenth century that earns German-speaking Europe special attention. Explorations of the history of sexuality before the eighteenth century have made important interventions in recent years, but these have largely emerged from Renaissance Italian and Elizabethan English examples. German-language vernacular poetry in medieval Europe and the fertile ground of Reformation Germany offer points of entry into new questions for the historiography of sexuality generally, and are presented here within a group of essays on the premodern and the question of periodization. That World War I and its aftermath bore precipitous consequences for shifts in the terrain of the history of sexuality was recognized on all sides, but it was felt particularly strongly in Germany.[7] The Roaring Twenties had implications for gender and sexuality everywhere, and yet the culture of sexual liberation (and concomitant conflict, as we will see later in this volume) looked to metropolitan Weimar Germany as a beacon. In particular, observers remarked on the lively development of lesbian and male homosexual subcultures, unparalleled elsewhere. The centrality of sexual politics to the National Socialist period is crucial, and has been the subject of a previous collection released by this publisher.[8] The two German states arising in the wake of World War II allow for comparison and contrast of the relationship of sexuality to capitalist and socialist systems, and we have included two essays relating to the GDR to help flesh out this relatively under-researched area. Finally, the radical left movements spanning over a decade but bearing the emblematic label "1968"—the set of movements in which the project of the *History of Sexuality* itself must be situated—produced unique experimental formations in Germany, where generational revolt was linked to the radical rejection of fascism. A crucial intervention in this volume seeks to restore this history and reevaluate the meanings of sexual revolution. The continuing presence of this venerable history of sexuality in Germany into the present is the focus of a postscript by Dagmar Herzog.

It goes without saying that these keystones of the history of sexuality in German-speaking Europe do not cover all important elements of that history. Notably, none of our contributions concerns German colonialism, for example.[9] The postwar period is included, but there is no article on the fall of the Berlin Wall and its aftermath. While two essays address German-speaking Switzerland and scattered references may roam to other parts of central Europe, little direct attention has been paid to the Habsburg Empire and its Austrian successor state.[10] The territory we set out to cover was chiefly conceptual.

♦ ♦ ♦

The main regions of inquiry organizing the pieces that follow are derived from three revolutionary proposals in Foucault's *History of Sexuality*. The first concerns the then radical claim of a periodicity of sexuality, and the insistence that not only the sciences of sex but also sexuality as such are peculiarly modern (and hence Western) phenomena. This claim has certainly determined the ground on which all histories of sexuality thereafter have been laid. It was a cornerstone of the debate that came to be characterized as a conflict between essentialists (believing in essential sexual identities persisting across time and space, albeit affected in their expression by changing historical circumstances), on the one hand, and social constructivists (believing that categories organizing sexual identity are themselves historical products, untranslatable to other periods). This arguably false binary clearly served to energize the field of the history of sexuality; the high-water mark of this presumed debate (too often a fantasized dialogue among straw men) is now behind us, even if its echoes can still be heard.[11]

Harder to get past is the question of periodicity. Foucault's apparent gesture in *History of Sexuality*—to mark a radical and sudden shift from one mode of understanding the world and oneself in relation to it—is of the same form (but not content) as the gesture behind all of his major interventions: the shift in definition of the normal and pathological, that behind the birth of the clinic, or the one governing disciplinary mechanisms. *The Order of Things* elevates the structure of this omnipresent gesture to the center of the argument.[12]

A related region of inquiry pertains to the claim that this complex of sexuality entailed the production of sexual subjects, not merely as objects of categorical analysis but as beings who understand themselves and speak for themselves in terms of categories of sexuality. This move was certainly influenced by Althusser's notion of "interpellation," or the way in which subjects are called into being by ideology.[13] In trading in epistemes and genealogies, though, Foucault discarded even so ample and complex a model of ideology as Althusser's, offering an image of power that—famously—entails resistance as much as discipline, and *subjectivation* incorporating the formation, expression, and subjection of individual persons. Nowhere in the Foucauldian corpus are the processes mobilizing all these apparently contradictory forces so expressly pronounced as in the work on the history of sexuality, yet the historical literature following it returns persistently to the image of repressive discourse(s) entrapping and disciplining subjects in its web. Foucault consistently rejected this characterization of his model of power and subjectivation.[14] Already in the first volume of *History of Sexuality*, Foucault makes no secret of the links among disciplinary discourse, sexual subjectivity or self-understanding, and emancipatory movements, but his focus remains on the first of these and on the domain of knowledge. In the latter two volumes (rendered in English as *The Use of Pleasure* and *The Care of the Self*), he turns to constructive processes of subject formation more directly, albeit only by escaping from the European modernity that is, after all, the home of "sexuality."

Arguably, historians working close to the material of specific moments and particular discourses may, in different ways, expose the micro-technologies pertaining to these claims about historical processes. To do so—to get close to the complex kind of history that the *History of Sexuality* demanded—it has been necessary to take a step away from the ready conclusions historians before us took for granted at the outset. This, of course, is precisely what critics like David Halperin have called for in work where the injunction to "forget Foucault" is in fact a call to remember him, to reread him and engage his text in different ways.[15] This has, very largely, also been the charge of the present volume.

As will fast become clear, the road back—or rather, forward—to Foucault has in many instances required a detour to other kinds of thinking about sexuality and subjects, including particularly psychoanalysis, critical theory, and Marxism, all intellectual contexts that Foucault had variously steeped himself in and that so often haunt his texts as silent discussants, opponents, or targets. In invoking them, it is useful to remain mindful of their different valences in our own historical context, where these bodies of thought have moved forward with the world to look very different from the way they presented themselves to Foucault in the mid twentieth century.

The authors of the following chapters are not of one mind as to the current state of the historiography of sexuality in relation to Foucault's work, and it is not desirable that they be so. Some clearly see impasses in the history of sexuality that emanate directly from that source and regard it as something to go beyond; others dwell upon the age-old tension between the broad gestures of theory and the particularities of historical research. The position I am articulating in this introduction is suggested in many, but not all, of the essays. They do, in sum, present a unity, but not a unanimity. That is very much in the spirit of the broader movement to write histories of sexuality that attend to the demands of Foucault's radical disruption of how we view sexuality, without projecting onto it a dogmatic program.

◆ ◆ ◆

The essays in this volume have been carefully focused through a series of correspondences and discussions, including centrally a workshop of six related panels at a meeting of the German Studies Association in San Diego. The history of sexuality workshop organized by Richard Wetzell at the German Historical Institute, in which some of the contributors, including two of the editors, participated, was a significant moment that has left its mark on the agenda here. Two of the essays make use of Edward Ross Dickinson and Richard Wetzell's historiographical overview, published to introduce some of the contributions to that workshop in a special issue of *German History* in 2005.[16] With a clear voice, the authors heralded what they saw as an "exciting new creative phase" in the historiography, one that gets beyond a rigid and limited "social-constructionist paradigm of the history of sexuality ... derived from the Foucauldian metanarrative of modernity." Elsewhere in the article, the authors parenthetically imply the point we have put at the center of our inquiry, namely that the focus on a more complex and contradictory picture of the historical production of sexuality, one involving sexual subjects and emancipation as well as "top-down" disciplinary discourses, is not *pace* Foucault, but was in fact the very model the *History of Sexuality* introduced.[17] It is, in other words, not Foucault that the new literature turns away from or moves beyond, as much as a Foucauldianism that amounts to a misconstrual of what is suggested by (but not presented in) the *History of Sexuality*.

The example of periodicity with which we begin is a case in point, albeit an unusually sticky one. For one thing, it is the particular target of those critics of Foucault who have come from the discipline of history. Furthermore, and stickier still: the historical claim that sexuality as we understand it came into being at a relatively recent date, and would be incomprehensible in other historical contexts, is a fundament of virtually all serious histories of sexuality since 1970. Yet the findings of many of those histories challenge what they take to be Foucault's or Foucauldians' historicizations.

This may be especialy the case for histories of sexuality focusing on the period before sexuality as such (or sexual "identity," or "modern sexuality") is thought to have emerged. If the "Great Paradigm Shift" (as Eve Sedgwick semi-ironically named it) that Foucault seemed to locate in the mid 1860s is not to be taken literally, what is left?[18] Are new chronologies to be produced, and if so, how are they to avoid the pitfalls of previous claims periodizing sexuality? In the interest of further thinking on these questions at the heart of periodizations of sexuality tout court, we begin the collection with five essays that explore medieval and early modern histories of sexuality.

The first three pieces in the first section, "When Was Sexuality? Rethinking Periodization," approach the general problem of periodization in the historiography from different vantage points. Helmut Puff's essay also complements the present introduction in that, through its specific focus on the historiography of homosexuality (chiefly but not solely of male homosexuality), it proposes that to think of periodicity differently from the way it has been considered in many historical works of sexuality is decidedly *not* a turn away from Foucault's original project, but a furthering of it. Puff employs a magnificently productive peripheral vision to observe historical moments at both temporal and geographical distance from a core moment of radical paradigm shift. He also dwells on contributions to the question of periodicity that have come from outside of the discipline of history. In these works he identifies "a history of homosexuality that engages the diachronic as well as the synchronic, the simultaneous and the non-simultaneous, the modern and the premodern in new configurations and constellations." The example of male homosexuality—the very one in which Foucault pinpointed a "date of birth"—shows that the most innovative histories of sexuality require a turn away from fundamental assumptions of the first wave of historical scholarship after Foucault.

As Merry Wiesner-Hanks's contribution meticulously demonstrates, revisions of the chronological marker when modern sexuality is understood to have come into existence are not enough to resolve the awkward problem of periodicity. She argues that the recent historiography of sexuality in Germany might demonstrate how the binary suggested by the "Great Paradigm Shift" (before/after the modern sexuality divide) may be dispensed with, while at the same time maintaining and indeed strengthening the argument for a radical historicity of the categories understood in relation to sex. She makes this argument with a similar double-movement, first slaying (or reminding readers of other historians' slaughter of) the beast of a definitive moment of paradigm shift either in the eighteenth, early nineteenth, or late nineteenth centuries, while then arguing for the ways in which the early modern period in the Holy Roman Empire may hold a key to the emergence of new conceptualizations.

An extraordinary example of the new chronological configurations suggested by the first two programmatic essays is Ulinka Rublack's piece on law and sexual subjectivity in Reformation Germany, which also reviews some recent innovative historiography along the way. Rublack presents evidence and interpretation that argues strongly that "the notion that sexual behavior made an essential statement about oneself as a moral subject, and that it needed to be expressed actively in one way only" was actually a novelty of Lutheranism. In doing so, she does not so much insist that the dating of sexual subjectivity be moved back to the sixteenth century as demonstrate that this alternative chronology needs to be tracked differently: not through the textual path of sciences of the body and mind, but through imagery related particularly to the disciplinary practices of law. Methodologically, Rublack's intervention suggests that the sexual in this context needs to be understood in terms of the "embodied" way in which it was experienced, and situated within a symbolic universe that connected the image of the body to concepts of personhood, and both of these to the order of good and evil.

In the remaining two pieces of the section, we shift to detailed explorations of single texts to test theses of periodization. Andreas Krass's lyrical essay, a more finely tuned literary analysis than others in this volume, is the only contribution on the medieval period and hence offers something none of the other studies can. In its adventurous interpretation of a canonical poem by Walther von der Vogelweide, it reads the dynamics of the repressive hypothesis and the incitement to discourse characteristic of the taboo back onto the erotic discourses promiscuously flowing through Walther's poem. In a quite different manner, Robert Tobin offers a reading of the cultured Swiss businessman Heinrich Hössli's early-nineteenth-century apology for male same-sex love, *Eros*, that charts the ways in which the text's apparent anticipation of modern categories of sexuality was an effect of its particular historical context, particularly its contemporary ideology of liberalism. In doing so, Tobin shows how the tension between Enlightenment and Romantic thought were echoed in the vessel of this early figure of male-male eros, just as the same would reverberate within the sexual politics of the twenty-first century.

The next section, "Whose Sexuality? Sexual Subjectivity, Surveillance, Emancipation," focuses on the core period between the fin de siècle and the Weimar Republic, and the figures of the male and female homosexual, the sexual woman, and the prostitute. Each of these studies directly addresses some aspect of the issue of the interrelation of disciplinary structures and the emergence of sexual subjects, along with their emancipation efforts. If we know from Foucault that these are actually manifestations of a single process, it is for historians to explore the micromechanics of that process. What are the scenarios that provide sexual subjects with an incentive to make themselves heard? What concepts and images are called forth, and how do institutions enable or disable historical actors 'in sexualibus'? The first wave of the historiography produced a well-rehearsed storyline of sexual science interpellating sexual subjects, but, as elucidated above, the most innovative recent studies, including each of the essays here, insist on a multiplication and complication of our grasp of these interrelations.

A generous opening of these questions is offered by Kirsten Leng's presentation of Anna Rüling, credited as the first lesbian activist. Rüling's landmark speech "What Interest Does the Women's Movement Have in Solving the Homosexual Problem?" represents a complicated case in which gender and sexual identity, sexual science eugenics, women's and queer emancipation are bound to one another in puzzling ways. Rüling's self-fashioning goes beyond Foucault's "reverse discourse," testing the boundaries of what he elsewhere called tactical polyvalence. In the space between her self-proclaimed compound identity—"female" and "homosexual"—Rüling confects a unique and telling form of resistance that either strategically appropriates or else succumbs to oppressive disciplinary discourse.

The case studies of this section continue with Robert Beachy's revision of the commonly assumed role of the "homosexual bureau" of the police in imperial Berlin in relation to the objects of their surveillance. Taking seriously the conjunction in its charge "to police *and* protect," Beachy meticulously follows the trajectory of the bureau's surveillance of homosexuals, its toleration and even sponsorship of gay spaces, and its pursuit of extortionists, seeking to complicate a view that has understandably focused on repression and punishment. Such repression is not so much disavowed as it is bracketed in this study, with its keen focus on the pivotal role police surveillance played in the nurturing of Berlin's early and rich homosexual subculture, thereby offering an inversion of the commonplace understanding of disciplinary power. Jeffrey Schneider looks at the male homosexual community in the same period, specifying the role of widespread prostitution by military personnel in it. While he explores dynamics of power and knowledge familiar to readers of the classic historical literature on sexuality, his focus is on an element often overlooked in it: fantasy. In order, again, to further rather than reject the implications of the *History of Sexuality*, Schneider turns to tools provided by psychoanalytic theorists (especially Slavoj Žižek) to speculate on the function of fantasies for homosexual subjects, soldier-prostitutes, ethnographers of gay Germany, and, not least, the reading public.

Julia Roos continues the discussion of exchanges of sex for money in Germany, moving however to the very different terrain of women prostitutes in the Weimar Republic and their efforts to participate in and ultimately wrest control of the public discourse on their regulation. Prostitutes organized them-

selves into an interest group that entered the public sphere, displaying remarkable skill at engaging active discourses of public health, labor emancipation,
and moral purity in order to achieve what they perceived to be maximum autonomy. Roos's research points to a moment in the late Weimar Republic where
this strategic engagement pushed at the given bounds of the apparatus of sexuality, thereby changing its shape. Marti Lybeck also looks at an emergent sexual
public sphere in Weimar Germany, the one that arose from the homosexual
women's movement. She examines love stories with particular attention to an
element that hardly played a role in the *History of Sexuality*: the emotion of
shame. Utilizing as principle sources a set of hundreds of love narratives from
three magazines aimed at the community, Lybeck uncovers hitherto unexpli-
cated dynamics of early emancipation strategies, which paradoxically required
tragedy and the renunciation of desire. Lybeck's case study thus harks back to
the paradoxes of subjectivation of Roos's prostitutes and Leng's lesbian activist,
just as her use of the category of shame resembles Schneider's turn to fantasy.

Philipp Sarasin, in an essay that aptly reflects upon methodological questions of a post-Foucauldian historiography, turns to the issue of trans- and
intersexuality. To do so, he poses the famous early-nineteenth-century case of
Herculine Barbin (unearthed and presented by Foucault in a set of published
documents with his commentary) against a large collection of letters from the
1980s to the capaciously tolerant Swiss advice column "Dear Marta," arguing
both with and against Foucault about the nature of "nature" and sexual subjectivity. Like Schneider, he marshals psychoanalytic theory to push Foucault's
insights in new directions, here calling upon Lacan rather than Žižek. The
mechanics of what Lacan refers to as "the Law" further complicate Foucault's
reading, as Sarasin postulates it: if many readers have understood Foucault's
position as idealist or "vitalist" (in Deleuze's words) in the inferred suggestion
that there may be a realm of pleasure outside of the regulatory mechanism of
symbolic systems, Lacan teaches that there is no escape from such a system,
the Law. This contribution hence ends our inquiries into subjectivation on a
provocative note: instead of moving "beyond Foucault" by broadening the ways
in which subjects may engage in resistance, Sarasin's Lacan restricts the field of
resistance further.[19]

The final set of essays revolves around questions of ethics and politics, moving through the twentieth century on to concerns of the present. Foucault's
insistence that sexuality constitutes an ethical field, and his comments in his
later writings and interviews especially, open up questions that have only recently been taken up in the historiography of sexuality. Sexual ethics itself has
a rich history in twentieth-century German-speaking Europe, as the opening
essay by Tracie Matysik explores. The more active subject who consciously negotiates the disciplinary mechanisms surrounding sex in what Foucault in his
late work would call "the care of the self" can be discerned in some of these

efforts to rethink and rework sexuality through the lens of the "ethical." In one sense, dynamic thinking about sexual ethics was intended by its authors to displace ossified and punitive moral codes; from the start, these efforts understood themselves as political. Matysik's focus on Helene Stöcker's "new ethic" of sexual emancipation, nested within a rich contextualization of these philosophical questions, provides a crucial background for sexual politics later in the twentieth and twenty-first centuries.

Andreas Pretzel looks into the discourse of "national moral renewal" of the 1930s in Germany and maps out a debate that echoes some of the tones of Matysik's ethics reform movement even as it foreshadows sexual liberation struggles and reactions later in the century. In response to a late-1929 parliamentary committee resolution (never enacted) that would partially decriminalize homosexual acts, newly unified Catholics, Protestants, and cultural conservative activists mobilized to restore what they decried as a collapse of morality. This contribution offers an important revision of assumptions that place a shift in the language of sexual ethics at the Nazi seizure of power, showing clearly that they were instead a major feature of the late Weimar Republic and the property of a broad spectrum of political actors. It also shows the tentative emergence of a self-consciously secular and liberal sexual ethic demanding a central place for individual freedom and responsibility.

The following two essays turn to the postwar period, chiefly in the Socialist German state, the GDR. Florian Mildenberger introduces us to Günter Dörner, the medical researcher whose endocrinological studies, of homosexuality in particular, spanned the better part of the twentieth century. Passing from racial to socialist eugenics and on to honored recognition in post-unification Germany, Dörner's science seems to demonstrate an ideological elasticity that masks its own necessary implications for sexual ethics and politics. The political drama surrounding his legacy complicates the case even further. Erik Huneke concentrates on sexual counseling in the GDR—marriage counseling centers in particular, but also advice manuals and clinics—to make sense of the complex terrain of the relations among personal sexuality, social policy, and the state. In doing so, he demonstrates how Foucauldian biopolitics is to be grasped not as a purely "totalitarian" realm of social control over individuals, but as the ground of affective bonding producing unpredictable social and political effects.

The sexual liberation movements of the 1960s and 1970s have special significance for the study of Foucauldian or post-Foucauldian sexual ethics, not least because they provided the immediate context and impetus for Foucault's original project. Furthermore, the history of the movements and their significance within the frame of the history of sexuality as a field has been mired in certainties and counter-certainties that have only recently begun to be challenged. We therefore allow more space for the volume's final essay, Massimo

Perinelli's enlightening analysis of the sexual politics of the German radical left. The periodical *Agit 883* is the chief source for a study of the push and pull surrounding the forging of a potentially revolutionary linkage of sexual pleasure and political emancipation. The documentary trail of these efforts gives the lie to a Foucauldianism that sees sexual liberation as a disciplinary regime, and points rather to a concrete historical example of what the late Foucault referred to as the sphere of ethics. Gilles Deleuze is the thinker in whom Perinelli finds a vehicle to carry Foucault beyond Foucauldianism: the "lines of flight," or potentially deterritorializing gestures of the utopian rethinking of sexuality, are, if we accept Perinelli's reading, worth rescuing from the enormous condescension of a historiography that would confine sexual liberation in the twin straitjackets of leftist sexism and feminist repression.

Perinelli's contribution brings out what is implicit in many of these essays, and indeed all historical work on sex after the *History of Sexuality*: namely, that the object of such histories is never only in the past. One can never recall often enough that Foucault's initial project emerged out of the very context of political upheaval Perinelli evokes, with all the promise and disappointment inherent in such moments. This reminder may lead us to another compelling question: What is the future of our history of sexuality? That one, however, will have to remain for those who come after.

Notes

1. Michel Foucault, from "Round Table of 20 May 1978," translated and reprinted as "Questions of Method," in M. Foucault, *Essential Works of Foucault 1954–1984*, vol. 3, *Power*, trans. Robert Hurley et al. (New York, 2000), 238.
2. For a classic example proximate to Foucault's first volume, consider Lawrence Stone, *The Family, Sex, and Marriage in England, 1500–1800* (New York, 1977).
3. The most concise statements of this commonly held, if obviously altered, position are found in Michel Foucault, "Nietzsche, Genealogy, History," in *Language, Counter-Memory, Practice: Selected Essays and Interviews*, ed. D. F. Bouchard, trans. D. F. Bouchard and Sherry Simon (Ithaca, NY, 1977), 139–64; and Friedrich Nietzsche's 1874 text, "The Use and Abuse of History for Life," in F. Nietzsche, *Werke in drei Bänden* (Munich, 1954), vol. 1, 209–85, respectively.
4. Foucault, "Nietzsche, Genealogy, History," 139.
5. Michel Foucault, *The History of Sexuality*, vol. 1: *An Introduction*, trans. Robert Hurley (New York, 1978), 43. Cf. idem, *Abnormal: Lectures at the Collège de France, 1974–1975*, ed. Valerio Marchietti and Antonella Salomoni, trans. Graham Burchell (New York, 2003), 310.
6. Foucault, *History of Sexuality*, vol. 1, 43n1. The author was Carl Westphal, the journal the *Archiv für Psychiatrie und Nervenkrankheiten* (not *Archiv für Neurologie*, as erroneously cited by Foucault in both instances above), and the editors in 1870 were the professors B. Gudden (Zurich), E. Leyden (Königsberg), L. Meyer (Göttingen), and Westphal himself (Berlin).

7. See, e.g., the monumental work arguing this thesis, Magnus Hirschfeld, ed., *Sittenge-schichte des Weltkrieges*, 2 vols. (Leipzig and Vienna, 1930). Research has shown the consciousness of such a shift elsewhere on the continent, especially France: see Carolyn Dean, *The Frail Social Body: Pornography, Homosexuality, and Other Fantasies in Interwar France* (Berkeley, 2000) and Mary Louise Roberts, *Civilization without Sexes: Reconstructing Gender in Postwar France, 1917–1927* (Chicago, 1994).

8. Dagmar Herzog, ed., *Sexuality and German Fascism* (New York, 2005).

9. Lora Wildenthal, *German Women for Empire, 1884–1945* (Durham, NC, 2001); cf. Ann Stoler, *Race and the Education of Desire: Foucault's History of Sexuality and the Colonial Order of Things* (Durham, NC, 1995).

10. This has been the subject of a recent volume; see Günter Bischof, Anton Pelinka, and Dagmar Herzog, eds., *Sexuality in Austria*, Contemporary Austrian Studies, vol. 15 (New Brunswick, NJ, 2007).

11. See, e.g., Graham Robb, *Strangers: Homosexual Love in the Nineteenth Century* (London, 2003), esp. 42–43.

12. See Foucault, *History of Sexuality*, vol. 1, 43; idem, *Madness and Civilization: A History of Insanity in the Age of Reason, Birth of the Clinic: An Archaeology of Medical Perception*, among other works. It is useful to note that even *The Order of Things* does not offer a theory of such "historical structures" as such, but rather an "account" of them, a "mode of being in order": Michel Foucault, *The Order of Things: An Archaeology of the Human Sciences* (New York, 1970), esp. xxi–xxiii, 50, 238.

13. Louis Althusser, "Ideology and Ideological State Apparatuses (Notes towards an Investigation)," in L. Althusser, *Lenin and Philosophy and other Essays*, trans. Ben Brewster (New York, 1971), 127–86.

14. Among these many refutations, the most influential in North America has been the compendious essay "The Subject and Power," *Critical Inquiry* 8, no. 4 (Summer, 1982): 777–95, which begins with a definitive statement that the "goal of [his] work during the last twenty years … has not been to analyze the phenomena of power … [but instead] to create a history of the different modes by which, in our culture, human beings are made subjects."

15. David M. Halperin, "Forgetting Foucault: Acts, Identities, and the History of Sexuality," *Representations* 63 (Summer 1998): 93–120; reprinted in idem, *How to Do the History of Homosexuality* (Chicago, 2002), 24–47, along with other essays along these lines, notably "Historicizing the Subject of Desire," 81–103.

16. Edward R. Dickinson and Richard F. Wetzell, "The Historiography of Sexuality in Modern Germany," *German History* 23, no. 3 (2005): 291–305. For the below points, see esp. abstract and 295–96. See also Richard Wetzell's conference report, "History of Sexuality in Modern Germany," *Bulletin of the German Historical Institute* 34 (Spring 2004): 137–46.

17. Dickinson and Wetzell, "Historiography of Sexuality," p. 298.

18. In one of the "axioms" introducing her classic *Epistemology of the Closet* (Berkeley, 1990), 44–48. Presciently, Sedgwick's work, which (with other works around the same time) launched what was to be "queer studies," began with a warning that Foucault's revolutionary and unsettling claim of the historicity of sexuality was threatening "inadvertently to refamiliarize, renaturalize, damagingly reify an entity that it could be doing much more to subject to analysis…" *Epistemology of the Closet*, p. 45.

19. One of the trenchant critiques of Foucault's late and influential discussion of the subject has come from Slavoj Žižek, who posited that the *History of Sexuality*, vol. 1, and

the late interviews such as those published in *Ethics: Subjectivity and Truth*, trans. R. Hurley, ed. Paul Rabinow (New York, 1997), merely created a paradox by offering distinct and incompatible models of the definition of the "subject" and the potential operations of "resistance." See Slavoj Žižek, *The Ticklish Subject: The Absent Centre of Political Ontology* (London, 1999), esp. 251–53. On this see also Peter Dews, "The Return of the Subject in Late Foucault," *Radical Philosophy* 51 (Spring 1989): 37–41.

SECTION I

~:~

When Was Sexuality?
Rethinking Periodization

Michel Foucault was a historical thinker par excellence. Yet the same Foucault has frequently been faulted for the multiple, often contradictory, ways in which he deployed chronologies or temporal schemas—the very stuff from which histories are made. Even historians who have taken inspiration from his writings, methods, or concepts have found this aspect of his work lacking in rigor or in need of correction. To be sure, many of Foucault's studies, essays, and lectures revolve around central moments of change toward the modern, discursive shifts that vary according to the particular problematic at hand, be it the history of psychiatry, of knowledge, or of the self. But this chronological maze manifests itself not only between different studies and subject matters; such multiplicity surfaces also within individual texts. In hindsight, it appears, temporalities in Foucault are disarmingly complex, opinions to the contrary notwithstanding.

Certain ambivalences associated with historical change are evidenced in the claim that the "new technology of sex" was novel "in that for the most part it escaped the ecclesiastical institution without being truly independent of the thematic of sin," to quote from the section of *History of Sexuality* devoted to "periodization,"[1] for instance: if one listens in closely, a lingering presence of the medieval, early modern, or premodern after the nineteenth-century "invention of sexuality" is evident, too. By casting their "period eye" on this same terrain, the one medievalist and four early modernists assembled in this section continue to build on, critique, and refine Foucault's thinking through historical time. "What happens to Foucault's chronologies when the technologies of sexuality are refigured for the imperial field?" The question Ann Stoler once asked in her *Race and the Education of Desire*[2] is echoed, with different accents, by our contributors. The Foucauldian placement of sexuality's invention in the nineteenth century has had lasting effects on the historiography of sexuality as well as early modern history, as Puff, Wiesner-Hanks, and Rublack argue in their contributions.

Revisiting the temporal thresholds that underwrite Foucault's work is all the more important since his period sensibility is rooted primarily in the French tradition. "The Classical Age," a description invoking the century of Colbert, Descartes, Poussin, Racine, and Rameau that is one of the most persistent turning points in his oeuvre, does not easily map onto the historical geography of German-speaking countries, where French classicism under the auspices of empire has little equivalent. As a result, German historians working with Foucault have had to productively recalibrate their temporal topography (Rublack). Dating the emergence of a selfhood anchored in sexuality is an issue that has persistently haunted the historiography on sexuality, and the answer to such a central period question hinges on what we mean by a sexual subject (Rublack; Tobin; see also section two). The investigation into the rise of sexual subjectivity may in fact lead us far from the metropolis and to the discovery of long gestation periods—a layered history that reaches back into the period before the nineteenth century (Tobin).

If we arrest a critical gaze fixated on historical movement or change, one text can be shown to stand at the confluence of different ways of speaking the tabooed matter of sex. Importantly, such rest from the flight to history allows us to take in the sound of words, their performance, and their literary resonances (Krass). *Quod erat demonstrandum.* Only a historiography that continually rethinks the conditions of its own period-making is a Foucault-inspired history. This is why thinking about alternate temporalities after the *History of Sexuality* is a history of sexuality with Foucault.

Helmut Puff

Notes

1. Michel Foucault, *The History of Sexuality*, vol. 1, *An Introduction*, trans. Robert Hurley (New York, 1978), 116.
2. Ann Stoler, *Race and the Education of Desire: Foucault's* History of Sexuality *and the Colonial Order of Things* (Durham, 1995), 6.

CHAPTER 1

~:~

After the History of (Male) Homosexuality

HELMUT PUFF

"Gender history is here to stay" was the opening salvo Lynn Hunt once fired for all historians to take note.[1] Today there is much reason to say the same about the historiography on homosexuality. Writings on male and female homosexuality have flourished since the 1970s. Arguably, it is one of the history of sexuality's prime movers. A stream of publications on hitherto neglected topics and unexplored geographies continues to reshape the contours of what we know of homosexual matters in history and how we come to know what is sexual in the first place. Gay and lesbian studies in history have embraced a bedazzling variety of subject matters, reaching from the vagaries of monastic friendship to the dialectic of the sexual enlightenment and the riddles of twentieth-century erotic subject positions. Like gender history, the history of male and female homosexuality is today at the forefront of discussions about themes and methods of relevance to many historians, the questions of subjectivity and agency as well as modernity chief among them. An area of knowledge that not too long ago would have been dismissed in disbelief, if not disgust, has established itself with remarkable resilience in the profession. Historical homosexuality studies are, I want to claim, here to stay.

While we can be relatively confident about the field's continued existence, at least in the North American academy, this success story has given rise to a number of certainties *within* the field—certainties I view as detrimental to the vitality of scholarly inquiry in sexuality studies. The history of sexuality's future depends on our ability to continually rewrite, revise, and redo existing research agendas. My essay issues a plea for a history of sexuality promiscuously open to strategic intellectual alliances. One of these certainties is the central position wielded by the premodern-modern divide in recent histories of, especially male, homosexualities. Texts foundational to the history of sexuality have consistently approached premodern sexualities through figurations of that which came after, or vice versa. Whatever their theoretical perspective, many researchers link their stories to the great transition to a modern sexual system. Whereas the notion of a great turning point has never worked well for lesbian history with its different set of entanglements—of which the nexus with male homosexuality is only one—narratives organized around the so-called invention of homosexuality have acquired an almost normative status with regard to males. This story defines who got there first, who came late, and what the "there" was in the first place. This model constructs centers and their various peripheries. Thus viewed, the history of male homosexuality is less at risk of wanting to know for sure whether people had sex with one another— the impulse Martha Vicinus once detected at the core of lesbian history writing.[2] With regard to the history of male homosexuality, the danger consists in thinking that we know already.

Let me briefly revisit the oft-cited locus classicus for the history of (male) homosexuality. In 1976, Michel Foucault could hardly have foreseen the effect a passage in his *La volonté de savoir* has had on historians of male (and female) homosexuality: "The sodomite had been a temporary aberration; the homosexual was now a species."[3] Or: "The sodomite was a renegade [or 'backslider']; the homosexual is now a species," as David Halperin captures this same sentence.[4] A generation of researchers translated a somewhat paradoxical formulation, especially in the standard English translation, into a road map on how to do research on the history of homosexuality—a productive misunderstanding, one might say, in which social histories often enough passed as histories of discourse and vice versa.

Yet the proviso to distinguish between sexual acts—acts committed without identities—and sexual selves centered in sociosexual identities has profoundly shaped the historiography on same-sex eroticism among males ever since. Wherever scholars have looked through this vaguely Foucauldian lens, the assumption of sexuality or homosexuality as a practically unchanging human experience did not stand up to close examination. "Sexuality" did not have a transhistorical presence; the concept emerged as part of a profound shift that revolved around changing ideas about bodies, subjects, and society. "Homosexuality moved from being a category of sin to a psychosocial disposition," as Jeffrey Weeks summarizes the transition in question.[5] More than three decades after Foucault's formulation, the invention of (male) homosexuality in mid-nineteenth-century Europe continues to resonate through the relevant literature, though its effects are often unacknowledged. In fact, the question of how to approach the history of (homo)sexuality "before homosexuality" has haunted the field of inquiry. Histories of homosexuality, or any sexualities for that matter, must fail, according to David Halperin in a groundbreaking article, "unless they also include as an essential part of their proper enterprise the task of demonstrating the historicity, conditions of emergence, modes of construction, and ideological contingencies of the very categories of analysis that undergird their own practice."[6] This caveat might well guide us, as we are building on past and imagining future histories.

It is imperative to remember that the historiography on homosexuality is not alone with regard to a categorical dilemma of this kind. History of art is a field whose titular concept, art, does not transcend the history the discipline covers. As Hans Belting and others have elaborated, art with its associations of artifice and connoisseurship emerged in Western Europe through a series of interrelated and overlapping shifts from icon to image, sacred spaces to personal devotion, patronage to market, agency of the image to the agency of the artist.[7] Such a comparison is instructive in that it points to why the issue of the history of sexuality's foundational category—(homo)sexuality—may remain so alive in the history that concerns us here. For one, it is uncomfortably close, one might say. Whereas art can be said to have emerged in the West over the course of the later Middle Ages, the invention of (homo)sexuality is recent, dated by most historians to the nineteenth century, separating vast historical terrains from the modern term's grasp as a result. Second, while the notion of art conjures up material objects, (homo)sexuality is intertwined with the question of how to study human society. These differences notwithstanding, disciplines such as art history may in fact provide important models for pursuing historical investigations of various kinds while interrogating concepts central to the discipline.

The opposition of acts vs. identities, to use shorthand for the complex shift circumscribed by the term homosexuality's invention, has had such a profound impact on the history of (male) homosexuality that it has persistently structured modes of inquiry into the past. Whether implicit or explicit, this focus on thresholds toward the modern has been so powerful that it has generated a plethora of other, similarly organized narratives of radical ruptures and breaks. A proliferation of threshold narratives has been the result. The invention of homosexuality was followed by the invention of heterosexuality, of homophobia, of heteronormativity, etc.[8] To complicate such claims, researchers such as George Chauncey, Gert Hekma, Jonathan Ned Katz, Harry Oosterhuis, and others have long "provincialized" the sexual histories of Europe and the so-called West (Dipesh Chakrabarty).[9] They have demonstrated the limits of "homosexuality's" reach in the very place where it had originated, instead fleshing out the simultaneity of different sexual mentalities and discourses at any given time. Yet their findings all too often appear as mere corrigenda to a well-rehearsed plotline.

In fact, David Halperin's *How to Do the History of Male Homosexuality* goes a long way in reconceptualizing our understanding of "homosexuality." Revising his own influential "Is There a History of Sexuality?" the author posits the term as a receptacle of a variety of premodern discourses.[10] Yet the examples undergirding the history of male homosexuality in Halperin strike one as uncannily familiar: ancient Greece and Rome or the Italian Renaissance, among other focal points. The Middle Ages barely make an appearance in this genealogy of male homosexuality, centered on the coinage of the word in 1868/69. As a result, homosexuality appears as something akin to Western civilization's underbelly with its progression from ancient times through the Renaissance/Reformation period to the modern. Needless to say, these waystations on the path to European modernity boast a particularly rich historiography. After all, they already served as treasure troves for sexologists eager to fill terminological slots with historical anecdotes and literary materials that resonated with their readers and therefore legitimated the sexological field of inquiry. With a library reaching back at least to the eighteenth century, ancient sexuality in particular, above all the well-documented erotic attachments of adult male citizens to young men in Athens, provided a, maybe the, model for approaching premodern homosexualities, with far-reaching consequences for our understanding of the breadth of premodern sexual practices.[11]

Put differently, the opposition of acts vs. identities has obfuscated the occlusions that inevitably arose with its structuring force.[12] With its multilayered associations of the medieval vs. the modern, collectivity vs. individuality, sexuality in the West vs. the non-Western, a set of oppositions entered into explorations of sexuality in history. Carla Freccero has recently cast critical light on the progressivism of accounts that rely on a distinction between premodern sexual acts and modern sexual selves. Even where the notion of a unifying one identity gives way to a more subtle notion of partial identities, such formulations are bound to "reinstate[] a notion of historical progression that makes modernity the culmination of identity, [even] as it attributes to modernity a unitary temporality and conceptual coherence across space/geography," she claims.[13] If deployed indiscriminately, the premodern-modern divide therefore risks flattening the complexities of so-called traditional and modern societies alike.

Multiple modernities were at play, for instance, in the transformation of Chinese sexualities in the twentieth century: an indigenous move toward reform, Western modernity, the Asian model modernization of Meiji Japan, and finally, a socialist modernity with its intellectual roots in the European Enlightenment, though in China's case this tradition was largely routed through the Soviet experience. Each of these reform ideas and movements introduced its own sets of binaries. After all, the modern, since its original coinage in late antiquity, has been a term deployed to generate relational opposites—opposites that habitually carry polemical overtones. The aforementioned reform projects resulted in a complex transformation that has made aspects of China's premodern sexual history, such as concubinage or the so-called men of the cut sleeve, virtually unintelligible for the majority of today's Chinese, reared under the aegis of sexual ideologies revolving around heterosexual monogamy and fortified by an ethical code centered on filial lines of descent.[14] To describe these webs of ideological practices and intersubjective mobilizations without favoring one modernizing story over another would be a way to write and simultaneously reflect this history of sexual modernization. The panacea I seek is not to move from a singular modernity to an equally elusive plural, however. Rather, I am suggesting that the grip of narratives of linear thresholds be suspended and the juxtapositions explicit or implicit in such a structure of thinking be relaxed in favor of multiple chronologies—chronologies that defy the temptation to order narratives around crises, breaks, and ruptures.

The censure of homoeroticism within the Ottoman Empire, for instance, did not result exclusively from an exposure to Western norms, notions, or invectives much focused on the supposed sexual doings among Turks. Such a response emerged from virulent strands of indigenous critique reinforced by Western ideas, especially from the nineteenth century on. In the early modern Ottoman Empire, the male pursuit of God's beauty through gazing at beardless youths became so popular that Sufis rallied against this spiritual-erotic practice, part of a "centuries-long battle for the soul of the community and for Islamic public morality"—a campaign Dror Ze'evi imaginatively compares to Reformation and Counter-Reformation Europe.[15]

To be sure, this diagnosis applies equally to studies of premodern sexualities. Here as elsewhere the notion of a modern sexual system has had a constraining effect on this historiography's contours. Researchers have struggled with existing models—models that prescribe sexual hierarchies for sexual actors in premodern societies. I remember the sense of bafflement at how few of the records I collected for my *Sodomy in Reformation Germany* reflected the model of intergenerational and asymmetrical sexual relations most commonly associated with early modern Europe. In part, this discrepancy resulted from the spottiness of existing trial records that, alas, were not written with historians' questions in mind. Civic notaries in late medieval and early modern Switzerland did not regularly record the age of the sexual actors that were prosecuted for *sodomitereyen* (though age was regularly mentioned if one or both of the actors were under age). Often, the sexual activity in question did not make it into the written documentation. From recorded sex acts we can infer, however, that anal sexuality might not have played the role it has often been accorded in the literature as an index of sociosexual relations. Rather than conjecture from lack of evidence that asymmetry in age and sexual roles prevailed, I sought to make a case for several social settings in which same-sex sexual behavior was noted: "it was practiced among adolescents; it existed in the milieu of workers or laborers with negligible age or social distinctions; and it flourished in cross-class and intergenerational relationships of masters with their dependents."[16]

Few scholars have, as Khaled El-Rouayheb proposes, emphasized the continuity "between premodern and modern conceptualizations" of sexual acts
between men. Among other interventions, this scholar suggests that the grand
awakening of the male homosexual may have mattered for the inserting partner
more than for the insertee, whose sexual role and desire were often denigrated
in Arab sexual discourses "before and after homosexuality": for the so-called
active partner, inserting constituted a sign of male privilege, at least until "after
homosexuality," when it was said to express a particular, homoerotic, desire.[17]

To think about alternate chronologies, different frameworks of thought,
and novel terminologies does not entail a return to "essentialism," the notion
that sexual categories are applicable throughout history. It does mean, however, to broaden our vocabulary and conceptual tools. El-Rouayheb advances
"inclination" as an important axis of understanding male-male erotic sociability, for instance.[18] Similarly, Wu Cuncun's "homoerotic sensibilities" captures
the nexus of artistic refinement and erotic tastes fashionable among Ming and
Qing literati in premodern China, an arena of male sexual privilege as well as
of conspicuous cultural choices that included the erotic pursuit of effeminate
male beauty. Such an approach is a far cry from canvassing a (homo)sexual system as a set of behavioral rules that could be flouted only at an actor's risk. For
elite males in late imperial China, erotic libertinage became a preferred mode of
experimentation and cultivation of the self through sensual indulgence. In the
milieu of male prostitutes and operatic performers, so-called *dan*-actors, male-
male intercourse lent itself to nostalgic idealizations in ways that sex between
men and women apparently did not. The author thus opens a window onto a
pliable cultural landscape with regional, social, and institutional specificities.[19]

As these examples demonstrate, studies on homoeroticism in the Near
East or Asia before the advent of modernities associated with the West have
launched new conceptual geographies. An introduction to a recent volume on
Islamicate Sexualities takes note that "we are now in a position to insist that
what is meant by sexual identity be more precisely defined, taking care to differentiate between such concepts as sexual inclination, tendency, preference,
predisposition, orientation, consciousness, subjectivity, self-perception, and
subculture."[20] So far, the traffic of academic terms and vocabulary has by and
large flowed in one direction: historians of homosexuality in Asia, Latin America, and Africa have adjusted, refitted, or rejected vocabularies current in the
field.[21] It is time to also reverse directions and work toward cross-fertilizing
these area-specific historiographies. After all, the vast terrain covered by the
label premodern has enabled novel dialogues across area specializations. Such
conversations will contribute to subverting persistent binaries such as East and
West, *ars erotica* and *scientia sexualis*, or before and after "sexuality."

Not all concepts will prove equally useful. The now ubiquitous "desire" may
count among the terms up for critical examination. Over the past two decades,

desire has forged links across a variety of discourses and modes of representation. One may add that it also has spawned many a conversation across temporal and geographic specializations. As James Schultz argues, "desire" has had too much of a good thing, a career in sexuality studies. In its infinite plasticity, "desire" denotes diverse phenomena, blurring important distinctions in its wake: "Medieval theologians' concupiscence, medieval doctors' appetite, and the courtly arrows of Lady Love are incommensurate explanations for what it is that causes individuals to seek what we call sexual relations [in medieval literature]."[22]

Queer studies has put tremendous critical pressure on grand narratives of how the modern came to be truly modern, at least those queer histories that wrestle with the *longue durée*. Whereas queer scholars have mostly treated a relatively recent history, critics such as Carolyn Dinshaw and Valerie Traub have treaded new paths in approaching the distant past. Dinshaw speaks of "Touching on the Past," Traub of "Practicing Impossibilities" when characterizing a critical, affective, and effective engagement of premodern histories from a decidedly anti-historicist vantage point.[23] These and other studies explore a history of homosexuality that engages the diachronic as well as the synchronic, the simultaneous and the non-simultaneous, the modern and the premodern in new configurations and constellations. Some queer critics in fact have shown a great affinity to the medieval with its promise of escape from the modern—a type of utopian medievalism that itself boasts a venerable pedigree among modern thinkers.[24] In a variety of ways, queer critics—most of whom are based in departments of literature—have called on historians to revisit the ways in which they have relied on unequivocal, unidirectional, standard time in their writings. Jonathan Goldberg and Madhavi Menon have urged us, one, to move away from histories focused on ruptures and sudden breaks, issuing a call "to resist mapping sexual difference onto chronological difference such that the difference between past and present becomes also the difference between sexual regimes; and two, to challenge the notion of a determinate and knowable identity, past and present."[25] Traub calls for a queer history that is attentive to the cyclical nature of certain recurrent sexual configurations.[26] Freccero has had us imagine "queer time"—a time whose flow is difficult to predict.[27] This time may lead forward, backward, or remain solidly still. These scholars posit a vision of the temporal *sans* the straitjacket of succession, instead foregrounding the queer critic or historian as a self-conscious organizer of time.

Such interventions have yet to spark sustained dialogues between queer and historical studies. The object many queer scholars have recently loved to attack goes by the name of historicism. Goldberg and Menon take "historicists" to task, for instance, for unduly favoring the alterity of the past over its similarities with the present—a sign of teleological and universalist aspirations, according to these critics.[28] Yet the historicism that figures in this and other queer writings is a historicism poorly historicized and rarely engaged. More often than not, it circumscribes a polemical phantasma, shored up with the one quote from Leopold von Ranke that supposedly encapsulates historicist practice, or spiced up by the occasional, though elusive, reference to recent historiographical debates. What many critics mean when they inscribe themselves into the annals of anti-historicism or "un-historicism," as Goldberg and Menon put it, would better be called a critique of teleology.[29]

To equate historicism with teleology, or historical practice with what passes as historicism, however, would be to downplay, if not dismiss, the breadth of historical work or to exaggerate its resistance to theory. Strange as it may seem, historicism, a historicism broadly understood, is the intellectual grounds from which calls for a different, a new history inescapably emerge. Historicist practice itself has relied on modes of identification as part of the hermeneutical process, a circulation of sympathetic energy between the researching subject and the researched object. Queer critics have both exposed and elaborated these forms of creating history via sympathies and antipathies. Both queer critics and practitioners of history alike rely on a balance of similarities and dissimilarities, sameness and otherness. Recent queer critics, however, have identified history too squarely with alterity while aligning queerness with similarity. Traub has in fact parted company with queer critics over their wholesale critique of empirical and historical work. Her forthcoming "The New Unhistoricism in Queer Studies" hopefully will enliven debates in history and queer studies alike.[30] To bring the ambivalent, elusive, multiple processes of disidentification and identification into the limelight when engaging historically situated materials is a worthwhile project—one that offers common grounds to queer critics and historians.

That writings on the history of homosexuality have come of age is also indicated by a spate of recent publications that synthesize decades of research into meta-narratives on the history of both male and female homosexuality. Louis Crompton's *Homosexuality and Civilization* (2003), Robert Aldrich's *Gay Life and Culture: A World History* (2006), and William Naphy's *Born to be Gay: A History of Homosexuality* (2004) are among several volumes that seek to attract new readerships to the historiographical gains made in recent decades. Importantly, these books explode the geographic horizons of the so-called West to cover sexual cultures around the world. (While ads and blurbs hail these books as first forays into the global history of same-sex sexuality, this distinction should go to historical sociologists such as Barry Adam and David Greenberg, whose 1988 *The Construction of Homosexuality* may well be the genre's pioneer.[31]) As meta-histories, these volumes productively reap the benefits of specialized studies. Yet their narratives reveal at times the persistence of well-trodden ideas, concepts, and trajectories.

Louis Crompton, for instance, is adamant that a comprehensive history of homosexuality can in fact be written: "To adopt Michel Foucault's view that the homosexual did not exist 'as a person' until this time is to reject a rich *and* terrible past."[32] Yet by covering the times between archaic Greece and Napoleonic Europe, he foregoes the challenge of how to write a history that would straddle the premodern-modern divide—an intriguing move, to be sure. While heralding a gallery of homosexual worthies—hence the word civilization in the book's title—Crompton seeks to improve on previous "universal histories" of homosexuality by setting the record straight on the rise and fall of persecutions: "a rich and terrible past." Somewhat surprisingly, the book's plotline therefore ends when executions for sodomy petered out in the so-called West around 1800, with Asia serving as an exotic backdrop to this largely European story. According to the author, China accepted homosexuality "as an inescapable fact of human existence."[33] Yet repression did not end with the end of executions, and the fact that men accused of same-sex sexual acts are occasionally executed in contemporary rural Iran is probably too far-fetched to merit attention. Such a progression from ancient acceptance to Christian non-acceptance and tolerance's constitution in the eighteenth century breathes life into a chronology whose stages are strongly reminiscent of humanism's tripartite vision of history with antiquity, the medieval period, and the age of a revival. Tellingly, we only get to see the dawn of the golden era we are fortunate—or doomed—to live in.

The anthology *Gay Life and Culture* takes "the panoply of same-sex behaviours, attitudes, and identities" in today's world as its starting point.[34] The various historical chapters read as an explanatory frame to the rise of difference and diversity associated with the "contemporary world."[35] Familiar and much-debated themes in sociology surface in this context: urbanization, the rise of consumer culture, and the emergence of civil society, to name just a few. But the question remains how to theorize difference and its history. How could we, for instance, approach the manifold contrapuntal relationships between sexual cultures organized around visibilities—with their meeting points, bars, and associations—and less public forms of same-sex practice on a global scale?

William Naphy is the author of the most ambitiously global of these recent histories of homosexualities. *Born to be Gay* systematically integrates materials on Africa and Asia in every of the book's chronologically arranged sections. After having us imagine a time before the destruction of Sodom and Gomorrah, Naphy traces the "birth of homophobia," as in one chapter's title, to the first millennium BCE and the emergence of monotheism among the ancient Hebrews. The author proceeds to chart how Western and non-Western minds alike have been and continue to be colonized (to adapt his own formulation) by homophobia.[36] If we follow this intriguing account, the birth of homophobia precedes the birth of the homosexual. Such a historical process lacks texture, however, as long as homophobia's appeal to elites and populaces across the world is left unexamined. The elusive question of subjectivity that has haunted much of the history of homosexuality therefore remains a desideratum in this context.

My cursory readings remind us of new departures and old certainties that continue to shape knowledge production with regard to the history of male and female homosexualities. Working toward new uncertainties means that we should be less concerned with guarding the impenetrability of the field and more involved in opening the history of homosexuality to other histories. In fact, some of the most seminal work in the field has embarked on a new permissiveness. Among the first and most important tasks at hand is to recalibrate the place of sex and sexual activity for the history of male and female homosexuality. Alan Bray's *The Friend* of 2003 may well be the most far-reaching of recent undertakings to shift the very grounds on which the history of homosexuality has been written. In this book, the author of the field-defining *Homosexuality in Renaissance England* (1982) proposes to dethrone sex as an organizing principle for the history of same-sex relations, offering affective intimacy as its centerpiece instead. The history of friendship may seem like a well-known storyline. Yet Bray rewrites its history from the bottom up, placing at its center the praxis, religious above all, among friends—not philosophical or literary discourses of friendship since ancient times. In one section of the book, though, Bray sheds light on precisely these discourses from the vantage point of friendship's praxology. To invoke the daringly singular friend of Bray's book title, the desire to erect a postmortem monument to *the* friend—the central axis of Bray's account—reveals a sensibility that is as much about the delights of companionship as it is about performance anxieties and loss. What emerges is a window onto the delicate scripts of male-male relations operative since the High Middle Ages and well into what we conventionally call the modern. (Same-sex friendships among women are the subject of Bray's concluding historical chapter.)

If we follow Bray, same-sex sociability before the advent of civil society rivaled the centrality of other, better researched social networks. In other words, social historians with their focus on demography, procreation, families, and marriage have blinded us to a world of same-sex intimacy we have indeed lost. As researchers have begun to show, same-sex sociability constituted a collective terrain marked by rituals, exchanges, investments, and affectivity as well as individual agency. Viewed thus, homosociality was anything but marginal to European or non-European societies of the past. On the contrary, same-sex social relations flourished in a culture where cross-sex sociability was often fraught. Yet while homosocial interactions mattered to both sexes in Renaissance Europe, the place of the sexual varied for men and for women, and so did the forms and meanings accorded male and female homosociabilities. Restoring these worlds to their proper place in a social history of medieval, early modern, and modern Europe or other parts of the world is one of the most alluring historiographical tasks awaiting us.[37]

Secondly, future studies will benefit from imbricating gender studies more intimately with histories of homosexuality. Under the umbrella of "love," George Haggerty's *Men in Love* on eighteenth-century masculinities and sexualities is an example of a study that brings gender and sexuality into conversation. After all, "love" is the concept that stood at the heart of the continuum of male-male desire in the eighteenth century. In this study of the intricate intersections of high class, gentlemanly masculinities, and emotional sensibilities in eighteenth-century Britain, love acquires a strangely subversive force, destabilizing the very social foundations on which its expression rested.[38] Afsaneh Najmabadi's work, to pick another example, may be said to have followed a trajectory inverse to Bray's. While the latter seemingly moved away from sex in *The Friend*—though he strikingly reintroduces the erotic through a chapter on *female* friendships, suggesting a narrative of sexuality's rise to more visibility in the early nineteenth century—the former, a gender historian of Iran, came to embrace sexuality in her work. Her study imaginatively explores how Qajar Iran reformed the social by regendering erotic desire. The beauty of the male adolescent, in whose image female beauty previously had been conceived, gave way to a new asymmetry of sexual attraction in which beauty ceased to be conceived of as masculine. Using Eve Kosofsky Sedgwick's insight about the omnipresence of the hetero/homo-distinction as constitutive of social relations, *Women with Mustaches and Men without Beards* demonstrates, among other things, how the rearticulation of same-sex desire into a brotherhood in the service of the state has never completely erased the homoerotic longing for male beauty at its roots.[39] We have, it seems, barely begun to read the history of masculinity and gender relations at large into the history of male homosexuality.

Thirdly, as I have argued throughout this essay, questions of periodization are up for rethinking. Future histories will not have to rely exclusively on the coinage and subsequent dissemination of homosexuality as the major structuring device for their narratives. The 1868/69 moment merits an in-depth exploration, the work of Klaus Müller, Hubert Kennedy, and others notwithstanding. Too many inaccuracies have been in circulation about the invention of the term homosexuality, starting with Michel Foucault's characterization of Karl Maria Kertbeny[40]—a state of affairs that is, at least in part, the result of this moment's function in upholding larger temporal schemes. Alain Corbin has recently reminded us of how richly textured medical discussions were before the advent of nineteenth-century sexology, Arnold Davidson's well-explicated claim of the Freudian revolution and its prehistory notwithstanding.[41] Bray, Halperin, Najmabadi, and Traub have offered fascinating models of how to narrativize historical difference across times and periods. So has Dagmar Herzog, whose *Sex after Fascism* draws an intricate portrait of National Socialism's complex legacy in postwar German history. This portrait of the inscription and reinscription of the sexual culture envisioned and created by National Socialists urges us to rethink watershed moments such as 1933, 1945, or 1968.[42]

What I have suggested here, finally, has implications for how we relate the history of male to that of female homosexuality. For many and good reasons, conventional wisdom has had it that these two histories be treated separately in order to develop the ineluctable specificities of gendered experiences as well as discursive regimes. Nonetheless, there have been common theoretical and historiographical grounds as well as conversations. The literature reviewed here suggests a new permeability. Most of the recent studies on homosexuality touch on significant aspects of lesbian history (the reverse does seem to be the case only rarely). Ultimately, histories of male homosexuality will have much to gain from modeling themselves in conversation with lesbian histories regarding the latters' attention to modes of friendship, their permeable chronologies, and their sophistication when it comes to not knowing for sure. The historiography on homosexualities is alive and well. Whether it will continue to have staying power will depend, among other things, on its practitioners' ability to incorporate new modes of inquiry, to find new intellectual alliances, and to forge new narratives.

Notes

1. Lynn Hunt, "The Challenge of Gender: Deconstruction of Categories and Reconstruction of Narratives in Gender History," in *Geschlechtergeschichte und Allgemeine Geschichte: Herausforderungen und Perspektiven,* ed. Hans Medick and Anne-Charlotte Trepp (Göttingen, 1998), 59. The following paragraph invokes Hunt's signature piece.
2. Martha Vicinus, "Lesbian History: All Theory and No Facts or All Facts and No Theory?" *Radical History Review* 60 (1994): 57–75.
3. Michel Foucault, *The History of Sexuality,* vol. 1: *An Introduction,* trans. Robert Hurley (New York, 1978), 43. Cf. Michel Foucault, *Histoire de la sexualité,* vol. 1: *La volonté de savoir* (Paris, 1976), 59.
4. David M. Halperin, "Forgetting Foucault," in D. M. Halperin, *How to Do the History of Homosexuality* (Chicago, 2002): 27; see also discussion ibid., 26–32.
5. Jeffrey Weeks, *Sexuality,* 2nd ed. (New York, 2003), 30.
6. David M. Halperin, "Is There a History of Sexuality?" in *The Lesbian and Gay Studies Reader,* ed. Henry Abelove (New York, 1993), 426.
7. Erwin Panofsky, "Three Decades of Art History in the United States," in E. Panofsky, *Meaning in the Visual Arts: Papers in and on Art History* (Garden City, NY, 1955): 322–24; Hans Belting, *Likeness and Presence: A History of the Image before the Era of Art* (Chicago, 1994).
8. Jonathan Ned Katz, *The Invention of Heterosexuality* (New York, 1996); William Naphy, *Born to Be Gay: A History of Homosexuality* (Stroud, 2004), 33–49 ("The Birth of Homophobia"); Karma Lochrie, *Heterosyncrasies: Female Sexuality When Normal Wasn't* (Minneapolis, 2005), esp. xxi.
9. George Chauncey, Jr., "Christian Brotherhood or Sexual Perversion? Homosexual Identities and the Construction of Sexual Boundaries in the World War I Era," in *Hidden from History: Reclaiming the Gay and Lesbian Past,* ed. Martin Bauml Duberman,

Martha Vicinus, and George Chauncey, Jr. (New York, 1989): 294–317, 541–46; Gert Hekma, "Homosexual Behavior in the Nineteenth-Century Dutch Army," *Journal of the History of Sexuality* 2 (1991): 266–88; Jonathan Ned Katz, "Coming to Terms: Conceptualizing Men's Erotic and Affectional Relations with Men in the United States, 1820–1892," in *A Queer World*, ed. Martin Duberman (New York, 1997): 216–35; Harry Oosterhuis, *Stepchildren of Nature: Krafft-Ebing, Psychiatry, and the Making of Sexual Identity* (Chicago, 2000). See also Anna Clark, "Twilight Moments," *Journal of the History of Sexuality* 14 (2005): 139–60.

10. David M. Halperin, "How to Do the History of Homosexuality," in Halperin, *How to Do the History of Homosexuality*, 104–37, 185–95.

11. While studies on sex in ancient societies are exceptionally sophisticated, the confrontation of ancient practices with modern sexuality has not required a sustained consideration of the social, economic, political, and religious transitions from the Roman Empire to what came thereafter. The ancient past has remained forever present in the so-called West, without historical genealogies having to establish its relevance. Few historians of sexuality have treated late antiquity's ruptures and the rise of Christian asceticism with the finesse of Peter Brown in *The Body and Society: Men, Women, and Sexual Renunciation in Early Christianity* (New York, 1988).

12. Carla Freccero, *Queer / Early / Modern* (Durham, 2006).

13. Ibid., 48.

14. Gail Hershatter, *Dangerous Pleasures: Prostitution and Modernity in Twentieth-Century Shanghai* (Berkeley, 1997); "Translating Feminisms in China," ed. Dorothy Ko and Wang Zheng, special issue, *Gender & History* 18, no. 3 (2006); Gail Hershatter and Wang Zheng, "Chinese History: A Useful Category of Gender Analysis," *American Historical Review* 113 (2008): 1404–21.

15. Dror Ze'evi, *Producing Desire: Changing Sexual Discourse in the Ottoman Middle East, 1500–1900* (Berkeley, 2006), 88.

16. Helmut Puff, *Sodomy in Reformation Germany and Switzerland, 1400–1600* (Chicago, 2003), 92.

17. Khaled El-Rouayheb, *Before Homosexuality in the Arab-Islamic World, 1500–1800* (Chicago, 2005), 45.

18. Ibid., 48–50.

19. Wu Cuncun, *Homoerotic Sensibilities in Late Imperial China* (London, 2004).

20. Valerie Traub, "The Past Is a Foreign Country? The Times and Spaces of Islamicate Sexuality Studies," in *Islamicate Sexualities: Translations across Temporal Geographies of Desire*, ed. Kathryn Babayan and Afsaneh Najmabadi (Cambridge, MA, 2008), 19–20.

21. With a reference to Jeffrey Weeks, Dror Ze'evi has recently revived John Gagnon's notion of "scripts," for instance. See Ze'evi, *Producing Desire*, 10 and passim.

22. James Schultz, "Love without Desire in *Mären* of the Thirteenth and Fourteenth Centuries," in *Mittelalterliche Novellistik im europäischen Kontext: Kulturwissenschaftliche Perspektiven*, ed. Mark Chinca, Timo-Reuvekamp-Felber, and Christopher Young, Beihefte zur Zeitschrift für deutsche Philologie 13 (Berlin, 2006), 130.

23. Carolyn Dinshaw, *Sexualities and Communities, Pre- and Postmodern* (Durham, NC, 1999); Valerie Traub, *The Renaissance of Lesbianism in Early Modern England* (Cambridge, 2002).

24. Bruce Holsinger, *The Premodern Condition: Medievalism and the Making of Theory* (Chicago, 2005).

25. Jonathan Goldberg and Madhavi Menon, "Queering History," *Publications of the Modern Language Association of America* 120 (2005): 1609.
26. Valerie Traub, "The Present Future of Lesbian Historiography," in *A Companion to Lesbian, Gay, Bisexual, Transgender, and Queer Studies*, ed. George E. Haggerty and Molly McGarry (Oxford, 2007), 124–45.
27. Freccero, *Queer / Early / Modern*, 5. See also the special issue on queer temporality edited by Elizabeth Freeman: *GLQ: A Journal of Lesbian and Gay Studies* 13 (2007): 159–325, especially Carolyn Dinshaw, Lee Endelman, Roderick A. Ferguson, Carla Freccero, Elizabeth Freeman, Judith Halberstam, Annamarie Jagose, Christopher Nealon, Nguyen Tan Hoang, "Theorizing Queer Temporalities: A Roundtable Discussion," 177–95.
28. Goldberg and Menon, "Queering History," 1608–17.
29. Ibid., 1609. See also Madhavi Menon, "Spurning Teleology in *Venus and Adonis*," *GLQ: A Journal of Lesbian and Gay Studies* 11 (2005): 491–519.
30. Valerie Traub, "The New Unhistoricism in Queer Studies" (forthcoming).
31. Barry D. Adam, "Structural Foundations of the Gay World," *Comparative Studies in Society and History* 27 (1985): 658–71; David F. Greenberg, *The Construction of Homosexuality* (Chicago, 1988).
32. Louis Crompton, *Homosexuality and Civilization* (Cambridge, MA, 2003), xiv (my emphasis).
33. Ibid., 243.
34. Robert Aldrich, ed., *Gay Life and Culture: A World History* (London, 2006), 8.
35. Ibid.
36. Naphy, *Born to Be Gay*.
37. Alan Bray, *The Friend* (Chicago, 2003); idem, *Homosexuality in Renaissance England* (London, 1982).
38. George E. Haggerty, *Men in Love: Masculinity and Sexuality in the Eighteenth Century* (New York, 1999).
39. Afsaneh Najmabadi, *Women with Mustaches and Men without Beards: Gender and Sexual Anxieties of Iranian Modernity* (Berkeley, 2005).
40. Klaus Müller, *Aber in meinem Herzen sprach eine Stimme so laut: Homosexuelle Autobiographien und medizinische Pathographien im neunzehnten Jahrhundert* (Berlin, 1991); Hubert Kennedy, *The Life and Works of Karl Heinrich Ulrichs, Pioneer of the Gay Movement* (Boston, 1988). Scott Spector has embarked on a study on fin-de-siècle sexuality.
41. Alain Corbin, *L'harmonie des plaisirs: Les manières de jouir du siècle des Lumières à l'avènement de la sexologie* (Paris, 2008); Arnold Davidson, *The Emergence of Sexuality: Historical Epistemology and the Formation of Concepts* (Cambridge, MA, 2001).
42. Dagmar Herzog, *Sex after Fascism: Memory and Morality in Twentieth-Century Germany* (Princeton, 2005).

CHAPTER 2

~∶∶~

Sexual Identity and Other Aspects of "Modern" Sexuality
New Chronologies, Same Old Problem?

MERRY WIESNER-HANKS

The influence of Michel Foucault on the history of sexuality remains staggering. Only recently have a few scholars begun to suggest that we might finally be entering a "post-Foucauldian" period—"post," that is, in the sense of "beyond" as well as "after"—noting a range of conceptual and methodological problems that have arisen because of the power of Foucault's theories. I would like to focus on one of the best known of these, the notion that there was one clear break in the history of sexuality when either sexuality itself or "modern" sexuality was born, created, or discursively constructed (the operative verb varies.) Foucault, of course, sees the beginning of "sexuality" in the nineteenth century, when sexual acts and desires began to be a matter of concern for political, educational, and medical authorities who wished to know, describe, and control them.

Foucault's notion that there was one dramatic break has been affirmed by many of the most influential authors on sexuality since. Much of this discussion has centered on what Eve Kosofksy Sedgwick has labeled "the Great Paradigm Shift," the point at which the notion of a "sexual identity," particularly the identity of "homosexual," developed.[1] Initially this appeared to be the late nineteenth century, but more recently it has moved backward into the eighteenth. Randolph Trumbach has been the most influential voice in tracing this shift, stating in vivid language that "[a] *revolution* [my emphasis] in the gender relations of Western societies occurred in the first generation of the eighteenth century."[2] The revolution Trumbach identifies is the creation of a third gender, a group of men identified as distinct from other men through both sexual actions and effeminate behavior, whereas "before 1700 *all* [my emphasis] western European men had desired women and adolescent males."[3] Other historians of western European sexuality in this era have not been quite as sweeping as Trumbach, and have in particular questioned his assertion of a link between male homosexuality and effeminacy, as well as his further contention that a "fourth gender"—sapphic women—developed only much later.[4] But Theo van der Meer, Jeffrey Merrick, Bryant Ragan, Michel Rey, Michael Sibalis, and others have all noted that, "the eighteenth century ... does stand out as the period in which 'modern' forms of sexual identity appeared."[5] Works on eighteenth-century German literature, including those by Robert Tobin and Susan Gustafson, affirm this, with Tobin titling one of the chapters in *Warm Brothers* "Made in Germany: Modern Sexuality."[6] In her work on female-female desire and sexuality, Angela Steidele also focuses primarily on the eighteenth century, though she is more cautious than Tobin and Gustafson about the emergence of sexual identity particularly in her latest work on the well-known case of Catharina Linck, the cross-dressing prophet, soldier, and husband who was executed in 1721.[7]

The beginning of "modern" sexuality is not understood to be simply a matter of sexual identities. Thomas Laqueur states categorically, "sometime in the late eighteenth century human sexual nature changed," the key change being that from a one-sex gender model to a two-sex gender model.[8] In an article that is largely critical of work that assumes Foucault denied the existence of sexual identities before the modern era, David Halperin still notes that "[s]exuality is indeed, as Foucault claimed, a distinctly modern production," part of a "large-scale transformation in social and personal life" in which "sex takes on new and individual functions, and assumes a new importance in defining and normalizing the modern self."[9] Halperin does not take a stance on the precise chronology of "the Great Paradigm Shift," noting only that it was sometime "between the end of the seventeenth century and the beginning of the twentieth."

Every theory positing one dramatic break has been criticized both for its chronology (hence Halperin's caution) and for the notion of a single break rather than gradual transformation.[10] As you can see from my examples, however, the assertion that there was a gulf between "modern" and "not-modern" sexuality is still very powerful. Even Sedgwick's ironic and trivializing label has not ended the search for a moment of origin. (Sedgwick is, by the way, primarily interested in arguing against a totalizing form for same-sex desire in *any* era, not specifically that there was no shift, a point reiterated by Carla Freccero in her recent *Queer/Early/Modern*.[11])

The break between modern and not-modern in sexuality leaves those of us who generally define ourselves as "early modernists" in a peculiar position. Though we may not think about the connotations of that term explicitly, we tend to identify it by things that are new in the era. If we study Europe, we point to the European voyages of discovery, the printing press, gunpowder weaponry, the development of nation-states, the expansion of preindustrial capitalism, and the Protestant Reformation, to name a few. If we are, or have become, world historians, we are often more conscious about our use of the term, challenged by those who stress the cultural imperialism in the whole notion of "modernity." The *Journal of Early Modern History*, for example, which began publication in 1998, is one of a number of academic journals with "early modern" in its title or subtitle. It is the only one to define its use of the term, however, no doubt because of its explicitly global purview: "'Early modern'" is a convenient description for the age that was marked by a quantum leap in the level of global interaction."[12]

Historians of areas other than Europe in this era also tend to explain (and thus defend) their use of the term more than Europeanists have, and to point to increased interaction as the defining characteristic. The South Asia historian Sanjay Subrahmanyam, for example, notes that the period "defines a new sense of the limits of the inhabited world, in good measure because it is in a fundamental way an age of travel and discovery, of geographical redefinition."[13] He sees the effects of these interactions in "complex changes in political theology" and "new and intensified forms of hierarchy, domination, and separation."[14] The historian of Ming China Evelyn Rawski agrees, noting that "elites, ideas, and religions moved across regions with greater frequency than ever before, significantly influencing intellectual and cultural life."[15] Not all historians of other parts of the world agree with this characterization of the era, or the use of the term at all. The historical sociologist Jack Goldstone has been particularly critical, viewing the term as overly teleological, appropriate only to Western Europe, and putting too great an emphasis on market exchange and modes of production.[16] But explicit discussion of its implications has been more evident among scholars of other areas than it has been among Europeanists, whose generally unreflective use of the term has led Randolph Starn to proclaim that we are in an "early modern muddle."[17]

Despite this conceptual muddle, and a muddle over the exact dates of the early modern period (each of the now many journals and book series with "early modern" in the title defines the era slightly differently), we are not muddled about change being its key quality. But if the key change in sexuality does not come until the nineteenth century, or at the earliest the eighteenth, where does that leave those of us who study sexuality in the sixteenth and the early seventeenth centuries, what we might term the "early early modern"? Are we back in a timeless "premodern" past? Doesn't this (an even more dreadful thought) lump us in with medievalists, against whom we often define ourselves?

I will leave it to medievalists to defend themselves, a task that has been boldly undertaken by David Wallace—fighting what he terms the "Renaissance/early modern Behemoth"—and Nancy Partner, who opposes what she calls "the rapacious maw of the Early Modern academic machine."[18] What I would like to do, much less dramatically, is to simply note some ways that recent scholarship, particularly that on German-speaking lands, has suggested that there was something distinctive about sexuality in the fifteenth, sixteenth, and seventeenth centuries. In this I will be making an argument similar to one I have made earlier about women's history, i.e., that investigating the Holy Roman Empire often leads to problems with chronologies that have been described as "European" but are really based on only one area.[19] (For women's history this is most often England or Italy, and for sexuality England or France.) Hence the title to my essay. This argument parallels one made recently by Lyndal Roper about gender and the Reformation, in which she, too, notes that there has been "an exaggerated significance [attributed] to the late seventeenth and eighteenth centuries as the crucial period of change," leaving the Reformation "elided with the non-modern."[20]

I see these changes emerging in several different areas. First are new discursive practices that emerged in the fifteenth and sixteenth centuries, not in the eighteenth or nineteenth. Rüdiger Schnell examines what he terms the "discourse of marriage" (*Ehediskurs*) along with the discourses directed at men and at women (*Frauendiskurs, Männerdiskurs*), paying particular attention to the ways in which sexual self-control and misbehavior appear in these three types of texts. He traces changes in discourses of marriage from the fifteenth century on, seeing these as a source, rather than a result, of what has generally been described as the "Protestant" championing of marriage.[21] They also serve as a (very distant) foundation source for what historians of the twentieth century would label "compulsory heterosexuality."

The switch from a one-sex to a two sex-model may also not have been as dramatic as Laqueur posited. Ulinka Rublack asserts that gender difference was indeed an "ontological category" well before the eighteenth century, and notes that Laqueur's positing of a one-sex model before then is limited by the fact that he looks only at "sexual intercourse in the reproductive process, ignoring gestation and parturition as part of female reproductive labour."[22] On the issue of sexual identity, scholars focusing on German-speaking areas, such as Helmut Puff and Bernd-Ulrich Hergemöller, have largely supported the idea that, in Puff's words, "sodomy was not thought of as a lifelong orientation, let alone a social identity."[23] They provide a few cases, however, of individuals, as well as actions, being labeled sodomitical or aberrant. The Basel chaplain Johannes Stocker, for example, used the phrase "priest and sodomite" to refer to himself in a 1475 confession of having had sex with a youth. Puff highlights the difficulties in interpreting the word "sodomite": Was Stocker boldly claiming an identity? Forced to use the word? Agreeing with its condemnatory tone? And whatever his motivation for using it, how did he (or those who made him use it) understand the word? Puff cautions that "the labeling of sodomites, as such, does not constitute them as a social group," but the use of the word for an individual does suggest at least a hint of what Theo van der Meer has rather satirically described as a "same-sex proto-something." [24]

Beate Schuster examines patterns of discourse surrounding "Dirnen" and "freie Frauen," words for which there are no good English equivalents. (As Schuster demonstrates, "prostitute" carries anachronistic conceptual baggage in both German and English.) Her conclusions stress the increasing sexualization of both marriage and prostitution in the late fifteenth century, the role played by brothels in political conflicts among guilds, city councils, and the citizenry, the growing hostility toward all unmarried women, and the development of what she terms a new "morality of settledness" (*Moral der Sesshaftigkeit*).[25]

Along with discursive formulations, Schuster examines legal and social issues involved in these changes in understandings of sexuality, as does Heide Wunder in her many publications. Wunder sees new ideas about marriage and new notions of masculinity and femininity resulting from a combination of social and economic changes that allowed a wider spectrum of the population to marry and also from "reconceptualizations of the sexes and gender relations" that resulted in the "creation of the modern couple [which] presupposes that man and woman are dependent upon each other." This familialization of work and life made the marital pair the basic production and consumption unit, as well as "the measure of all things."[26]

While Wunder, Schnell, and Schuster all stress changes that began before the Reformation and shaped Reformation sexual ideology, other historians emphasize discourses that resulted from the Protestant Reformation. Susan Karant-Nunn includes extensive discussion of sexual metaphors and meaning in her analyses of changes in ritual brought about by the Protestant Reformation, describing Protestant attempts to "tame and domesticate the wild beast of sexuality" through engagement and marriage ceremonies, and to reunite women to the "body of man"—including the body of their husbands—through the ritual of churching.[27] In a classic article, Lyndal Roper notes the sharp distinction between Reformation understandings of the "common man" and the "common woman." The former was a hero who both understood the true meaning of Christianity and reflected this through the governance of his family and household; the latter, a woman sexually available to all.[28] This championing of proper Christian households was a central element in the efforts by which, after the Reformations, Protestant and Catholic religious authorities worked with rulers and other secular political officials to make people's behavior more orderly and "moral." This process, termed "social discipline" or "the reform of popular culture," has been studied intensively over the last several decades, especially in German-speaking areas. Such analyses provide a second area of scholarship suggesting there was something distinctive about sexuality in the sixteenth and seventeenth centuries.

The initial conceptualization of "social discipline" and early scholarship in this area, though aware of class differences, were largely blind to gender, which seems particularly odd given the fact that so much about social discipline related to sex.[29] That has changed, and most of the newer scholarship focuses on issues related to gender and sexuality. This recent scholarship recognizes the medieval roots of such processes as the restriction of sexuality to marriage, the encouragement of moral discipline and sexual decorum, the glorification of heterosexual married love, and the establishing of institutions for regulating and regularizing behavior, but also emphasizes that all of these processes were strengthened in the sixteenth century. The enormous body of scholarship on marriage, divorce, the family, and sexuality in the context of the Reformations makes clear that the roots of this heightened attention to social discipline are complex, and include much more than theology.[30] Though most studies are not directly comparative, as a whole they make it clear that these changes occurred in Catholic areas as well as Protestant, and that they involved church bodies as well as secular courts and other institutions.

The intensification of social discipline brought changes in men's lives as men. For craft masters, merchants, and other middle-class men, the qualities of an ideal man increasingly centered on their role as heads of household: permanence, honesty, thrift, control of family members and servants. Manhood was linked to marriage, a connection that in Protestant areas even included the clergy. This notion of masculinity became increasingly hegemonic and was enforced by law as well as custom. Men whose class and age would have normally conferred political power but who remained unmarried did not participate to the same level as their married brothers; in some cities they were barred from being members of city councils. Unmarried men were increasingly viewed as suspect, for they were also not living up to what society viewed as their proper place in a gendered social order. Scholarship on masculinity in early modern Germany, such as that of Martin Dinges and Ann Tlusty, has examined these processes, though as in so much else in early modern history, work on German-speaking areas has been eclipsed by a flood of studies on English masculinity.[31] (By my last count, there were six book-length studies of early modern English masculinity published in the last decade, not including those that focused solely on literature; this represented a healthy share of the *thirty* books on British masculinity that have appeared recently.[32])

The enforcement of social discipline had an even greater impact on women's lives. Laws regarding such issues as adultery, divorce, "lascivious carriage" (flirting), monastic enclosure, and interdenominational and interracial marriage were rarely gender-neutral. The enforcement of such laws was even more discriminatory, of course, for though undisciplined sexuality and immoral behavior of both women and men were portrayed from the pulpit or press as a threat to Christian order, it was women's lack of discipline that was most often punished. The idealization of marriage contributed to suspicion of unmarried women as deviant and dangerous, and to laws prohibiting unmarried women from moving into cities or living on their own, ordering unmarried female servants to take positions only in households headed by men, and even ordering unmarried daughters to leave the household of their widowed mothers to find a position in a male-headed household.[33] Renate Dürr, for example, has traced the demonization of female servants in the writings of Protestant moralists and the authors of urban law codes, who denounced them for immorality, sloth, laziness and disobedience.[34]

As with masculinity, studies of the social disciplining of women's lives have not been limited to German-speaking areas, but scholarship on Germany has been central in suggesting that there was a significant break with earlier patterns. Recent work has underscored the fact that social discipline is a long-term process, but it has also emphasized that this is no reason to discount its significance—no more than in the case of more familiar long-term processes such as "the rise of the nation-state" and "the growth of proto-industrial capitalism."

Puff ends his most recent book on sodomy in Germany and Switzerland with a hope that it might help "thwart our obsessions with telling histories that lead us toward what is commonly, though rather obtusely, called modern sexuality," an obsession that he, like most everyone, lays at Foucault's door. Like Sedgwick, Freccero, and many others, he highlights the artificial and constructed nature of the modern–not-modern divide and calls for queering this as well as other binary categories. His call to resist teleology is not absolute, however, but qualified by the comment that "we should not refrain from inserting temporality, the messy stuff from which history is made, into the equation."[35]

Puff's own work, and that of the other scholars of early modern Germany that I have cited, can actually help us accomplish both of these goals, which are not as contradictory as they might seem. This scholarship might also help us reconcile the conclusions of two recent commentators on the notion of "early modern," Randolph Starn and Wolfgang Reinhard. Both authors comment on ways in which the early modern period has been seen as distinctive, and they also point to limitations in these conceptualizations. They agree on many points but take diametrically opposed positions on the period's importance in German historical scholarship. Starn dismisses it in one sentence, noting that "'frühe Neuzeit' … was and has remained historiographically dispensable," with its usage "described as purely pragmatic and pedagogical."[36] Reinhard, on the other hand, comments that "the most elaborate arguments in favor of a particular 'Early Modern History' have been produced by Germans."[37] Interestingly, both cite many of the same works to establish their points, including a 1957 article by the philosopher Wilhelm Kamlah and Johannes Kunisch's comments on the founding of *Zeitschrift für historische Forschung*.[38]

Starn and Reinhard differ on another point. Starn highlights the use of "early modern" in gender studies and notes that the first book by literary scholars to use the term was *Rewriting the Renaissance: The Discourses of Sexual Difference in Early Modern Europe*, published in 1986.[39] Reinhard does not mention gender or sexuality (or women) at all. My brief series of examples here nonetheless suggests that Reinhard is right, but in part for reasons that Starn provides. In scholarship on sexuality, *Frühneuzeit* is not "historiographically dispensable." To pick up on Puff's two goals, I think we are stuck with the ungainly and teleologizing label "early modern," but we do not have to let the questions we ask about "our period" (however we exactly define it) be primarily those posed by historians of more recent eras looking for origins of what they find interesting. We can follow the lead of the world historians I cited earlier, approaching sexuality in the "früh-Frühneuzeit" not simply as a prologue to "the Great Paradigm Shift" of the eighteenth or nineteenth century, but as an era of significant transformation itself.

Notes

1. Eve Kosofsky Sedgwick, *Epistemology of the Closet* (Durham, NC, 1993), 44.
2. Randolph Trumbach, *Sex and the Gender Revolution, vol. 1, Heterosexuality and the Third Gender in Enlightenment London* (Chicago, 1999), 1.
3. Randolph Trumbach, "Blackmail for Sodomy in Eighteenth-Century London," in "Eighteenth-Century Homosexuality in Global Perspective," ed. Bryant T. Ragan, Jr. and Jeffrey Merrick, special issue, *Historical Reflections/Réflexions Historiques* 33 (Spring 2007): 23.
4. On the issue of effeminacy, see Jeffrey Merrick, "Sodomitical Scandals and Subcultures in the 1720s," *Men and Masculinities* 1 (1999): 365–84. On constructions of female same-sex desire, see Valerie Traub, *The Renaissance of Lesbianism in Early Modern England* (Cambridge, 2002); her critique of Trumbach is on 29–31.
5. Bryant T. Ragan, Jr. and Jeffrey Merrick, introduction to "Eighteenth-Century Homosexuality in Global Perspective," 1. Along with the article by Trumbach, this collection includes one by Theo van der Meer that includes references to his large body of scholarship on homosexuality in eighteenth-century Amsterdam. Jeffrey Merrick's recent analysis and translation of a 1666/67 case also, in his words, "underscores the significance of the changes in practices and attitudes that emerged in Paris, as in London and Amsterdam, around 1700." Jeffrey Merrick, "Chaussons in the Streets: Sodomy in Seventeenth-Century Paris," *Journal of the History of Sexuality* 15, no. 2 (May 2006): 167–203, quotation on 179.
6. Robert Tobin, *Warm Brothers: Queer Theory and the Age of Goethe* (Philadelphia, 2001); Susan E. Gustafson, *Men Desiring Men: The Poetry of Same-Sex Identity and Desire in German Classicism* (Detroit, 2002).
7. Angela Steidele, *In Männerkleidern: Das verwegene Leben der Catharina Margaretha Linck alias Anastasius Lagrantinus Rosenstengel, hingerichtete 1721* (Cologne, 2004). Her comments about sexual identity are on 142–49.

8. Thomas Laqueur, "Orgasm, Generation, and the Politics of Reproduction Biology," in *The Gender/Sexuality Reader,* ed. Roger N. Lancaster and Micaela di Leonardo (New York, 1997), 219. Laqueur first proposed this idea in *Making Sex: Body and Gender from the Greeks to Freud* (Cambridge, MA, 1990), a book that has been widely and rightly criticized, most recently in Michael Stolberg, "A Woman down to Her Bones: The Anatomy of Sexual Difference in the Sixteenth and Early Seventeenth Centuries," *Isis* 94 (2003): 274–99.

9. David Halperin, "Forgetting Foucault: Acts, Identities, and the History of Sexuality," *Representations* 63 (Summer 1998): 93–120, reprinted in his *How to Do the History of Homosexuality* (Chicago, 2002), as well as in Kim M. Phillips and Barry Reay, eds., *Sexuality in History: A Reader* (New York, 2002). The quotations appear in the latter collection on 45 and 46.

10. See, for example, Ruth Karras, "Prostitution and the Question of Sexual Identity in Medieval Europe," *Journal of Women's History* 11 (1999): 159–77. Katharine Crawford provides a succinct summary of these in her *European Sexualities, 1400–1800* (Cambridge, 2007), 200–206.

11. Carla Freccero, *Queer / Early / Modern* (Durham, NC, 2006). Chapter 3 is a critique of Halperin's article and the entire acts vs. identities debate.

12. *Journal of Early Modern History,* prospectus http://www.hist.umn.edu/~jemh/prospect .html (accessed 20 March 2007).

13. Sanjay Subrahmanyam, "Connected Histories: Notes toward a Reconfiguration of Early Modern Eurasia," *Modern Asian Studies* 31 (1997): 737. For a particularly forceful articulation of this view, see Jerry Bentley, "Early Modern Europe and the Early Modern World," in *Between the Middle Ages and Modernity: Individual and Community in the Early Modern World,* ed. Charles H. Parker and Jerry H. Bentley (London, 2007), 13–32.

14. Subrahmanyam, "Connected Histories," 739. Along with increasing interaction, Joseph Fletcher and Victor Lieberman have also identified common developments in many societies that, in Lieberman's words, "distinguished all or part of the period c. 1400–1800 from antecedent and succeeding eras." Victor Lieberman, "Introduction," *Modern Asian Studies* 31 (1997): 452. Joseph F. Fletcher, "Integrative History: Parallels and Interconnections in the Early Modern Period, 1500–1800," in J. Fletcher, *Studies on Chinese and Islamic Inner Asia* (Aldershot, 1995), item X.

15. Evelyn S. Rawski, "The Qing Formation and the Early-Modern Period," in *The Qing Formation in World-Historical Time,* ed. Lynn Struve (Cambridge, MA, 2004), 211.

16. Jack A. Goldstone, "The Problem of the 'Early Modern World,'" *Journal of the Economic and Social History of the Orient* 41 (1998): 249–84, with replies by Peter van der Veer and David Washbrook; see also "Early Modernities," ed. Shmuel N. Eisenstadt and Wolfgang Schluchter, special issue, *Daedalus: Journal of the American Academy of Arts and Sciences* 127 (1998).

17. Randolph Starn, "The Early Modern Muddle," *Journal of Early Modern History* 6 (2002): 296–307.

18. David Wallace, "Carving Up Time and the World: Medieval-Renaissance Turf Wars; Historiography and Personal History," University of Wisconsin-Milwaukee, Center for Twentieth Century Studies, Working Paper No. 11, 1990–91, 6, 7; Nancy F. Partner, "Did Mystics Have Sex?" in *Desire and Discipline: Sex and Sexuality in the Premodern West,* ed. Jacqueline Murray and Konrad Eisenbichler (Toronto, 1996), 297.

19. See Merry Wiesner-Hanks, "Gender and Power in Early Modern Europe: The Empire Strikes Back," in *Chloe: Beihefte zum Daphnis*, vol. 19, *The Graph of Sex and the German Text: Gendered Culture in Early Modern Germany 1500–1700*, ed. Lynne Tatlock (Amsterdam, 1994), 201–23 and "The Holy Roman Empire: Women and Politics Beyond Liberalism, Individual Rights, and Revolutionary Theory," in *Women Writers and the Early Modern British Political Tradition*, ed. Hilda L. Smith (Cambridge, 1998), 305–323. I have also addressed some of the issues discussed here in "Disembodied Theory? Discourses of Sex in Early Modern Germany," in *Gender in Early Modern German History*, ed. Ulinka Rublack (Cambridge, 2002), 152–73, though in that article the thrust was the way recent theoretical perspectives in sexuality have played out in Germany, rather than the other way around.

20. Lyndal Roper, "Gender and the Reformation," *Archiv für Reformationsgeschichte* 92 (2001): 299.

21. Rüdiger Schnell, *Frauendiskurs, Männerdiskurs, Ehediskurs: Textsorten und Geschlechterkonzepte in Mittelalter und Früher Neuzeit* (Frankfurt am Main, 1998). Schnell has also edited two collections of essays on marriage literature, some of which discuss sexual issues: *Text und Geschlecht: Mann und Frau in Eheschriften der frühen Neuzeit* (Frankfurt am Main, 1997) and *Geschlechterbeziehungen und Textfunktionen: Studien zu Eheschriften der Frühen Neuzeit* (Tübingen, 1998).

22. Ulinka Rublack, "Pregnancy, Childbirth and the Female Body in Early Modern Germany," *Past and Present* 150 (1996): 84–100, quotation on 86.

23. Helmut Puff, "Early Modern Europe, 1400–1700," in *Gay Life and Culture: A World History*, ed. Robert Aldrich (London, 2006), 86. This collection also has an essay by Bernd-Ulrich Hergemöller on the Middle Ages, one by Michael Sibalis on the period 1680–1850, and one by Laura Gowing on "lesbians and their like" in early modern Europe. See also Puff's longer work, *Sodomy in Reformation Germany and Switzerland, 1400–1600* (Chicago, 2003) as well as Bernd-Ulrich Hergemöller, "Sodomiter: Schuldzubeschreibungen und Repressionsformen im späten Mittelalters," in B.-U. Hergemöller, *Randgruppen der spätmittelalterlichen Gesellschaft* (Warendorf, 1990), 338–43 and his *Männer, 'die mit Männern handeln', in der Augsburger Reformationszeit* (Munich, 2000).

24. Helmut Puff, "Localizing Sodomy: The 'Priest and Sodomite' in Pre-Reformation Germany and Switzerland," *Journal of the History of Sexuality* 8 (1997): 165–95, quotation on 191. Theo van der Meer, "Sodomy and Its Discontents: Discourse, Desire and the Rise of a Same-Sex Proto-Something in the Early Modern Dutch Republic," in Merrick and Ragan, "Eighteenth-Century Homosexuality," 41.

25. Beate Schuster, *Die freien Frauen: Dirnen und Frauenhäuser im 15. und 16. Jahrhundert* (Frankfurt am Main, 1995).

26. Heide Wunder, "What Made a Man a Man? Sixteenth- and Seventeenth-century Findings," in *Gender in Early Modern German History*, ed. Ulinka Rublack (Cambridge, 2002), 22 and 23. Wunder has addressed these issues at greater length in *'Er ist die Sonn', sie ist der Mond': Frauen in der frühen Neuzeit* (Munich, 1992).

27. Susan C. Karant-Nunn, *The Reformation of Ritual: An Interpretation of Early Modern Germany* (London, 1997), 7 and 84.

28. Lyndal Roper, "'The Common Man,' 'The Common Good,' 'Common Women': Reflections on Gender and Meaning in the Reformation German Commune," *Social History* 12 (1987): 1–21. See also her *The Holy Household: Women and Morals in Reformation Augsburg* (Oxford, 1989).

29. The concept of "social disciplining" was first discussed by Gerhard Oestreich in his essays published as *Geist und Gestalt des frühmodernen Staates* (Berlin, 1969), a modified version of which has been translated into English as *Neostoicism and the Early Modern State*, ed. Brigitte Oestreich and Helmut G. Koenigsberger, trans. David McLintock (Cambridge, 1982). There is a good English-language discussion of the issue, and an extensive bibliography of both English- and German-language works, in R. Po-Chia Hsia, *Social Discipline in the Reformation: Central Europe 1550–1750* (London, 1989). A survey of the more recent literature may be found in Ralf-Georg Bogner, "Arbeiten zur Sozialdisziplinierung in der Frühen Neuzeit: Ein Forschungsbericht für die Jahre 1980–94; Erster Teil," *Frühneuzeit-Info* 7 (1996): 127–42. For a recent theoretical discussion, and a survey of scholarship on other parts of Europe, see the "Focal Point: Confessionalization and Social Discipline in France, Italy, and Spain," with articles by James R. Farr, Wietse de Boer, and Allyson Poska, in *Archiv für Reformationsgeschichte* 94 (2003): 276–319.

30. Representative monographs on social discipline in German-speaking areas include Thomas W. Robisheaux, *Rural Society and the Search for Order in Early Modern Germany* (Cambridge, 1989); Joel F. Harrington, *Reordering Marriage and Society in Reformation Germany* (Cambridge, 1995); Siegrid Westphal, *Frau und lutherische Konfessionalisierung: Eine Untersuchung zum Fürstentum Pfalz-Neuburg, 1542–1614* (Frankfurt am Main, 1994); Heinrich R. Schmidt, *Dorf und Religion: Reformierte Sittenzucht in Berner Landgemeinden der Frühen Neuzeit* (Stuttgart, 1995); Scott Dixon, *The Reformation and Rural Society: The Parishes of Brandenburg-Ansbach-Kulmbach, 1528–1603* (Cambridge, 1996).

31. B. Ann Tlusty, "Gender and Alcohol Use in Early Modern Augsburg," *Social History/ Histoire Sociale* (November 1994): 241–59, and *Bacchus and Civic Order: The Culture of Drink in Early Modern Germany* (Charlottesville, VA, 2001). Martin Dinges, ed., *Hausväter, Priester, Kastraten: Zur Konstruktion von Männlichkeit in Spätmittelalter und früher Neuzeit* (Göttingen, 1999) and *Männer-Macht-Körper: Hegemoniale Männlichkeit vom Mittelalter bis heute* (Frankfurt am Main, 2005). See also Lyndal Roper, "Blood and Codpieces: Masculinity in the Early Modern German Town," in L. Roper, *Oedipus and the Devil: Witchcraft, Sexuality, and Religion in Early Modern Europe* (London, 1994), 107–24; Merry Wiesner-Hanks, "The Religious Dimensions of Guild Notions of Honor in Reformation Germany," in *Ehrkonzepte in der Frühen Neuzeit: Identitäten und Abgrenzungen*, ed. Sibylle Backmann, Hans-Jörg Künast, Sabine Ullman, and B. Ann Tlusty (Berlin, 1998), 223–33; Scott Hendrix and Susan Karant-Nunn, eds., *Masculinity in the Reformation Era* (Kirksville, MO, 2008).

32. Mark Breitenberg, *Anxious Masculinity in Early Modern England* (Cambridge, 1996); Elizabeth Foyster, *Manhood in Early Modern England: Honour, Sex and Marriage* (London, 1999); Tim Hitchcock and Michele Cohen, eds., *English Masculinities* (London, 1999); Philip Carter, *Men and the Emergence of Polite Society in Britain 1660–1800* (London, 2001); David Kuchta, *The Three-Piece Suit and Modern Masculinity: England, 1550–1850* (Berkeley, 2002); Alexandra Shepard, *Meanings of Manhood in Early Modern England* (Oxford, 2003).

33. Merry Wiesner-Hanks, "Having Her Own Smoke: Employment and Independence for Unmarried Women in Germany, 1400–1700," in *Singlewomen in the European Past*, ed. Judith Bennett and Amy Froide (Philadelphia, 1999), 192–216.

34. Renate Dürr, *Mägde in der Stadt: Das Beispiel Schwäbisch-Hall in der Frühen Neuzeit* (Frankfurt am Main, 1995).

35. Puff, "Sodomy," 181, 182.
36. Starn, "Early Modern Muddle," 300.
37. Wolfgang Reinhard, "The Idea of Early Modern History," in *Companion to Historiography*, ed. Michael Bentley (London, 1997), 283.
38. Wilhelm Kamlah, "'Zeitalter' überhaupt, 'Neuzeit' und 'Frühneuzeit,'" *Saeculum* 8 (1957): 313–32; Johannes Kunisch, "Vorwort," *Zeitschrift für historische Forschung* 1, no. 1 (1974): 1.
39. Edited by Margaret Ferguson, Maureeen Quilligan, and Nancy Vickers (Chicago, 1986).

CHAPTER 3

~:·~

Interior States and Sexuality in Early Modern Germany

ULINKA RUBLACK

State-building in early modern Europe was based on a new order of the intimate, the "love laws" of Christian states that defined who was allowed to have sex with whom, when, and how this would affect their social privileges.[1] Classifications of what was legitimate or illegitimate sex underpinned statebuilding and its politics of shame, its rituals of inclusion and exclusion. Courts had to manage sex on an entirely different scale from that of the Middle Ages, and the language of domestic affect and sexuality was prominent in startling ways throughout society. Not only do we therefore have to challenge Foucauldian chronologies, which hold that sexuality only became central to state rule in the eighteenth century, but we also need to develop a sense of different but fundamentally embodied meanings of sexuality and subjectivity in this period. The sexual was part of a whole range of ways in which people accounted for their bodies and selves. "Discourses" here interest me primarily in their appropriation by common people and in the resistance to them, to show what particular groups understood to be passions or emotions and to what effect. I thus ask about the ways in which the history of state-building and the law is more widely connected to the history of emotions, beyond, though intimately connected with, the sexual. This chapter hence seeks to show how we might approach the history of sexuality as part of a history of subjectivity, and not just in terms of a history of public interest in sexuality.

Policing Sex in Early Modern Europe

Historians generally agree that after the mid-fifteenth century, secular authorities interfered much more determinately than previously to establish their understandings of proper femininity and masculinity. Urban magistrates and territorial princes began to vigorously regulate most forms of verbal and physical violence, disobedience, theft, and "improper lifestyle" due to excessive gambling or drinking, as well as sodomy and prostitution.[2] Sodomy was prosecuted as a capital crime, while prostitution was institutionalized and controlled in civic brothels. Legitimized prostitutes were labeled "common women," while other women suspected of prostitution were called *unendliche Frauen*, literally "never-ending women," and usually exiled. This went hand in hand with what Beate Schuster terms the new morality of "settledness": the right to stay in a community was now linked to the demand that a woman should clearly belong to a social institution under male control.[3] This institution was to be a household or—in Catholic territories after the Council of Trent—an enclosed convent. Correspondingly, the more regulative governmental authority began to be naturalized as paternal: magistrates and territorial lords steadily referred to themselves as fathers appointed to ensure the honor of the commune, which alone would grant it divine favor.[4] This made their policies part of a religious endeavor that was to ensure collective purity and salvation. During military conflicts, this understanding lent additional significance to symbolic politics identifying the city with a virgin. If she defended her honor, enemies would be unable to conquer her. This symbolism had real effects in several cities, where licentious women were seen to make the civic body vulnerable and invite invasion.[5]

Historians also agree that this specific moralization of communal life was integral to the success of Protestant reform movements.[6] Beginning in the 1520s, these movements challenged not only the sexual and judicial privileges of the substantial caste of clerics, but the validity of canon law and legitimacy of ecclesiastical courts. Moreover, just as the Augustinian monk Martin Luther abandoned the idea that fasting connected one to purity and had be practiced regularly, so he rejected the notion that celibacy should be embraced by sexually mature men and women and should be privileged. For the very first time in Christendom this move institutionalized the notion that sexuality was human and could not be transcended, contained, or relegated to particular occasions. It proclaimed mature humans to be sexual always. The fact that marriage for Luther no longer was a sacrament equally enforced the construction of sexuality as normal and mundane. Luther thus presented a turning point toward making prominent the "modern" notion that man was inescapably a sexed, desiring subject. Hence sexuality needed to be securely placed, and Luther firmly thought the only possible such place was a parentally approved marriage.[7]

At the same time, the view that celibacy hosted perversions became integral to anti-Catholic propaganda. The attack on celibacy was the key bodily referent to orchestrate claims for a reorganization of church and society. Its currency and political importance can be seen, for instance, in the grievances the German estates presented to the emperor at the Diet of Worms in 1521, which listed as its seventh complaint that "Rome awards German benefices to unqualified, unlearned, and unfit persons such as gunners, falconers, bakers, donkey drivers, stable grooms, and so on, most of whom know not a word of German" and claimed that "German benefices should be awarded to native Germans only."[8] Helmut Puff shows brilliantly how this rhetoric was further developed by Lutherans, and Caspar Hirschi underlines the extent to which it built on the foundations of a nationalist rhetoric developed by fifteenth-century German humanists. Rome was depicted again and again as a whorish city filled with sodomites and prostitutes; offices were obtained through sexual favors among men.[9] A caste of powerful Italian aristocrats who had legitimated their claim to spiritual authority through alleged sexual purity now needed to be dethroned; Luther did this by radically rejecting the whole basis of their claim—that one might be celibate and that such a life should be more sacred than clerical life.

If we take visual media to be not only passive representations of ideas but active agents in their construction, then the development of the Wittenberg court artist Lucas Cranach's visual satire "The Papal Ass" between 1523 and 1545 is another important example of the ways in which Protestants sexualized anti-Catholic as anti-Roman propaganda. A small, plump monster that allegedly had been found in the Tiber was first drawn in Bohemia. The drawing was sent from there to Wittenberg, where Cranach further accentuated its breasts in 1523, fully sexualizing it in 1545 for the final Lutheran campaign against a church council. The tightened body and alluring naked breasts, as well as the fact that this monster was not clearly recognizable as either male or female, were all taken as exhibiting Rome's perversion and falseness.[10] This sexualized monster was meant to fascinate and then disgust its audiences; it became an icon of Protestant propaganda, which did much to build up emotional reactions against the papal "Antichrist" among those sympathetic to Lutheranism. Mass-produced woodcuts invited an active imaginative engagement with this creature and the customization of ownership through the process of coloring, or the commissioning of its coloring.[11]

Ideas about respectable manhood, femininity, and conduct were thus at the heart of the social order envisaged by the Reformers and given visual and textual prominence. Heterosexuality, the choice of socially respectable partners, marriage, and procreation became constitutive of German Protestant manhood. It was frequently linked to the rhetoric of national honor, which equated the sodomite with duplicity and linked honest and virtuous German-ness to heterosexual fidelity.[12] In Foucauldian terms, then, the notion that sexual behavior made an essential statement about oneself as a moral subject and that it needed to be expressed actively and in one way only was newly characteristic of Lutheranism and influenced sixteenth-century German society.

Apart from visual media, such constructions were disseminated through marriage sermons, as studied by Susan Karant-Nunn, through the extensive marital literature, and through the courts. "New in the sixteenth and seventeenth centuries," Karant-Nunn affirms, "were the scale, frequency and vigour with which [marriage sermons] were preached to the entire lay population."[13] By the end of the seventeenth century, this genre affirmed that heartfelt love was integral to the choice of a marriage partner and positively acknowledged the role of conventional sexual intimacy in creating a bond between spouses. The "holy household" of the *Biederleute* (proper people)—a label that began to be used regularly in the fifteenth century—was meant to be sexually active. The household supposedly constituted a remedy against fleshly lust to prevent sin, of course, but also enacted an understanding of sexual difference and proper balance of hierarchy, pleasure, and bondedness within marriage. Sermons highlighted enduring fidelity as a pleasure in itself. This value could be symbolized through the flowers *Je-länger-je-lieber* and *Vergißmeinnicht* (honeysuckle, and other common plants with the romanticized vernacular names "The-longer-the-more-loving" and "Forget-me-not") in the garden of love. At the same time, Georg Gottlieb Pitzmann, a Silesian pastor in the late seventeenth-century, would warn his parishioners and pious readers to avoid "the poisonous Tunisian flower or little Turkish nail."[14] In a period in which the import of exotic flowers for patrician and bourgeois gardens in Germany as elsewhere had become a meaningful cultural pursuit and plants were studied on an unprecedented scale, a sermon of this kind endorsed a worldview privileging European plants in new visions of the domestic against the exotic, rare, colorful, non-Christian corrupt trade that would promise only momentary pleasure. Religious identities were about practices that embodied and built up specific ideals about the ways in which a community of believers located themselves on earth in relation to the divine. It implicated the religious self physically as well as intellectually, and it intriguingly imbricated sexual, religious, cultural, and political ideals.

As Lyndal Roper, Merry Wiesner-Hanks, and Sheilagh Ogilvie argue most strongly, apart from looking at the church, it is important to emphasize the particularly enduring strength of other German social institutions, above all communes and guilds, to enforce and regulate norms in daily life. Roper's pioneering work shows how the urban Reformation movements in Augsburg were from the very beginning supported by artisan groups within the citizenship whose defense of respectable masculine and feminine behavior formed part of a wider social and economic ethic of "fairness," local control, and domesticity. Secular judges were now entrusted with the regulation of sexuality and the "holy household."[15] The activity of such courts, which in particular called upon unmarried men and women who had had intercourse and punished them, has to be understood as collective practice of particular groups of men to affirm and reaffirm their moral values. As institutions, courts thus were not removed; rather, they could gain an unprecedented presence in communal life, involving a considerable percentage of the population through hearings. This much enlarged activity of judging and observing moral behavior from the sixteenth century onward led to legally sanctioned understandings of good and bad femininity and masculinity.

Ogilvie's research on the large Lutheran southwestern territory of Württemberg in particular demonstrates the extent to which local communities regulated migration and marriage patterns, economic activities, household positions, and political rights, in cooperation with state and church officials. The authorities' as well as the guilds' decisions disadvantaged women. They restricted opportunities for women to find employment outside the household and in labor markets unregulated by guilds. Increasingly, permissions to marry and form a household were strictly regulated by the state and local communities, leading to higher emigration rates among men.[16] This, as Ogilvie sums up, contributed to "high female celibacy, male scarcity in the prime working ages, and strong economic incentives to move into 'men's work.'" But these incentives were "partially choked off by these very social networks and the social capital they generated, concerned to protect their male members against female competition."[17] In other words, even though marriage was privileged as the ideal norm, this society also made it extremely difficult for most women to be in a position to marry or for widows to remarry. Around 10–15 percent of women thus never married at all, a figure in line with celibacy rates in central and western Europe.[18] Around 15 percent of households were headed by poor widows.[19] Courts, in turn, needed to deal with the stable number of those men and women who did not meet the requirements of celibacy before late marriage, or during all of their unmarried or widowed lives. Social institutions thus shaped demographic and social structures, making women more likely to experience longer periods of imposed celibacy and greater legal vulnerability throughout their life cycle.

One important continuity to the rulings of courts in the Middle Ages was the extremely restricted understanding of what constituted rape: women were honorable and trustworthy victims only if they were virgins, and usually of minor age. Men who raped small girls were harshly sentenced. This made immediately obvious the idea of legislating men and their supporters that any more mature woman might be likely to consent to intercourse. While convictions for rape remained steadily low, there were now considerably more accusations of sexual abuse within the family, for which women were held as responsible as men and severely punished. Another crime that was more vigorously prosecuted was infanticide. It illustrates clearly different evaluations of male and female violence against innocent victims, as homicide remained relatively common. Homicide was understood as unpremeditated murder and typically as a crime resulting from understandable anger between men. It was usually settled with a compensation of the victim's family; the victims' sufferings were never described. In infanticide cases, by contrast, the state of the baby was described at length and evidence sought to suggest that the killing had been planned. There was little sympathy for the emotional or social situation of the mother. The crime was constructed as an offense against God, who had given life to the child.[20]

Taken together, the sixteenth and seventeenth centuries in the German-speaking lands in these respects witnessed a tightening of patriarchal values in that those who upheld order newly problematized female sexual behavior outside marriage. They affirmed the importance of virginity before marriage and of sacrificial motherhood, despite the stigmatization of single mothers. Divorce remained almost impossible to gain in Catholic and Protestant territories alike.[21] Secular authorities also became more interventionist than the Church had been about misplaced sexuality within the "holy household," accusing men and their female victims alike of incest and punishing incestuous couples harshly. Secular authorities prosecuted sexual intimacy with animals more harshly and more frequently than at any time before.[22]

In addition, there was the specter of witchcraft. A curious division of labor has separated historians of witchcraft from historians of sexuality and female deviance more generally. Witchcraft, for instance, is omitted from Isabel Hull's discussion of the states' interest in sexual regulation in her important study *Sex, State and Civil Society in Germany*, to which I shall return.[23] But fears about witchcraft and the concern with sexual regulation were intrinsically linked. Such fears characterize the way in which gender relations were constructed and female and male sexuality were given meaning. It is particularly important to note that the accelerated number of witchcraft accusations in sixteenth- and seventeenth-century Germany, which were followed up by many territorial and civic courts, had as their theme not only the anti-housewife, but the anti-householding couple. In a peculiar way, historians have looked rather narrowly at the problem of "men in witchcraft cases" by examining the cases in which men were accused, and constructions of femininity in witchcraft cases by looking at the vast majority of cases in which women were accused. But if we ask how witchcraft cases were gendered, and more specifically how they reflect anxieties about the proper ordering of gender relations, we find that the male was always there—in the figure of the devil.

The devil, of course, was the very model of bad male sexuality and courtship. He was the man who seduced through false promises of money and power and looks. Witchcraft narratives typically described him as wearing beautiful, costly, soft, seductive—and either expensive black or colorful—clothes and accessories, such as feathers. Sex was foremost on his mind and it was not intimate. Sexual acts usually took place in outdoor spaces or stables, rough and fast. Afterward he immediately disappeared, but having sex had bound the woman to him. In one Würzburg case, the woman and the devil poignantly later sat at a table like a real husband and wife, but they merrily ate up children instead of raising them.[24] If, following Lyndal Roper's recent work, we think of femininity and fertility as key themes in witchcraft cases, then it is worth bearing in mind that masculinity and fertility again featured through the figure of the devil.[25] If the witch was associated with dry postmenopausal women, the devil matched her because he was cold and hard, his semen infertile. He had no heat and passion, which explained why he was immune to the fire of hell. No feeling could flow from the heart inside the hard, bitter, thin, and envious witch, and the devil had hardened her further.[26]

This was the image of coupledness that early modern Catholic and Protestant people and authorities alike so extensively came to fear and sought to find resolve against. The symbolic place of witchcraft thus was related to the new emphasis on procreative marriage and role of the *Hausvater* and *-mutter* across German society. It problematized the demanding behavior of older single or widowed women and their recourse to supernatural power. Such policies made it crucial for women to affirm their respectability by distancing themselves from the immoral behavior of women who would seek pleasure and act primarily for their own good. They, too, widened the gap in the status, rights, and emotional safety of married and single or widowed women—and, as noted earlier, German social institutions kept many women in this latter category.

There is a whole and fascinating semiology of temperatures embedded in such understandings, which followed on from Galenic ideas and connected medical ideas with a language of somatically manifest emotion. Just as hell was linked to fire, so the passions were linked to an overheating inside the body. Desire was thought to burn selfishly and extinguish any concerns about others. Conceptualized as being outside the order of moderation, it could only take over, extinguish, and possess, whereupon it had accomplished its cause. On the other hand, since only temperate heat made the semen fertile, both bodies, male and female, needed to have the right temperature and flow inside them. This condition also enabled one to open oneself to others and to material and spiritual nourishment, and to live in intimate connection with people and God in a healthy state of body, mind, and social relatedness.[27]

Protestantism thus, on the one hand, developed the specter of bourgeois heartfelt love and enjoyment of intimacy as integral to sexual identity, a complex linked to a whole set of norms about a pleasurable, pious civility and an aesthetics of German home-grown *Biedermännlichkeit*. Yet sermons continued to point out that very few women would be able to achieve such virtue.[28] On the other hand, Protestantism contributed to making sexual morality a key regulatory issue in the German lands.

Since attacks on Catholicism focused on the abuses of celibacy, it should come as little surprise that Catholic territorial states such as Bavaria, and arch-

bishoprics led by zealous Counter-Reformation bishops such as Julius Ech-
ter in Würzburg, were similarly concerned to fight illegitimacy as well as to
support a definition of virginity that rested on strict celibacy and thus had to
be enclosed. As Ulrike Strasser brilliantly argues, after Duke Maximilian I,
Catholicism in Bavaria furnished a gendered "idiom of meaning" that Bavarian rulers used to modernize political life. While tertiary nuns were enclosed,
the English Ladies of Mary Ward's teaching order were welcomed in Munich
to dedicate themselves to educating girls for their domestic and religious roles
as wives and nuns.[29] "Bavarian state authorities," Strasser concludes, "recruited
female virgins to demarcate legitimate and illegitimate forms of sexuality, to
maintain hierarchies of gender and class, and to endow power politics with
the aura of the sacred and natural."[30] She rightly emphasizes that the sexualizing effects of state regulation affected lower-class women particularly harshly
and demonstrates that Catholics responded to the Protestant concern that the
constantly sexed subject needed to be constantly regulated. Strasser affirms
that "understandings of gender and sexuality appear to be among the most far-
reaching and long-term effects of the German confessionalization process."[31]
It located passion as outside of marriage, something to be feared by but also
attractive to men and to be associated with lower-class, unrespectable behavior by women.[32] Confessional ideologies in the wake of Protestant attacks on
celibacy thus made sexual behavior the cornerstone of religious and political
morality in practice as much as in theory across confessional divides. The same
social institutions—guilds and communities—supported these moral values in
Protestant and Catholic lands to privilege men's access to economic and social
benefits.

Historians mainly agree in their analysis of these important shifts. As Merry
Wiesner-Hanks shows, this demonstrates that sexuality was turned into a political field two centuries before Foucault proposed it did, and that it affected
female identities in particular.[33] Historians have followed Foucault in showing
how these ways of imagining desire, masculinity, and femininity influenced relationships throughout society.

Reading Sexual Difference

A central issue historians have disagreed about is whether we can read criminal
records and other contemporary records only as documents of such a gendered
instantiation of values, and thus point to their standardized discursive nature,
or whether historians can capture how sexuality could be given meaning by
concrete people within specific relationships in more nuanced ways. The second part of my chapter therefore introduces some important studies that have
participated in this debate and then goes on to suggest a method of "responsive

reading" of early modern texts to render legible early modern subjectivities and the place of sexuality within languages of affect.

The first study of the construction of gendered sexualities through court trials was Ulrike Gleixner's *"Das Mensch" und "der Kerl,"* published in 1994 with the subtitle *The Construction of Gender in Fornication Trials of the Early Modern Period.* Her introduction strikingly remarks that "after reading several hundred interrogation protocols I began to think that I had always read about the same woman and the same man."[34] Even though the men and women who appeared before eighteenth-century courts in rural Prussia had very different life stories, Gleixner finds that they were forced to abstract from the contexts of their daily life so as to adapt to the courts' definition of "male" and "female" virtue as rigid categories with only one possible meaning. Whereas villagers evaluated illegitimate pregnancies in a contextual way—how a woman behaved generally, who the father was, etc.—the court was not interested in contexts and uniformly imposed a sense of dishonor and guilt on women. It therefore constructed the understanding that a woman could be recognized as good only if she always guarded her sexual honor and only had sex within a marriage. Women were held more responsible for seduction than men, and they were publicly pilloried if they "re-offended," whereas men simply had to pay a fine. All that was expected of men was to accept financial responsibility for a child they had fathered, while their sexuality was not seen as sinful and their honor not as polluted by premarital sex. Men in turn used the narrative of female seduction to reduce their financial responsibility.

Susanna Burghartz's 1999 study of "times of purity, places of fornication" (*Zeiten der Reinheit, Orte der Unzucht*) focuses on the Basel marriage courts during the sixteenth and seventeenth centuries and, like Gleixner, points out that illegitimacy did not decline as a result of disciplining.[35] First of all, she emphasizes that court activities produced illegitimacy discursively by defining specific sexual activities as either legitimate or illegitimate. They made these constructions a feature of the way in which morality was imagined. Courts were engaged in a permanent effort to exclude what they had come to regard as polluting society. Burghartz uses Mary Douglas's contention that activities that clearly define and distinguish "inside and outside, high and low, masculine and feminine, for and against" more generally serve to create order in a world experienced as chaotic and threatening. Since marriage had become so crucial to reformers' understanding of an anti-Catholic social order, it followed that sexuality outside marriage had to be stigmatized continuously.[36] In this way authorities staged their moral politics and Christian honor. Men and women, Burghartz concludes, told the marriage court about their relationships by using stereotypical images and stories. Their formula did not serve the expression of their experiences, but "led to the construction of gender and gender stereotypes."[37] Once more, the notion of women as sinful sexual seductresses and the lack of emphasis on male violence were disturbing and enduring features of this construction.

These discourses therefore produced an abundance of language that increasingly began to focus on sexual intercourse, rather than other modes of intimacy in a relationship. Helmut Puff's work has pointed out the silencing of homosexual experience through the activities of courts as equally relevant. His 2003 monograph *Sodomy in Reformation Germany and Switzerland* shows how it was explicitly argued that public punishments could "implant the seed" of sodomy by making people think of it as a possibility, and therefore advised that it was better "to silence this vice completely," true to its name "the mute sin."[38] Whereas before the Reformation there was no standardized language yet for speaking about sodomy, and trials against women or men entailed extensive descriptions of, say, a wooden dildo on a woman, trial documents became more overtly moralistic in the sixteenth century. Faced with capital crimes, the accused likewise represented themselves as seduced by someone of the same sex. Their self, Puff concludes, needed to be devoid of individual experiences and personhood to defend themselves as susceptible to evil, un-Christian influences by others.

On the basis of the particular records they have consulted, all of these authors thus affirm the power of courts to impose a collective, uniform narrative on subjects. Other historical work, however, has suggested that even trial records can provide us with a sense of how sexuality was imagined as part of a specific relationship with a wider way of being in the world and thus lead us to a richer understanding of past people's subjectivity. In her book *The Village in Court*, focused on crimes in rural Bavaria before and after 1800, Regina Schulte was the first to introduce the distinction between a "manifest" and "latent" dimension of criminal behavior that can be deduced from a reading of other cultural sources, such as songs or objects.[39] On a manifest level, poaching, for instance, was a lucrative, male business. On a latent level, however, Schulte argues that poaching songs reveal a world of young men who in their everyday lives had to cope with strict sexual regulations and domesticated females—the world created since the fifteenth century, we might say. The songs eroticized game, hunting, and wilderness. This kind of analysis seeks to look at crime as a meaningful and sometimes highly symbolic cultural practice. But the sources enabling such readings come from outside the courtroom. Historians therefore need to decide whether and how they think they are connected to collective experiences of a group involved in crime. In fact, Schulte treats the three groups she discusses—farmhands responsible for arson attacks, maidservants who committed infanticide, and young poachers—very much as collective cultural actors with a common mentality.

Lyndal Roper, by contrast, most clearly upholds that it is possible to encounter subjective experiences through an analysis of trial documents. In an important article entitled "Beyond the Linguistic Turn," published in the journal *Historische Anthropologie* in 1999, Roper argues against the notion that only language and discourses can structure reality. For her, gender entails pre-discursive elements—elements rooted in the body and the unconscious. Moreover, what interests her in court documents is not only the use of standardized narrative strategies, but also the ways in which individuals use discourses differently to express some of their experiences. "Subjectivity," Roper sums up, "is about the way in which a person structures their experiences emotionally and mentally. Subjectivity is partly framed by culture.... But it is also individual, since we do not react in identical ways to the same situations."[40] Roper takes the narrative of a Swiss man in 1667 as an example. He told the magistrate that the devil had asked for his body, promised him a beautiful woman, and tried to seduce him into committing suicide. The way he told the story related to fairy tales and dreams, but he assembled the elements, Roper argues, to unconsciously express his conflicting feelings about sexuality, age, longing, and despair. His emotional and physical experiences—desire—and his fantasies were the reason for his confessions, and need to be taken seriously as a historical force.

Susanna Burghartz, in an article published in the same year, likewise provides a reading of a late sixteenth-century Basel case in which a woman accused a man of violently attacking her, asking for compensation.[41] Maria Veborgen's language evoked powerful images that express her distress and fantasies of resistance: she said that the man had chased her so hard in a garden that her legs had been covered with nettle stings such "that it was a disgrace." "The nettle stings," Burghartz suggests here, "may be read as an expression of disgrace, which became manifested in a physical sign visible to all and a displaced account of the physical pain and injury she suffered in the garden."[42] Verborgen also said that her male companion had grabbed her by her plaits and that she had only managed to escape by cutting them off with a knife. The narrative symbolically reenacted the loss of her virginity she had experienced, since plaits were only worn by virgins. Ultimately, Verborgen was "successful," for the judges believed that her honor had been violently taken and asked for a compensation payment. Burghartz therefore stresses that there was at least some narrative scope that women used to eloquently give voice to their emotional and physical pain as well as their change of identity through male violence. It is also clear that judicial interrogations often tended to be open to a language of the unconscious, because questions pertaining to evidence such as where did you have a knife, where did the plaits fall, etc., were not rigorously asked.

In reflecting on these approaches, it is useful to draw on an essay by Kathleen Canning entitled "Difficult Dichotomies: 'Experience' between Narrativity and Materiality."[43] As a result of the debates surrounding the "linguistic turn," Canning contends, the concepts "discourse" and "experience" have often been evoked as different realms: "Experience became the unspoken, the implicitly materialized and oppositional counterpart of the discursive."[44] Alternatively, historians have regarded "experience" as completely shaped by regulatory norms and practices. In Canning's view, this has meant to deploy a "sanitized notion of experience, divested of its complexity, of the layers of memory and emotion, of the passions and positionings that propelled historical change at crucial turning points, such as desire, rage, grief, despair, resistance."[45] She points to the work of feminist philosophers such as Elizabeth Grosz and Toril Moi who ascribe an irreducible agency to the body, which expresses pleasure or pain as well as registers resistance.[46] Moreover, Canning stresses that it is important to historicize categories such as experience, alerting us to categorical dichotomies such as discourse and experience.[47] In a different article on the history of the body, she argues against the notion that subjects and bodies are simply passive surfaces, ready for social inscription, but equally against the notion that bodies are outside the social as an authentic "material" realm, just as, pace Judith Butler, it no longer makes sense to oppose the terms "sex" and "gender." Canning's work thus encourages historians to think in terms of an inflection of how subjects and bodies are formed by and exposed to ideas about proper behavior and their differential absorption and reworking of such practices.

But how are we to read those sources that are open enough to provide a window onto subjective experience? Like a psychologist listening to a person's story, historians, I would argue, can train themselves in the reading of texts in which a subjective involvement appears, listening for moments of contradiction, resistance, or uncertainty. Again, it is important to stress that the purpose is not to recover a more authentic nondiscursive voice, but to use court records and other narrative documents to see how early modern subjects worked their way through the gendered dimensions of norms and relationships, through conflicting demands, fears, and emotions. We need to ask how men and women gave norms about sexuality meaning and what narrative forms this could take. This, surely, is what must be implied in our limited attempt to encounter past people as humans. Such readings, in short, are not based on any wish to establish identificatory relationships between the historians and particular individuals—they serve to show how people in the early modern period made sense of or related to being, and how they experienced and resisted the conventions of their time.

In my own attempts to become a more sensitive reader of early modern texts, I have found it useful to take note of the work feminist scholars Lyn Mikel Brown and Carol Gilligan have done with girls, from which they developed a guide to responsive reading and "listening."[48] Despite the increasing attention that historians have paid to trial records, diaries, personal letters, and other types of what are called ego-documents, there seems to be little methodological discussion of exactly how historians should go about the business of reading them and arrive at a "thick" account of what the people whose voices we hear through them are trying to say.[49] Historians might therefore be well advised to approach this problem by learning from the social sciences. Brown and Gilligan's study first of all emphasizes the need to repeatedly read through the document and to pay special attention to different elements within the narrative each time. First, they listen to get a sense of what is happening, to follow the unfolding of events, to listen "to the drama (the who, what, when, where, and why of the narrative). Like a literary critic or a psychotherapist," they explain, "we attend to recurring words and images, central metaphors, emotional resonances, contradictions or inconsistencies in style, revisions and absences in the story, as well as the shifts in the ... narrative position. In this way we locate the speaker in the narrative she tells." At a second reading, Brown and Gilligan listen for the "voice of the 'I' speaking in this relationship." They describe this practice as an attempt to responsively encounter the power, creativity, suffering, and conflicts particular to a person. This has a political dimension, because one asks, "Who is speaking, in what body, telling what story of relationships— from whose perspective, in what social and cultural frameworks?" In a third and fourth reading of the text, Brown and Gilligan focus on the way in which people "talk about relationships—how they experience themselves in the relational landscape of human life." They ask "which institutional restraints and cultural norms and values become moral voices that silence voices, constrain the expression of feelings and thoughts, and consequently narrow relationships, carrying implicit or explicit threats of exclusion, violation, and, at the extreme, violence." This leads them to an analysis of "when relationships are narrowed and distorted by gender stereotypes or used as opportunities for distancing, abuse, subordination, invalidation, or other forms of psychological violation, physical violence, and oppression, and when relationships are healthy, joyous, encouraging, freeing and empowering."[50]

Obviously, reading early modern sources differs significantly from conducting an interview. But despite the constraints of the historical genres and social frameworks that allow us to encounter a person's account of her or his relational world in a particular context, Brown and Gilligan nonetheless provide useful suggestions for a methodology of reading our sources. Roper's and Burghartz's careful close analysis of particular trials, for instance, is implicitly informed by such tools—the attention to recurring images, inconsistencies, the sufferings and conflicts, but also the potential for a creative use of narrative forms for people in particular relationships and within particular institutional constraints.

We can link this technique with how Gabriele Jancke and Claudia Ulbrich have used feminist and postmodern debates to change the ways in which narratives of personhood—*Selbstzeugnisse*—are commonly approached. Jancke and Ulbrich argue that we need to read for different concepts of personhood that particular genres and a wide selection of authors (male and female, of different social backgrounds and religious beliefs) furnish. Instead of looking for the emergence of autonomous individuality, it makes far more sense to look at the emergence of personhood through the way in which people see themselves in relation to others, to the supernatural, to their body, to institutions, or even to things. Such an analysis of early modern texts can open up a spectrum of ideas and practices that gave meaning to masculinity and femininity. The question remains to what extent these differences form patterns that neatly correspond to the social, religious, or gender profile of particular groups.[51]

By Way of Example: Martin Luther and Katharina von Bora, 1545

Let me then provide an example of what it might mean to work with the technique of responsive reading to understand more widely how sexual difference acquires meaning in the early modern period.

In 1545, one month before he died, the aged Martin Luther wrote to his wife Katharina von Bora on an icy February day from the town of Eisleben—a place-name that literally translates as "icy life." The letter provides another fascinating glimpse into the way in which thinking through temperatures—the hot, the cold, and the temperate—was often made central to contemporary perceptions of micro- and macrocosm as well as embodied experience. The letter almost at the outset—and uniquely so—alludes to Katherine's knowledge that her husband of twenty years was impotent now: "Grace and peace in Christ, and my old, poor love, and as your Grace knows, impotent."[52] Luther relates his weakness during the trip from Wittenberg to Eisleben, and regards the fifty resident Jews in a village near Eisleben as a cause of this:

> Dear Kethe. I was weak along the way, just before we got to Eisleben. It was my fault. But if you had been there, you would have said that it was the Jews' fault or the fault of their god. For we had to travel through a village close to Eisleben where many Jews live, and perhaps they blew hard upon me. At this very hour over fifty Jews are resident here in the city of Eisleben. And it is the truth that, as I went past the village, such a cold wind blew back into the wagon onto my head and through my hat, as though it wanted to turn my brain to ice. This may have helped me to become dizzy. But now, God be praised, I am in good shape, with the exception that the beautiful women cannot tempt me as much, and I have neither concern for nor fear of unchastity.[53]

Later in the letter, Luther comments once more on the cold that makes one unable to do anything but freeze. For the first time, he signed as "old little love."[54]

To speak about impotence in the early modern period meant to say that a male body had lost the necessary heat to produce and consummate desire. For

Luther this was linked to an experience of age and feebleness. In his relation-ship with Katharina, Luther could allow himself to become "little" and still feel assured of love. He was playful and joking about his newly gained immunity to female beauty and temptation. This provides a strong sense of how he oth-erwise had experienced himself, namely as being exposed to sexual temptation through women; he always connected this to fears about unchastity. That is to say, Luther saw humans as sexual always and marriage as the religiously accept-able remedial institution for lust. At the same time, marriage did not obliter-ate the confrontation with extramarital lust. Only impotence—the end of the sensation in the flesh—could put a stop to that. But while impotence liberated him from temptation and guilt, Luther also felt ambivalent about this finitude. This unease presumably explains why in the same letter he commented so ex-tensively on the bodily effects of the cold and the porousness of his body and mind to evil, cold, non-Christian forces. The cold was connected to immobility and stagnancy—the end of pleasure and process.

Jewish activity always signified the coming of the Antichrist at the end of the world for Luther. The letter from Eisleben related the presence of embodied evil to a fear of bodily invasion and the disintegration of his mind. He attrib-uted to Jews the power of physical violation, knowing that Katharina regarded Jews as aggressors against Christians in this way. Luther's own feebleness, in other words, evoked fears of corruption and fantasies of annihilation, but in his following letter he also revealed that his heart was "chilled" because Wit-tenberg people still behaved so immorally and mocked God's word through their behavior. He wrote that he would rather stay away for longer and even live as a beggar than to return to Wittenberg and expose himself to "anger and dislike."[55] If body and mind were so cold, then negative passions might freeze him, because the range of positive, warming passions he could now experience had been so reduced.

In Conclusion

A source of this kind demonstrates that early modern subjectivity was experi-enced as deeply embodied, that is interlinked with the physical and emotional and equally interrelated with the external world. This shows that the history of sexual difference cannot be adequately reconstructed only through a history of social regulations, church, and state interest. It needs to flesh out the place of the sexual more widely in a symbolic universe, considering images of the body, concepts of personhood, and its imagined relatedness to good and evil. Doing so will make us understand how sexuality and sexual difference simultaneously gained meaning from physical experience, cultural perceptions of affect, and discursive constructions. Early modern German society was clearly fascinated by themes such as male sexual power or fertility. Fears of political immorality could be communicated through the language of female adultery, infanticide, and disruptive virility. Languages of virginity and motherhood symbolically communicated claims for political purity and liberty.[56] This was the result of the intensified politicization of ideas of sexual difference and regulation since the mid fifteenth century, when the "familiarization" of work and life had begun to widely characterize a growing society and posed new problems of order.[57] The resolution to these issues was to strengthen the guilds' and communes' control over who could reside in them via specific economic, political, legal, and social rights, and the resulting conditions served to disadvantage women.

Therefore much of the research reviewed and presented in this essay, in conclusion, suggests a revision of Isabel Hull's influential account of the character and effect of sexual regulation through early modern courts in her landmark *Sex, State and Civil Society in Germany, 1700-1815*, published in 1996.[58] Hull sets out to understand how sexual behavior was "shaped and given meaning to by institutions" in the early modern "absolutist" regime and subsequently by the earliest forms of the modern state in the eighteenth century. She argued that public interest in sexual behavior changed most strongly in this later period. Moreover, Hull proposes that "absolutism's actual interest in sexual regulation was extremely limited compared to that of the church" and, further, that "despite its Reformation-inspired pretension that it was the caretaker of its subjects' morals, the ancien régime restricted its active intervention generally to out-of-wedlock births."[59] In sum, she regards absolutism as more "inclined toward gender equality than ... the liberal, civil society that succeeded it."[60] Sex, she goes on to explain following a Foucauldian genealogy, was not regarded as integral to human nature, but as a privilege linked to status. Sexual dissatisfaction was not psychologically problematized. Desire expressed itself in customary ways that were often not merely genital, and that officials understood and tolerated in practice. The key mark of absolutist sexual regulation, moreover, was its failure in implementation.[61]

In this essay I have tried to show why it is misleading to use the notion of "gender equality" in connection with sixteenth- and seventeenth-century legislation, which needs to be understood as part of a whole set of institutional controls that served to disadvantage women in German society in striking ways.[62] I have argued that it is important to note that territorial and civic courts continued a policy of nonintervention against rape and that all these authorities agreed on strong measures against prostitution, which were implemented in practice. The abolition of civic brothels and campaigns against sexual licentiousness generated a new climate of suspicion against unmarried women. This needs to be related to a more widespread understanding that celibacy was impossible for sexually mature human men, and especially for women. Married women, in turn, found it easier to claim respectability, but were nonetheless more easily suspected of and far more harshly punished for adultery than men.

Public interest in sexual regulation found another expression in the prosecution of witchcraft, which projected fears about the corruption of the Christian household onto fantasies about older women's desire for the male devil. In this, as in other cases, fantasies about corruption were often linked to the idea that an older woman would lead a younger woman into sin. And such fears could turn into psychic realities, as they were taken on and adapted by women in these centuries. Scripts of fear and corruption that interacted with perceptions of sexual difference and its symbolization were broadly disseminated across urban and rural society. Women increasingly were made to pay the price for the shame that out-of-wedlock births caused. Perhaps one of the biggest changes in attitude concerned illegitimate births. While illegitimate children were a common feature of social reproduction not least among the elites up to the early sixteenth century, "bastard" children became stigmatized and a mark of lower-class immorality for the remainder of the early modern period. Instead of being ineffective, the increasing amount of sexual legislation led to increased pleading, negotiating, and bargaining, which gave mediating officials a powerful position and fractured any sense of communal cohesion.[63]

All these processes had a deep impact on the experience of sexuality and personhood in early modern Germany. The Reformation movements had enforced a sense that sexuality was a key regulatory problem for social order. In a city like Basel, the new institution of a marriage court continued to operate for centuries.[64] In a territory such as Württemberg, new "church-convent-courts," staffed by local elites, began to operate even in villages by the mid seventeenth century.[65] Religious ideas of purity and fears of divine punishment continued to underpin regulatory policies by secular and religious authorities and were likewise disseminated through sermons. Public interest in effectively distinguishing between legitimate and illegitimate sexual behavior thus rose markedly after the mid fifteenth century. It was biased to be predominantly rooted in the social and cultural experiences and interests of particular groups of men, and finally, it could profoundly shape experiences of body, self, and society for men and women in the early modern German lands.

This is testified to, not least, by the language of resistance to which some women resorted against experiences of male violation and degradation. One of them was the wife of a carpenter in northern Germany, Friderica Soht. As late as 1752, she wrote a letter to the Lutheran pastor of her village, explaining why she had illegally deserted her violent husband. "It is not my business to be hit by Detlef Soht," she summed up, adding determinedly, "I can justify myself before God for not thanking him for such wonderful deeds, but he has to know whether he can justify how he has acted. Women have not been created so that they lie fully under male feet. A human being will walk in a human way—*Ein Mensch geht ein Menschen Gang.*"⁶⁶

Notes

1. The expression love-laws is aptly adopted from the writings of Arundahti Roy by Carol Gilligan and David A. J. Richards, *The Deepening Darkness: Patriarchy, Resistance, and the Democratic Future* (Cambridge, 2009).
2. An outstanding introduction to the extensive literature is Merry E. Wiesner-Hanks, *Christianity and Sexuality in the Early Modern World: Regulating Desire, Reforming Practise*, 2nd ed. (Abingdon, 2010).
3. Beate Schuster, *Die freien Frauen: Dirnen und Frauenhäuser im 15. und 16. Jahrhundert* (Frankfurt am Main, 1995); Peter Schuster, *Das Frauenhaus: Städtische Bordelle in Deutschland 1350–1600* (Paderborn, 1992).
4. Joel F. Harrington, "*Hausvater* and *Landesvater*: Paternalism and Marriage Reform in Sixteenth-Century Germany," *Central European History* 25 (1992): 52–75.
5. Ulinka Rublack, "Wench and Maiden: Women, War and the Pictorial Function of the Feminine in German Cities in the Early Modern Period," *History Workshop Journal* 44 (1997): 1–22.
6. Two particularly important publications are Lyndal Roper, *The Holy Household: Women and Morals in Reformation Augsburg* (Oxford, 1989); and R. Po-Chia Hsia, *Social Discipline in the Reformation: Central Europe, 1550–1750* (London, 1989).
7. The best introduction in English is Susan C. Karant-Nunn and Merry E. Wiesner-Hanks, eds., *Luther on Women: A Sourcebook* (Cambridge, 2003), 88–136; for a recent more general discussion see Katherine Crawford, *European Sexualities, 1400–1600* (Cambridge, 2007), 55–99.
8. Gerald Strauss, *Manifestations of Discontent on the Eve of the German Reformation* (Bloomington, 1971), 54.
9. Helmut Puff, *Sodomy in Reformation Germany and Switzerland 1400–1600* (Chicago, 2003), 107–78; Caspar Hirschi, *Wettkampf der Nationen: Konstruktionen einer deutschen Ehrgemeinschaft an der Wende vom Mittelalter zur Neuzeit* (Göttingen, 2006), 326–47.
10. Konrad Lange, *Der Papstesel: Ein Beitrag zur Kultur-und Kunstgeschichte des Reformationszeitalters* (Göttingen, 1891); Robert W. Scribner, *For the Sake of the Simple Folk: Popular Propaganda for the German Reformation* (Cambridge, 1981), 129–32.
11. For an example of such coloring, see the cover of Ulinka Rublack, *Reformation Europe* (Cambridge, 2005).
12. Ibid., 47
13. Susan Karant-Nunn, "'Fragrant Wedding Roses': Lutheran Wedding Sermons and Gender Definition in Early Modern Germany," *German History* 1 (1999): 25–41.
14. Ibid., 34.
15. Roper, *Holy Household*, 7–88.
16. Sheilagh C. Ogilvie, *A Bitter Living: Women, Markets, and Social Capital in Early Modern Germany* (Oxford, 2003), 64.
17. Ibid., 74.
18. Ibid., 42.
19. Ibid., 177.

20. Ulinka Rublack, *The Crimes of Women in Early Modern Germany* (Oxford, 1999), 163–96, on incest see 231–54.
21. Ibid., 197–230.
22. For a preliminary exploration of Württemberg see Karl Wegert, *Popular Culture, Crime and Social Control in 18th Century Württemberg* (Stuttgart, 1994).
23. Isabel Hull, *Sex, State and Civil Society in Germany, 1700–1815* (Ithaca, NY, 1996).
24. Laura Kounine, *Witch-Hunting and Attitudes to Gender in Counter-Reformation Würzburg* (MPhil diss., Cambridge University, 2007), 82.
25. Lyndal Roper, *Witch Craze: Terror and Fantasy in Baroque Germany* (New Haven, 2004).
26. This theme is further explored in Ulinka Rublack, "Fluxes: The Early Modern Body and the Emotions," *History Workshop Journal* 53 (2002): 1–16.
27. Ibid.
28. Karant-Nunn, "'Fragrant Wedding Roses,'" 40. For the domestic ideal of marriage see Ulinka Rublack, *Dressing Up: Cultural Identity in Early Modern Germany* (Oxford, 2010), chap. 6.
29. Ulrike Strasser, *State of Virginity: Gender, Religion, and Politics in an Early Modern Catholic State* (Ann Arbor, 2004), 150.
30. Ibid., 173.
31. Ibid., 176.
32. Ibid., 178; for the same conclusion see also Rublack, *Crimes of Women*, 260.
33. Merry E. Wiesner, "Disembodied Theory? Discourses of Sex in Early Modern Germany," in *Gender in Early Modern German History*, ed. Ulinka Rublack (Cambridge, 2002), 162.
34. Ulrike Gleixner, *"Das Mensch" und "der Kerl": Die Konstruktion von Geschlecht in Unzuchtsverfahren der Frühen Neuzeit (1700–1760)* (Frankfurt am Main, 1994), 9.
35. Susanna Burghartz, *Zeiten der Reinheit, Orte der Unzucht: Ehe und Sexualität in Basel während der Frühen Neuzeit* (Paderborn, 1999), 8.
36. Ibid., 286.
37. Ibid., 289.
38. Puff, *Sodomy*, 75–104.
39. Regina Schulte, *The Village in Court: Arson, Infanticide and Poaching in the Court Records of Upper Bavaria, 1848–1910*, trans. Barrie Selman (Cambridge, 1994).
40. Lyndal Roper, "Jenseits des Linguistic Turn," *Historische Anthropologie* 3 (1999), 452–66, here 457.
41. Susanna Burghartz, "Tales of Seduction, Tales of Violence: Argumentative Strategies before the Basle Marriage Court," *German History* 1 (1999): 41–56.
42. Ibid., 49.
43. Kathleen Canning, "Difficult Dichotomies: 'Experience' between Narrativity and Materiality," in K. Canning, *Gender History in Practice: Historical Perspectives on Bodies, Class, and Citizenship* (Ithaca, NY, 2006), 101–20.
44. Ibid., 102.
45. Ibid., 103.
46. Ibid., 116.
47. Ibid., 120.
48. Lyn Mikel Brown and Carol Gilligan, *Meeting at the Crossroads: Women's Psychology and Girls' Development* (Cambridge, MA, 1992), 25–30.

49. See Mary Fulbrook and Ulinka Rublack, eds., "Egodocuments," special issue, *German History* 3 (2010): introduction.
50. Brown and Gilligan, *Meeting at the Crossroads*, 27–28.
51. Gabriele Jancke and Claudia Ulbrich, "Vom Individuum zur Person: Neue Konzepte im Spannungsfeld von Autobiographietheorie und Selbstzeugnisforschung," *Querelles: Jahrbuch für Frauen- und Geschlechterforschung* (Göttingen) 10 (2005): 25.
52. Karant-Nunn and Wiesner-Hanks, *Luther on Women*, 193.
53. Ibid.
54. Ibid.
55. Ibid., 194.
56. Ulinka Rublack, "State-formation, Gender and the Experience of Governance in Early Modern Württemberg," in Rublack, *Gender in Early Modern German History*, 213.
57. Heide Wunder, *He Is the Sun, She Is the Moon: Women in Early Modern Germany*, trans. Thomas Cunlap (Cambridge, MA, 1998), 1–15.
58. Hull, *Sex, State, and Civil Society*.
59. Ibid., 3.
60. Ibid.
61. Ibid.
62. In spite of Hull's remarks on the theme, ibid., 85. See also Ogilvie, *Bitter Living*.
63. Rublack, "State-formation, Gender and the Experience of Governance," 211.
64. Burghartz, *Zeiten der Unreinheit*; on Bern see Heinrich R. Schmidt, *Dorf und Religion: Reformierte Sittenzucht in Berner Landgemeinden der Frühen Neuzeit* (Stuttgart, 1995).
65. In addition to Ogilvie, *Bitter Living*, and Rublack, *Crimes of Women*, these have also been explored by David Warren Sabean, *Property, Production, and Family in Neckarhausen, 1700–1870* (Cambridge, 1990). For the activities of courts in Baden see André Holenstein, "*Gute Policey*" *und lokale Gesellschaft im Staat des Ancien Régime: Das Fallbeispiel der Markgrafschaft Baden(-Durlach)* (Epfendorf, 2003).
66. Alexandra Lutz, *Ehepaare vor Gericht: Konflikte und Lebenswelten in der Frühen Neuzeit* (Frankfurt am Main and New York, 2006), 187.

CHAPTER 4

~:~

Saying It with Flowers
Post-Foucauldian Literary History and the Poetics of Taboo in a Premodern German Love Song (Walther von der Vogelweide's "Lindenlied")

ANDREAS KRASS

The Poetics of Taboo: The Will to Knowledge

In Michel Foucault's introductory volume to his discursive history of sexuality, *La volonté de savoir* (*The History of Sexuality*, vol. 1, *An Introduction*), he criticizes what he calls the "repressive hypothesis." Victorian taboos, according to Foucault, did not silence speaking about sexuality, but rather enabled it in the first place: "There was installed rather an apparatus for producing an ever greater quantity of discourse about sex, capable of functioning and taking effect in its very economy."[1] Taboos do not determine *whether* sexuality is talked about, but rather *how* sexuality is talked about. They are a strategic instrument in the interplay between discourses, practices, and institutions, which Foucault labels the deployment (*dispositif*) of sexuality. This deployment emerged in the second half of the nineteenth century when medicine, which engendered "sexuality" in the first place, achieved a superior position among the discourses dealing with sexuality. During the Middle Ages and Renaissance, the church and the judiciary determined how sexuality was talked about even before there was such a term, as recent scholarship has shown. Back then the discourse centered on sodomy, which, in a narrow sense, meant anal penetration between men, but in a broader sense meant any sexual practice that did not uphold the reproductive mandate of Christian marriage.[2] Sexual misconduct was judged as a sin and a crime, and not, as would later be the case, as an illness according to pathological indices.

A further development accompanied this discursive shift. The modern phenomenon of sexuality is no longer merely a matter of acts committed, but also a matter of one's existence. It is no longer concerned with mere practices, but also identity. Sexuality provides information about a person's psyche. Sexual conduct is characteristic of a personality type and assigns a person to a to a particular group with certain characteristics. The modern deployment of sexuality delineates a typology for sexual aberrations that can be read as a distorted image of the bourgeois nuclear family. Alongside the Malthusian couple, the deployment incorporates the onanistic child, the hysterical woman, and the adult pervert whose perversions can be divided into a broad spectrum of subtypes.[3]

As Dagmar Herzog shows in her study *Sex in Crisis*,[4] the deployment of sexuality persists even in the twenty-first century. It continues to be centered on marriage and the family and still operates by pathologizing individuals and groups. Yet, as far as the situation in the United States is concerned, the unholy alliance of evangelicals and the Republican Party has induced a transformation that can be described as a politicization of sexuality (and a sexualization of politics). Queer theory provides the decisive analytic category for this transformation, namely heteronormativity.[5] In the view of right-wing sexual politics, sexuality in heteronormative channels is "good" sexuality. Not only is "good" sexuality tolerated, but it is moreover propagated with the help of practical guidebooks and pamphlets. Conversely, sexuality that breaks with the heteronormative framework continues to be pathologized, though now the range of pathologization is growing considerably. The psychiatrist no longer simply has cases of homosexuals, whose cure is guaranteed so long as they receive therapy. According to this point of view, every heterosexual who does not keep to the rules of "good" sexuality reveals a lack of self-esteem and incurs mental damage. The cautionary tale of a young woman who did not have the inner strength to save her precious virginity until marriage brings to mind the jaundiced images of the onanistic child and the hysterical woman. The girl who engages in sex prematurely not only conducts herself in a morally reprehensible way but also squanders her psychic health and bars herself from the promise of sexual satisfaction in matrimony.

Walther von der Vogelweide draws a completely different picture of a young woman in his "Lindenlied," the most famous medieval German love song. The lyrics depict a young woman meeting her lover out in nature for a round of lovemaking. This song shows the kind of contribution that literary history can make to the discursive history of sexuality.[6] The song does not sing of spiritual frailty or squandered joy. Instead, it sings of the joys of consummated love. Walther sings the song in the persona of a woman who is thoroughly aware of the moral taboo that looms over extramarital love affairs. The taboo induces her to produce discourse. Indeed, her discourse *plays* with the taboo that it breaks. The song provides an excellent example for the kind of *ars erotica* that Foucault juxtaposes with *scientia sexualis*. Foucault sees it as a foregone conclusion that *scientia sexualis* can function as *ars erotica*. The success of Richard von

Krafft-Ebing's classic work in the science of sexuality, *Psychopathia sexualis*, first published in 1886, was due to its dual reception as not only an academic work but also a pornographic one. A similar phenomenon appears in the medieval penitentials, which list every imaginable sexual practice. The penitentials also risked spreading information about non-normative sexual practices. Walther's song, however, represents a different case, in which the inversion of the taboo is not an inversion of an aesthetic of reception, but of an aesthetic of production. The song documents a form of discursification that Foucault does not take into consideration, namely the option of a poetic eroticizing of the taboo. Walther does not subscribe to the sexual taboo. Instead, he uses it as an aesthetic medium. He quotes fragments from discourses that gain energy from the taboo in question, and shapes the fragments into a poetic language of love that eludes the heteronormative order.[7]

1 ‚Under der linden an der heide,
dâ unser zweier bette was,
dâ mugent ir vinden schône beide
gebrochen bluomen unde gras.
Vor dem walde in einem tal,
tandaradei,
schône sanc diu nahtegal.

2 Ich kam gegangen zuo der ouwe,
dô was mîn friedel komen ê.
dâ wart ich enpfangen, hêre frowe,
daz ich bin sælic iemer mê.
Kuster mich? wol tûsentstunt,
tandaradei,
seht, wie rôt mir ist der munt.

3 Dô hât er gemachet alsô rîche
von bluomen eine bettestat.
des wirt noch gelachet innechîche,
kumt ieman an daz selbe pfat,
Bî den rôsen er wol mac,
tandaradei,
merken, wâ mirz houbet lac.

4 Daz er bî mir læge, wessez iemen,
nun welle got, sô schamt ich mich.
wes er mit mir pflæge, niemer niemen
bevinde daz, wan er und ich,
Und ein kleinez vogellîn,
tandaradei,
daz mac wol getriuwe sîn.'[8]

"Under the linden tree on the heath,
where we two had our bed,
there you may find lovely, both
broken flowers and grass.
In a dale, at the edge of the woods,
tandaradei,
beautifully sang the nightingale.

I came walking to the field,
my lover was there before me,
there was I received, Blessed Lady,
so that I am joyous evermore.
Did he kiss me? Many times!
tandaradei
See how red my mouth is.

There he made so splendidly
A bed out of flowers.
One would laugh to himself
should he take that same path.
By the roses he could well
tandaradei
note where my head lay.

That he lay by me, if anyone knew,
God forbid, I would be ashamed.
What he did with me, may no one ever
find out, except for him and me,
and a small little bird,
tandaradei
Which, I trust, will be true."[9]

Clerical Discourse: Kisses on the Mouth

Foucault designates confession as the central practice in medieval sexual discourse as well as in the modern deployment of sexuality.[10] The investigation of the believer's conscience, conducted by the father confessor, provides an incentive to speak about lust. A handbook for confessors from the year 1330 demonstrates just how forceful the pastoral will to knowledge is. With extramarital sexual intercourse in mind, the author demands that the father confessor inquire about the precise circumstances of the act in question: "whether the sexual sin had been committed with an unwedded or wedded woman, with a widow or a virgin; whether the woman had been raped or had she given herself over voluntarily; whether the sinner had violated marriage only once or frequently; whether he slept with a variety of people, when and where he incurred the guilt of adultery."[11]

Walther invokes these types of clerical speech acts when he has his singing persona make a confession of her love. She divulges information on her breaking the erotic taboo, in full realization that she has done something forbidden. Instead of an avowal laden with guilt and remorse, however, hers is full of happiness and joy. The forms of speech, along with the speech act, point toward clerical discourse. Walther refers to biblical texts, which he quotes word for word, and to biblical situations, which he evokes through associative allusions. The song draws on three episodes from the Bible that, in their own various ways, each deal with erotic encounters: the meeting of the lovers in the Song of Songs, the Fall of Adam and Eve in the Book of Genesis, and the Annunciation to Mary in the Gospel of Luke. Walther's references to Holy Scripture are not at all about making theological declarations. Instead, they eroticize the song. The quoted passages not only provide Walther with vocabulary, but at the same time enable a semantic contrast that uses the holy words to stage an unholy event.

Scholarship about Walther's love song has frequently addressed the *Canticum Canticorum* quotation.[12] The parallel to the "Lindenlied" resides in the two pairs of lovers' encounter in nature. In an allegorical exegesis of the Bible, the encounter is usually said to refer to an encounter between Christ and Mary, Christ and the Church, or Christ and the soul, thereby barring from view the profane erotic content of the encounter, which is in the foreground of Walther's song. The resonances are distributed throughout the first three stanzas of the song: the bed of flowers (3.3: *von bluomen eine bettestat;* cf. 1.2: *dâ unser zweier bette was*),[13] the anticipation of the lover (1.3: *mîn friedel*),[14] the return to nature (2.1f.: *Ich kam gegangen zuo der ouwe / dô was mîn friedel komen ê*),[15] and the profusion of kisses (2.7, 9: *Kuster mich? wol tûsentstunt, [...], seht wie rôt mir ist der munt*).[16]

The Fall of Man and the Annunciation are communicated more through association than through quotation. Walther demonstrated mastery of religious allusions in his political songs, and the same technique also appears in his erotic songs.[17] The allusion to the Fall of Man is woven into the fourth stanza. The parallel here resides in the configuration of similar motifs: the paradisiacal tree (1.1: *Under der linden*),[18] the ensuing shame (4.2: *sô schamt ich mich*),[19] and the fear of being discovered (4.1: *wessez iemen*; 4.4: *niemer niemen bevinde daz*).[20] In the "Lindenlied" the transgression relates to concupiscence, which accord- ing to theological interpretations is a *result* of the Fall (4.1: *Daz er bî mir læge*). The themes of knowledge (*wessez*) and discovery (*bevinde*) indicate the same themes that brought about the Fall.[21] In the "Lindenlied," the mention of God preventing the exposure of the lovers (4.2: *nun welle got*—"God forbid") is an ironic inversion of the biblical situation. God is not presented as a judge, but as an accomplice to the malefactors.[22] The nightingale who graces the Fall with its aphrodisiacal "tandaradei" (1.5–7) takes over the role of the seductive snake who whispers suggestions of transgression.

The allusions to the Annunciation are in the second stanza. Here, again, the allusion involves an audacious role reversal. The Virgin, without ever hav- ing "known" a man, *receives* the angel and then, through the angel's salutation, *conceives* (in German "empfangen" means both) the son of God. By contrast, the persona in the "Lindenlied" bears in mind the overwhelming reception that her lover gave her. The virgin does not conceive/receive, instead she is received—and in a sexually gratifying way. The motifs of homage (2.3: *hêre frowe*),[23] gratification (2.4: *daz ich bin sælich iemer mê*),[24] arrival (2.1 f.: *Ich kam gegangen* [...] *dô was mîn friedel komen ê*),[25] and reception/conception (2.3: *dâ wart ich enpfangen*)[26] further point in this direction.

Courtly Discourse: The Shadow of the Linde

By alluding to the speech act of confession and to biblical speech in the "Lin- denlied," Walther invokes clerical discourse, which treats marriage as the only place for sexual love and sees reproduction as love's only purpose. The "Linden- lied" creates erotic tension all the more because it plays with taboos; it conjures up the very boundary that it transgresses. The courtly discourse of love differs from the clerical discourse of love insofar as the former does not yoke love to marriage and reproduction, but rather has pleasure as its goal, independent of the lovers' marital or familial status.[27] Tristan and Isolde, the most famous pair of courtly lovers, are adulterers and have no children. Things look quite dif- ferent in the lyric poetry of courtly love, in the so-called *Minnesang*. Whereas *Minnesang* also considers the goal of courtly love to be pleasure, it is marked by one-sidedness. *Minnesang* relies upon the generic rule that the lady never yields to the knight who is wooing her. The failure of love's labors is requisite for a higher success: the knight's and court society's ethical and aesthetic ennoblement. To the extent that there are no provisions for sexual satisfaction, the courtly deployment of love in *Minnesang* is also based on taboo. The authority that the courtly taboo establishes is on the one hand the self-restraining lady herself, and on the other hand court society, to the extent that it controls the relationships between the sexes. Court society achieves its control through chaperones, or *huote*, which as social instruments protect the lady's reputation.

The "Lindenlied" further plays with this taboo by staging a situation that recalls Tristan and Isolde more than *Minnesang*. But how is Walther, within the *Minnesang* genre itself, capable of turning its one-sided model for love into a passionate one that is based on reciprocity and includes sexual gratification? To this end, he makes use of the same strategy he already used in his encounter with the clerical taboo, namely the technique of quotation. Walther quotes the stanzaic form and the concept of love from an earlier phase in the lyric poetry of courtly love. The "Danubian *Minnesang*" (*Donauländischer Minnesang*), as it is called, propagated the reciprocity of love and gave voice to the lady's desire. Through quotation Walter draws from this tradition in order to modify the concept of love in classic *Minnesang*.

This can readily be deduced from the song's form. As in romance literatures, the classic *Minnesang* follows the complex form of the canzone, while the Danubian *Minnesang* is made up of simple stanzas called "long-line verses," which consist of two short-line verses divided by a caesura. Walther used a hybrid form of the two for the "Lindenlied." Its lines can be read both as long-line verses (as in the edition by Maurer)[28] and as canzone verses (as in the edition by Cormeau).[29] It is also significant that Walther borrowed language from another "Lindenlied" that served as a model for him. The song is by Dietmar von Aist, one of the most prominent purveyors of Danubian *Minnesang*. Carl von Kraus, in his 1939 commentary on Dietmar's "Lindenlied," asserts that "When you think of Walther's song 39.11, then pretty much all the same things come up again: *Under der linden … bette … bluomen … vor dem walde … sanc diu nahtegal … rôsen … ein kleinez vogellîn*. Thus it seems to me that it is not only 'by all means possible,' but rather quite certain that Walther was familiar with our stanzas."[30]

Let us have a closer look at their correlation:

1. *Ûf der linden obene*
   dâ sanc ein kleinez vogellîn.
   vor dem walde wart ez lût.
   dô huop sich aber daz herze mîn
   an eine stat, dâ ez ê dâ was.
   ich sach dâ rôsebluomen stân,
   die manent mich der gedanke vil,
   die ich hin zeiner vrouwen hân.

   Upon the linden tree, there sang a little bird. At the edge of the woods it could be heard. At that my heart leapt to a place where it had been before. I saw roses standing there; they call to mind many memories I have of a certain lady.

2. ‚Ez dunket mich wol *tûsent jâr*,   It seems like a thousand years to me
    daz ich *an liebes arme lac*.   since I last lay in the arms of my love.

    sunder âne mîne schulde   Through no fault of mine he has been
    vremedet er mich menegen tac.   away from me for many a day.

    sît ich *bluomen* niht ensach   Since then I have seen no flowers, nor
    noch enhôrte der *vogel sanc*,   have I heard the song of the little birds,

    sît was mir mîn vröide kurz   since then my joy has been short-lived
    und ouch der jâmer alzelanc.'[31]   and my pining all too long.[32]

Whereas Dietmar accentuates what happens *upon* the linden tree, Walther emphasizes what happens *under* it. Upon the linden there is singing; under the linden there is loving. Dietmar prefigures the relation between these acts. He places the bird's singing and the lovers' copulation in the second half of the first long-line verse of each stanza (1.1: *dâ sanc ein kleinez vogellîn*—2.1: *daz ich an liebes arme lac*). Walther quotes the motif of the singing bird twice from Dietmar's second short-line verse: word for word in the fourth stanza (4.5: *ein kleinez vogellîn*) and with modifications in the first stanza, in which he specifies that the bird is a nightingale (1.7: *schône sanc diu nahtegal*). The doubling of the motif corresponds to its qualitative appreciation in value. The bird is given the narrative role of a discreet witness that divulges its secret only in a concealed manner through its chirping "*tandaradei.*" The third short-line verse presents the motif of the woods. Again Dietmar and Walther literally coincide here: *vor dem walde* ("At the edge of the woods"). Further parallels can be found in the floral motifs of the two songs. Both poets speak generally of flowers (Dietmar 2.3: *bluomen*; cf. Walther 1.4, 3.2: *bluomen*) and specifically of roses (Dietmar 1.3: *rôsebluomen*; cf. Walther 3.5: *rôsen*). While Dietmar's roses *stand* (1.3: *rôsebluomen stân*), Walther's roses are—with symbolic importance—*broken* (1.4: *gebrochen bluomen*). Thus, with its typical props (linden trees, heath, woods, nightingale, and flowers) the site of love marks the act of love. Talk of copulation (4.1: *bî mir laege*) is also present in Dietmar's "Lindenlied": *daz ich an liebes arme lac* (2.1). Walther's metaphorical circumlocution of the flowers as *bettestat* (3.2, cf. 1.2: *bette*) also has its precedent here. The bed of flowers is a specification of the *stat* (place) in Dietmar's song (1.3). The loving figures who accompany the site and act of love are once again borrowed from Dietmar: the lady (2.3: *frowe*; cf. Dietmar 1.4) and the lover (2.2: *friedel*).

The lover's motif in Walther's song derives from another famous song attributed to Dietmar, namely the first stanza of his aubade (*Tagelied*). The song also brings together the motifs of the linden, the bird, and consummated love: "Are you sleeping, dear love? / Alas, we will be woken soon; / a sweet little bird / just lighted upon the linden branch" (*Slâfest du, vriedel ziere? / wan wecket uns leider schiere; / ein vogellîn sô wol getân / daz ist der linden an daz zwî gegân*).[33]

In Walther, an archaic address is used for the lover—*friedel*, an uncommon word that at the time of his writing was already disappearing from courtly language.[34] Apart from Dietmar and Walther's songs, the word appears in the *Nibelungenlied* (also from the Danubian tradition), in which it takes on sexual connotations yet again. Kriemhild shows Brünhild the stolen ring and berates her as Siegfried's mistress: "My love brought me this ring after having been the first to lie with you" (*daz brâhte mir mîn vriedel, do er êrste bî iu lac*).[35] Walther even takes the heath motif, again word for word, from another of Dietmar von Eist's stanzas. In Dietmar's song he depicts a vernal ensemble that, on top of bird, linden, and flowers, also includes the heath: *an der heide*.[36]

Yet another linden casts its shadow from the genre of the *pastourelle*. The macaronic German and Latin song *Ich was ein chint sô wolgetân*, from the *Carmina Burana*, provides the most readily available contrastive example.[37] The song is about the rape of a girl under a linden tree. In terms of form, Walther's "Lindenlied" has a parallel refrain (*Hoy et oe!*). In terms of content, the two have parallels in their *locus amoenus* (including linden, heath, and path), as well as the defloration motif (stanza 2: *ibi deflorare*; cf. 2.4: *gebrochen bluomen*). Walther turns the violent situation constitutive of the pastoral genre into a tryst between voluntary lovers. His "Lindenlied" thus alludes to the pastoral genre without belonging to the genre itself.

Travesty: The Knight as Lady

The poetics of taboo that Walther formulates in his "Lindenlied" incorporates three aesthetic strategies. The first consists of quoting speech acts and forms of speech from deployments that establish sexual taboos. Walther uses quotations, taken from moral theology and from the lay discourse of *Minnesang*, as fragments of a poetic language of love that eludes the deployment. The second strategy Walther employs is camouflage. If all the quotations and allusions are stripped from Walther's song, what is left are numerous words from the semantic field of hermeneutics. They deal with themes of finding (1.3: *vinden*), seeing (2.7: *seht*), tracking (3.4: *kumt ieman an daz selbe pfat*), noticing (3.7: *merken*), knowing (4.1: *wessez*), and recognizing (4.4: *bevinde*). Walther stages the Fall of the lovers as a paradoxical game of divulging secrets, in which the perpetrator reveals his deed to the degree that he conceals it.

The third strategy relies upon the travesty that comes to bear upon the circumstances of the song's performance. The performing singer is male; the role he performs is female. Walther emphasizes the song's ambiguous quality through a telling gesture that can be read as a stage direction for the singer: *seht, wie rôt mir ist der munt* (2.7). One imagines how, after having told of the lover's thousand kisses while in the role of the lady, the singer points out his reddened mouth as proof of the passionate encounter. In this performative gesture, the real body of the male singer and the imaginary body of the female role coincide. As Judith Butler has shown through the modern-day example of drag queens, a male performer's ability to perform a female role underlines the fundamental performativity of gender roles.[38]

But who is this persona to whom Walther lends his voice? Because the song is addressed to a *friedel*, that is to say, a male lover, one presumptuously draws the conclusion that the persona must be a woman. The reasoning relies upon the heteronormative expectation that whoever loves a man must be a woman. Yet it remains to be seen whether or not the text gives explicit evidence as to the gender of the textual subject, for the persona must be clearly identifiable as a female in order to successfully pull off the travesty as such. In the Dietmar songs to which Walther makes reference, the distribution of gender roles is marked in express terms.[39] This is not the case in Walther's "Lindenlied." Everything depends on how the formulation *hêre frowe* (2.3) is understood. Those who argue for a religious reading label it an exclamation of joy ("Virgin Mary!"). Those who argue for a courtly reading see it as an apostrophe ("sublime lady!"), an apposition ("there I, the sublime lady, was received"), or a comparison ("there I was received as a sublime lady is received"). The performed role is only explicitly designated as a lady in the case of apostrophe and apposition. But there is another problem. The variant *hêre frowe* is documented only in the *Codex Manesse* (*Große Heidelberger Liederhandschrift*) (C), which often alters original texts by leveling out their style and content.[40] The *Weingartner Liederhandschrift* (B) provides an alternative, and perhaps the original, variant—namely, *herre frowe* ("lord lady"). Here the gender of the knight and the gender of the lady collide. If B is taken seriously, then the possible readings that *hêre frowe* engenders can also be played through with *herre frowe*. The religious interpretation for this case has already been considered. In 1860, Franz Pfeiffer pondered, "Could this not be the true way of reading it: *herre frowe!* an impetuous 'Jesus and Mary!' still common today in catholic countries; more akin to an exclamation of fear, but also of joyful surprise."[41] But if read according to courtly indications of rank, *herre frowe* denotes the textual subject as at once knight and lady. This doubling corresponds to the circumstances of the performance, for indeed the "I" presents itself as two genders: as male, in the role of the performing singer, and as female, in the role that is being performed.

If one decides to follow the interpretation that says the textual subject is female, then Walther's wording, *herre frowe*, highlights the aspect of travesty. But if one surmises that Walther leaves the gender of the enacted role open, then the ambiguity should be estimated as a calculated effect, brought about through the concrete circumstances of the performance. The fact that the singer is unequivocally male, while the gender of the role he sings remains ambiguous, opens up the possibility of understanding the song as a knight's recollection of a lover's tryst with his *friedel*.[42] Cramer, who speaks of "androgynous stanzas" in such cases, derives from this indeterminacy a need for further research methods: "Androgynous stanzas offer varied and new readings for many poems. It would be a profitable task to systematically test them and to think through their consequences."[43] The same is true of Walther's "Lindenlied." It all depends on whether the recipient follows heteronormative expectations or eludes them. Walther's "Lindenlied" invites both manners of reading.

A fourth strategy that comes into play at this point could be considered a staggered arranging of taboos: as one infringement of a taboo is revealed, another one is concealed. This is camouflage proper. In divulging the supposed secret—the illegitimate rendezvous in nature—the actual secret remains hidden. This relation results from the indeterminacy of the persona's gender. Is she a woman (in contrast to the gender of the singer), and thus we are dealing with a sexual offense between a knight and a lady? Or is she a man (in keeping with the gender of the singer), and thus we are dealing with a sexual offense between two knights? In the language of moral theology, is this a case of *fornicatio simplex* or *peccatum contra naturam*? While the first breach of taboo can be articulated as an open secret, the second presents a sin that is not allowed to utter its own name. Ostensibly much speaks in favor of the female persona interpretation, but the recessive option, namely that the persona is a male figure, is not denied. An unspeakable taboo is evoked in order to add more tension to the speakable taboo. The song follows a logic of substitution by allowing the comparatively harmless breach of taboo to participate implicitly in the stigmatization of an unmentionable breach of taboo.

Here again the bird comes into play: it refers to the singer through a poetic metaphor. In Gottfried von Straßburg's literary excursus in *Tristan*, he compares minnesingers (*Minnesänger*) to nightingales and calls Walther their "leading lady" (*leitevrouwe*). Gottfried plays with the literal meaning of the singer's name and, it appears, with the diction of the "Lindenlied." Walther is the "Nachtigall von der Vogelweide" ("nightingale from the bird-pasture") whose voice rings out across the heath (ln. 4803: *über heide*). Perhaps Gottfried is playing with the poet's ambiguous gender: as the singer he is a man, but as the nightingale he is the most eminent of all ladies: "*she* of the bird-pasture" (ln. 4802: *diu von der Vogelweide*).

Translated by Japhet Johnstone

Notes

1. Michel Foucault, *The History of Sexuality*, vol. 1: *An Introduction*, trans. Robert Hurley (New York, 1978), 23.

2. Cf. Sven Limbeck and Andreas M. Thoma, eds., *"Die sünde, der sich der tiuvel schamet in der helle": Homosexualität in der Kultur des Mittelalters und der frühen Neuzeit* (Ostfildern, 2009); Helmut Puff, *Sodomy in Reformation Germany and Switzerland, 1400–1600* (Chicago, 2003); Glenn Burger and Steven F Kruger, eds., *Queering the Middle Ages* (Minneapolis, 2001); Jonathan Goldberg, ed., *Queering the Renaissance* (Durham, NC, 1993).

3. Foucault, *History of Sexuality*, 104–5.

4. Dagmar Herzog, *Sex in Crisis: The New Sexual Revolution and the Future of American Politics* (New York, 2008).

5. See Annmarie Jagose, *Queer Theory: An Introduction* (New York, 1997); Andreas Krass (ed.), *Queer Studies in Deutschland: Interdisziplinäre Beiträge zur kritischen Heteronormativitätsforschung* (Berlin, 2009).

6. This is James A. Schultz's concern in his seminal work, *Courtly Love, the Love of Courtliness, and the History of Sexuality* (Chicago, 2006). Schultz focuses on the courtly poetry of the High Middle Ages in Germany—the genre and period to which Walther's "Lindenlied" belongs.

7. Cf. Anna Babka and Susanne Hochreiter (eds.), *Queer Reading in den Philologien: Modelle und Anwendungen* (Göttingen, 2008); Andreas Krass, "Queer lesen: Literaturgeschichte und Queer Theory," in *Gender Studies: Wissenschaftstheorien und Gesellschaftskritik*, ed. Caroline Rosenthal, Therese Frey Steffen, and Anke Väth (Würzburg, 2004), 233–48; Christoph Lorey and John Plews (eds.), *Queering the Canon: Defying Sights in German Literature and Culture* (Rochester, 1998); Eve Kosofsky Sedgwick (ed.), *Novel Gazing: Queer Reading in Fiction* (Durham, NC, 1997).

8. Walther von der Vogelweide, *Leich, Lieder, Sangsprüche*, ed. Christoph Cormeau (Berlin, 1996), 77–78; see note 28 for more on alternative verse arrangements. For the current state of research cf. Mary M. Paddock, "Speaking of the Spectacle: Another Look at Walther's 'Lindenlied,'" *The German Quarterly* 77 (2004): 11–29; Jan-Dirk Müller, "'Gebrauchszusammenhang' und ästhetische Dimension mittelalterlicher Texte: Nebst Überlegungen zu Walthers Lindenlied (L. 39,11)," in *Das fremde Schöne: Dimensionen des Ästhetischen in der Literatur des Mittelalters*, ed. Manuel Braun and Christopher Young (Berlin and New York, 2007), 281–305. In the following references to the poems, the first number of every textual reference refers to the stanza, the second to the verse in question; 2.1, for instance, refers to the first line in the second stanza.

9. English translation quoted from Paddock, "Speaking of Spectacle," 15 (st. 1), 17 (st. 2), 18 (st. 3), 19, 23 (st. 4).

10. Foucault, *History of Sexuality*, 68.

11. Cf. Rüdiger Schnell, *Frauendiskurs, Männerdiskurs, Ehediskurs: Textsorten und Geschlechterkonzepte in Mittelalter und Früher Neuzeit* (Frankfurt am Main, 1998), 158. The quoted passage is in reference to the cleric Guido de Monte Rocherii's *Manipulus curatorum* (Paris, 1473).

12. Volker Mertens, "Reinmars Gegensang zu Walthers *Lindenlied*," *Zeitschrift für deutsches Altertum* 112 (1983): 161–77, see 172.

13. Cf. Cant 1:15: *lectulus noster floridus* ("our bed is green"); here and in the following, I quote the Latin Vulgate and for the English translation the *King James Version*.

14. Cf. Cant 1:12: *dilectus meus* ("my well-beloved").

15. Cf. Cant 7:1: *Veni, dilecti mi, egrediamur in agrum* ("Come, my beloved, let us go forth into the field").

16. Cf. Cant 1:1: *Osculetur me osculo oris sui* ("Let him kiss me with the kisses of his mouth").
17. The second verse of "Der erste Philippston" provides a striking example (L. 19.5: "Magdeburger Weihnacht"). Walther plays liberally with the trinity, the Virgin Mary and the Magi, in order to place Philipp, his wife, and his entourage in perspective; see *Leich, Lieder, Sangsprüche*, 37.
18. Cf. Gen 2:9: *omne lignum pulchrum visu* ("every tree that is pleasant to the sight").
19. Cf. Gen 2:25: *non erubescebant* ("they were ... not ashamed").
20. Cf. Gen 3:10: *abscondi me* ("I hid myself").
21. Cf. Gen 3:5: *scientes bonum et malum* ("knowing good and evil").
22. Cf. the ordeal in Gottfried von Straßburg's *Tristan*.
23. Cf. Lk 1:28: *benedicta tu in mulieribus* ("blessed art thou among women").
24. Cf. Lk 1:28: *gratia plena* ("thou that art highly favoured").
25. Cf. Lk 1:28: *et ingressus [...] ad eam* ("came in unto her").
26. Cf. Lk 1:31: *ecce concipies* ("behold, thou shalt conceive").
27. Cf. Schultz, *Courtly Love*, 157: "In the history of European thinking on these matters, the gradual shift from an ideology of sex for procreation to an ideology of sex for pleasure is one of the most important long-term developments."
28. The first segment of the stanza contains a double shift from long-line to short-line verses, while the second contains three short-line verses. The long-line verses are characterized by heavily accented syllables: *Ùndèr der líndèn án dèr héidè* (ln. 1) and *dâ mùgent ìr víndèn schônè béidè* (ln. 3). The refrain can be read as both *tándàradéi* or *tándàrádèi*. This creates an animated rhythm to which all stanzas freely conform; in fact, they virtually require it. Cf. Walther von der Vogelweide, *Sämtliche Lieder*, ed. Friedrich Maurer (Munich, 1972), 122–125.
29. According to the Cormeau edition, the first segment of the stanza ("Aufgesang") contains six lines that divide into two identical halves ("Stollen"); the second segment of the stanza ("Abgesang") comprises three lines, one of which is an unrhymed refrain. The rhyme scheme is abc abc dxd; double accented lines alternate with quadruple accented lines (224, 224, 424).
30. Carl von Kraus, *Untersuchungen* (= *Minnesangs Frühling*, vol. 3, part 1) (Stuttgart, 1981 [Leipzig, 1939]), 80. Joachim Heinzle confirms the finding: "Indeed, there are key elements from the *Lindenlied* found together there: the lover's tryst in nature, the scenery of the *locus amoenus vor dem walde* with lindens, roses, and bird song—and the *vrouwe* who reminisces." Heinzle prefers not to settle the matter "whether Walther was familiar with the Dietmar stanzas. But they show his point of reference: set against this foil, the '*Lindenlied*' appears as a virtuoso 'variation on a theme from the early Minnesang.'" Joachim Heinzle, "Mädchendämmerung: Zu Walther 29.11 und 74.20," in *Verstehen durch Vernunft*, ed. Burkhart Krause (Vienna, 1997): 145–58, see 156f. (trans. J.J.).
31. *Des Minnesangs Frühling*, vol. 1: "Texte," ed. Hugo Moser and Helmut Tervooren (Stuttgart, 1988): 58 (MF 34.3).
32. English translation quoted from Paddock, "Speaking of Spectacle," 21.
33. *Minnesangs Frühling*, 66 (MF 39.18).
34. *Das Nibelungenlied*, ed. Helmut de Boor, 22nd ed. (Wiesbaden, 1996), 143 (commentary on stanza 847).
35. Stanza 847.3. Cf. stanza 2372.3 in relation to Siegfried's Schwert: *daz truoc mîn holder vriedel, dô ich in jungest sach.*
36. *Minnesangs Frühling*, 57 (MF 33.15).

37. Ingrid Kasten, ed., *Frauenlieder des Mittelalters* (Stuttgart, 1990), no. XLIX (CB 185), 148–53 (text), 275–77 (commentary).
38. Judith Butler, *Gender Trouble: Feminism and the Subversion of Identity* (London, 1990).
39. In Dietmar's "Lindenlied," the man speaks of the love that he has for *zeiner vrouwen* (1.4), and the woman speaks of how *er* ("he" 2.2) avoids her—he, in whose arms she lay. In Dietmar's aubade, gender roles are marked by the alternating forms of address of *vriedel* (1.1) and *vriundin* (2.4) as well as by a hint of epos (3.1: *Diu vrouwe begunde weinen*).
40. The variation of *Er kuste mich*, instead of *Kuster mich*, is similarly leveled out.
41. Franz Pfeiffer, "Über Walther von der Vogelweide," *Germania* 5 (1860): 1–44, here p. 41; cf. Heinzle, "Mädchendämmerung," 152n30. Ingrid Kasten also follows this interpretation in *Frauenlieder des Mittelalters*, 116 (text), 263 (commentary).
42. In courtly novels the motif of the thousandfold kisses appears as an expression of love between friends among men. When the Arthurian knights Ywain and Gawain recognize one another after a duel, they express their joy of being reunited by kissing each other thousandfold on the eyes, cheeks, and mouth: *si underkusten tûsentstunt / ougen wangen unde munt* (1.7503f.); see Hartmann von Aue, *Iwein*, ed. Ludwig Wolff et al. (Berlin, 2001).
43. Thomas Cramer, "Was ist und woran erkennt man eine Frauenstrophe?" in *Frauenlieder: Cantigas de amigo*, ed. T. Cramer et al. (Stuttgart, 2000), 19–32, see 24. On this point, Kasten comments that due to heteronormative expectations the complementary gender is presumed. She adds, however, that such a presumption is far from certain. Kasten, "Zur Poetologie der weiblichen Stimme: Anmerkungen zum Frauenlied," in Cramer, *Frauenlieder*, 3–18, see 14.

CHAPTER 5

~:~

Early Nineteenth-Century Sexual Radicalism
Heinrich Hössli and the Liberals of His Day

ROBERT DEAM TOBIN

From 1836 to 1838, Heinrich Hössli published a massive two-volume, roughly 650-page defense of sexual love between men, called *Eros: Die Männerliebe der Griechen, ihre Beziehung zur Geschichte, Erziehung, Literatur und Gesetzgebung aller Zeiten* (Eros: The Male Love of the Greeks, Its Relationship to the History, Pedagogy, Literature and Legislation of All Times). In this apology for same-sex desire, Hössli seemingly relies on concepts of sexuality that would be half a century too early if one were to take Foucault's claims about the birth of the homosexual literally.[1] Because of this inconsistency— and frankly also because of the obscurity and at times tediousness of Hössli's writing—*Eros* has generally been relegated to the museum of freakish and inexplicable oddities of sexual history. In this situation it is tempting to reclaim Hössli as a sexual innovator, celebrating the original and forward-thinking contributions of *Eros*. It is perhaps more interesting, however, to emphasize—with all due respect for Hössli's achievements—the ways in which he lacks originality. In fact, Hössli's *Eros* is deeply embedded in early nineteenth-century liberal thought. But although this post-Enlightenment worldview had openings to the acceptance of same-sex desire, Hössli found that he constantly pushed up against the limits of his era's liberalism and had to reach for more radical formulations to articulate his sexual politics.

The claim that Hössli was working with modern notions of sexuality in the 1830s should certainly awaken suspicion in the mind of any historian of sexuality. Hössli does indeed use the word "sexuality" (*Sexualität*), which at this time was probably not more than fifty years old.[2] In the first volume of *Eros* (1836), he cites an 1834 lecture by Joseph Hermann Schmidt, published in the 1835 issue of *Magazin für die gesammte Heilkunde* (Magazine for All Medicine):

"The concept of sexuality (*Sexualität*) is no longer derived exclusively from the sexual organs, but rather from the entire organism."[3] Typically, Hössli relies on current scholarly and critical work to bolster his claims. This vocabulary of a sexuality that emerges from the entire body, not just the genitalia, sounds like a modern conception of sexuality that is more comprehensive than simply a penchant for certain sexual acts. However, if one reads the citation further, it turns out that Schmidt (and by citation Hössli) uses this term differently than one would now: "Woman," he continues, "is primarily vegetative, man primarily animalistic, and within the more restricted confines of the latter, the masculine sex emerges from irritability, while the feminine sex emerges from sensibility."

While this might look like a casual assessment of the psychic states of men versus those of women, it actually refers to a serious strain of scientific thought. In the eighteenth century, Albrecht Haller had attempted to distinguish between purely mechanical responses of the body, which were a product of "irritability" (*Irritabilität* or *Reizbarkeit*), and bodily actions determined by the soul, which were a product of "sensibility" (*Sensibilität* or *Empfindlichkeit*).[4] Schmidt therefore relies on this eighteenth-century framework to argue that male genitalia respond more mechanically, while female genitalia require the active participation of the soul.[5] But the more important point here is that Schmidt is not actually using the word *Sexualität* to describe "sexuality" in the sense of a sexual drive or orientation. Instead he is using the term to describe the sex of an individual—whether the person is primarily masculine, animalistic, and irritable or whether the person is feminine, vegetative and sensible. His usage is typical for the late eighteenth and early nineteenth centuries, following Carl Linnaeus's studies of botany, which outlined the "sexual life" of plants in graphic detail that shocked readers.[6] But here too the "sexual" really meant "having a sex": The discussion of "sexual life" consisted in describing how the plants were sexed—how the stamens were masculine and the pistols feminine, etc. So when Schmidt argues that a person's *Sexualität* emerges from their entire organism, it seems that he is actually arguing that biological sex informs the entire organism, not just the genitals.[7]

Nonetheless, Hössli does seem to work with a modern notion of sexuality, even if he does not use the word "sexuality" to describe what he is talking about. By the end of his first volume, Hössli believes that he has proven that there is "a male-loving, purely humane, specific masculine human nature (*eine männerliebende, rein menschliche, bestimmte, Männermenschennatur*)."[8] This "masculine human nature" is "specific" to indicate that there is a certain group of men who have this desire—it is not the case that any man might have occasional temptations to fall in love with other men. Only some men do, and those who do, do so out of reasons that are "purely humane"—Hössli emphasizes that this love is in no way to be derided as crude or animalistic. In addition, this sexual nature is immutable. In convoluted German, Hössli declares at the beginning

of the second volume, "The large and general portion [of the human popula-
tion] that loves the other sex cannot be the sort [literally, 'the nature'] that does
not love the other sex, and the sort [again, literally, 'the nature'] that loves its
own sex cannot be lovers of the other sex."[9] The passage indicates that people
have, or in fact *are*, an orientation in their sexual nature that is unchangeable.
Hössli fairly consistently contests the notion that people *have* a sexuality that is
distinct from their being, asserting instead that people *are* their sexuality.[10] He
implies with this phrasing that the sexual nature of a person is identical with
that person—that there is not even the distinction that exists between a person
and the nature that he or she has.

When Hössli does use language that suggests someone *has*, rather than *is*,
a sexuality, he attributes that language to his intellectual opponents. Critics of
male love argue that the men-loving men have "laid aside" their original nature, while Hössli believes that it would be impossible to lay such a nature
aside.[11] In Hössli's world, it is—somewhat surprisingly—men who are sexually
attracted to women who say things like, "I was born with my sexual love (*Ge-
schlechtsliebe*)," implying that their sexuality is an attribute separate from their
being.[12] In his writings, Hössli's men who love men tend to say that they "are"
their sexuality, rather than that they "have" or are "born with" a sexuality. Their
sexuality is an essence that constitutes them. By the end of the second volume,
Hössli concludes that questions about a person's sexual nature are "questions
about the individuality, the foundational essence, the original depths of human
disposition, about his innermost, unchangeable nature and being."[13] He moves
here in the direction of what Foucault would call the "truth" of sex in a modern
society that defines a person at the deepest and most profound level by his or
her sexuality. For Hössli, natural sexual desire is specific in its focus on men or
women, it is unchangeable, and it gets at the essence of the individual—all of
which suggest that he is working with a concept of sexuality.

But how might this more or less modern concept of sexuality emerge from
the intellectual developments of the early nineteenth century? In order to answer this question, it is instructive to focus on Hössli's life. Hössli, who lived
from 1784 to 1864, was not an academic, but rather an entrepreneur, a milliner
and hatter in the small central Swiss town of Glarus, where his fashions were
always the *dernier cri*. Nowadays the profession seems eccentric, but it is perhaps most useful simply to think of him as a Swiss bourgeois, sympathetic to
many of the concerns of the early nineteenth-century central European bourgeoisie and imbued with many of the political leanings of that group. His family life, however, sheds some light on the bourgeoisie of the period. He did not,
for instance, actually live with his wife Elisabeth Grebel, who chose to reside in
Zurich. Nonetheless, they had two sons, both of whom emigrated to America.
According to Ferdinand Karsch, who wrote a biographical essay about Hössli

for the 1903 edition of Magnus Hirschfeld's *Jahrbuch für sexuelle Zwischen-stufen* (Yearbook for Sexual Intermediary Types), Hössli's son, Johann Ulrich, was sexually attracted to men and wrote about the subject to his father. Johann Ulrich sponsored a number of young men from Switzerland who wanted to immigrate to the United States, and at least one of the fathers of these young men accused him of inappropriate behavior.[14]

Conceivably, the elder Hössli's sympathies with his son's desires encouraged him to write *Eros*. Hössli himself gave a different reason: he was horrified by the execution of Franz Desgouttes, a 32-year-old man convicted in 1817 of murdering Daniel Hemmeler, the 22-year-old man whom he loved and with whom he had sexual relations. Desgouttes was "broken at the wheel," which means executioners tied him to a wheel, broke the bones in his arms and legs, and left him to die a slow and excruciating death in public. Hössli did not focus on the fact that Desgouttes had murdered his beloved Daniel—instead he understood the events as a crime of passion that merited understanding and sympathy, rather than a grotesquely violent punishment. Part of Hössli's reaction certainly had to do with an abhorrence of forms of the death penalty that emphasized deliberate cruelty. His opposition to cruel punishment reflects the liberal soil in which his thoughts developed.[15]

Hössli's class background as an independent entrepreneur and his Swiss training made him open to liberal thinking of the time.[16] There is almost as much risk of projection and anachronism in talking about liberalism at the beginning of the nineteenth century as there is in talking about sexuality at that time. As Jean de Grandvilliers reports, the words "liberal" and "liberalism" first entered the German political vocabulary in 1812.[17] James Sheehan opens his classic study, *German Liberalism in the Nineteenth Century*, with the admission that liberalism is "impossible to define simply," especially in the early nineteenth century, when "political terminology was extremely imprecise or inconsistent."[18] Scholars such as Jonathan Knudson conclude that for this time period, "liberalism consisted of a loose family of ideas which could be creatively combined in a local and often idiosyncratic manner."[19] Although Hössli does not use the word "liberal," his ideas clearly fit into the family of ideas that was coming to identify with that nomenclature.

To begin with, he engages with thinkers such as Charles de Montesquieu, whose 1748 *De l'esprit des lois* (On The Spirit of the Laws) is often considered a founding text of liberalism.[20] Interestingly, though, he underscores the inadequacy of Montesquieu's approach for certain sexual matters:

> In our world, Montesquieu could not say in his book *On the Spirit of the Laws*: "In the Orient male-male love is neither a sin nor a crime, nor considered unnatural." He can't say that, he can only say what he actually says: "In the Orient, pederasty and sodomy are very popular."[21]

His citation of Montesquieu suggests not only that he is well-read in the emerging liberal tradition, but also that he is willing to critique liberalism's inability to think through sexual rights. Hössli insists that progressive thought emerging from the Enlightenment needs to move forward in the realm of sexuality.

The brief critique of Montesquieu helps explain Hössli's relationship with Heinrich Zschokke (1771–1848). Zschokke is one of many literary and cultural figures who have been overshadowed by the sheer number of famous authors writing in the Age of Goethe. Nowadays, he shows up in literary histories primarily because he took part in a trip with Heinrich Geßner (son of the poet Salomen Geßner), Ludwig Wieland (son of the novelist Christoph Martin Wieland), and Heinrich Kleist, which resulted in the writing of the beloved play *Der zerbrochene Krug* (The Broken Jug). But Zschokke was a prolific writer in his own right, involved with a variety of liberal journals and newspapers. His *History of Switzerland* is a classic defense of the liberal values that the country claimed as its moral justification.[22] He founded *Der Schweizerbote* (The Swiss Intelligencer), which ran from 1804 until 1879 and continued to be published long after its founder's death. Politically active in the Helvetic Republic, he occupied a series of important positions in government at various points in his life. Generally interested in increasing the rights of the citizenry, he developed—with help from the innovative Enlightenment pedagogue Johann Heinrich Pestalozzi—a number of schemes to edify the public. He ran a school in Switzerland and then held various administrative positions in Aarau, Unterwalden, and eventually Uri, Schwyz, and Zug. He oversaw the reorganization of the educational systems in the Italian cantons of Switzerland. At one point he was also lieutenant governor of Basel.[23]

Hössli met Zschokke through a mutual friend, Ignaz Troxler, a physician who had become a professor of philosophy in Bern and proposed using the United States constitution as a model for reforming the Swiss Confederation.[24] Troxler's mediation between the two emphasizes the liberal circles in which Hössli and Zschokke were traveling. Hössli assumed that a man of such spotless credentials as Zschokke would paint the plight of men who loved other men in the most sympathetic light. He commissioned Zschokke to write a story based on what he perceived to be the tragedy that resulted in Desgouttes's murder of Hemmeler. Zschokke came through with "Eros," published in 1821 in a collection of short stories titled *Erheiterungen* (Exhilarations), one of the earliest stories in the German tradition explicitly trying to elucidate the mysteries of male-male love. In the narrative, a judge named Holmar (based on Hössli) tries to convince a small group of bourgeois couples that the recent execution by breaking on the wheel of a certain Lukasson (based on Desgouttes) for murdering his beloved Walter (based on Hemmeler) was unjust because society did not understand love between men. Holmar recounts the glory days of ancient Greece, when men like Lukasson were honored poets, philosophers, and politicians, not criminals subject to archaic punishments.[25]

Hössli detested the story because it betrayed all of the principles for which he stood. In Zschokke's version, Holmar's interlocutors ponder his arguments in defense of Greek love, but ultimately reject them. They conclude that the male-male love of the ancient Greeks was not sensual and that any sensual same-sex love must be pathological and should be prohibited by law. To add insult to injury, Zschokke's Holmar is an odd and eccentric fellow, the only man in the group without a wife or fiancée present. In fact, the narrator asks Holmar if he too is one of the men who love other men, which the judge denies.[26] From Hössli's perspective, it seems that the voices of the liberal bourgeoisie—voices like Zschokke's—were unable to incorporate sexual freedom into their political vision and ultimately resorted to ad hominem attacks.

For Hössli, this failure was all the more striking because sexual freedom should in fact emerge from that loose collection of Enlightenment ideals that was coming to be known as liberalism. As Hössli framed the debate, sexual emancipation should result from such causes as (1) the removal of the church from politics, (2) the emancipation of the Jews, and (3) the extension of rights to women. With at least the third of these points, though, Hössli had moved beyond the liberal thought typical of his era and embraced more radical positions.

In Hössli's case, one standard for progressive liberalism that emerges clearly is the principle of secularism—the rejection of superstition and those aspects of religion that are deemed superstitious. As Sheehan documents, "demands for religious freedom, therefore, became part of the liberal effort to create a free public in which men would be able to follow the dictates of their own enlightened opinion."[27] In his thorough study of German liberalism, Dieter Langewiesche concludes that "a secular state was at the heart of liberal beliefs."[28] The emphasis on the separation of church and state explains why Hössli—building on Enlightenment values—begins his book *Eros* with a discussion, not of male-male sexual love but rather of the persecution of witches. In fact, there is enough material on the subject in *Eros* that one of the two volumes in the reorganized and reedited 1892 reprint of his work published by Barsdorf press of Leipzig was devoted primarily to witches and called *Hexenproceß und Glauben, Pfaffen und Teufel: Als Beitrag zur Cultur- und Sittengeschichte der Jahrhunderte* (Witch Trial and Faith, Priests and Devils: A Contribution to the Cultural and Moral History of the Centuries).

The subject matter must have been particularly significant for Hössli because, two years before his birth, a woman who was executed for being a witch lived in the very house in which he was born, according to his biographer Karsch.[29] Hössli himself cites from the death certificate, dated 21 July 1782, of this unfortunate woman, whose name he gives as Anna Güldin.[30] Although her family name is spelled in a variety of ways (Goldin, Göldin, Göldi), Anna is well-known as the last woman executed as a witch in Europe.[31] Expounding on his concerns about the persecution of witches, Hössli reminds readers of the burning of what he refers to as "hysterical" nuns in Würzburg in 1749 and in West Prussia in 1779.[32] Alluding to the execution in 1766 of someone who claimed to be able to change the weather, he stresses the contradictions between such executions and the Enlightenment:

> As late as 1766, in the little town of Buchloe in Swabia, a human among humans was sentenced to die as a weather witch (*Wettermacher*) and in fact executed. In precisely that century witches were burned at the stake and beheaded—and precisely that century called itself the enlightened, the philosophical century. And we are now in the nineteenth century and don't murder people as weather witches or sorcerers anymore, but as for the rest, most is as it was and that's just fine for most people.[33]

While Hössli suspects bitterly that many of his contemporaries long for the good old days, the point of his critique is that the Enlightenment has not yet been realized.

Hoping to appeal to other Enlightened readers, Hössli therefore begins his analysis of "Greek love" with an extensive report on the witch hunts, without immediately spelling out the connections between witchcraft and "male love." He commences with references to witch hunts and witch trials, spelling out the gory details of various medieval exploits, emphasizing the extremes to which religious fanaticism can lead. By the end of his study, after he has addressed male-male desire explicitly, he still makes allusions to witchcraft to show the way that superstitious beliefs can damage people and societies.[34] Hössli alludes to the sexual underpinnings of some of the witch hunts when he mentions Pope Innocent VIII's bull against "carnal intercourse with the devil."[35] But more generally Hössli finds the comparison to witches useful as a way to set up his polemic against what he considers to be superstitious and outdated religious prejudices against same-sex love.

Framing his discussion of same-sex erotic love in terms of superstitious persecutions of witches allows Hössli to also make an implicit comparison between Jews and men who love men—a comparison based on the unjust application of Christian morality to state law. He does permit himself the occasional anti-Semitic exclamation. In rejecting the claim that male-male desire is an exclusively pagan phenomenon, he exclaims, "that really smells like the spirit of Israel!"[36] But generally, he attempts to marshal sympathy for the sufferings of the Jews. While his allusions to the persecutions of Jews are more cursory than his intensive study of witch hunts, his reports on their misfortunes are nonetheless focused and full of detail. He describes their medieval scapegoating as plague-bearers and movingly outlines a series of horrendous atrocities that befell them: the burning of large numbers of Jews in Basel, Freiburg, Bern, Zürich, Constance, Strasbourg, and Mainz; the desperate self-immolation of Jews in Speyer and Esslingen; the torture of Jews in Geneva. Hössli concludes, "and all this happened in Switzerland, throughout Germany, Italy, Spain, France, in 1349, by and for European Christianity."[37] Medieval anti-Judaism filled him with a sense of liberal outrage at religiously inspired bias in law and culture. The fact that the pogroms of 1349 were undertaken as a response to the plague stands in implicit contrast to what Hössli would see as an appropriate medical and scientific response to a health crisis. Hössli's reader can infer that a medical, scientific approach to male-male love would also be much more suitable than any superstitious religious response.

By the 1830s, the emancipation of the Jews was a cause widely supported by liberals in the German-speaking world.[38] Many of those who were moved by the plight of the Jews hoped that their emancipation would lead to their social improvement. In his 1781 treatise, "Ueber die bürgerliche Verbesserung der Juden" (On the Civil Improvement of the Jews), Christian von Dohm, for instance, had argued along Rousseauean lines that Jewish culture and society were in decay because of the political and legal mistreatment of the Jews, not because of any inherently bad qualities. Hössli would make the same argument regarding men who sexually loved other men. He insists that deleterious social conditions can alter the appearance of male-male love by perverting it through oppression. Asserting that Plato's writing is a product of ancient Greek society's positive treatment of male-male love, Hössli argues that the philosopher today would have "succumbed to misdeeds, internal battles and misery and ruin and would have ended on the cart, in jail and—perhaps on the gallows."[39]

Whereas "Greek love" had flourished in the time of Plato, today, according to Hössli, "it creeps about as vice under the burdens of general condemnation, destroyed and destroying, without blessing, power or deed, full of guilt and torture, beyond all concept and dignity of humanity, mostly in repulsive, not Greek, figures." It constitutes, he continues, "its own special circle of corruption, vice, sin and waste."[40] This mistreatment is a "rich but tainted spring of humiliation and misery." Wallowing in melodramatic despair, he declares, "Greek love today dwells among thousands of innocent families as a terrible riddle, squalid, shattered and lost in itself; it howls as an outcast in thousands of prisons on our continent, cursing itself and the hour of its birth, hidden in the darkness of night, a self-consuming monster that renews itself daily and contradicts itself constantly."[41] Today, "it provides in this form work and bread to prison masters and hangmen," as well as leading to "suicides inexplicable to us."[42] "Thus waves," he bitterly and sarcastically concludes, "our victory palm, our psychology (*Seelenkunde*), over Greece's poor old humanistic arts and science."[43] Through the Romantically tinged prose, Hössli's argument emerges: sexuality, while not irradicable, can assume new and terrible forms as a consequence of societal oppression and persecution. And in the context of his comparisons between men who love men and Jews, he seems to be picking up on early nineteenth-century rhetoric concerning the social regeneration of the Jews.

The locus of the allusions to the similarity between women, Jews, and men who are sexually attracted to men is a fascinating passage that Hössli quotes twice—first, prominently on the frontispiece of volume 1, and secondly in the text itself. The source is a review published on 4 June 1834 by Wolfgang Menzel in his *Literatur-Blatt* (Literature Review). According to Menzel, "the Rabbinical doctrine of the soul has a curious characteristic: namely, it explains the contradictions in the character of the sexes and their often strange sympathies and antipathies through the transmigration of souls, such that female souls in male bodies repel women and male souls in female bodies repel men, as identical magnetic poles would. Conversely, they attract each other despite having the same bodily sex, on account of the differing sexes of their souls."[44] If anything, Menzel has even more difficulty articulating his ideas than Hössli, who had clearly thought much longer about them. But Menzel's point is that a man with a female soul will not be interested in other women, and a woman with a male soul will not be interested in other men, while women with male souls will be attracted to other women and men with female souls will be attracted to other men. Hössli does not push this idea uncritically, noting that there have been very masculine men who were sexually attracted to other men, but the fact that he introduces this early explanation of same-sex desire as a product of gender inversion in the context of rabbinical doctrine is significant, given that later German thinkers, from Karl Heinrich Ulrichs to Otto Weininger, would strongly emphasize both the comparability of Jews and homosexuals and the gender inversion of homosexuals.

Hössli's reference to gender inversion points in the direction of women's rights, a final source for his thinking on sexual rights. Here he moves the farthest away from the standard liberal politics of his time, which—as Dagmar Herzog has noted—rarely found room for women's rights.[45] One of the implications of the belief that men who love men have female souls is that female souls are capable of sexual desire. If many of Hössli's thoughts regarding the emancipation of male-male love have roots in Enlightenment critiques of religious superstition and in beliefs in cultural tolerance, this particular aspect of Hössli's argument is undoubtedly heavily influenced by Romantic thought. Particularly early on, texts such as Friedrich Schlegel's *Lucinde* of 1799 had represented female sexual desire positively. By the 1830s, Schlegel's depiction of female sexuality and Friedrich Schleiermacher's defense of that depiction had been reprised by Karl Gutzkow in essays and in his *Wally, die Zweiflerin* (Wally the Skeptic). In this 1835 novel, the character Wally particularly admires Delphine, a Jewish woman who is able to live out her love fully, ignoring societal conventions that limit a woman's love to one man who must also be of the same faith. Wally wishes that she lived in a country where French law took precedence, because then people could marry without interference of the church.

This celebration of Jewishness, critique of Christianity and preference for Napoleonic law aroused as much controversy in 1830s Germany as did the call for sexual freedom of women. Critics of the novel quickly resorted to anti-Semitic slurs. In *Das Literatur-Blatt*, Menzel declared, "I would like very much to know what the Jewry (*die Judenschaft*) imagines it will get from such literary lackeys in the somewhat delicate question of their emancipation, as one must hear everywhere that the so-called Young Germany is really Young Palestine."[46] The novel about a sexually active Jewish woman who preferred Enlightenent legal codes to the rule of Christianity raised the hackles of Menzel, who increasingly trained his editorial sights on German-Jewish writers.[47]

And this is where Hössli comes back into the picture. The first volume of Hössli's *Eros* was printed one year after Gutzkow's *Wally* appeared in 1835. The attacks and defenses of the novel took place in the following years, as Hössli was completing and publishing his study of male-male desire. As previously indicated, Menzel had spearheaded the polemics against *Wally*. It is clear that Hössli was reading the *Literatur-Blatt* at precisely this time because he cites these particular issues of the periodical repeatedly in his *Eros*. Hössli has extended discussions of the meaning of male-male love in a play by Sigismund Wiese called *Die Freunde* (The Friends). Wiese is now quite obscure, although his 1844 play *Jesus* did make it to the Vatican's index of forbidden works. *Die Freunde* deals with two friends, the Prussian Philipp and the French Eugen, who—in a classic trope of friendship discussed by the German Romantic author Jean Paul and the French poststructuralist Jacques Derrida[48]—must fight each other to the death. Hössli learned about *Die Freunde* from a review in the *Literatur-Blatt* of 19 September 1836, which declared that "*Die Freunde* is a drama that in Holland and England could not be performed, without the author's and the actors' risking their healthy limbs. The two friends speak exactly like two lovers and awake even in the most tolerant reader a feeling of disgust."[49] Hössli takes from this negative review the belief that the play is indeed about a sexual and erotic friendship: "if my idea about the play is inaccurate why does Menzel's *Literatur-Blatt* say 'in many places the author and the actors of this play would be stoned'?"[50] Anticipating the argument that the play is about non-sexual friendship rather than sexual love, he begins his analysis of the play by saying, "I can already predict that people will incorrectly claim that another spirit governs Wiese's drama than the Greek-erotic one."[51] Despite its implicit resort to threats of violence against those involved with the play, the *Literatur-Blatt* is useful to Hössli because it confirms the notion that the play is dealing with sexual friendship.

In addition to this extended discussion of the *Literatur-Blatt*'s 1836 review of Wiese's *Die Freunde*, Hössli's references to Menzel's discussion of supposedly Talmudic beliefs in the transmigration of souls all come from the same source, again precisely when the journal was the scene of considerable debate about Gutzkow's *Wally*. Although Hössli does not mention Gutzkow or the controversy around his novel, he does pick up on a variety of passages in the *Literatur-Blatt* that have to do with issues of sexual emancipation.[52] Hössli's citations of this journal suggest that he was aware of calls for the emancipation of women and the flesh, which were themselves at the radical edge of liberal thought in the 1830s. His tentative analysis of same-sex love as the product of gender inversion allows him to take these calls for the emancipation of female desire further than even the most radical thinkers of his day, by implying that, if women should be able to express their sexual desires, then men with female souls should also be able to express their love.

In his critique of the persecution of witches, in his sympathy with the Jews, and in his tentative discussion of female sexual desire, Hössli stands rooted in the liberal and progressive thought of his era. In all cases, though, his application of these liberal principles to men who sexually loved other men was a radical innovation. But as radical as his innovation was, it is even more significant that the arguments he makes have connections to liberal and progressive thought of his era. If his arguments are indeed the logical extension of Enlightenment and Romantic thought, then subsequent developments in the history of sexuality have some of their roots in the eighteenth and early nineteenth centuries. Very specifically, the Enlightenment's secularism underscored its faith in science rather than religion, a faith that helped establish a tendency among homosexuals to turn to scientifically quantifiable evidence in order to legitimize their sexual identity. Efforts to emancipate the Jews, which emerged out of the Enlightenment, provided a minoritizing, identity-based model for homosexual activists of the nineteenth and twentieth centuries. And Romantic depictions of female desire lent credence to gender inversion as an explanation for *urnings* (Ulrichs's word for people with male bodies and female souls who sexually desire men) and male homosexuals. More broadly, the tensions between the Enlightenment roots of many of Hössli's demands and the radical challenges that his claims posed to society foreshadow that continuing debate between liberal activism on behalf of gay rights, such as the right to marry or the right to serve in the military, and the radical queer critique of the political system that encompasses such activism.

Notes

1. I refer here of course to the oft-cited claim that "the psychological, psychiatric, medical category of homosexuality was constituted from the moment it was characterized—Westphal's famous article of 1870 on 'contrary sexual sensations' can stand as its date of

birth." Michel Foucault, *The History of Sexuality*, vol. 1: *An Introduction*, trans. Robert Hurley (New York, 1978), 43.

2. The German word *Sexualität* does not appear in the *Deutsches Wörterbuch* of Jacob and Wilhelm Grimm. The earliest citation for the English word "sexuality" in the *Oxford English Dictionary* comes from 1800, in a piece William Cowper wrote on Erasmus Darwin's "Lives of Plants," which was about Carl Linnaeus's discussion of the "sexual lives" of plants.

3. The original is in Joseph Hermann Schmidt, "Ueber die relative Stellung des Oertlichen zum Allgemeinen," *Magazin für die gesammte Heilkunde* 45, no. 2 (1835): 166. Cited by Heinrich Hössli, *Eros: Die Männerliebe der Griechen, ihre Beziehung zur Geschichte, Erziehung, Literatur und Gesetzgebung aller Zeiten* (Glarus, 1836/St. Gallen, 1838; reprinted in 3 vols. Berlin, 1996), vol. 1, 302. Translation is my own.

4. Albrecht von Haller, *Von den empfindlichen und reizbaren Teilen des menschlichen Körpers*, trans. and ed. Karl Sudhoff (Leipzig, 1922).

5. Not all that different from what the *New York Times* would argue in 2009. See Daniel Bergner, "What Do Women Want?" *New York Times*, Sunday magazine, 22 January 2009.

6. Patricia Fara, *Sex, Botany and Empire: The Story of Carl Linnaeus and Joseph Banks* (New York, 2003).

7. Cf. Thomas Laqueur, *Making Sex: Body and Gender from the Greeks to Freud* (Cambridge, MA,1990).

8. Hössli, *Eros*, vol. 1, 267.

9. Ibid., vol. 2, 6–7.

10. Here he interestingly diverges from the modern American pattern that Judith Butler identifies, according to which people "are" a gender, but "have" a sexuality. See Judith Butler, *Undoing Gender* (New York, 2004), 16.

11. Hössli, *Eros*, vol. 2, 227.

12. Ibid., 200.

13. Ibid., 230.

14. Ferdinand Karsch, "Heinrich Hössli (1784–1864)," *Jahrbuch für sexuelle Zwischenstufen* 5, no. 1 (1903): 449–556.The Karsch essay is reprinted in the third volume of the Verlag rosa Winkel edition of Hössli: Ferdinand Karsch, "Heinrich Hößli (1784–1864)," in Hössli, *Eros*, vol. 3, 35–142. See also Bernd-Ulrich Hergemöller, *Mann für Mann: Biographisches Lexikon zur Geschichte von Freundesliebe und mann-männlicher Sexualität im deutschen Sprachraum* (Hamburg, 1998), 366–67.

15. The prohibition of the death penalty in the enumeration of basic rights of Germans (*Grundrechte des deutschen Volkes*) issued by the avowedly liberal National Assembly that convened in Frankfurt in 1848 shows the importance of this issue for liberals. Article I, paragraph 5 and Article III, paragraph 9, of the *Grundrechte des deutschen Volkes*; see Jean de Grandvilliers, *Essai sur le libéralisme allemande* (Paris, 1914), 41–43.

16. James Sheehan discusses the sociological demographics of liberals in the early nineteenth century in *German Liberalism in the Nineteenth Century* (Chicago, 1978), 24.

17. Grandvilliers, *Essai*, 7.

18. Sheehan, *German Liberalism*, 5.

19. James Knudson, "The Limits of Liberal Politics in Berlin, 1815–1848," in *In Search of a Liberal Germany: Studies in the History of German Liberalism from 1789 to the Present*, ed. Konrad H. Jarausch and Larry Eugene Jones (New York, 1990), 111.

88 ~: *Robert Deam Tobin*

88 ~: *Robert Deam Tobin*

20. Grandvilliers, for instance, cites Montesquieu as an important intellectual ancestor of German liberalism in particular (*Essai*, 20).
21. Hössli, *Eros*, vol. 1, 300.
22. Heinrich Zschokke, *The History of Switzerland*, trans. Francis George Shaw (New York, 1875).
23. For more information on Zschokke, see Klaus H. Bongart, "Heinrich Zschokke: Volksschriftsteller und Volkserzieher," in *Analecta Helvetica et Germanica: Eine Festschrift zu Ehren von Hermann Boeschenstein*, ed. Achim Arnold et al. (Bonn, 1979), 137–53.
24. Hössli, *Eros*, vol. 3, 72; Karsch, "Heinrich Hößli (1784–1864)," 486.
25. The Zschokke story is reprinted in the third volume of the Verlag rosa Winkel edition of Hössli, *Eros*, vol. 3, 201–56.
26. Hössli, *Eros*, vol. 3, 327.
27. Sheehan, *German Liberalism*, 38.
28. Dieter Langewiesche, *Liberalism in Germany*, trans. Christiane Banerji (Princeton, 2000), 199.
29. Hössli, *Eros*, vol. 3, 40.
30. Ibid., vol. 1, 62.
31. Anna's case has inspired a considerable body of creative work in recent years, including the novel by Kaspar Freuler, *Anna Göldi: Die Geschichte der letzten Hexe* (Bern, 1947), the novel by Eveline Hasler, *Anna Göldin, Letzte Hexe* (Zurich, 1982), the play by Stephanie Bernhard, *Das Schicksal der Anna Göldi: Bühnenstück in 5 Akten* (Gundeldingen-Ost, 2008), the opera by Kaspar Freuler and Martin Derungs, *Anna Göldi: Stationen eines verpfuschten Lebens: Musiktheater in 12 Bildern nach dem Göldi-Roman von Kaspar Freuler*, and the Swiss film directed by Gertrud Pinkus, *Anna Goldin— letzte Hexe* (1991). Scholarly research includes Walter Hauser, *Der Justizmord an Anna Göldi: Neue Recherchen zum letzten Hexenprozess in Europa* (Zurich, 2007). See also Susanne Kord, "Ancient Fears and the New Order: Witch Beliefs and Physiognomy in the Age of Reason," *German Life and Letters* 61, no. 1 (2008): 61–78.
32. Hössli, *Eros*, vol. 1, 54.
33. Ibid., 14.
34. Ibid., vol. 2, 259.
35. Ibid., vol. 1, 11.
36. Ibid., vol. 2, 264.
37. Ibid., vol. 1, 59–60.
38. See Sheehan, *German Liberalism*, 41, and Langewiesche, *Liberalism*, 13. But despite liberal support, complete emancipation was slow to come: the reorganization of the Habsburg Empire as Austria-Hungary in 1867 brought with it the emancipation of the Jews; in Germany, the constitution of the empire in 1871 wiped away the last vestiges of anti-Jewish laws; and Switzerland finally eliminated legal limitations on non-Christians (i.e., Jews) in all cantons in 1874. For a basic outline on the subject, see the entry, "Emancipation," *The New Standard Jewish Encyclopedia*, 7th ed. (New York, 1992), 301–2.
39. Hössli, *Eros*, vol. 1, 192.
40. Ibid., vol. 2, 239.
41. Ibid. Hössli's comparison of "Greek love" to a self-destructive monster that renews itself daily and contradicts itself constantly (*ein täglich sich erneuendes, selbstverzehrendes*

und unaufhörlich widersprechendes Ungeheuer) harks back to Werther's description of nature in Johann Wolfgang Goethe's *Die Leiden des jungen Werthers* (The Sorrows of Young Werther) as "an eternally swallowing, eternally chewing monster" (*ein ewig verschlingendes, ewig wiederkaeuendes Ungeheuer*). Johann Wolfgang von Goethe, *Werke: Hamburger Ausgabe in 14 Bänden*, ed. Erich Trunz (Munich, 1981), vol. 6, 53.

42. Hössli, *Eros*, vol. 2, 239.

43. Ibid.

44. Hössli, *Eros*, vol. 1, 295, see also frontispiece.

45. Dagmar Herzog, "Liberalism, Religious Dissent, and Women's Rights: Louise Dittmar's Writings from the 1840s," in Jarausch and Jones, *In Search of a Liberal Germany*, 55; idem, *Intimacy and Exclusion: Religious Politics in Pre-Revolutionary Baden* (Princeton, 1996), 85–110, 140–66. See also Langewiesche, *Liberalism*, 12.

46. Wolfgang Menzel, "Unmoralische Literatur" (originally in *Literatur-Blatt* 1835). Here cited from Alfred Estermann, ed., *Politische Avantgarde 1830–1840: Eine Dokumentation zum 'Jungen Deutschland,'* vol. 1 (Frankfurt am Main, 1972), 64.

47. For useful insights and further leads on Menzel and his attacks on Jewish writers in the *Literatur-Blatt*, see Todd Samuel Presner, *Mobile Modernity: Germans, Jews, Trains* (New York, 2007), 166 and 177–79.

48. See Robert Tobin, *Warm Brothers: Queer Theory and the Age of Goethe* (Philadelphia, 2000), 48.

49. Cited by Hans Krah, "Freundschaft oder Männerliebe?" *Forum Vormärz Forschung: Jahrbuch 1999*, vol. 5, *"Emancipation des Fleisches": Erotik und Sexualität im Vormärz*, ed. Gustav Frank and Detlev Kopp (Bielefeld, 1999), 186.

50. Hössli, *Eros*, vol. 2, 328.

51. Ibid.

52. For Schlegel, Gutzkow, and Hössli, see also my essay, "The Emancipation of the Flesh: The Legacy of Romanticism in the Homosexual Rights Movement," in *Romanticism on the Net*, no. 36/37 (November 2004): "Queer Romanticism," ed. Michael O'Rourke and David Collins, http://www.erudit.org/revue/ron/204/v/n36-37/011143.14.html.

SECTION II

✵

Whose Sexuality?
Subjectivity, Surveillance, Emancipation

Studies of sex in history—its social formations, the play of permissiveness and repression, its formal regulation, and so on—were not unknown, or even uncommon, before Foucault wrote the *History of Sexuality*. The radical innovation of the three-volume work was not the historical consideration of sex, but rather of the uniquely modern domain of sexuality, which bound together two "elements that do not usually fall within the historian's practice or analysis": these were the categories of the "subject" and "truth."[1] The entire project can be seen as an illustration of the peculiar way in which we have come to formulate the question of the true self. This was and remains at once a question of expert determination, volitional community-formation, and authentic self-knowledge; the process of "subjectivation" famously entails oppression and discipline at the same time that it provides ground for claims to emancipation, however problematic. The historical formation of the truth of the subject had been a concern of Foucault's since his earliest work, yet it was the domain of "sexuality" that brought him to focus on this self-contradictory potential of the subject. It is here, in the domain of the process of subjectivity, that there is a possibility of ethical action. Reviewing the history of sexuality, we see moments where the subject and the relations formed among subjects remain linked to, but are more than effects of, "capillary power."

Attending more closely to this potential requires historical work on the precise ways in which disciplinary power—surveillance, regulation, oppression, penalization—was produced as part of the same process that called forth self-understandings, communal ties, and the will to liberation, vexed though these may have been. The six individual historical cases that follow track particular aspects of how these highly ramified and interconnected processes unfolded. In some, we are presented with classic apparatuses of surveillance and regulation, such as Beachy's imperial Berlin police bureau, the Department of Black-mailers and Homosexuals; or the regulation of Roos's Weimar-era registered prostitutes ("Kontrollmädchen"). In each of these cases, the authors detect the production of active subjects and communities through the processes of discipline. Whether this was an unintended effect of the control process (as Beachy suggests occurred in tandem with practices of police "protection") or a strategic appropriation of disciplinary discourses (as Roos sees in prostitute activists' maneuvers among liberal and Marxist social advocates and police) may be matters for further interpretation or debate.

The same is true of subjects' tactical appropriations and manipulations of authoritative knowledge. This is clearest in the first essay in this section, Leng's subtle analysis of Anna Rüling's important intervention in homosexual science, where psychiatric and other knowledges of the gendered and sexualized body are a source of self-empowerment. Authoritative knowledge also takes the form of liberal counsel in Sarasin's analysis of a mid-twentieth-century Swiss advice columnist's acceptance of intersex subjects. This is deftly juxtaposed to Foucault's Herculine Barbin, the intersex subject whose place outside of the "symbolic order" is idealized, according to Sarasin. The sexual image of the imperial German soldier is the object of Schneider's attention in an essay that uses the pivotal moment of the Eulenburg scandal and its exposure of homosexual prostitution in the military to explore the dynamics of public and private fantasy in relation to ideology. This deployment of sexuality differs from what Foucault presented, to be sure, and it expands the view of both disciplinary discourse and conceptions of subjectivity. In Lybeck's contribution, in particular, popular culture emerges in the form of fictional narratives depicting lesbian love, offering the possibility of sexual self-fashioning that does not entail submission to a psychoanalytic model of the self.

These contributions also suggest that the focus on the subject in early twenty-first-century scholarship is enriched by theorists emerging from humanistic psychoanalytic criticism, on the one side, and post-Marxism on the other. Lacan, Žižek, Butler, and others appear in these essays, each as they engage with, rather than undermine, the Foucauldian concept of subjectivation. Together, they raise a new set of questions concerning the role conscious-ness may play in the interaction of disciplinary, subjective, and activist spheres. As Leng reminds us, Foucault's military metaphors of tactics, strategies, and deployments raise the question of what kind of war this was—a battle for the subject? Or are these all merely further iterations of what Foucault called not discourses but discourse, for which, but also within which, a kind of struggle takes place?

Scott Spector

Notes

1. *Hermeneutics of the Subject: Lectures at the Collège de France 1981–1982*, 2.

CHAPTER 6

~:~

Anna Rüling, Michel Foucault, and the "Tactical Polyvalence" of the Female Homosexual

KIRSTEN LENG

The writings of Michel Foucault have provided historians of sexuality with invaluable methodological and conceptual tools with which to read, analyze, and better understand their subject matter. Foucault's conceptualization of the emergence of the sexual subject as the product of modern relations of "power-knowledge," so provocatively elaborated in *The History of Sexuality*, vol. 1: *An Introduction*, is especially helpful for students of the sexual reform movements of the early twentieth century.[1] Centrally, Foucault asserts that sexual subjectivity is not only the effect of a hegemonic, medico-scientific "will to knowledge," but also the result of resistance on the part of sexual subjects themselves. He contends that sexual subjects have often articulated this resistance using the very vocabularies and categories of the medical and scientific authority they ostensibly refuse; he refers to this phenomenon of discourse serving "both as an instrument of, and point of resistance to, power" as tactical polyvalence.[2]

In later essays, the figure of resistance took on a greater role in Foucault's understanding of the processes by which human beings are transformed into subjects, sexual or otherwise.[3] However, what Foucault meant by resistance was left only vaguely explicated in subsequent texts; in "The Subject and Power," for example, he defines resistance as the promotion of "new forms of subjectivity" opposed to the "kind of individuality which has been imposed on us for several centuries."[4] In light of the historically contingent and continually contested character of both subjectivation and resistance, as suggested by tactical polyvalence, one is forced to ask what possibilities realistically exist for the creation of such "new forms of subjectivity" detached from their contemporary configurations of power-knowledge. One may also ask what kind of ethical imperative is implied in the directive that subjects transcend their historically conditioned consciousness in order to create such new forms of subjectivity. Indeed, when confronting the texts of resisting subjects, the historian of sexuality working within a Foucauldian methodological framework is left with a number of fundamental, troubling questions: If a subject is constituted in and through discourses of power-knowledge—even as he or she resists them—how can one accurately identify resistance on the part of the subject? Is it always "power-knowledge" itself that is—and must be—resisted? What are the implications of Foucault's understanding of resistance and subjectivation for the politics and ethics of writing the history of sexuality? And how can or should the historian evaluate forms of resistance that appear to be politically retrograde?

This essay confronts the questions provoked by Foucauldian notions of resistance and tactical polyvalence, but it also complicates them by analyzing a sexual subject who not only resists sexual, but also gendered, subjectivation. As feminist theorists have noted, Foucault failed to account for the difference gender makes when analyzing the sexual subject, and at times dismissed the need to understand lesbian subjectivity apart from the subjectivation of the homosexual as such. However, feminist scholars such as Biddy Martin have argued that an understanding of gender is crucial to understandings of sexuality.[5] In her essay "Extraordinary Homosexuals and the Fear of Being Ordinary," Martin takes particular issue with the exclusion of the feminine from theorizations of homosexual women's identity and demonstrates the difference gender makes through a reading of two texts from turn-of-the-century Germany, including Anna Rüling's 1904 speech to the Wissenschaftlich-humanitäres Komitee (Scientific Humanitarian Committee),[6] "Welches Interesse hat die Frauenbewegung an der Lösung des homosexuellen Problems?" (What Interest Does the Women's Movement Have in Solving the Homosexual Problem?).

Martin's choice of Rüling's speech to demonstrate this problem is fitting. As one of the first documented examples of a person speaking publicly as an *Urninde*, or homosexual woman,[7] "What Interest Does the Women's Movement have in Solving the Homosexual Problem?" is a remarkable document.[8] Although the declared purpose of Rüling's speech is to identify common ground between the early twentieth-century German homosexual rights and women's movements, Rüling's speech constitutes one of the first public efforts to construct the Urninde as a legitimate political subject in her own right. This construction is, however, made problematic by the fact that the Urninde simultaneously occupied two subordinate categories, those of "homosexual" and "woman," and yet, given the masculine definition of the former and the heterosexual definition of the latter during Rüling's time, the Urninde did not belong fully to either category as hegemonically defined, and neither movement viewed the Urninde as a constituent.[9]

Over the course of Rüling's speech one can detect multiple points of what could be called resistance, as the Urninde attempts to speak her own truth about a compromised and overdetermined subjectivity. Though Rüling contests the dominant and overwhelmingly negative constructions of female homosexuality propagated by scientific experts, her characterization of the Urninde draws extensively on the very discourses that in other contexts are used to subordinate and pathologize her, particularly those of sexology and eugenics. Indeed, the greatest resistances present in Rüling's speech are directed toward the consideration of the Urninde as a potentially feminine woman. Rüling thus draws upon expert knowledge in her speech to resist the Urninde's identification with the feminine by insisting on her fundamental masculinity. As such, Rüling's speech provides a compelling example of resistance through the mechanism of tactical polyvalence, and enables us to evaluate the strengths and limits of the Foucauldian methodology for the history of sexuality. In what follows, I analyze Rüling's construction of the Urninde to identify the many ways in which expert scientific knowledge provides Rüling with opportunities—and difficulties—in establishing the Urninde as an independent and legitimate political subject. I also pay close attention to Rüling's negotiation of the categories of "homosexual" and "woman" to illuminate the complexities of resistance when one takes both sex and gender into account. By way of conclusion, I consider the merits and limits of Foucauldian methodology for the history of sexuality, in particular the difficulties of thinking about the ethics of sexual politics from within a Foucauldian framework.

Representing the Urninde: Sexological Accounts

In the first volume of *History of Sexuality*, Foucault maintains that the nineteenth century witnessed a transformation in the ways in which sex was ordered in relation to "the medical institution, the exigency of normality, and … the problem of life and illness."[10] By the end of the century, according to Laura Doan and Chris Waters, "a series of distinct scientific, clinical and discursive practices established a new taxonomy of 'deviant' sexual behavior predicated upon the existence of a normative heterosexuality."[11] The burgeoning *scientia sexualis* was comprised of contributions from emerging disciplines vying for legitimacy, including psychiatry, criminology, and anthropology. Sexologists disseminated their taxonomy of deviant sexual behavior to a broader European and North American public through the fields of medicine, law, and popular journalism. Indeed, by the turn of the century, sexological understandings of homosexuality had accrued an influence beyond their immediate, tiny readership and came to constitute the dominant framework for scientific, legal, and popular discourses on same-sex love and desire. In effect, sexology became what Arnold Davidson calls the "dominant style of reasoning" regarding sexuality during the early twentieth century.[12]

At the time of Rüling's speech there existed within sexology numerous theories of homosexuality, which often overlapped at many points. Among these were the "sexual inversion" model, attributed to Havelock Ellis, and the "third sex" or "sexual intermediate" model pioneered by Karl Heinrich Ulrichs and elaborated by Edward Carpenter, Otto Weininger, and Magnus Hirschfeld.[13] Both theories aimed to distance themselves from earlier understandings of homosexuality as a disease; both insisted that homosexuality was congenital, that is, a product of nature, although both still considered it a psychological condition;[14] and both, to varying degrees, helped to legitimize homosexual desire and identity.[15] However, these theories exhibit a general confusion within sexology regarding whether homosexuality could be read on the body, through physiognomy and performance, or whether it was a psychological condition that lurked below the surface of a "normal" exterior; some insisted both phenomena existed simultaneously. According to Havelock Ellis, homosexuality manifested itself anatomically, sartorially, and performatively. In *Sexual Inversion*, Ellis identifies the female "invert" by pointing to her deep voice, firm muscles, and absent soft connective tissue, as well as her predilections for male attire, athletics, and smoking, and her disdain for domestic work.[16]

Alternatively, Karl Heinrich Ulrichs asserted that homosexual preferences were the product of a psychic, rather than a physical, sexual inversion, famously encapsulating this concept in the phrase *anima muliebris virili corpore inclusa*, a feminine soul enclosed in a male body.[17] Other sexual theorists such as Otto Weininger understood homosexuality as a result of a fundamental, genetic bisexuality, with bisexuality here understood as the presence of both male and female characteristics, which could both be found at the level of the cell. Such an understanding of bisexuality thus postulates a diversity of sexed and gendered subjectivities between the pole of male and female, and heterosexual and homosexual; thus, in the first "preparatory" part of his *Sex and Character*, Weininger insists that, "[b]etween Man and Woman there are *innumerable gradations*, or 'intermediate sexual forms.'"[18] Much like Weininger, Magnus Hirschfeld, cofounder of the WhK, derived his understanding of homosexuality from his belief in a fundamental physiological bisexuality; however, Hirschfeld went much further in synthesizing third sex and sexual inversion positions. In his essay "The Objective Diagnosis of Homosexuality," he insisted that "[t]he most valuable result of research into homosexuality is the determination that, between man and woman, *in all spiritual and physical points* only gradual, quantitative differences exist."[19] Indeed, in diagnosing homosexuality, Hirschfeld argued that one must consider the development of the germ cells, the nature of the individual's physical features, his/her intellectual nature, and the direction of his/her sex drive.[20]

Despite the debates among sexologists regarding the locus of homosexuality, it is worth stressing that the majority of sexologists agreed that the key to understanding female homosexuality was to understand her fundamental masculinity, whether this masculinity was physical or psychological.[21] Furthermore, despite the talk of sexual intermediaries among some, sexologists continually referred to sexual "types" that ultimately depended on a heterosexual understanding of what it meant to be a man and a woman. As she was a member of the WhK, it should not be surprising to us that Rüling's construction of the Urninde most closely approximates Hirschfeld's synthetic approach; however, traces of all the aforementioned approaches, with all of their assertions, contradictions, and uncertainties regarding the relationship of sex and gender, mind and body, are present in Rüling's speech. Though Rüling at times challenges the authority of scientists' expertise, she frequently engages their ideas, moving strategically between the theories, for the purpose of constructing the lesbian subject. Most importantly, sexual scientific discourse enables Rüling to define her sexual subjectivity in resistance to the heterosexual woman by asserting a fundamental difference between the Urninde and the feminine woman by virtue of the former's masculinity.

Representing the Urninde: Rüling's Account

Rüling's use of the term "Urninde" as signifier and self-descriptor clearly places her within the referential realm of "third sex" theories of homosexuality. Beyond taxonomy, Rüling's indebtedness to the third sex model is evinced by her claim that homosexuality is not only a fact of nature but also "the natural and obvious link between men and women."[22] It is further present in her claim that "in people with primarily masculine characteristics, it naturally directs itself toward women and vice versa, regardless of the actual physical sex of the person."[23] Relying on the third sex model is strategically significant, for it enables Rüling to compare the Urninde's sociopolitical plight with that of the Urning or male homosexual. Rüling asserts that "the mental stress that Urninden endure is just as great, or greater, than the burden under which Uranian men suffer," because "[t]o the world which bases its judgment on outward appearances, these women are much more obvious than even the most effeminate man," making them the objects of "misdirected morality ... scorn and mockery."[24]

Rüling vacillates on the question of whether homosexuality can be read via external cues throughout her speech. At times she draws upon sexual inversion theories that stress the visibility of homosexuality, insisting that "homosexual proclivities express themselves often unconsciously and unintentionally in appearance, speech, deportment, movement, dress, etc," and are visible to a degree that is "obvious to all onlookers."[25] Rüling valorizes the lesbian subject by asserting that "anyone with the slightest bit of familiarity with *homosexual traits* who has been following the women's movement at all or who knows any of its leading women *personally or by pictures*, will find the Uranians among the suffragettes and recognize that Uranians are often noble and fine."[26] However, Rüling elsewhere acknowledges that sometimes the Urninde's homosexuality is not immediately legible, stating: "Of course not all homosexual women show masculine exteriors that harmonize with their inner selves. There are many Uranian women with completely feminine appearance, which they accentuate with very feminine behavior in order to escape being detected as homosexuals. This is a comedy which is bitter and painful to those who must participate."[27] Such a statement suggests she believes that some correlation should exist between one's external self-presentation and one's subjective, self-understood identity, as though the feminine threatens to undermine the presence of homosexuality. Such a statement also suggests that one's external appearance is unreliable as a marker of sexual difference. Thus, like Ulrichs, Rüling insists that fundamental psychological differences distinguish the Urninde from the feminine, heterosexual woman.

Importantly, the distinction Rüling seeks to make cannot be made without continual comparisons to the feminine woman—comparisons which tended to legitimize the Urninde, but which also threaten to undermine the independence of the Urninde's subjectivity. Like Hirschfeld and Weininger, Rüling insists on the existence of innumerable gradations of the sexed personality. Between the poles of man and woman, she asserts, "we can differentiate between a feminine personality in which feminine characteristics dominate; a masculine one, in which the masculine characteristics dominate; and finally, a feminine-masculine or a masculine-feminine personality with equally masculine and feminine qualities."[28] In advancing such an argument, Rüling calls into question the category of woman; however, her purpose is not to broaden the category to include Urninde, but to limit it to the feminine woman only. Rüling insists that despite a shared corporeality, the category of woman is not unified, and that the body itself betrays great psychological diversity. In light of such claims, it is not surprising that Rüling asserts, "[w]hen nature created the different sexes ... the intention was for each person to fill the role appropriate to his or her own traits and abilities."[29]

Thus, like many proponents of the third-sex model, Rüling works with ideal types while simultaneously appealing to the notion of sexual intermediaries. At this point the reader can identify not only tensions within sexological understandings of sex and gender, but also the strategic possibilities of tactical polyvalence. According to Rüling, the "predominant and deciding trait" of the heterosexual woman is emotionality; conversely, "clear reason rules the Urninde." In making this claim, she maintains that the Urninde is instead more like "the average man," and is, like him, "more objective, energetic, and goal oriented than the feminine Woman." Rüling goes as far as to claim that, in terms of the Urninde's thoughts and feelings, "she does not imitate man"; rather, she is "inherently similar to him."[30] Like the normal, "that is, the completely virile man," who is similarly ruled by qualities of reason, objectivity, and ambition, the Urninde too is "is *physically* more suited for a rugged life's struggle than a Woman." Conversely, according to Rüling, "The feminine woman has been designed by nature to become first of all wife and mother."[31]

Even in the realms of education and the professional studies, Rüling also asserts that an absolute gendered difference between the Urninde and the feminine woman exists. The Urninde is especially suited for the study of the sciences and other "manly" professions, such as "medicine, law, agricultural professions, and the creative arts,"[32] because of her "possess[ion] of those qualities lacking in feminine women: greater objectivity, energy, and perseverance."[33] Conversely, she insists that, if given access to education, feminine women will pursue studies more suited to their duties as wife and mother; indeed, Rüling insists, "under favorable conditions most heterosexual women choose marriage. They seek a broader, more comprehensive education in order to be esteemed companions for their husbands, not just sensual love objects, and to be wives who are respected by their husbands as intellectual equals, and accordingly granted equal rights and responsibilities in the marriage."[34] While such statements may recall the misogyny of Otto Weininger's claim that "studying becomes a *fashion* among women ... intended to ensnare a man,"[35] it is worth noting that although education was a primary objective of the women's movement, even the most radical feminists maintained that woman's highest destiny was motherhood.[36]

But perhaps the most important instance in which the Urninde's difference from woman is mobilized is in Rüling's discussion of the former's relationship to the women's emancipation movement. Rüling claims, "Contrary to the belief of the anti-feminists that women are inferior and that only those with strong masculine characteristics are to be valued, I believe that women in general are equal to men." However, in the very next sentence, she asserts, "I am convinced, however, that the homosexual Woman is particularly capable of playing a leading role in the international women's movement for equality."[37] "With her androgynous characteristics," Rüling claims, "she was often the one who initiated action because she felt most strongly the many, many injustices and hardships with which laws, society, and archaic customs treat women." This assertion would seem to suggest that Rüling viewed the public sphere of law and politics as exclusively male, and that the Urninde, by virtue of her closeness to man, suffered this exclusion more keenly. "Without the active support of the Uranian women," Rüling further asserts, "the women's movement would not be where it is today—this is an undisputable fact."[38] Indeed, Rüling insists that it is "through [her] energy" that the Urninde can awake "the *naturally indif-*

ferent and submissive average women to an awareness of their human dignity and rights."[39] Despite her criticisms of Otto Weininger, one cannot help but remark on the similarity between this comment and Weininger's claim that "[a]ll those women who really strive for emancipation … always display many male properties."[40]

Sexological understandings of homosexual woman seem to have provided Rüling with the intellectual tools with which to create the Urninde as a politically legitimate, independent subject—one who is both "noble and fine." Yet the logic of tactical polyvalence could not allow such a construction to exist without complications. Sexology's diagnosis of homosexuality as a psychological condition, or abnormality, also contributes to Rüling's construction of the Urninde. It is this aspect of sexological thinking that leads Rüling to engage with eugenics, the hereditary "science" of "improving stock,"[41] in yet another tactically polyvalent maneuver, namely illustrating the "national" and "racial" consequences of the failure to liberate the Urninde. It is here that the pathologizing sting of sexological discourse reveals the trap of tactical polyvalence: while Rüling's appeal to eugenic arguments may seem not only disturbing but also sudden, it is less surprising when we recall Foucault's recognition of sexology and eugenics in the *History of Sexuality* as "the two great innovations in the technology of sex of the second half of the nineteenth century." Indeed, he argues that they "merged together quite well, for the theory of 'degenerescence' made it possible for them to perpetually refer back to one another."[42] Rüling's appeal to eugenics should also seem less surprising given its currency among her social reformist contemporaries. From the vantage point of the twenty-first century, the popularity of eugenics seems unfathomable; nevertheless, we must acknowledge that eugenic arguments were extremely influential among sex reformers, feminists, socialists, and left-liberals as well as those on the extreme right.[43] Like these social reformers, Rüling appeals to eugenics to argue that the recognition of the Urninde's individual rights and unique subjectivity can serve a larger national and "racial" good.

We find evidence of eugenic thought in Rüling's arguments surrounding the "marriage question," which she takes up to argue the Urninde's right to sexual, social, and economic independence.[44] After pointing out that in a heterosexual partnership the Urninde can fulfill her "marital duties" only "with aversion or, at best, indifference," and that enabling homosexuals to remain single would leave more husbands "for those women whose natural inclinations are satisfied by the role of wife, housekeeper and mother," Rüling argues that the matter of homosexual liberation is of greater social importance.[45] According to Rüling, "the marriage of homosexuals is a triple crime; it is a crime against the state, against society itself, and against an unborn generation, for experience teaches us that the offspring of Uranians are seldom healthy and strong." Indeed, she attributes "a large percentage of the mentally disturbed, retarded, epileptics, tuberculars, and degenerates of all kinds," as well as "[m]orbid sexual drives such as sadism and masochism" to homosexuals who "procreated against their nature."[46] Thus, Rüling maintains, "The state and society should have an urgent interest in preventing Uranians from marrying, since it is the state and society who bear the burden of these sick and weak beings who are unable to make any contribution in return."[47] To ensure that homosexuals do not act against their nature, Rüling suggests that the women's movement, concerned as it is with the "moral fiber and health of our people," ought to explain "the nature of homosexuality rationally and sensibly to older children and young people in whom homosexual tendencies have been detected"—in consultation, of course, "with a physician who is knowledgeable in this area."[48]

Although Rüling posits this educational program as liberatng—a means of freeing homosexual children from heterosexual paths—in light of the preceding arguments, she also represents it as a means of preventing racial degeneration. Suddenly, it would seem that knowing and acting within one's nature becomes an extremely limiting thing indeed, returning us to the questions, stated in the introduction, of exactly how we can identify resistance, and how we can evaluate it. Even if Rüling's willingness to subordinate the Urninde's freedom to the imagined "greater social good" is a purely strategic move, it should lead us to question the independence and legitimacy of the Urninde as a political subject, as such a move ultimately undermines the Urninde's unique *entitlement* to the individual rights for which Rüling argues so forcefully.

Conclusion

What can we ultimately make of Rüling's speech as an example of resistance through the mechanism of tactical polyvalence? Let us first consider the relationship between gender and tactical polyvalence. What is clear throughout Rüling's speech is that she does not resist expert knowledge so much as resist the Urninde's identification with the feminine; indeed, she embraces expert discourses insofar as they help to establish the Urninde's fundamental masculinity vis-à-vis the "womanly woman." Although queer theorists such as Gayle Rubin have suggested that separating sexuality from gender could be an emancipatory move that could challenge the binary structure of masculinity/femininity established by the patriarchal system,[49] such a challenge is not what is sought in Rüling's speech. Rüling clearly seeks the privileges of patriarchy, here defined as access to education and the professions. Upon reflection, we can see that in all instances where Rüling identifies common cause between the women's movement and the homosexual rights movement, she frames these commonalities in terms of the Urninde's liberation from the strictures of the category of woman, and legitimates this move through recourse to the claim, first pioneered by Ulrichs, and later echoed by Hirschfeld and Weininger, that all should have a right to live "according to their natures."

After acknowledging Rüling's resistance to the feminine along with the ways in which sexology facilitates this resistance, we must further ask what real possibilities for liberation from the strictures of the feminine existed for the Urninde during Rüling's time. Despite Rüling's attempt to effect such a separation, throughout her speech the body acts as bulwark to total masculine identification. The material, female body must be considered a *limit* on Rüling's ability to resist the category of woman and all it entailed. For those gendered female by virtue of their body who yet dissociated with this gender by virtue of their sexual desires, resistance involved both a rejection of the traits associated with the female body and an embrace of alternative sites of subjectivity. Rüling's resistance to being subsumed within the category of woman and the femininity and heterosexuality it implied; her insistence on the psyche as the site of the Urninde's unique, masculinized subjectivity; and her problematic handling of the body within her definition of the Urninde should force us to recognize that resistance is itself a gendered practice whose nature varies according to the historical context of its deployment.

While it is important to acknowledge resistance as a practice that simultaneously implicates gender and sexuality, this recognition leaves unanswered the question of the larger ethical implications of Rüling's form of resistance, as well as the historian's role as ethical adjudicator of such discursive practices. Certainly, her eugenic arguments beg such a consideration from German historians. This question in particular illuminates some of the merits and limits of Foucauldian methodology. Foucauldian concepts such as tactical polyvalence help us to better understand and represent the historical contexts within which subjects operated, and to acknowledge that the forms their resistance took may not be those chosen by political subjects of the twenty-first century. Tactical polyvalence in particular illuminates the strategic significance for subordinate political subjects of seizing the authority and legitimacy of science in particular instances for subordinate subjects. Furthermore, Foucault's definition of power provides us with a more complicated understanding of the political, which facilitates a richer, more complex historical reconstruction of sociopolitical movements and struggles. However, it is worth stressing here that Foucault himself continually insisted, in both writings and in interviews, that he was primarily interested in process; that is, in questions of *how* power operated and *how* struggles unfurled.[50] Tellingly, as an interviewer once pointed out, he conceptualized these processes through military metaphors such as tactics, strategies, and deployments.[51] He was thus significantly less interested—or perhaps less comfortable—in considering questions of "to what end" or "with what legacy" vis-à-vis tactics and strategies; clearly his stronger interest lay in the battle and not the outcome of the war. Consequently, the historian drawing primarily upon Foucauldian methods and analyses is left at a loss when attempting to ethically evaluate the consequences of a sexual subject's particular mode of resistance, or to conceptualize an ethical sexual subject that could serve as the foundation for a just sexual politics.

It is possible that the tools needed for such tasks are beyond the scope of Foucauldian methodology. Foucault's reluctance to engage with the ethical consequences of past political practices, particularly those conducted under the banners of progress and emancipation, raises questions about the place of politics and ethics in the writing of history, particularly histories of sexuality. The historian working within a Foucauldian framework is confronted with the difficult question of whether it is just to impose an ethical imperative upon marginalized subjects to somehow rise above historical circumstances. Certainly the concept of tactical polyvalence suggests that, for subjects like Anna Rüling, there were few perceived options other than to work with the discursive materials at hand. Still, one cannot help but ask whether appeals to discourses that posited homosexuality as degenerative constitute resistance. In the end, despite our analyses and methodological sophistication, we are left with questions perennial to ethically minded counter-hegemonic movements: Are there forms of resistance that are completely unproblematic? Or are we, as political subjects, regardless of intention, caught in a trap of perpetual ethical compromise?

Notes

1. Michel Foucault, *The History of Sexuality*: vol. 1: *An Introduction*, trans. Robert Hurley (New York, 1978), 56–57; see also 103, and part 4, chaps. 3 (Domain) and 4 (Periodization).
2. Foucault, *History of Sexuality*, 101. For a more concrete elaboration of the concept, see "Power and Sex," in Michel Foucault, *Politics, Philosophy, Culture: Interviews and Other Writings, 1977–1984*, ed. Laurence D. Kritzman (London, 1988), 115.
3. See especially Michel Foucault, "The Subject and Power," in *Beyond Structuralism and Hermeneutics*, ed. Hubert L. Dreyfus and Paul Rabinow (Chicago, 1982).
4. Foucault, "The Subject and Power," 216.
5. See "Sexual Choice, Sexual Act: Foucault and Homosexuality," in *Politics, Philosophy, Culture*, 291.
6. Founded in 1897 by Dr. Magnus Hirschfeld, Max Spohr, Eduard Oberg, and Franz Joseph von Bülow, the Wissenschaftlich-humanitäres Komittee was the first organization in history to publicly campaign for the decriminalization of homosexual acts between men and for the social recognition of homosexual and transgendered men and women. Producing and disseminating "scientific" work to clarify homosexuality and identify the "true homosexual" was central to their political work.
7. Throughout this paper, I have used the term "Urninde" to signify a subjectivity that today would be termed "lesbian". Rüling herself used this term in her speech interchangeably with a variety of other terms, including "homosexuelle Frau," "weibische Urning," "urnische Fraue," "homogene Frau," and "Uranier." See Anna Rüling, "Welches Inter-

esse hat die Frauenbewegung an der Lösung des homosexuellen Problems?" *Jahrbuch für sexuelle Zwischenstufen* 7 (1905): 131–51. However, I prefer Urninde over other options because it gestures to Rüling's theoretical indebtedness to the third sex model of homosexuality, as well as indicating a subjectivity apart from that of the homosexual male and heterosexual woman.

8. Rüling's speech was first delivered at the annual convention of the WhK at the Prince Albrecht Hotel on 8 October 1904; it was subsequently reprinted in the WhK's *Jahrbuch für sexuelle Zwischenstufen.*

9. It was not until 1909 that sections of the women's and homosexual rights movements joined forces in fighting the criminalization of same-sex relations between women. On this moment of collaboration, see Tracie Matysik, "In the Name of the Law: The 'Female Homosexual' and the Criminal Code in Fin de Siècle Germany," *Journal of the History of Sexuality* 13, no. 1 (2004): 26–48. If anything, the German women's movement, particularly its moderate wing, sought to distance itself from the homosexual movement, given the suspicions of some sexologists—and the assertions of Rüling herself—that the women's movement was led by, and actually organized for, lesbians. In the 1900 volume of the *Jahrbuch für sexuelle Zwischenstufen*, a DPhil Arduin argued that the women's movement was led by, and appealed to, "virile" homosexual women, and that consequently, the demands of the women's movement appealed little to the "true" woman. See Dr. phil Arduin, "Die Frauenfrage und die sexuellen Zwischenstufen," *Jahrbuch für sexuelle Zwischenstufen* 2 (1900): 211–23. The fear of being associated with homosexuality may explain the anonymous attack (later attributed by Margit Göttert to Marie Stritt) on Rüling's speech in the 1904–05 edition of the *Centralblatt des Bundes deutscher Frauenvereine*, which blasted its "Shamelessly Cheeky Agitations." Even as late as 1926, feminists like Helene Lange blamed Rüling for the propagation of "anti-feminist" views. See Christine Leidinger, "Anna Rüling, A Problematic Foremother of Lesbian Herstory," *Journal of the History of Sexuality* 13, no. 4 (2004): 493–94.

10. Foucault, *History of Sexuality*, 117.

11. Laura Doan and Chris Waters, "Homosexualities: Introduction," in *Sexology Uncensored: The Documents of Sexual Science*, ed. Lucy Bland and Laura Doan (Chicago, 1998), 41.

12. Davidson defines a "style of reasoning" as "a set of concepts linked together by specifiable rules that determine what statements can and cannot be made with concepts." According to Davidson, the "style of reasoning" concept helps us to understand "what was conceptually possible in a given historical period and how a change in constraints could lead to a reorganization of the limits of the possible." See Arnold Davidson, *The Emergence of Sexuality: Historical Epistemology and the Formation of Concepts* (Cambridge, MA, 2001), 68, 140–41.

13. Doan and Waters, "Homosexualities: Introduction," 42.

14. See, for example, Havelock Ellis, "Studies in the Psychology of Sex, vol. 2: Sexual Inversion" (1897) in Bland and Doan, *Sexology Uncensored*, 57.

15. See for example Karl Heinrich Ulrichs, *The Riddle of "Man-Manly" Love: The Pioneering Work on Male Homosexuality*, vol. 1, trans. Michael A. Lombardi-Nash (Buffalo, NY, 1994), 39, 41, 109, 137–48; and Otto Weininger, *Sex and Character: An Investigation of Fundamental Principles*, trans. Ladislaus Löb (Indianapolis, 2005), 42, 44–45.

16. Havelock Ellis and John Addington Symonds, *Sexual Inversion* (London, 1897), 94–97.

17. Ulrichs, *The Riddle of Man-Manly Love*, 36.
18. Weininger, *Sex and Character*, 13.
19. Hirschfeld, "Die objektive Diagnose der Homosexualität," *Jahrbuch für sexuelle Zwischenstufen* I (1899), 4-35, see p. 5 (emphasis added).
20. Ibid., 8.
21. Indeed, this pronouncement can be found in strikingly similar statements by Ellis and Ulrichs. See Ellis, *Sexual Inversion*, 94–95, and Ulrichs, *The Riddle of Man-Manly Love*, 81.
22. Anna Rüling, "What Interest Does the Women's Movement Have in the Homosexual Question?" (1904), in *We Are Everywhere: A Historical Sourcebook of Gay and Lesbian Politics*, ed. Mark Blasius and Shane Phelan (London, 1997), 143. I note here that, although my analysis of Rüling's speech is based on the German text published in the *Jahrbuch für sexuelle Zwischenstufen*, I cite from the English translation already provided in Blasius and Phelan's volume.
23. Rüling, "What Interest," 144.
24. Ibid., 143.
25. Ibid., 148.
26. Ibid., 148. Emphasis added.
27. Ibid., 148.
28. Ibid., 147.
29. Ibid., 147.
30. Ibid., 144.
31. Ibid., 146.
32. Ibid., 147.
33. Ibid., 146.
34. Ibid., 147.
35. Weininger, *Sex and Character*, 61–62.
36. See Edward Ross Dickinson, "Reflections on Feminism and Monism in the Kaiserreich, 1900–1913," *Central European History* 34, no. 2 (2001): 191-230, see esp. p. 198.
37. Rüling, "What Interest," 148.
38. Ibid., 150.
39. Ibid., 149. Emphasis added
40. Weininger, *Sex and Character*, 58.
41. For a helpful definition of eugenics, drawing extensively on founder Francis Galton's own writings, see Carolyn Burdett, "The Hidden Romance of Sexual Science: Eugenics, the Nation and the Making of Modern Feminism," in *Sexology in Culture: Labeling Bodies and Desires*, ed. Lucy Bland and Laura Doan (Chicago, 1998), 44–59.
42. Foucault, *History of Sexuality*, 118.
43. With specific reference to the role of eugenics in German feminism, see Dickinson, "Reflections on Feminism and Monism," and Ann Taylor Allen, "German Radical Feminism and Eugenics, 1900–1908," *German Studies Review* 11, no. 1 (February 1988): 32–56. See also Edward Ross Dickinson, "Biopolitics, Fascism, Democracy: Some Reflections on Our Discourse About 'Modernity,'" *Central European History* 37, no. 1 (2004): 1–48.
44. Further evidence of eugenic thought can be further found in her discussion of prostitution and venereal disease. See Rüling, "What Interest," 149.
45. Ibid., 145.

46. Ibid.
47. Ibid.
48. Ibid., 145–46.
49. See Gayle Rubin, "Thinking Sex: Notes for a Radical Theory of the Politics of Sexuality," *Pleasure and Danger: Exploring Female Sexuality*, ed. Carole Vance (London, 1984), 267–93.
50. Foucault, "The Subject and Power," 216–17, 219; "Power and Sex," in *Politics, Philosophy, Culture*, 111.
51. Foucault, "Power and Sex," 123.

CHAPTER 7

∽:∼

To Police *and* Protect
The Surveillance of Homosexuality in Imperial Berlin

ROBERT BEACHY

In February 1893, the Swedish playwright August Strindberg attended a homosexual ball at the Café National in Berlin, which he depicted in his short story *The Cloister*.[1] Referring to himself in third person as "the author," Strindberg—accompanied by a Berlin "Police Inspector" and other friends—offers a revealing description:

> It was the most horrible thing he had ever seen. In order that a better check might be kept on them, the perverts of the capital had been given permission to hold a fancy-dress ball. When it opened everyone behaved ceremoniously, almost as if they were in a madhouse. Men danced with men, mournfully, with deadly seriousness.... The one playing the lady's role might have the moustache of a cavalryman and pince-nez, he might be ugly, with coarse, masculine features, and not even a trace of femininity.... The Police Inspector and his guests had seated themselves at a table in the centre of one end of the room, close to which all the couples had to pass.... The Inspector called them by their Christian names and summoned some of the most interesting among them to his table, so that the author could study them![2]

Apart from his visceral repulsion, Strindberg's strongest reaction was to the openness of the ball and the official surveillance. The affair received formal sanction, as Strindberg claimed, so officials could monitor more easily "the perverts of the capital." The "Police Inspector" did not even disguise his presence and actually knew and greeted the participants by name.

This toleration of same-sex sociability accompanied by careful surveillance was a deliberate strategy of the Berlin police. More than likely, Strindberg's chaperone was Berlin Police Commissioner Leopold von Meerscheidt-Hüllessem (1849–1900), founder and director of the Department of Blackmailers and Homosexuals (*Erpresser- und Homosexuellendezernat*), the police unit responsible for infractions related to the German anti-sodomy statute, Paragraph 175 of the Imperial Criminal Code. A relic of premodern Prussia, Paragraph 175 threatened fines and imprisonment for both bestiality and certain sexual acts between men. Criminalized sex acts were generally conducted in private, of course, so successful prosecutions under Paragraph 175 required either confession or the testimony of witnesses. The chance of discovery *in flagrante delicto* was minimal, but the law facilitated sexual blackmail, posing the greater risk to middle-class and elite homosexuals. For this reason, Hüllessem's department was also responsible for thwarting those who blackmailed homosexual men, which explains the cumbersome title of his department. Since blackmail affected potentially innocent citizens and threatened greater criminality and disorder than actual violations of Paragraph 175, Hüllessem and his officers practiced a watchful tolerance. By about 1890, Berlin officials permitted large same-sex balls, including the one Strindberg attended; they likewise tolerated same-sex bars, clubs, and restaurants.[3] These semipublic spaces gave the police—as well as observers such as Strindberg—access to an inherently secretive same-sex milieu that was otherwise largely invisible.

As Michel Foucault might argue, these venues were little more than nodal points in a larger "carceral" that facilitated "perpetual surveillance." This is confirmed by Strindberg, whose party of observers occupied a central table, allowing inspection of those who attended the ball.[4] Through the creative interpretation of Paragraph 175, Hüllessem and his officers developed self-serving strategies for coping with an impractical legal code through—arguably—lax enforcement. This official toleration had the tremendously significant if unintended influence of providing visibility for an incipient community of men—but also some women—who sought the sexual companionship of their own sex. Strindberg's account is just one of the many that described not only the costume balls but also the same-sex bars and other entertainments of imperial Berlin. The visibility created by these reports contributed to a new urban identity, which emanated from the same-sex sociability of a burgeoning milieu of bars, clubs, and dances tolerated by the Berlin police.

Yet many interpreters of Foucault have failed to appreciate the creative role of police surveillance in the construction not merely of deviance but also of new identities. Certainly a range of scholars have analyzed the "carceral" society that emerged in the nineteenth century, including the scientific discourses of psychology, psychiatry, sociology, criminology, sexology, and the institutions they inspired. A range of studies have applied Foucault's insight to explain how police surveillance helped to identify and entrench an underclass of prostitutes, the working poor, petty criminals, and sexual "deviants."[5]

Foucault's "discovery" of sexuality has stimulated even greater debate on the "birth" of the homosexual: can we claim that there were no sexual identities corresponding to same-sex erotic practices, as Foucault *seemed* to suggest, before the coining of the word "homosexuality" around 1870?[6] Certainly recent scholarship has moved beyond constructivist analyses that view power as something that can be held, controlled, and imposed, whether by medical professionals or the police. Foucault himself explained power as an interactive process in which "acting subjects by virtue of their acting" might influence the state and elude or manipulate its controlling agencies.[7] This insight has informed more nuanced accounts of sexual subjectivity and its emergence in the late nineteenth century: the "feed-back loop" created between "subjects" and the psychiatric professions, for example, or between "sexual deviants" and the popular press, contributed powerfully to the elaboration and diffusion of incipient social and sexual identities.[8] Berlin's Department of Blackmailers and Homosexuals was another critical institution that fostered this dynamic. The official toleration of same-sex bars and costume balls permitted the emergence of a minority sexual community; it likewise gave access to medical professionals, writers, and journalists whose scientific and popular accounts of this milieu accelerated its growth and visibility.

Same-Sex Sociability

Berlin officials had long contended with violations of the Prussian anti-sodomy statute. As early as 1782, one guidebook devoted a short chapter to Berlin's "Warme Brüder" ("Warm Brothers") and the prevalence of male prostitution, an income source for garrisoned soldiers.[9] This reputation was well established by the mid nineteenth century. One of the most telling accounts, an 1846 volume on prostitution published by the future Berlin police director Wilhelm Stieber (1818–1882), identified the favorite cruising areas of male prostitutes and their patrons, which included Unter den Linden, the Tiergarten Park, and a grove of chestnut trees just north of the neoclassical Guardhouse.[10] No later than 1900 the unlit Tiergarten path favored by homosexual men had gained the moniker of the "schwule Weg" (gay path).[11]

By 1900 there were bars and restaurants that catered exclusively to homosexual men. The first documented locales, however, faced significant police harassment, and at least two were closed down. In the early 1880s Lachmine was raided and its guests escorted to a nearby police precinct for identification.[12] The Seegert'sche Restaurant, run by Carl August Seeger, was visited several times by a plainclothes officer and then raided by police in February 1885. Seeger, his barkeep, and eight other patrons were arrested. None of the men was charged under Paragraph 175, but Seeger and his employee were cited for "procurement" and "inciting criminal activity." For these offenses they received eight- and four-month prison sentences, respectively. Seven others—three merchants, two artisans, a manservant, and a *rentier*—received three- to four-month prison sentences for disturbing the peace. The basis for this charge was testimony from the undercover officer, who reported the behavior he had witnessed: the men flirted, kissed, and fondled one another, and used women's nicknames.[13]

Soon after closing the Seegert'sche Restaurant, however, the Berlin police must have resolved to tolerate same-sex sociability, since discreet gay venues had become commonplace. There is no evidence that "procurement" or "disturbance" charges were leveled for merely congregating in specific bars. This incipient bar culture was well documented in many publications. According to one published account, numerous gay watering holes were opened in the last decades of the nineteenth century, most clustered a few blocks south of Unter den Linden. One of the first city guides, *Führer durch Berlins Nachtlokale* (Guide Through Berlin's Night Spots) (1869), had hinted at the presence of a homosexual nightlife.[14] An anonymous guidebook from 1886 went much further, describing the prevalence of homosexual cruising and prostitution in parks, public toilets, and in the busiest streets of central Berlin. The author also claimed that the police largely tolerated all-male establishments and dancing events.[15] More scurrilous tracts devoted entirely to the Berlin demimonde—straight and homosexual—were quickly censored after publication and unfortunately are no longer extant.[16]

In 1891 psychiatrist Albert Moll published *Die Conträre Sexualempfindung* (*Perversions of the Sex Instinct*), the first scientific study devoted entirely to the phenomenon of homosexuality. Moll completed his medical degree under Rudolf Virchow at the University of Berlin, and his monograph synthesized the literature on same-sex eroticism—including the work of Johann Ludwig Casper, Carl Liman, Carl Westphal, Richard von Krafft-Ebing, and others—while providing the first documented, ethnographic description of Berlin's homosexual subculture. Moll's fieldwork was assisted by Berlin Police Commissioner Hüllessem and the editor Adolf Glaser. In the book's foreword, Moll thanked Glaser—identifying him by the pseudonym "N. N."—as an "Urning" (homosexual) and expert. Glaser's bona fides had been bolstered by a scandal in 1878, when he was arrested in Berlin on Paragraph 175 charges. Both Glaser and Police Commissioner Hüllessem escorted Moll through Berlin's homosexual subculture. As Moll's subtitle suggested—*Mit Benutzung amtlichen Materials* (*Based on Clinical Data and Official Documents*)—he was able to consult official documents from the Berlin Police Headquarters, for which he also thanked Hüllessem.[17]

Moll's account—not to mention Hüllessem's assistance—attested to the tacit tolerance that homosexual locales enjoyed by 1891. Moll emphasized this point by citing the "proceedings against one restaurateur and his guests" (the raid of the Seegert'sche Restaurant and his subsequent trial) a few years earlier,

a police action Moll that claimed "appears to happen seldom now in these locales."[18] The public venues and nightlife Moll described included small pubs but
also restaurants and a number of *Bierkeller*. Although the most popular venues
changed frequently, especially when patrons grew too rowdy or numerous, decorum had improved "in comparison to early times." Overtly sexual behavior
was not tolerated, Moll suggested, but there was no mistaking the homosexual
character of the clientele and their interactions. At some bars the patrons appeared in drag, and many adopted female nicknames—most used the labels
Schwester or *Tante* to refer to friends and lovers.[19]

Moll's ethnographic impulse inspired many subsequent students of Berlin's
gay subculture—medical professionals (like Moll), investigative journalists,
and urban raconteurs whose academic and popular accounts created a broad
and detailed panorama of homosexual life before the First World War.[20] One
of the most important chroniclers of gay Berlin, the sexologist and homosexual rights activist Magnus Hirschfeld, identified no fewer than fifteen bars
and restaurants in 1904.[21] In his monumental study of homosexuality from
1914, Hirschfeld claimed to know of at least thirty-eight Berlin locales that
catered almost exclusively to homosexuals and lesbians.[22] A handful of these
had opened before 1900, and several remained open into the 1920s. The bar
Hannemann in the Alexandrinenstraße, named for the manager and eventual
owner Gustav Hannemann, celebrated its thirty-second anniversary of continuous operation in 1924, dating Hannemann's management of the locale to
at least 1892.[23] The "Schöne Müllerin" was opened in 1906 by the pianist Otto
Müller and did not close until 1921. According to *Das perverse Berlin*, Müller
had played piano and entertained in several other establishments before opening his own. The feminized name "Müllerin" alluded to the woman's garb that
he habitually wore.[24]

Another signal feature of Berlin's same-sex cultural life was the large transvestite balls held in public venues like concert halls and theaters, as well as
private clubs. Perhaps the earliest mention of a same-sex costume ball comes
from the homosexual rights activist Karl Heinrich Ulrichs, who described a
private affair sponsored by a Polish count in 1868 in a Berlin restaurant.[25] The
chronicler of nineteenth-century gay Berlin Hugo Friedländer confirmed this,
claiming in 1914 that homosexual and transvestite balls had been common
since at least the 1860s.[26] Moll, Hirschfeld, Krafft-Ebing, and many others who
reported attending such events portrayed the balls as seasonal, well-organized
affairs that attracted over 500 participants to the most prominent Berlin theaters and banquet halls.[27]

As August Strindberg suggested in *The Cloister*, the homosexual balls of
Wilhelmine Berlin were clearly public events that enjoyed official sanction.
And like any public entertainment, including concerts or theater productions,
they required formal permission. Throughout the prewar period, the individual

Berlin police precincts were responsible for reviewing permit requests, which required a detailed description of time, venue, the character of the event, and a waiting period of at least two days. Bar and restaurant concessions generally excluded dancing permits, and owners faced fines if they failed to enforce this prohibition. Owners of the largest theaters and dance halls were able to apply for annual permits allowing them to rent their spaces to event planners.[28]

The impresarios who organized the balls are rarely identified, though they were likely owners or managers of other homosexual locales. Hugo Friedländer mentioned the balls in the Dresdener Kasino planned by "N.," and those of "L." held in the Central-Theater, as especially popular. The frequency of the "Homo-Bälle" is also difficult to determine, but by 1900 they appear to have followed the patterns of the conventional ball season, commencing weekly in November with special themed and costume balls held throughout the season in Berlin's most prestigious addresses. The largest of these spaces accommodated up to 1,000 people. Particularly opulent evenings would begin with a sumptuous buffet dinner, followed by dancing and concluding with an early morning breakfast. The expense was likely formidable, and a large costume ball could generate remarkable demand for hospitality services, musicians, tailors, and even coach drivers.

The Wilhelmine balls established a large following, but without visible marketing. As the Berlin journalist Konstantin Grell explained: "If one goes, perhaps in the company of a well-known police official, one is astonished to encounter many familiar faces, who of course only wanted to witness the scandal first hand but were able all the same to acquire tickets through an acquaintance. The tickets are nowhere on offer, and the promoters sell them only to insiders. Of course there are no announcements for such original entertainments."[29] Whether the many acquaintances Grell surprisingly encountered were merely "slumming," as they claimed, or perhaps more intimately involved in Berlin's gay nightlife is unclear. In any case, as Grell implied, advertising was by word of mouth, and admission tickets were likely vended directly by the event planners, perhaps in the homosexual locales that they owned or managed. (Only with the advent of Berlin's gay press in the 1920s were entertainments publicly advertised.)

Grell's account also suggests how the balls became a magnet for journalists, authors, and other urban ethnographers. Like Grell himself, Oscar Méténier, a naturalist author and former Parisian police officer, explored Berlin's homosexual subculture for a French-language work published in 1904 on the emergent "German vice." Naturally, Méténier's study required the requisite visit to a homosexual ball:

> We were deposited in front of the brilliant façade of a theater known as the Dresdener Casino. In a broad vestibule the bouncer took our coats, and another determined that we had the necessary invitations. Finally we were admitted

through double doors into an enormous, richly decorated hall flanked by columns. I remained standing, dazzled and stupefied. Before me was a crowd of four or five hundred, dancing to an orchestra—excellent like all German orchestras—hidden behind a platform. All or nearly all the dancers were wearing costumes. Only here and there in the swirl of color could one detect the black jacket of the police officers. We slowly made our way to an unoccupied table not far from the buffet. Many of the dancers were wearing women's clothing.[30]

Certainly Méténier had been briefed before attending and had some idea what to expect. Yet his astonishment is palpable; not even the rumors in Paris conveyed adequately what transpired in Berlin.

Those without writerly pretensions were also drawn to the spectacles. The retired Prussian officer Paul von Hoverbeck recalled an early twentieth-century visit to one East Berlin *Balllokal* in his 1926 memoir: "I'll never forget the scene. Hundreds of men and women of all ages, most made-up, many of the men attired as women and many of the women as men. As we entered the brightly lit hall, the entire crowd knew that we were curiosity seekers accompanied by police officials."[31] The common element in all these accounts, strikingly, beginning with Moll's 1891 study, was an obvious police presence (which in turn facilitated visits of outside observers). Why, in fact, did Berlin officials tolerate the organized activities of a group defined by its tendency to engage in illicit sexual acts? What was the point of regulating and controlling homosexual locales and ball events so closely?

Enforcing Paragraph 175

Certainly tacit forbearance did not signal official indifference to the activities of Berlin's sexual minorities. In 1876 the Berlin police officer Leopold von Meerscheidt-Hüllessem inaugurated the *Verbrecheralbum* to collect photos of arrested suspects. These images were then organized in separate mug shot albums by crime—murderers, thieves, cat burglars, pickpockets, con artists, rapists, and so on—to aid investigations. A former army lieutenant, Hüllessem joined the police in 1873 at the age of twenty-four. More generally, his interests in science and the application of new investigative techniques were important factors in his professional success, and throughout his career he continued to trumpet new methods or technologies, often adapted from innovative French practices. He promoted the anthropometry of French enforcement officer Alphonse Bertillon, for example, whose tutelage he sought in Paris in 1895 before introducing a similar system in Berlin. He also spearheaded the use of fingerprinting.[32]

In 1884 Hüllessem introduced a new mug shot album devoted to "pederasts" (homosexuals). The decision to photograph pederasts—habitual lawbreakers by definition—was a natural extension of the special lists that the Berlin police had kept since at least the 1860s.[33] The pederast label was ambiguous, of course, and the police register likely recorded names of suspected homosexuals, cross-dressers, pedophiles, and male prostitutes. At its inception, the album for pederasts included thirty-four images, but this number had grown sixfold by 1890, and by a factor of nearly ten to reach over 300 images by 1895. The number of photos increased dramatically into the twentieth century, reaching nearly 1,000 on the eve of World War I.[34] It is clear that police officials photographed most men detained under suspicion of illicit sexual activity related to Paragraph 175, and included many more than were ever successfully charged. Like the original lists, undoubtedly the mug shot album included adult men and adolescents suspected of prostitution, sexual cruising, cross-dressing, and blackmail. Hüllessem continued to play a central role in shaping strategies for policing Berlin's homosexual subculture, and in 1885 he became the first director of the newly created Department of Homosexuals (Homosexuellen Dezernat). In 1896 Hüllessem expanded the department's formal function to include sexual blackmail, changing the title to the Department of Blackmailers and Homosexuals.[35] The formal bailiwick of the department, according to a handbook published in 1921, was "pederasty and offenses related to this, including blackmail and the creation of a public nuisance through exhibitionism."[36]

The history of the Homosexuellen Dezernat and its policing strategies is not well documented, and the earliest accounts come from French observers intrigued by Berlin's thriving subculture. In his 1904 study, Oscar Méténier offered his French readers a brief description of this curious Berlin task force.[37] Two French journalists, Henri de Weindel and F. P. Fischer, published a more extensive study in 1908 that periodized the development of Berlin's policing policies. According to their account, the first decade after German unification was characterized by the use of paid informants and denunciations. This policy was intensified by about 1880 with the use of plainclothes investigators and agents provocateurs, who investigated suspicious locales or actively entrapped homosexual men. By about 1890, however, Hüllessem redirected the Homosexual Department to focus on surveillance and determined to tolerate same-sex locales and entertainments.[38] The timing of this new strategy corresponds roughly with the undercover investigation that led to the raid of the the Seegert'sche Restaurant in 1885. The installation of Bernhard von Richthofen—widely rumored to have been homosexual himself—as the new Berlin police president in 1885 might have been an additional factor in this apparent liberalization.[39]

Hüllessem's engagement was of tremendous relevance, and he powerfully shaped the priorities of the Department of Blackmailers and Homosexuals. Like the attention he paid to the forensic advances of French criminologists, Hüllessem exhibited a keen interest in those doctors, sexologists, and others who made it their business to study the homosexual milieu. As we have seen,

Hüllessem developed a firsthand familiarity with Berlin's homosexual subculture, which he shared readily with Albert Moll and Konstantin Grell. Along with these others, Krafft-Ebing thanked Hüllessem for sharing his expertise in the 1893 edition of *Psychopathia Sexualis*.[40] Remarkably, Hüllessem was also involved in the initial organization in 1897 of the Scientific Humanitarian Committee (Wissenschaftlich-humanitäres Komitee, WhK), the world's first homosexual rights organization, led by Magnus Hirschfeld.[41] This support won Hüllessem the trust of many who later turned to the police when threatened by blackmail. Although he ended his own life in 1900—a response to a personal scandal involving money and corruption (but no personal sexual misconduct)—his successor Hans von Tresckow continued his work.

It is the city's criminal statistics that most strikingly demonstrate the relative tolerance of Berlin officials.[42] Published annually in the Berlin city almanacs beginning in 1876, arrests for sodomy remained remarkably low throughout the imperial period (likewise during the Weimar Republic). Before 1890 the greatest number recorded for a single year was only eleven (in 1882), and 1911 set the record with just thirty-five. As Magnus Hirschfeld claimed, it was "not the act, but rather bad luck" that was punished.[43] In 1920, the Berlin police commissioner Dr. Heinrich Kopp, who had worked in the Department of Blackmailers and Homosexuals since 1904, reported that the beat officers in his division "had happened upon only one situation in sixteen years that actually represented a violation of the law." In other words, only once between 1904 and 1920 had two men been caught *in flagrante delicto* in a sex act that violated Paragraph 175.[44] The rapidly growing number of denunciations further underscores the difficulty of enforcing the law. While the tips given to police of suspected homosexual activity increased fivefold from 1890 to 1910 (from 67 to 349), the number of arrests increased only modestly. This figure—the number of denunciations—also suggests the growing visibility of a homosexual milieu. If we consider the city's significant population growth, from 825,000 inhabitants in 1871 to just over 2,000,000 in 1914, the per capita number of arrests remained virtually constant.

Policing Male Prostitution

The Department of Blackmailers and Homosexuals was far less tolerant of homosexual prostitution, another striking feature of imperial Berlin. According to American sociologist Abraham Flexner, who wrote an authoritative comparative study, Berlin was Europe's "main mart" for boy prostitutes.[45] Dive bars catering to male (and female) prostitutes and their patrons were Berlin fixtures, and the general toleration of them reflected both the German law governing *female* prostitution and local policing practices. Formally, the imperial law code banned procurement (*Kuppelei*) and empowered police to force suspected female prostitutes to submit to medical exams, a policy of "regulationism" adapted from the French. In practice, the policing of female prostitution varied dramatically from place to place, and Berlin officials created their own specific regulations: brothels had been abolished by the mid nineteenth century and were no longer tolerated, but inscription was voluntary, and while prostitutes were allowed to live throughout the city, streetwalking was prohibited on main thoroughfares like Unter den Linden.[46] The Berlin Sittenpolizei or morals police monitored female prostitution within its own administrative division, completely separate from the Department of Blackmailers and Homosexuals, a subdivision of the criminal police. Still, the Berlin policies for regulating female prostitution ultimately influenced the city's homosexual subculture. Both the prohibition of heterosexual brothels and the absence of internment or "ghettoization" policies prevented the growth of a concentrated red light district in Berlin. This promoted a geographic diffusion of the city's gay cruising and bar culture, spreading out from Friedrichstrasse and the inner city in all directions.

As the regulation of female prostitution suggests, Berlin officials worked assiduously to thwart boy brothels and the procurement of male prostitutes. One out-of-work actor and would-be pimp, Gustav Haupt, formed a partnership with the merchant Karl Moscholl and then opened for business in a dingy apartment in 21 Mohrenstraße, located a few blocks south of Unter den Linden. Recruiting "staff" straight off the streets, Haupt and Moscholl established a wealthy clientele. They enhanced profits by robbing their disrobed johns, who, not surprisingly, avoided the police for fear of a second and more figurative exposure. By the time an anonymous tip led to their apprehension in 1902, they had operated the boy brothel for nearly two years.[47] Another enterprising merchant, a cigar retailer named Fritz Geßler, used the back room of his tobacco shop as a boy bordello. A newspaper account described the reaction of neighbors, who marveled at the traffic in and out of his small shop and the apparent uptick in his business. Geßler was finally arrested in May 1905, but only because he and his rent-boys had become greedy and begun blackmailing their patrons.[48]

These stories illustrate the characteristic link between male prostitution and sexual blackmail. As Police Commissioner Tresckow commented, homosexuals were targeted increasingly in the opening years of the twentieth century.[49] After 1900 the phenomenon was spurred by sensational reports in the daily press. The practice of protecting victims' privacy was first violated in 1901, when the trial of a male prostitute who extorted money from Count Friedrich von Hohenau, a cousin of ruling Emperor Wilhelm II, was published in the *Berliner Morgenpost*. Soon after, Maximilian Harden identified "Fritz von Hohenau" by name as the blackmailer's victim in his weekly news magazine *Die Zukunft*.

These press reports cost Hohenau his career in the Prussian diplomatic service, and he soon fled to Italy. It also inspired a host of copycat extortionists, who used the threat of public disclosure in the popular press to intimidate wealthy or prominent victims. The scandals reported in the Berlin papers in the first decade of the twentieth century besmirched a range of industrialists, politicians, and judges, but these represented no more than a small fraction of those victimized. Magnus Hirschfeld estimated in 1914 that nearly 30 percent of Berlin's homosexual community had been blackmailed at some point.[50]

Many blackmail reports published in the Berlin papers mentioned Tresckow specifically as a counselor or investigator. During his tenure as director of the Homosexuellen Dezernat, Tresckow actually received an annual stipend for the separate office in his apartment where he held daily *Sprechstunden* between 5:00 and 6:00 P.M. to counsel blackmail victims. In one case, Tresckow succeeded in helping several victims identify eight members of a larger gang, who made friendly overtures to apparent foreigners and then demanded money on threat of blackmail.[51] One older fellow, a man of modest means, was threatened and robbed by a new acquaintance brought home from the Friedrichstraße. The victim admitted frankly that his understood purpose was a sexual assignation with the young man, but he denied, improbably, that the sex involved a monetary exchange. Upon arriving in the apartment, however, the blackmailer demanded payment and promptly left with the old man's cash. With the help of the mug shot album, the victim identified the thief, who was apprehended the following day.[52] An American visitor "not familiar with local conditions" brought home a hustler he had met at the symphony. In his hotel room, the tourist was forced to hand over his valuables and cash. He then reported his experience to the police and identified his blackmailer from the photo album. The hustler was quickly apprehended, and the watch and chain were returned to the American before he left the city.[53]

If we concede the moderate success of the Berlin police in *protecting* and not merely policing homosexuals, we might also argue that the real beneficiaries were elites. It surely oversimplifies, however, to describe these enforcement strategies for coping with Paragraph 175 as little more than a form of class-based justice. Almost certainly petty criminals and rent-boys were overrepresented among the photos of the mug shot album. But elite homosexuals were also monitored. As reported by Tresckow in his memoirs, Hüllessem had maintained a collection of index cards with the names of aristocrats, military officers, and commercial elites whom he suspected were homosexual. Their disclosure as homosexuals, he feared, could directly affect affairs of state. Without doubt, Count Hohenau was included in Hüllessem's card file, as were dozens of others, including many who would eventually be exposed. Shortly before his suicide in 1900, Hüllessem entrusted a close friend to deliver a packet of some one hundred of these cards to the emperor. Allegedly, however, Wilhelm II refused to open Hüllessem's envelope and simply sent it on to the police president.[54] The special attention given to these figures reflected heightened concern for their privacy and a willingness to provide them with all possible protection. Hüllessem's index cards also represented the reality that aristocrats and other elites could no longer indulge their "perversions" indiscriminately. The threat of blackmail and exposure in the daily press made elite men the most vulnerable, arguably, and proved to be a powerful leveling force. No longer could wealth or title protect, for even those with great resources might one day be branded homosexuals.

Hüllessem recognized that Paragraph 175 exposed homosexual men to the risk of blackmail, and he tailored enforcement strategies accordingly. Since homosexual association—if it avoided creating a "public nuisance"—was never formally criminalized and could be thwarted only with great difficulty, the officers of the Department of Blackmail and Homosexuals monitored and observed but, after 1890, no longer prohibited same-sex venues and entertainments. Since the law inspired sexual blackmail, the Berlin police targeted male prostitutes and attempted increasingly to provide support to its victims. Arguably, the investigative technologies developed by the Berlin police reduced in at least some small measure the vulnerability of men who sought the sexual companionship of other men.

The passive enforcement of Paragraph 175 had equal if not greater significance in the way it gave visibility and definition to what had formerly been a shadowy, indistinct group of sexual minorities. For the sake of surveillance and control, Hüllessem tolerated homosexual sociability. Certainly he and his officials monitored and "disciplined" the patrons of gay bars and transvestite balls, as most interpreters of Foucault would argue. But the acceptance of same-sex entertainments and venues also permitted same-sex loving men and women to congregate and forge an incipient community. Of equal significance, Hüllessem and his successors then granted access to this exotic world to literary figures, medical professionals, and journalists, who theorized and broadcast the emergence of a new sexual community and identity. In short, these policing strategies played a critical role in the creation of a homosexual milieu, which became an established cultural feature of prewar Berlin.

Notes

1. Strindberg's biographer Michael Meyer dates the Berlin ball event to 23 February 1893 in *Strindberg: A Biography* (Oxford, 1985), 245.
2. Quoted from *The Cloister*, trans. Mary Sandbach (New York, 1969), 12–13.
3. Magnus Hirschfeld claimed that the Berlin police never employed *agents provocateurs*. Hirschfeld, *Berlins Drittes Geschlecht* (Berlin, 1904; repr. 1991), 73.
4. Michel Foucault, *Discipline and Punish: The Birth of the Prison*, trans. Alan Sheridan (New York, 1977), esp. "Panopticism," 195–308.

5. Representative titles include Jacque Donzelot, *The Policing of Families* (New York, 1979); Alain Corbin, *Women for Hire: Prostitution and Sexuality in France after 1850* (Cambridge, MA, 1996); Mitchell Dean, *Gevernmentality: Power and Rule in Modern Society* (London, 1999; 2nd ed., 2010).

6. See *The History of Sexuality*, vol. 1: *An Introduction* (New York, 1978), 43. The literature on this question is voluminous, and I cite sparingly. For the emphatically "constructivist" position on the "medicalization" of homosexuality see Arnold Davidson, "Sex and the Emergence of Sexuality," *Critical Inquiry* 14 (1987): 16–48 and "How to Do the History of Psychoanalysis: A Reading of Freud's *Three Essays on the Theory of Sexuality*," *Critical Inquiry* 14 (1987): 252–77. David Halperin offers a nuanced reading of Foucault's claim. See "Forgetting Foucault," *Representations* 63 (1998): 93–120.

7. Quoted from Foucault, "The Subject and Power," in Herbert Dreyfus and Paul Rabinow, *Michel Foucault: Beyond Structuralism and Hermeneutics* (Chicago, 1983), 220.

8. Consider Harry Oosterhuis, *Stepchildren of Nature: Krafft-Ebing, Psychiatry, and the Making of Sexual Identity* (Chicago, 2000), or Scott Spector, "The Wrath of the 'Countess Merviola': Tabloid Exposé and the Emergence of Homosexual Subjects in Vienna 1907," in *Sexuality in Austria*, ed. Günter Bischof, Anton Pelinka, and Dagmar Herzog (New Brunswick, NJ, 2006), 31–48.

9. Johann Friedel, *Briefe über die Galanterien von Berlin* (Gotha, 1782).

10. *Die Prostitution in Berlin und ihre Opfer: In historischer, sittlicher, medizinischer und polizeilicher Beziehung beleuchtet* (Berlin, 1846), 209–10. See also Adolph von Schaden, *Berlins Licht- und Schattenseiten* (Dessau, 1822), 72–73.

11. Magnus Hirschfeld, *Die Homosexualität des Mannes und des Weibes* (Berlin, 1914), 698.

12. Hugo Friedländer, "Aus dem homosexuellen Leben Alt-Berlins," *Journal für sexuelle Zwischenstufen* 14 (1914): 55–58.

13. See the reports in *Berliner Börsen-Zeitung*, no. 561 (1 December 1885), 7–8; *Berliner Tageblatt*, no. 609 (1 December 1885), 5; and *Norddeutsche Allgemeine Zeitung*, no. 562 (1 December 1885), 2. The trial is also documented in Ferdinand Karsch-Haack, *Erotische Großstadtbilder als Kulturphänomene* (Berlin, 1926), 56–71.

14. Max Marcus, *Führer durch Berlins Nachtlokale* (Berlin, 1869); this was also republished in new editions into the 1880s.

15. [Gustav Otto], *Die Verbrecherwelt von Berlin* (Berlin, 1886), 173–77.

16. I have not been able to locate *Die Geheimnisse der Berliner Passage* (1877), and *Die Männerfreunde von Berlin* (1880) in German or American libraries, but both are mentioned and described in twentieth-century publications. Magnus Hirschfeld discusses *Männerfreunde* in *Berlins Drittes Geschlecht*, 145, and Iwan Bloch mentions *Geheimnisse* in *The Sexual Life of our Time* (New York, 1937), 290.

17. Moll, *Die Conträre Sexualempfindung: Mit Benutzung amtlichen Materials* (Berlin, 1891), vii–viii. On the Glaser scandal and his identification as "N.N." see Friedländer, "Aus dem homosexuellen Lebens Alt-Berlins," 61–62; and Anonymous, *Das perverse Berlin: Kulturkritische Gänge* (Berlin, 1910), 62–63.

18. Moll, *Die Conträre Sexualempfindung*, 190.

19. Ibid., 190–96.

20. The titles are too numerous to review here, but of particular note are the fifty volumes edited by Hans Ostwald for "Großstadt-Dokumente," devoted primarily to Berlin's seamy underbelly and published between 1904 and 1908. See Ralph Thies, *Ethnograph des dunklen Berlin: Hans Ostwald und die "Großstadt-Dokumente" (1904–1908)* (Cologne, 2006).

21. Hirschfeld, "Das Ergebnis der statistischen Untersuchungen über den Prozentsatz der Homosexuellen," *Jahrbuch für sexuelle Zwischenstufen* (1904): 121.
22. Hirschfeld, *Die Homosexualität des Mannes und des Weibes*, 682–83.
23. *Die Fanfare*, no. 39 (1924), and *Das perverse Berlin*, 130.
24. *Das perverse Berlin*, 133–34.
25. Ulrichs, *Memnon* (Leipzig, 1868), 77–78.
26. "Aus dem homosexuellen Leben Alt-Berlins," 45–63.
27. [Otto], *Die Verbrecherwelt von Berlin*, 175; Moll, *Conträre Sexualempfindung*, 84; Paul Lindenberg, *Berliner Polizei und Verbrechertum* (Leipzig, 1892), 105–6; Otto Podjukl, *Die Enterbten des Liebesglücks* (Leipzig, 1893), 183; Hirschfeld, *Berlins Drittes Geschlecht*, 103–11; Hans Ostwald, *Männliche Prostitution* (Leipzig, 1906), 9–12.
28. "Polizei-Verordnung über öffentliche Lustbarkeiten," *Ministerial-Blatt für die gesammte innere Verwaltung in den Königlich Preußischen Staate* 45, no. 8 (1884): 213; Friedrich Retzlaff, *Vorschriften über den Geschäftsbetrieb der Immobilien-Makler, Trödler, Gesindevermieter und Stellenvermittler, Theater-Agenten ...* (Recklinghausen, 1906), 39–40.
29. Grell, "Männliche Prostitution," *Die Kritik: Monatschrift für öffentliches Leben* 2, no. 30 (27 April 1895): 788.
30. Oscar Méténier, *Vertus et Vices allemands* (Paris, 1905), 85–87.
31. Paul von Schoenaich (pseud.), *Mein Damaskus: Erlebnisse und Bekenntnisse* (Hamburg, 1926), 76.
32. Jens Dobler, "Leopold von Meerscheidt-Hüllessem (1849–1900)," *Archiv für Polizeigeschichte* 9 (1998): 73–79.
33. The existence of Berlin's *Päderastenlist* came to light during the 1869 trial of the alleged sexual deviant Carl von Zastrow, who was convicted of raping and mutilating a young boy. See Manfred Herzer, "Zastrow—Ulrichs—Kertbeny: Erfunden Identitäten im 19. Jahrhundert," in *Männerliebe im alten Deutschland*, ed. Rüdiger Lautmann (Berlin, 1992), 61–80.
34. The annual municipal almanacs tallied not only criminal statistics but also the number of photos included in each of the separate "criminal albums." See *Statistisches Jahrbuch der Stadt Berlin* (Berlin, 1876–1918). Also consider Edward Ross Dickinson, "Policing Sex in Germany, 1882–1982: A Preliminary Statistical Analysis," *Journal of the History of Sexuality* 16, no. 2 (2007): 204–50.
35. GStA, Rep. 84a, no. 7646.
36. Wilhelm Stieber and Hans Schneikert, *Praktische Lehrbuch der Kriminalpolizei* (Potsdam, 1921), 31.
37. Méténier, *Vertus et Vices allemands*, 112–13.
38. Weindel and Fischer, *L'Homosexualité en Allemagne: Étude documentaire et anecdotique* (Paris, 1908), 81–96.
39. One of Richthofen's underlings, Hans von Tresckow, who directed the Homosexuellen Dezernat after Hüllessem in 1900, claimed in his best-selling memoir that Richthofen was not only gay but also secretly monitored by his own men. See *Von Fürsten und anderen Sterblichen: Erinnerungen eines Kriminalkommissars* (Berlin, 1922), 55.
40. Richard von Krafft-Ebing, *Psychopathia Sexualis*, 8th ed. (Stuttgart, 1893), 428.
41. Jens Dobler, "'Nicht nur Verfolgung—auch Erfolge: Zusammenarbeit zwischen Schwulenbewegung und polizei in der Kaiserzeit und in der Weimarer Republic," *Comparativ* 9, no. 1 (1999): 48–60; and Dobler, "Zum Verhältnis der Sexualwissenschaft und der homosexuellen Emanzipationsbewegung zur Polizei in Berlin," in *Verqueere Wissen-*

schaft? Zum Verhaältnis von Sexualwissenschaft und Sexualreformbewegung in Geschichte und Gegenwart, ed. Ursula Ferdinand, et al. (Münster, 1998), 329–36.

42. *Statistisches Jahrbuch der Stadt Berlin,* 1876–1918.
43. Hirschfeld, *Berlins Drittes Geschlecht,* 133.
44. *Die Freundschaft,* January 1920, nos. 2–3.
45. *Prostitution in Europe* (New York, 1914), 31.
46. Richard Evans, "Prostitution, State and Society in Imperial Germany," *Past and Present* 70 (1976): 106–29; Sybille Krafft, *Zucht und Unzucht: Prostitution und Sittenpolizei im München der Jahrhundertwende* (Munich, 1996); Regina Schulte, *Sperrbezirke: Tugendhaftigkeit und Prostitution in der bürgerlichen Welt* (Frankfurt am Main, 1984).
47. *Vorwärts,* 20 August 1905, no. 194.
48. *Deutsche Warte,* 15 May 1905, no. 134.
49. Tresckow, *Von Fürsten und Anderen Sterblichen,* 77–78.
50. Hirschfeld, *Homosexualität,* 897.
51. *Berliner Morgenpost,* 2 June 1899, no. 127.
52. *Vorwärts,* 11 June 1905, no. 135.
53. *Vorwärts,* 7 December 1906, no. 285.
54. Tresckow, *Von Fürsten und Anderen Sterblichen,* 114–16.

CHAPTER 8

~:~

Soliciting Fantasies
Knowing and Not Knowing about Male Prostitution by Soldiers in Imperial Germany

JEFFREY SCHNEIDER

By the end of the nineteenth century, a subculture organized around sex between civilian men and uniformed members of the armed forces arose in a number of major cities, including London, St. Petersburg, Stockholm, New York, and Berlin.[1] In his popular 1904 guidebook to gay Berlin, *Berlins Drittes Geschlecht* (Berlin's Third Sex), Magnus Hirschfeld, a sexologist and leading figure in the modern homosexual emancipation movement, cites an informant who contends that "except in London … there is no city in the world with such a choice of soldiers from so many different branches of the military than in Berlin."[2] Without a doubt, the German capital offered soldiers and homosexual civilians alike an ideal setting for an underground sex market, since, together with nearby Potsdam, Berlin contained the largest single metropolitan concentration of military personnel in Germany. As a large city with nearly two million inhabitants and an additional 1.5 million living in the surrounding suburbs, the capital also afforded anonymity while diminishing the authorities' ability to police all areas.[3] Finally, Berlin had one of the most developed gay subcultures in existence at the time, boasting not only the world's first organized modern gay emancipation movement but also numerous gay balls, "jour fixes," private salons, and more than twelve gay bars.[4]

Though gay Berlin and military Berlin were worlds apart, the city offered at least three points of intersection. First, homosexual civilians frequented so-called soldier bars that regularly sprang up near the numerous barracks located throughout the city. While often short-lived, because the army would ban them for all military personnel, these bars made it possible for civilians to curry favor with soldiers by buying them drinks and food, since their miserably low pay left them with little or no spending money of their own.[5] Much like female prostitutes, soldiers could also be found strolling the city streets in the late evening looking for customers. Men in uniform regularly canvassed the streets near the bars as well as certain paths in the Tiergarten, a massive park located in the center of Berlin.[6] Finally, there was at least one male brothel operating out of an apartment in the middle of the city. The police commissioner Hans von Tresckow, who raided the operation in the summer of 1907, claimed that it "had been known for years as a gathering place for homosexuals who celebrated their orgies with soldiers there."[7]

Despite its apparent prevalence, however, there is little official evidence with which to reconstruct the sexual relations between soldiers and civilian men. Though police assisted the army in identifying and patrolling bars and streets where soldiers and homosexuals came together, there is little documentary evidence in Berlin's criminal police archives, which largely went missing after 1945.[8] Because the military had legal jurisdiction over soldiers at all times, even in the case of criminal acts committed outside the barracks or while off-duty, any soldiers caught by the police engaging in sexual activity with other men would have been turned over to the military authorities for judicial or disciplinary proceedings.[9] Ute Frevert, however, reports that the military archives that survived World War II lack any documented "evidence of homosexuality" from this time.[10] Yet the topic of male prostitution by German soldiers did emerge briefly, if spectacularly, as part of a larger series of homosexual scandals that rocked the German Empire from 1907 to 1909. Typically called the Eulenburg Scandal after Kaiser Wilhelm II's most influential civilian adviser Prince Philipp Eulenburg, the scandal's prime political target, the series of allegations and revelations also enveloped a few top military officers, several of whom were investigated and dismissed for having pressured their subordinates into providing sexual services.[11] It was during the first of several high-profile trials against General Kuno von Moltke, one of Eulenberg's closest friends and confidantes, that prostitution by soldiers became front-page news in German papers. The issue spurred debates in the Reichstag, during which War Minister Karl von Einem acknowledged that soldiers were in fact exchanging sex for money.[12]

Yet relying on these published accounts for an accurate picture of *Soldatenprostitution* also poses problems. Hirschfeld, for instance, depicts relations between civilian homosexuals and soldiers as innocent friendships in which sexual acts and the outright exchange of money were rare occurrences. His editor Hans Ostwald, who authored numerous popular exposés of the metropolitan underworld, saw things differently.[13] In his *Männliche Prostitution im kaiserlichen Berlin* (Male Prostitution in Imperial Berlin), published in 1906—just two years after Hirschfeld's *Berlins Drittes Geschlecht* and one year before the Eulenburg scandal broke—Ostwald chastised Hirschfeld for "sugarcoating" the issue.[14] As a counterpoint, Ostwald paints a bar scene in which older, wealthy, lascivious civilians prey upon young soldiers hard up for cash.

And whereas the war minister's official account in 1907 blamed prostitution by male soldiers on sexually aggressive and dangerous homosexual civilians, an anonymous author felt compelled to correct Einem's "slandering" of homosexuals just one year later in his own underground guidebook, *Das perverse Berlin* (Perverse Berlin).[15]

But rather than lament the dearth of reliable information with which to adjudicate these competing versions, I want to suggest that the significance of *Soldatenprostitution* lies less in the actual acts themselves than in the heated debates, titillating descriptions, and ambitious theorizing they provoked. Indeed, the competing accounts of these illicit sexual relations offer valuable material for unpacking some of the strange and productive intersections between the politics of militarism and what Foucault calls "the endlessly proliferating economy of the discourse on sex."[16] Nevertheless, the discourse on *Soldatenprostitution* raises methodological questions about Foucault's account of sexuality as that "strange endeavor ... to tell the truth of sex," for despite their sexological pedigree and their claims to offer an insider's guide into a hidden subculture, published accounts such as Hirschfeld's and *Das perverse Berlin* seem in fact better designed to obfuscate than reveal.[17] Foucault, of course, acknowledges that *scientia sexualis* exhibited "systematic blindnesses" and deployed a range of "tactics" for "evading this truth, barring access to it, masking it," what he calls "a stubborn will to nonknowledge."[18] He does not, however, elucidate these mechanisms, preferring instead to emphasize their structural place within the overall strategy for producing the truth of sex: "Choosing not to recognize was yet another vagary of the will to truth."[19]

It is striking, of course, how Foucault's characterization of the tactics of nonknowledge—evading, barring, and masking—borrows so explicitly on the vocabulary of psychoanalysis, in particular, the Lacanian account of fantasy. In what follows, I want to focus on the role of fantasy in the discourse of *Soldatenprostitution* to expand Foucault's account of sexuality beyond his familiar rubric of "power-knowledge." To do so, I draw on the work of Slavoj Žižek, whose Lacanian approach treats social fantasies as ideological operations that mask deep structural antagonisms in society. Žižek contends that fantasy emerges in response to disturbances, gaps, and ruptures in discourse. The existence of an illicit underground sexual economy involving soldiers not only disturbed the military leadership, which was relentlessly concerned about breakdowns in discipline, but also the German public, whose sons entered the army as conscripts. By constructing an alternative understanding of disturbing phenomena, fantasies about *Soldatenprostitution* enabled the military leadership, homosexual civilians, and society as a whole to avoid recognizing or acknowledging what they did not want to know. These fantasies, however, were neither pure propaganda nor merely figments of the imagination, that is, the opposite of reality. Indeed, Žižek contends that fantasy serves as the very means by which reality is apprehended—it is, in fact, our account of reality: "in the opposition between dream and reality, fantasy is on the side of reality: it is, as Lacan once said, the support that gives consistency to what we call 'reality.'"[20] Fantasy thus operates as a support mechanism for "truth," but only to the extent that we do not take its version of events as fantasies, but rather mistake them for a true account of how things are. In the history of sexuality, then, we might say that the tactics of the "will to nonknowledge" emerges at those points when the will to truth threatens to break down as a strategy of power. To re-paraphrase Žižek through Foucault, fantasy is a blindness within discourse operating on the side of power.

In his speech in front of the Reichstag, for instance, War Minister Karl von Einem began by acknowledging publicly "that whole regiments are contaminated": "There may be an exaggeration or two in such claims. But the facts are indeed quite clear that our soldiers resist only with great effort the assaults that scoundrels (*Buben*) from civilian circles are making against them."[21] At one level, Einem's public statement amounts to a surprising concession on the part of a leadership known for its maniacal need for secrecy.[22] Nevertheless, his explanation involves some less surprising but no less interesting turns, in particular his move from the metaphor of "contamination," which he acknowledges to be an exaggeration, to the "fact" (*Tatsache*) that homosexual civilians are the aggressors and that military personnel can barely defend themselves against them.

On the one hand, by designating such sexual advances as an attack, Einem absolves soldiers of any responsibility for their involvement. Indeed, his representation of the soldiers as essentially defenseless victims reconfigures the army's mission from one of disciplining its wayward personnel to one of protecting them. The army's countermeasures, for instance, which placed restrictions on wearing the distinctive and erotically charged dress uniforms after dark, were "necessary in order to protect these people from the attacks perpetrated by perverse members of the civilian population (*vor den Angriffen der pervers veranlagten Teile des Zivilpublikums*)."[23] We might see the final act of protecting such troops—and redefining the discourse of *Soldatenprostitution*—in the metaphor of "attack," which desexualizes these encounters by recasting them in a military-like metaphor. On the other hand, Einem's emphasis on the army's defensive role also shifts the discursive focus from the soldiers to the homosexuals:

> Gentlemen, until now I have never read anything about such things; they were foreign to me, and they were disgusting. But I have been moved to read about this issue in brochures and scientific texts, and from those it is quite clear that the men who are afflicted with this passion search out those men who appear to them to be the strong, the perfect ones in terms of masculine potency (*die starken, die vollkommenen an Manneskraft*). For example, porters, coachmen, and

draymen (*Lastträger, Rollkutscher, Bierkutscher*) are supposed to be special objects of their desire, and one of the most famous experts in this scientific-medical question, Dr. Moll, has written that these people encounter bravery and strength in the soldier, quasi in the uniform, and that is exactly what they are looking for.[24]

Albert Moll's sexological research on homosexuality enables Einem to pathologize the homosexual for his desire, explaining the secret of his desire—his uniform fetish—in his persistent search for ideal masculinity.

It is not difficult to see the war minister's emphasis on "homosexual aggression" as the kind of fantasy that flies in the face of reality rather than the kind that actually structures it. Just one year later, then, the anonymous author of the book *Das perverse Berlin* returns to Einem's speech in order to ridicule the idea that manly soldiers were barely capable of defending themselves against civilian homosexuals. He notes that while the latter were seen as essentially weak and effeminate, the former were actually armed with daggers, trained to kill, and could easily—and legitimately—have resorted to violence to protect themselves.[25] Moreover, he claims, "if homosexuals really do dare to approach soldiers, the former only do so because they know that such advances are not unwelcome to the latter."[26] Finally, he also questions the war minister's claim of ignorance by alluding to an incident that occurred just months before the first trial in the Eulenburg scandal, when the Prussian Minister of the Interior Theobald von Bethmann Hollweg was propositioned by a soldier one evening while strolling through the Tiergarten.[27] "Does Herr von Einem," he provocatively asks, "know nothing about that?"[28]

Nevertheless, I want to suggest that for all its flimsiness, Einem's characterization of these sexual trysts as homosexual "aggression" does accurately represent the military's sense of its powerlessness vis-à-vis homosexual desire. Most significant, however, is the implication that the homosexuals' aggressiveness constitutes an assault of knowledge against the innocence of ignorance. By claiming not to have any knowledge of homosexual desire prior to these revelations, Einem suggests that his own sexual innocence, that is, his ignorance of (homo)sexual matters as well as the innocent ignorance of the entire German public, which has been forced to reach about such "disgusting" matters (Einem) in the newspapers, has been defiled in much the same manner that the innocence of the troops has been defiled by the homosexuals' advances. This investment in innocence, in a lack of knowledge, also extends to the troops themselves. Rather than training them to decline unwanted solicitations from homosexual civilians or encouraging them to use their training in deadly force, the army's relatively recent uniform regulations sought not only to prevent such advances but also to effectively shield the soldiers from the knowledge of homosexuality that an aggressive response would require.

But it is not merely the case that the anonymous but well-informed author of *Das perverse Berlin* has replaced Einem's ignorance or lies with "real" knowledge. For now, in place of the homosexual's desire, there is the need to account for the soldier's motivations. In response to Einem's version of events, then, *Das perverse Berlin* proposes two possible scenarios. In the first, a soldier "tells his (mostly younger) comrades that one can earn some easy money in a certain way. Such a promise awakens their curiosity—as well as their desire for money."[29] In the second scenario, a young male prostitute named "Hans" actually enlists in the army in order to use the uniform to increase his appeal and his illicit income. His newfound wealth, however, eventually awakens a jealous curiosity in his comrades. In response to their queries, "next time, Hans takes his curious comrade with him, and since he's a pretty boy—everyone, after all, looks nice in a uniform—within just a short time he has a relationship—or even more than one!"[30] In both of these quite imaginative scenarios, the actively desiring homosexual, who played such a prominent role in Einem's account, has been removed from the picture entirely and replaced by a knowledgeable peer—either one who infiltrates the military ranks or one who is already on the inside. Thus, rather than being victims of homosexual advances, the soldiers are led astray by their insatiable appetite for money.

As an account offered by a homosexual informant, however, these two scenarios tell us less—indeed, probably nothing—about the actual desires and motivations of the soldiers or, for that matter, the overall libidinal economy of the military itself. According to Žižek, the "army community relies on a thwarted/disavowed homosexuality as the key component of the soldiers' male bonding."[31] This contention is problematic, however, not least because it runs the risk of making homosexual desire among soldiers too constant and fixed, and their camaraderie merely repressed male-male desire. Such a claim is dangerously close to the familiar homophobic reading of fascism as repressed homosexuality.[32] Moreover, if some of the soldiers who exchanged sex with men for money might also have enjoyed it, we would have to ask what, exactly, they would have been enjoying: The pleasure in earning easy money? The pleasure in subverting the disciplinary reach of a totalizing institution? The unanticipated (or even highly anticipated) thrill of sexual contact with another man? Or some combination of all three?

Because we don't have any records from them that might indicate their motivations, the question is essentially moot. But as George Chauncey points out, prior to the homosexual emancipation movement, masculine men who took the active role in sexual encounters with other men could initiate and consummate such sexual acts without considering themselves homosexual—or, for that matter, being considered such by others, including the passive homosexual partner.[33] Since none of the texts about *Soldatenprostitution* ever questions the soldiers' presumed heterosexuality, it seems likely that they assumed the active role. But with a lively homosexual emancipation movement operating in Berlin, it is also not entirely unlikely, following Allan Bérubé's work on the emergence of gay culture in the wake of the mass mobilization of the U.S. in World War II, that some rural recruits may have "realized" that they were homosexual during their two-year obligation.[34] Certainly, many recruits did remain in the city after their service.[35]

But while the two scenarios spun out in *Das perverse Berlin* tell us little about the soldiers or the military, they do tell us much about the structure of the civilian homosexuals' desire for soldiers. As Žižek contends, "fantasy does not simply realize a desire in a hallucinatory way: rather ... a fantasy constitutes our desire, provides its co-ordinates; that is, it literally 'teaches us how to desire.'"[36] The first set of coordinates is, of course, already clear from the start: the soldiers' masculinity and the erotic appeal of the uniform. But it is also apparent that the soldiers' innocence, in particular their sexual innocence, served as another important coordinate of desire. In both imagined scenarios in *Das perverse Berlin*, this innocence derives from their desire for money, which, while a desire in its own right, is not a *sexual* desire, and certainly not a desire for sex with another man. By emphasizing the characteristic of prostitution as the soldiers' fundamental motivation, the author of *Das perverse Berlin* brackets and implicitly dismisses the possibility that soldiers might themselves also be seeking sexual satisfaction with other men.

The next coordinate of desire is related to the previous one: in both fantasy scenarios offered by *Das perverse Berlin*, the desire for money is never a desire that appears alone, within an individual soldier, but instead arises out of his interactions with his fellow soldiers—and invariably reinforces their camaraderie through their new shared secret about *Soldatenprostitution*. Thus, the scene of Hans's imagined interrogation is the communal setting of the barracks, and the interrogators are the "one or the other soldiers who sleep in the same room," a curious detail that seems to imbue the setting with an additional erotic subtext.[37] But while seduction into prostitution at the hands of an older or more experienced comrade is, of course, a seduction into sex work, the seduction does not itself constitute a sex act. This distinction is critical because it casts the homosexual as somehow tangential to the practice of *Soldatenprostitution*. Here the fantasies stage not only the soldiers' (hetero)sexual innocence, but their essentially nonsexual bonds with their fellow soldiers as well. Thus, the image of the heterosexual soldiers bonding—in this case through their shared secret about how to earn money through prostitution—also underwrites the homosexual's desire.

In essence, then, the fantasy of the soldiers' innate, unchanging, and incontrovertible heterosexuality must be sustained against any facts that could—and, speaking from our vantage point today, perhaps legitimately should—indicate otherwise. But as these two scenarios in *Das perverse Berlin* make clear, the fantasy of the "military chaser," as such men are called today, is not to have sex with a *gay* man in the military, and thereby participate in the army's purportedly libidinal *homosexual* economy (as Žižek's erasure of any substantive difference between homoeroticism and homosexuality might have it), but rather to have sex with a straight man in uniform, and thereby have access, even if only indirectly, to a libidinal economy marked as *heterosexual* male bonding. As the self-described military chaser Steven Zeeland admits: "most military chasers are at least as eager as conservative gay activists to believe in the existence of true, oh-so-rigid *heterosexuals* whose same-sex experiences *don't really count.* Indeed, it is precisely this sense of difference that drives us on. Without it, there would be no space to chase."[38] That "oh-so-rigid" heterosexuality stems in part from the soldiers' "*unstudied* masculinity," though, as Zeeland notes, the fantasy requires overlooking how men "who *learn* how to become masculine at boot camp [can] be termed 'unstudied.'"[39] But it also derives from a fetishized notion of military camaraderie, since, from the vantage point of military chasers today, "the military love of comrades is something that gay life can't offer."[40]

The military chaser's eroticization of heterosexual male bonds in *Das perverse Berlin* is structured along the lines of Žižek's analysis of the medieval church's accounts of sex in the Garden of Eden. According to Žižek, in St. Augustine's account,

> far from being the sin which caused man's Fall, sexuality is on the contrary, the *punishment, penitence* for the sin. Original sin lies in man's arrogance and pride; it was committed when Adam ate from the Tree of Knowledge.... if Adam and Eve had stayed in the Garden of Eden they would have had sexual intercourse, but they would have accomplished the sexual act in the same way as they accomplished all other instrumental acts (ploughing, sowing...).[41]

In Aquinas's account, on the other hand, Žižek contends that "there *was* sex in Paradise, Adam and Eve *did* copulate, their pleasure was even greater than ours ... the only and crucial difference being that, while copulating, they maintained proper measure and distance, and never lost self-control ... it was the kingdom of perversity."[42] Though contradictory, both accounts of Edenic sex presume that sex is not the problem, but rather any inherent excess—a loss of distance and self-control—that would distinguish it from instrumental acts like farming or its instrumental purpose in procreation. This quality, however, is not inherent within the sexual acts themselves (which are already perverse and pleasurable). Instead, the excess is a function of knowledge: knowledge of that perversity, which results in the loss of innocence.

In the case of *Das perverse Berlin,* the camaraderie between Hans and his nameless fellow soldiers is perverse to the extent that it leads to prostitution and provokes the desire of homosexuals. But it is essentially innocent to the extent that the soldiers are themselves unaware of what they are doing, or rather that they are presumably not motivated by sexual desire but by instrumental reasons: to earn money. Moreover, their bonds with each other are more fundamental than any connection they might experience in sexual contact with homosexuals. The camaraderie with their fellow soldiers is itself significant and pleasurable, but achieving such bonds is not the soldiers' intentional goal—rather, such bonds arise out of the thoroughly militarized (though here entirely unsanctioned) rites of initiation, in this case, the initiation into prostitution.

There are two important insights to be gleaned from this extended analysis of the military chaser's fantasies. The first is that *Das perverse Berlin*'s fantasy scenarios, for all their claims to explain the phenomenon of *Soldatenprostitution*, rely less on a will to knowledge than on a will *not* to know: not to know about the soldiers, to pursue their motivations, to subject them to the "careful" analysis of *scientia sexualis*, to compel them to confess the secrets of their own desires. In place of that knowledge, *Das perverse Berlin* offers up a fantasy of a pre-lapsarian "Barracks of Eden" in which soldiers are perversely bonding and desiring, but are innocently unaware of that perversity. Thus, in accounting for the "truth" of the soldiers' desire, this explanation articulates instead the desire of homosexual civilians who pay for sex with supposedly heterosexual soldiers who, in current parlance, are merely "gay for pay." The second is that for all its insistence on offering a fundamentally different account, *Das perverse Berlin* essentially corroborates the war minister's key claim in front of the Reichstag: that manly soldiers are essentially innocent and thus implicitly heterosexual, and that it is exactly this fundamental "truth" that makes them so desirable to homosexuals.

As I have already indicated, though, the war minister's emphasis on this "truth" is itself structured by a will not to know, which we now have the tools to explore more fully. This non-knowledge does not lie in his convenient suppression of evidence, as *Das perverse Berlin* suggests, nor is it entirely located in the careful diversion in his parliamentary report from the activities themselves to the "truth" of the homosexuals' desire. Rather the truth that must not be known, that must remain the object of a fundamental misunderstanding (*méconnaissance*, as Foucault puts it),[43] is the pleasure that those on the political side of the army—the army leadership as well as the broader German public—*also* take in the "innocent" masculinity, the "innocent" camaraderie of the rank-and-file soldiers, and the thrilling sight of the military uniform. On the one hand, what Einem's fantasy of the military chaser does not seem to acknowledge is how much his description of homosexual desire corresponds to the military's own recruitment policies. Like the homosexual "scoundrels," the military also "searched out" exactly such strong, fit, and masculine men, primarily menial laborers from the nonindustrialized lower classes, to fill its ranks.[44]

But unlike *Soldatenprostitution*, whose supposedly clandestine pleasures were regularly put on display as one of the sordid secrets of the Berlin metropolis, the militaristic pleasure in the uniform was neither repressed nor disavowed but instead found expression in numerous public venues, perhaps most especially in the annual military spectacles that grew in size and importance after German unification in 1871. According to Jakob Vogel, "the colorful military 'performance' attracted masses of spectators to these events that up to then had been staged as purely military exercises."[45] As he points out, the authentic popularity of these events brought about changes in the exercises, which had to be moved to larger cities to accommodate the ever larger crowds of watchers, many of whom, especially the well-to-do and local notables, paid for the privilege of sitting in bleachers with guaranteed sightlines. Despite the spectacle's character as a broad and increasingly commercialized *Volksfest* where families and groups drank and dined before and after the parade, the soldiers themselves remained the draw. As Ute Frevert contends, "in contrast to later military parades where the technology of weaponry took centre stage, Imperial Germany's military parades accentuated the physical presence of troops and officers, an effect the colorful uniforms underlined. The message to be conveyed was that the army's strength lay in the men's physique, their vitality and youth, their smart posture and sharp precision."[46] For both Vogel and Frevert, such public rituals not only garnered popular support for the military but also functioned ideologically to hide from the public the soldiers' ultimate purpose: killing in warfare. And though this purpose was "precisely what gave [the parading soldiers] that unique aura, an equal mix of fear and awe,"[47] both historians suggest that the soldiers' dress uniforms, which were clearly so impractical for modern warfare, provided the screen behind which this truth was covered.

Implicit in both Vogel's and Frevert's analyses is a psychoanalytic notion of fantasy. We can thus augment their explanation of the spectacle's ideology by drawing more substantially on psychoanalytic theory. In Lacanian parlance, the soldiers' murderous potential is the Real, that is, the horror—unarticulated because unsymbolizable—whose emergence in discourse and knowledge would seem to threaten the very viability of the social fabric in general and German militarism in particular. But rather than entirely hiding the Real under a pleasant veneer (as Frevert suggests), fantasy draws its strength from the horror of the Real. Thus, military spectacles only too clearly incorporate everything necessary for battle: the deadly weapons, the powerful bodies, the rigid discipline, and even, I would contend, the showy uniforms—which, however impractical they might have been for battle in the early twentieth century, referred back to a long tradition of warfare (when colorful uniforms were an essential part of strategy) and, even more importantly, clearly marked their wearers as different from civilians. In these military parades, then, the soldiers' murderous potential was visible, even pronounced, but through the parade it was redirected into a dance whereby the horrible chaos of war was replaced by a reassuring order: precisely choreographed steps, orchestrated to marches, with weapons as props.

Yet the key component missing from Frevert's and Vogel's accounts is that the murderous potential is not merely disavowed, but rather covered up—the *méconnaissance*—through its simultaneous eroticization. Indeed, it was the public's phantasmic pleasure in these events that ensured that the will to knowledge would be short-circuited by a "stubborn" and "systematic blindness." The effect of nearly identical men marching past in uniform conveyed "a primeval power, tamed by discipline" with enough "aura," as Frevert terms it, to ensure that recollections found their way into nearly every "memoir by contemporaries of the Wilhelminian era, whatever their gender or class."[48] That such displays inflamed the passions of young single women was, even then, a cliché.[49]

It would be naïve, of course, to imagine that such pleasure took hold only in women and girls. But that does not mean that the men who experienced this pleasure were latent, closeted, or repressed homosexuals, for such designations—"heterosexual" desire in women or "homosexual" desire in men—would merely be, as Foucault points out in his genealogy of the homosexual, discursive labels applied after the fact to give coherence to the phenomenon being scrutinized.[50] The point is that such phantasmic pleasures were *not* labeled—that the impetus to label them was blocked by a "will to nonknowledge." Thus, most civilian men's pleasures at military parades were probably not latently homosexual, if by this term we refer to a man's repressed or disavowed desire to have sex with these soldiers. But it is nevertheless the case that German society's phantasmic pleasure in the parading and uniformed rank-and-file soldiers was, in fact, structurally the same as the fantasies of the "military chasers," for they too, like both the German public and military leadership, took intense pleasure in the display of these bodies and in the fantasies—forever being called up in hagiographic terms—of their profound camaraderie, itself the embodiment of selfless service to the nation. Militarism's ideological "hold" over German society, then, operated in part through the fantasy that the rank-and-file soldiers were "innocent," that they exemplified the possibility of honor and duty in a modern society increasingly "corrupted" by capitalism, materialism, and socialism. In the eyes of German society, the value of their military service existed beyond or even in spite of the dubious political machinations of the military leadership.

Thus, when the phenomenon of *Soldatenprostitution* emerged into the broad light of day, the public's excessive outrage indexed its sense that homosexuals were defiling and stealing (even if buying) the source of their pleasure: the soldiers' essential innocence. It was for this reason that one of the outcomes of the Eulenburg scandal in general and *Soldatenprostitution* in particular was the demonization of the homosexual and the abrupt end to Hirschfeld's dream that homosexual emancipation was close at hand. Indeed, because the homosexual fantasy underlying *Soldatenprostitution* never challenged but instead reinforced the fantasy that all soldiers were incontrovertibly heterosexual, the only solution to the crisis of too much knowledge was to make abject and to expel the "criminal" homosexual. As Police Commissioner Tresckow concludes, "In any case, the trials with all their disclosures have damaged the homosexuals' cause more than they helped, since public opinion has quite rightfully been outraged over their brash behavior."[51]

Thus, it is unsurprising that despite its flimsiness, it was Einem's account and its logic that ultimately sutured the rupture caused by the public's awareness of *Soldatenprostitution*. This act of sealing up, however, was not secured primarily by a will to knowledge about homosexuals' desires, but rather by a will to non-knowledge about militarism's own desires. As the Reichstag deputy and former military officer Max Liebermann von Sonnenberg asserted after Einem's speech, though his was by no means a lone voice: "I, at least, must admit that I was as excited as a child at Christmas by the Christmas present that the war minister gave us yesterday. (Bravo calls from the right!) The clear, sharp words of a soldier (*Soldatenworte*) have shooed away (*verscheucht*) like a fresh wind the stench of putrefaction hovering over our people. The power of lies is frighteningly big."[52] Liebermann's claim about the power of lies was, of course, directed against those who "mistakenly" believed the revelations issuing from the Eulenburg scandal and had spoken their outrage prior to hearing from the war minister. But the sentence more accurately characterizes the power of fantasy to shape and reshape reality, even in the face of facts that, from another point of view, clearly say otherwise. For the "gift" that the war minister gave was not any new knowledge, but rather the occlusion of knowledge, and hence the ability of the discourse of militarism to keep, wrapped up and under wraps, what it "stubbornly" refused to see. The circularity of Liebermann's claim points to the power of the militarist fantasy, since the integrity of the war minister's military words—"the clear, sharp words of a soldier"—vouches for the integrity of the soldiers themselves and excises any need to make the prostituting soldiers an object of scrutiny. As Žižek contends, fantasy does not merely obfuscate these ruptures or antagonisms but derives its force from them: "An ideology really succeeds when even the facts which at first sight contradict it start to function as arguments in its favour."[53]

Foucault may be right to claim that the will to nonknowledge can function as another "vagary of the will to truth." But it is a mistake to see it only as subordinate to and supportive of the operations of power-knowledge. Instead, it seems more important to recognize that the will to nonknowledge—that is, fantasy—also has powerful effects of its own. As psychoanalysis explains, fantasy operates less as an absence of knowledge than as a force with its own structures and mechanisms. As a result, "the will to nonknowledge" not only functions differently from the "will to truth" but is just as likely to subvert power-knowledge as to support it. Moreover, its "stubbornness" suggests that "the will to nonknowledge" is not easily vanquished. Indeed, fantasy's tenacity, which derives from the deep pleasure we take in it, makes it quite resistant to "facts" and rational argument. As Liebermann's own words reveal, the victory of "nonknowledge" takes place through a reversal of the terms, whereby "lies" become "truths," and fantasy—as ideology—appears on the side of "reality." We might see this "frighteningly big" "power of lies" as the unconscious of power itself. Thus, despite the antagonistic relationship between Foucault and psychoanalysis, it may be not only possible but also necessary to think "Foucault with Lacan"—even if the project of ultimately reconciling their theoretical differences might itself constitute a fantasy of sorts.[54]

Notes

1. For New York, see George Chauncey, *Gay New York: The Making of the Gay Male World, 1890–1940* (New York, 1995). For London, see Matt Houlbrook, "Soldier Heroes and Rent Boys: Homosex, Masculinities, and Britishness in the Brigade of Guards, circa 1900–1960," *Journal of British Studies* 42 (July 2003): 351–88; Jeffrey Weeks, "Inverts, Perverts, and Mary-Annes: Male Prostitution and the Regulation of Homosexuality in England in the Nineteenth and Early Twentieth Century," in J. Weeks, *Against Nature: Essays on History, Sexuality, and Identity.* (London, 1991), 46–67. For St. Petersburg, see Dan Healey, "Masculine Purity and 'Gentlemen's Mischief': Sexual Exchange and Prostitution between Russian Men, 1861–1941," *Slavic Review* 60, no. 2 (2001): 233–65.
2. Magnus Hirschfeld, *Berlins Drittes Geschlecht,* ed. Manfred Herzer (Berlin, 1991 [1904]), 96–97.
3. Peter Fritzsche, *Reading Berlin 1900* (Cambridge, MA, 1996), 7.
4. See Hirschfeld, *Berlins Drittes Geschlecht,* 65–114; Andreas Sternweiler, "Leben in der Unterdrückung," in *Goodbye to Berlin? 100 Jahre Schwulenbewegung. Eine Ausstellung,* ed. Schwules Museum and Berlin Akademie der Künste (Berlin, 1997), 70–74, here 71.
5. Hans Ostwald, *Männliche Prostitution im kaiserlichen Berlin* (Berlin, 1991 [1906]), 85.
6. Hirschfeld, *Berlins Drittes Geschlecht,* 97.
7. Hans von Tresckow, *Von Fürsten und anderen Sterblichen. Erinnerungen eines Kriminalkommissars* (Berlin, 1922), 181.
8. See Jens Dobler, *Zwischen Duldungspolitik und Verbrechensbekämpfung: Homosexuellenverfolgung durch die Berliner Polizei von 1848 bis 1933,* Schriftenreihe der Deutschen Gesellschaft für Polizeigeschichte e.V. (Frankfurt, 2008), 5.
9. On the jurisdiction of military courts, see Günter Gribbohm, *Das Reichsmilitärgericht: Teil deutscher Rechtskultur in wilhelminischer Zeit* (Münster, 2007), 15.
10. Ute Frevert, *A Nation in Barracks: Conscription, Military Service and Civil Society in Modern Germany,* trans. Andrew Boreham and Daniel Brückenhaus (New York, 2004), 177.
11. The best English-language accounts of the Eulenburg scandal are I.V. Hull, *The Entourage of Kaiser Wilhelm II., 1888–1918* (Cambridge, 1982); James D. Steakley, "Iconography of a Scandal: Political Cartoons and the Eulenburg Affair," *Studies in Visual Communication* 9, no. 2 (1983): 20–51; Harry F. Young, *Maximilian Harden. Censor*

Germaniae. The Critic in Opposition from Bismarck to the Rise of Nazism (The Hague, 1959).

12. *Stenographische Berichte über die Verhandlungen des Reichstags* (Berlin, 1908), vol. 229, 1913–1916.

13. For information on Ostwald, see Peter Fritzsche, "Vagabond in the Fugitive City: Hans Ostwald, Imperial Berlin and the Grossstadt-Dokumente," *Journal of Contemporary History* 29, no. 3 (1994): 385–402; Dietmar Jazbinsek, Bernward Joerges, and Ralf Thies, "The Berlin 'Großstadt-Dokumente': A Forgotten Precursor of the Chicago School of Sociology" (Berlin, 2001) http://skylla.wzb.eu/pdf/2001/ii01-502.pdf

14. Ostwald, *Männliche Prostitution*, 84.

15. Anonymous, *Das perverse Berlin. Kulturkritische Gänge* (Berlin, 1908), 103.

16. Michel Foucault, *The History of Sexuality*, vol. 1, *An Introduction*, trans. Robert Hurley (New York, 1978), 35.

17. Ibid., 57.

18. Ibid., 55.

19. Ibid.

20. Slavoj Žižek, *The Sublime Object of Ideology* (London, 1989), 44.

21. *Stenographische Berichte*, vol. 229, 1913.

22. Prince Chlodwig zu Hohenlohe-Schillingfürst, imperial Germany's third chancellor (1894–1900), recalled in his memoirs General Wilhelm von Hahnke, chief of the Military Cabinet from 1888–1901, asserting "the army must remain an insulated (*abgesonderter*) body into which no one dare peer with critical eyes." Quoted in Gordon A. Craig, *The Politics of the Prussian Army, 1640–1945* (Oxford, 1955), 247.

23. *Stenographische Berichte*, vol. 229, 1913.

24. Ibid. Einem is most likely referring to Albert Moll, *Die Conträre Sexualempfindung*, 3rd ed. (Berlin, 1899).

25. Anon., *Das perverse Berlin*, 104.

26. Ibid., 105.

27. Tresckow, *Von Fürsten und anderen Sterblichen*, 185.

28. Anon., *Das perverse Berlin*, 105.

29. Ibid., 106.

30. Ibid., 108.

31. Slavoj Žižek, "The Seven Veils of Fantasy," in S. Žižek, *The Plague of Fantasies* (London, 1997), 3–44, here 24.

32. Klaus Theweleit takes leftist-Marxist critics like Adorno and Brecht to task for their homophobic attempts to connect fascism with homosexuality, as in Adorno's aphorism: "Totalitarianism and homosexuality go together." Klaus Theweleit, *Male Fantasies: Women, Floods, Bodies, History*, trans. Stephen Conway in collaboration with Erica Carter and Chris Turner, 2 vols. (Minneapolis, 1987), vol. 1, 55. See also Andrew Hewitt, *Political Inversions: Homosexuality, Fascism, and the Modernist Imaginary* (Stanford, CA, 1996).

33. Chauncey, *Gay New York*, 65–97.

34. Allan Bérubé, *Coming Out under Fire: The History of Gay Men and Women in World War Two* (New York, 1990).

35. Frevert, *A Nation in Barracks*, 191.

36. Žižek, "The Seven Veils of Fantasy," 7.

37. Anon., *Das perverse Berlin*, 108.

38. Steven Zeeland, *Military Trade* (New York, 1999), 12.
39. Ibid., 5.
40. Ibid., 1.
41. Žižek, *The Sublime Object of Ideology*, 222.
42. Žižek, "The Seven Veils of Fantasy," 15.
43. Foucault, *The History of Sexuality*, vol. 1, 56.
44. Work on recruitment policies has tended to focus primarily on the army's preference for men from the rural peasantry and its practice of declaring large numbers of men from the urban proletariat unfit ("untauglich"). See Stig Förster, "Militär und staatsbürgerliche Partizipation. Die allgemeine Wehrpflicht im Deutschen Kaiserreich 1871–1914," in *Die Wehrpflicht. Entstehung, Erscheinungsformen und politisch-militärische Wirkung,* ed. Roland G. Foerster (Munich, 1994). Though Förster explains that many of the urban proletariat were dismissed as "unfit" primarily for political reasons, many eugenicists at this time expressed alarm about the number of unfit men in the urban, industrial centers and began studying and debating the causes of the supposedly growing physical shortcomings of the German male population. See Paul Weindling, *Health, Race and German Politics between National Unification and Nazism, 1870–1945* (Cambridge, 1989), 99–100, 259.
45. Jakob Vogel, "Military, Folklore, Eigensinn: Folkloric Militarism in Germany and France, 1871–1914," *Central European History* 33, no. 4 (2000): 487–504, here 492.
46. Frevert, *A Nation in Barracks*, 212.
47. Ibid.
48. Ibid.
49. See, for instance, Jakob Vogel, "Stramme Gardisten, temperamentvolle Tirailleurs und anmutige Damen. Geschlechterbilder im deutschen und französischen Kult der 'Nation in Waffen,'" in *Militär und Gesellschaft im 19. und 20. Jahrhundert,* ed. Ute Frevert (Stuttgart, 1997), 245–62, esp. 252–56.
50. Foucault, *The History of Sexuality*, vol. 1, 43.
51. Tresckow, *Von Fürsten und anderen Sterblichen*, 163.
52. *Stenographische Berichte*, vol. 229, 1945.
53. Žižek, *The Sublime Object of Ideology*, 49.
54. Charles Shephardson, "History and the Real: Foucault with Lacan," *Postmodern Culture* 5, no. 2 (1995), doi: 10.1353/pmc.1995.0015.

CHAPTER 9

~:~

Between Normalization and Resistance
Prostitutes' Professional Identities and Political Organization in Weimar Germany

JULIA ROOS

In February 1922, more than sixty registered prostitutes (*Kontrollmädchen*) in Frankfurt am Main signed a petition to the Prussian district president in Wiesbaden protesting the planned closing down of their city's licensed brothels. The petition highlighted the social misery prostitutes evicted from the brothels faced, "because the lengthy isolation has rendered most girls incapable of moving about freely in the streets." Given the acute housing shortage and the police's rigid restrictions on prostitutes' choice of apartments, many *Kontrollmädchen* would become homeless. The petitioners denied that they were exploited by their madams and stressed the brothels' beneficial economic functions in generating tax revenue and sustaining small businesses. If Frankfurt's police chief followed through with his plan to abolish the brothels, they warned, "chaos" would ensue in public health: "Authentic police materials prove that unlicensed streetwalking contributes to a far greater extent to the spread of venereal diseases than possible under the conditions of confined prostitution." The *Kontrollmädchen* expressed their dismay "that in the German republic, which according to leading personalities is supposed to have the most liberal constitution in the world, ... an institution, which has existed for decades and has proven itself to be useful, can be removed without any good reason."[1]

Like many of their colleagues in other German cities, Frankfurt's *Kontrollmädchen* participated collectively in Weimar-era conflicts over prostitution reform. Similar to registered prostitutes elsewhere, the authors of the 1922 petition felt deeply ambiguous about the system of state-regulated prostitution: while they defended the licensed brothels, they simultaneously admitted that these establishments brutally isolated their residents. By invoking Germany's new constitution, Frankfurt's registered prostitutes suggested at least implicitly that the recent expansion of democratic and civil rights should act as a check on the police's powers; this was a potentially radical demand. And yet, the petitioners approvingly cited "authentic police materials" to buttress their rather conventional claims about the hygienic advantages of licensed prostitution. Given the marked tensions in registered prostitutes' attitude toward state-regulated prostitution, how should we evaluate the political nature of their protests?

This essay argues that Weimar-era *Kontrollmädchen* engaged in significant acts of resistance against state-regulated prostitution despite their identification with select aspects of the system. Indeed, the successful hygienic normalization of prostitutes' sexuality within the confines of police-controlled prostitution played a crucial role in the initial formation of political organizations among *Kontrollmädchen*. Regarding the contradictory relationship between prostitutes and the system of state-regulated prostitution, Michel Foucault's notion of power as developed in the first volume of *The History of Sexuality* offers vital insights for analysis.

Foucault conceived of power as a ubiquitous microphysics functioning *not* according to a negative mode of repression, but rather through the incitement of "the will to knowledge" about the "truth" of sex and the resultant proliferation of sexual discourse. Power, he argued,

> must be understood in the first instance as the multiplicity of force relations immanent in the sphere in which they operate and which constitute their own organization; as the process which, through ceaseless struggles and confrontations, transforms, strengthens, or reverses them; as the support these force relations find in one another, thus forming a chain or a system, or on the contrary, the disjunctions and contradictions which isolate them from one another; and lastly, as the strategies in which they take effect, whose general design or institutional crystallization is embodied in the state apparatus, in the formulation of the law, in the various social hegemonies…. [P]ower is not an institution, and not a structure; neither is it a certain strength we are endowed with; it is the name that one attributes to a complex strategical situation in a particular society.[2]

Within this analytical framework, resistance is an integral part of the "strategic field of power relations." Like power, resistance is multicentered, changeable, and politically ambivalent. While Foucault conceded that occasionally, resistance could lead to "massive binary divisions," he believed that it more typically remained "mobile and transitory … producing cleavages in a society that shift about, fracturing unities and effecting regroupings, furrowing across individuals themselves."[3]

The sexual discourses supporting state-regulated prostitution generated a complex microcosm of power relations and resistances. In many ways, 1920s prostitutes' movements conform to Foucault's conception of the immanent, fractured nature of resistance. Official justifications of state-regulated prostitution emphasized the system's importance for containing the spread of "venereal disease" (*Geschlechtskrankheiten*, hereafter VD) by imposing rigid medical controls on prostitutes.[4] As they began to organize collectively in defense of their professional interests, licensed prostitutes adopted select socio-hygienic arguments about the dangers of VD and clandestine prostitution. In doing so, they to some extent helped confirm fears of "venereal pollution" that were central to their own social marginalization; they also contributed to branding nonregistered streetwalkers a "public health hazard." Simultaneously, however, their sense of superior hygienic expertise led many *Kontrollmädchen* to develop a self-confident professional identity fundamentally at odds with prevalent moral norms and female role prescriptions. This shared professional identity played a crucial role in uniting registered prostitutes in efforts at self-organization.

The system of state-regulated prostitution produced many vital preconditions for the emergence of prostitutes' movements in Weimar Germany. Yet not all factors spurring *Kontrollmädchen* into political action came from within the enclosed world of police-controlled prostitution. Broader changes in Germany's political constitution after 1918—and especially also the introduction of woman's suffrage—opened up new possibilities for prostitutes to contest their marginalized status. After the abolition of state-regulated prostitution in 1927, the protection of their newly won legal rights moved to the center of prostitutes' political agenda. This focus on issues of legal rights marked an important qualitative shift in the nature of prostitutes' resistance. Before turning toward a more detailed analysis of 1920s prostitutes' activism, it is helpful to take a brief look at key elements of state-regulated prostitution and the system's role in creating a separate class of professional prostitutes.

State-Regulated Prostitution and the Making of 'Kontrollmädchen'

Until 1927, many German cities operated local systems of state-regulated prostitution, or regulationism.[5] Under the conditions of this system, prostitution in principle was illegal, yet prostitutes registered with the morals police (*Sittenpolizei*) were tolerated. Some cities practiced solely voluntary registration of prostitutes; others also used compulsory inscription. Typically, women arrested for street soliciting had no recourse to a lawyer or court of law. Even for women who had registered voluntarily with the police, the price of toleration was high: *Kontrollmädchen* had to submit to frequent medical exams for VD and, if found infected, to compulsory treatment and hospitalization. Local police ordinances for prostitutes generally banned streetwalkers from major urban spaces like downtown areas, theaters, and parks, as well as from the use of public transportation. Many cities confined *Kontrollmädchen* to specific streets or houses, a practice known as "putting them into barracks" (*Kasernierung*).[6] In most places, prostitutes had to obtain police permission if they wanted to move or leave town. Regulationism imposed tight controls on prostitutes' personal and family life: especially *Kontrollmädchen* restricted to specific areas like brothel streets were prohibited from sharing apartments with male partners or children. Release from police surveillance was conditional upon proof of steady employment and the successful return to an "honest life"; both requirements were often extremely difficult to meet and left substantial room for discretionary police powers. In these ways, regulationism made manifest and continuously reproduced prostitutes' status as legal and social pariahs.

Unlicensed streetwalkers certainly had reason to fear the morals police—among other things, arrest inevitably resulted in compulsory medical exams for VD. However, illegal streetwalkers were not subject to the many petty restrictions regulationism imposed on registered prostitutes, and thus they were able to move more easily between different social identities.[7] *Kontrollmädchen* were acutely aware of this difference, and their own articulations of professional identity often entailed a rather dismissive, even resentful attitude toward amateur "interlopers."

Prostitutes' Political Mobilization in the Early Weimar Republic

With Germany's democratization and women's enfranchisement after November 1918, regulationism faced new political pressures. Prostitutes seized this opportunity to intervene actively in the debate over prostitution reform. A flyer distributed during the early 1920s underlined the inadequacy of projected changes to prostitution laws. It appealed to streetwalkers to organize in defense of their rights, "because only through unity and competent leadership ... can we stop the bureaucrats' senseless hustle and bustle and achieve changes in the legislation."[8] Several major cities witnessed the emergence of prostitutes' unions. According to sex reformer Magnus Hirschfeld, himself a member of the executive council of the Auxiliary Club of Berlin Prostitutes (Hilfsbund der Berliner Prostituierten), the various local unions represented "at least one hundred women each."[9] Their members regularly convened to discuss issues such as prices and competition, the conduct of the police, and effective protections against professional hazards. Berlin's Auxiliary Club issued membership cards and collected monthly fees of four marks per person. A special fund supported needy members. The colorful spectrum of people elected to the organization's executive committee showed that prostitutes' political initiatives gained support from certain liberal-minded individuals. Next to a number of prostitutes, one of whom "had obtained official permission to wear men's clothes," the committee included Hirschfeld and two other men, among them one "Mr. M.," who claimed to be an official in the Catholic Church.[10]

Another center of prostitutes' political activism was Hamburg. In January 1921, Hamburg's morals police supervised 114 brothels concentrated on eight streets in the inner city and in the harbor area of St. Pauli, respectively. The average number of inmates ranged between 550 and 600, which meant that roughly half of the city's more than 1,300 registered prostitutes lived in licensed brothels.[11] Attempts to organize prostitutes focused on these brothel residents. In January 1920, Communist Party members Ketty Guttmann and Ehrenfried Wagner initiated the founding of a union for registered prostitutes, the Council of Hamburg-Altona's Registered Prostitutes (Vertrauensrat der Hamburg-Altonaer Kontrollmädchen).[12]

On 7 January, approximately two hundred prostitutes attended the union's first meeting.[13] Among the main demands of the Vertrauensrat were fixed rents in regulated brothels, the abolition of the obligation to sell alcohol to clients (*Bierzwang*) and of punishments for soliciting from the doorway (*Türestehen*), access for registered prostitutes to theaters and other restricted public spaces, and better treatment in the hospitals.[14] Reminiscent of the structure of industrial trade unions, each of the brothel streets elected a representative (*Vertrauensperson*) who functioned as an intermediary between the residents and the Vertrauensrat. The *Vertrauensperson* was responsible for passing on prostitutes' complaints to the union. Upon being notified of such complaints, the union first tried to negotiate with brothel keepers and the authorities. If peaceful negotiations failed, the Vertrauensrat then turned toward more militant tactics. To mobilize prostitutes and appeal to a wider public audience, the union had its own newspaper called *Der Pranger: Organ der Hamburg-Altonaer Kontrollmädchen* (The Pillory: Organ of the Regulated Prostitutes of Hamburg-Altona).[15] The weekly's editors were Guttmann and Wagner, who also contributed the lion's share of articles.

A central aim of *Der Pranger* was to expose the abuses of regulationism and brothel life. The paper attacked the inhumane conditions in licensed brothels as manifestations of women's inferior status in German society.

> It is shattering to hear of the dramas taking place daily in these so-called "houses of joy" (*Freudenhäuser*). The unscrupulous manner in which the girls are being exploited here seems to be the most shameless of all forms of exploitation. It is proof of the fact that while one has given woman equal suffrage, one still considers her legally and morally man's object of exploitation. The slave-like treatment of women in the brothel is an insult to all women. And to protest against such a shameless exploitation of the female body *has to become the business of each and every woman*.[16]

Few women, the editors maintained, entered a life of prostitution "out of vanity, shallowness, or due to a pathological sexual predisposition."[17] The vast majority of prostitutes were "victims of the economic disparities and of an abysmally unjust (*abgrundtief schlecht*) society."

In its critique of regulationism, *Der Pranger* emphasized aspects of class conflict. Thus it consistently depicted madams and brothel keepers as greedy parasites thriving on prostitutes' impoverished situation. In January 1921, under the somewhat ominous headline "Pig Slaughter in the Brothel," *Der Pranger* featured an exposé about a brothel madam in Meissen who frequently treated herself to lavish pork roasts: "Brothel owners can afford such things. While their girls have to go on the man hunt rain or shine and are forced to end their day's work with a shabby kipper, their fattened exploiters sit by the warm stove and dig into a luscious pork roast."[18] The madam's extravagant diet, the article suggested, underlined the deep social divisions between brothel owners and prostitutes. For Guttmann and Wagner, regulationism constituted a perfect microcosm of the injustices of capitalist society.

Der Pranger tried to appeal to streetwalkers by offering them alternative interpretations of their role in society that deemphasized aspects of personal guilt. This was crucial for motivating prostitutes to speak out about their experiences. Unfortunately, it is impossible to establish the authenticity of prostitutes' anonymous contributions to *Der Pranger*. Letters to the editor complained about the exploitative situation in licensed brothels, police harassment, and streetwalkers' humiliating treatment in local hospitals. Such complaints rang true enough—after all, they addressed typical grievances also expressed in other written sources by prostitutes. Still, it has to remain unclear to what extent the letters represented prostitutes' original voices. Even if a substantial number of the letters to the editor may have been fictitious, however, the public forum *Der Pranger* created for the discussion of prostitutes' interests stirred considerable controversies at the local and national levels.

Conservatives strongly objected to the content and aims of *Der Pranger*. In September 1920, the nationalist Young Bismarck League (Jung-Bismarck-bund) urged the Hamburg senate to outlaw the paper. In a petition, members of the right-wing youth association expressed outrage that "under the eyes of city authorities, an immoral and dirty rag (*Schund- und Schmutzblatt*) like *Der Pranger* is sold to youths on the streets of Hamburg."[19] The league threatened to resort to vigilante measures if the government failed to intervene. Similarly, in December 1920, representatives of the conservative German National People's Party (DNVP) in Hamburg's parliament, the Bürgerschaft, demanded the harsh suppression of *Der Pranger* and other "indecent" periodicals.[20] In her response to the motion, the conservative politician Emma Ender outlined the rigid controls already imposed on *Der Pranger*. The police reviewed every new issue immediately upon publication; if any of the articles grossly violated "common sentiments of decency and propriety," the entire issue was confiscated.[21] At the time of the Bürgerschaft debate, three separate charges for violating public morality were pending against Ketty Guttmann. Several issues of the weekly were confiscated in the course of 1920.[22] Ender's statement suggested that *Der Pranger* reached a substantial national audience. As she stressed, Hamburg officials regularly exchanged information concerning the paper with police departments in Berlin, Hanover, Cologne, and Munich. In December 1920, Berlin's chief of police banned *Der Pranger* from sale by street vendors.[23]

The public controversies about *Der Pranger* attested to the paper's important role in challenging prostitutes' exclusion from society. They also revealed a growing rift between the editors and certain groups of registered prostitutes. In the fall of 1920, *Der Pranger* criticized streetwalkers' reluctance to support the Vertrauensrat.

> The organization of prostitutes lacks the support it deserves. If things do not work out immediately the way some people expected, they just throw in the towel. Believe us, *Kontrollmädchen*, you could not do the brothel owners a bigger favor than deserting your organization.... [It] is difficult to create unity among you.... Your divisions and envy against each other enable the brothel owners to dominate you![24]

The author (probably Guttmann) reminded prostitutes that *Der Pranger* fought for their interests and reprimanded those who "whine that [the paper] ruins your business." Nowhere else, the article stressed, did prostitutes have a newspaper dedicated to the defense of their rights. The author's frustration at times bordered on resentment: "Your 'profession,' girls, is nothing but a mockery of humanity—it is the flip side of this 'godly world order.'" To liberate themselves, streetwalkers had to overcome their "lethargy and stupor."[25]

The conflict between the editors and registered prostitutes over the role of the brothel highlights certain weaknesses in the Marxist analysis of prostitution. For communists like Guttmann, madams and brothel owners were typical capitalists who exploited the labor of prostitutes. Therefore, the latter's liberation required the brothel owners' expropriation. From this perspective, prostitutes who sided with the proprietors of brothels lacked proper class consciousness and were potential reactionaries. However, the communist interpretation of the political economy of the brothel neglected important practical needs of prostitutes. Residential restrictions and laws against procuring made it extremely difficult for registered prostitutes to find housing outside the regulated brothel. Moreover, while conflicts of interest clearly existed between madams and brothel residents, both groups shared a similar experience of social ostracism and formed part of the same precarious community of outcast women. This special gender identity often superseded economic differences.

The ensuing battle over the closing of Hamburg's brothels underlines the relevance of Foucault's notion of resistance's fluidity and immanence to predominant sexual discourse. The conflict showed that *Kontrollmädchen*, far from being politically apathetic, actively fought for their own conceptions of beneficial prostitution reforms. To realize their goals, registered prostitutes entered strategic alliances with brothel owners and conservative citizens concerned about the specter of the spread of "immorality" after the abolition of locally confined prostitution. This alliance indeed differed dramatically from the big binary divisions posited in Marxist theories of class struggle. Hamburg prostitutes' political compromises testified to the extent to which they identified with certain aspects of the regulationist system; they also shed light on the ways in which prostitutes' precarious legal status limited their ability to engage in modes of resistance more radically opposed to prevailing moral and sexual norms.

On 17 June 1921, the Bürgerschaft voted to abolish Hamburg's regulated brothels.[26] By mid November, the police had closed down three of the city's eight brothel streets.[27] The measure stirred considerable public opposition and led to an unlikely political alliance comprised of concerned citizens, respectable members of the business community, and representatives of the "underground economy" of prostitution.[28] In late September, five hundred people attended a protest meeting against the closure of the brothels. According to the Social Democratic *Hamburger Echo*, "in the end decent citizens, regulated prostitutes, and brothel proprietors voted in cozy harmony (*trauter Harmonie*) for the resolution against the removal of the brothels."[29]

During the debate, many participants criticized the deterioration of the "streetscape" (*Straßenbild*) since the beginning of the crackdown on public houses. The dispersion of prostitutes had turned commercial sex into a highly conspicuous spectacle that endangered public safety and Hamburg's youth. Others emphasized the hardships the Bürgerschaft's decision had created for brothel residents. Most speakers, a police report noted, supported demands for the postponement of prostitutes' eviction, so that the women would not "be thrown into the streets … and impoverished to such an extent that the opposite of the proclaimed goals of the closing-down of the houses would be achieved."[30] A representative of *Der Pranger* attacked liberal politician Frieda Radel, the author of the motion to shut down the brothels: "You, Mrs. Radel … promised us a mild treatment of the girls in the public houses…. You broke your promise in the most despicable way."[31] When Radel tried to respond to these criticisms, an audience filled with prostitutes, madams, and pimps shouted her down with "vulgar heckling" (*pöbelhafte Zwischenrufe*) and bursts of laughter.[32] In the conflict over the abolition of Hamburg's brothels, prostitutes and female reformers sat on opposite sides of the fence.

Prostitutes turned to the German League for the Reform of Criminal Justice (Deutscher Bund für Strafreform) for support in their struggle against eviction. They also closed ranks with their employers. As the league's president, John Krüger, informed the Hamburg senate in October 1921, the league represented the association of registered prostitutes alongside the brothel owners' organization.[33] In the name of both groups, Krüger demanded that the former brothels be converted into "private hotels for prostitutes." A petition signed by ninety-six prostitutes who still lived in the former brothel streets welcomed the decision to remove the system of licensed brothels: "We, too, support the view that we do not need brothels or brothel streets and are grateful to the senate and the Bürgerschaft for liberating us from the classification of regulated prostitutes."[34]

The *Kontrollmädchen* agreed that regulationism contradicted "the principle of legal equality and woman's status today." However, they protested against being expelled from their homes and appealed to the senate "to convert the houses into licensed hotels where we can remain and take up lodgings without this causing our landlords or us any legal disadvantages." In an affidavit, the petitioners confirmed that "our landlords neither exploit us nor do they force us to consume excessive amounts of alcohol." They also sharply criticized "the notion propagated in the Bürgerschaft and in the press that we are indebted to our landlords" and emphasized that they were free at any time to leave the brothels. The petition stressed the discrimination against prostitutes on the housing market: "we regret to say that for some time now we have tried unsuccessfully to find alternative lodgings. Private landlords charge usurious rates (*Wuchermieten*) we cannot afford; most of them refuse altogether to take us in." Due to the harsh penalties for procuring, many landlords hesitated to accept prostitutes as tenants. Those who did often demanded exorbitant rents to cover their risk. Prostitutes' difficulties were further exacerbated by Hamburg's dramatic housing shortage: in 1925 it was estimated that up to 6,600 apartments in the city were severely overcrowded.[35]

For many women, the brothel provided an important "safety net." The abolition of Hamburg's public houses threatened to render former residents homeless and destitute. In a petition of November 1921, registered prostitutes and brothel keepers drew attention to insurmountable obstacles faced by women who tried to return to a normal life.[36] They reported that "most of the employers whom we asked for work for the girls have refused in the most decisive manner to hire regulated prostitutes, because the respectable workers do not want to work alongside prostitutes." For a majority of the women it was extremely difficult to find jobs outside prostitution, because they lacked professional experience and credentials. Moreover, many of them had long passed "the youthful age." As the petitioners pointed out, the situation was especially

precarious for old ex-prostitutes who earned their living as housekeepers, re-
ceptionists, or charwomen in the brothels.[37]

The November petition suggested a modified and somewhat less repressive
system of public supervision of prostitution. This plan would convert all former brothels into lodging houses for registered prostitutes. While every house
would have a certain number of permanent tenants, the "private hotels" were
also supposed to accommodate nonresident streetwalkers and their clients.
Prostitutes who did not live in one of the lodging houses had to register with
the landlord. This, the petitioners emphasized, would enable the police to exert
"a certain control over street prostitution."[38] All women who used the lodging
houses had to prove that they were not infected with VD. The petition argued
that by offering streetwalkers legal accommodations to which they could resort
with their clients, the lodging house system made it easier for them "to return
to an ordered private life, since they now could reside anywhere in a respectable
fashion." In the eyes of prostitutes, the institution of the lodging house was
preferable because it allowed them "to change at any time the places where they
can legally solicit, so that they would be free in every respect."[39]

Registered prostitutes and brothel keepers were clearly concerned about
reducing competition from unlicensed prostitutes. To achieve this goal, they
utilized certain regulationist arguments about the greater hygienic safety of supervised hotels. As they explained, the establishment of official lodging houses
also would constitute an effective means of suppressing illegal brothels, whose
proliferation "gravely endangers Hamburg's tourism and the reputation of our
hometown." These references to illegal prostitution highlight another reason
why registered prostitutes aligned themselves with their employers: for brothel
owners and regulated prostitutes alike, clandestine streetwalkers posed an economic threat. From the perspective of licensed prostitutes, illegal streetwalkers
were "free riders" who were able to avoid the rigid hygienic and police controls
they themselves were subjected to. Therefore, they supported plans for a system that would treat different groups of prostitutes in a more equal way. Ironi-
cally, this meant that registered prostitutes favored the extension of certain
state controls over women who engaged in prostitution.

Prostitutes' resistance against the closure of regulated brothels in Hamburg
was no isolated incident. In June 1927—four months before the nationwide
abolition of regulationism—twenty-four Berlin *Kontrollmädchen* petitioned
the Prussian government to uphold state regulation.[40] All of the women had
enrolled prior to World War I and thus were long-term professionals. The petitioners stressed regulationism's hygienic advantages. Illegal streetwalkers, they
argued, tended to avoid medical treatment for VD due to their "ignorance and
false shame." By contrasting the "amateurish" behavior of their unlicensed com-
petitors with their own hygienic expertise, the *Kontrollmädchen* highlighted
professional prostitution's beneficial functions for society.

How many married men come to us because their own wives are incapacitated by diseases. Single men cannot always afford a serious relationship because at the moment everyone is suffering financially. The consequences [of abolition] will be illegitimate children creating a burden for the state. And how many more sexual murders (*Lustmorde*) will be recorded ... as a result of an overstraining of the nerves.[41]

By providing a hygienically and morally "safe" outlet for the sexually deprived, *Kontrollmädchen* viewed themselves as fulfilling vital roles in preventing social disorder and "venereal pollution." The Berlin and Hamburg examples underscore the powerful impact of normalization on prostitutes' conceptions of their sexuality. In Weimar-era prostitutes' own accounts, prostitution typically is cleansed of any potentially subversive erotic associations; rather, venal sex is presented as a sanitized, strictly functional activity.

In the years prior to the decriminalization of prostitution, Weimar-era *Kontrollmädchen* frequently turned regulationism—a system originally devised to isolate prostitutes from respectable society in an effort to protect the latter against the moral and hygienic dangers emanating from the prostitute body— into a vehicle for claiming a special, socially indispensable expertise. This hygienically trained sexual expertise formed the basis of registered prostitutes' claims for recognition as useful members of the community with legitimate expectations for the protection of their professional and economic interests. Registered prostitutes' partial reshaping of regulationist rhetoric sheds light on the limited parameters of resistance within the system of state-regulated prostitution. Regulationism's nationwide abolition offered prostitutes expanded opportunities for challenging dominant sexual discourse and for advancing new demands for legal rights that differed qualitatively from earlier modes of prostitutes' protests.

From the Protection of Professional Interests to the Defense of Legal Rights: The Impacts of Decriminalization on Prostitutes' Political Activism

The Law for Combating Venereal Diseases (Gesetz zur Bekämpfung der Geschlechtskrankheiten, or anti-VD law) of October 1927 upheld the criminal code's ban on brothels yet decriminalized most forms of prostitution.[42] Street soliciting remained illegal in towns smaller than 15,000 and in the vicinity of schools and churches. The morals police was abolished, and laws against procuring relaxed. Henceforth, landlords charging prostitute tenants standard rents no longer risked criminal punishment.[43] This provision made it easier for streetwalkers to find apartments; it also offered them a certain protection against exploitation. In the area of hygienic supervision, gains in streetwalkers' rights were more limited. Clause 4 of the anti-VD law specified that public health authorities could require medical documentation (*Gesundheitszeugnis*) from "persons urgently suspected of being infected with a venereal disease and of spreading the disease to others." This provision often functioned as a legal basis for requiring regular health tests of women suspected of prostitution. However, clause 4 also stipulated that, barring exceptional cases, people under supervision of the health office had the right to choose private physicians who examined them for VD. Based on this provision, major cities—including Berlin, Breslau, Leipzig, Dresden, Chemnitz, Bochum, and Bremen—permitted prostitutes to visit private specialists instead of public health facilities.[44]

The decriminalization of prostitution energized streetwalkers to resist attacks on their legal and economic rights. Leipzig prostitutes founded an association that employed legal counsel to defend its members against the police. In March 1931, the Saxon Ministry of Labor and Welfare (Sächsisches Arbeits- und Wohlfahrtsministerium) reported that "[a] large number of Leipzig prostitutes have submitted a petition to the city magistrate and chief of police protesting against unduly repressive police measures. They argue that they have the right to pursue their business like any other tradesperson, since they pay taxes and would become dependent on social welfare if the severe controls continued."[45] In the city-state of Bremen, prostitutes also challenged what they considered illegal forms of police harassment. According to the Bremen health office, streetwalkers there had founded "a kind of protective association which represents the supposed rights of its members ... through a certain lawyer."[46] After July 1932, the Bremen police arrested streetwalkers on the basis of the Law for the Temporary Arrest and Detention of Persons (Gesetz betreffend das einstweilige Vorführen und Festhalten von Personen), which allowed the police to detain individuals for a period of up to twenty-four hours if this appeared necessary to protect the person's own or the public's safety. Prostitutes opposed this practice as incompatible with the decriminalization of prostitution and sued the police for false imprisonment and grievous bodily harm.[47] Bremen police officials were exasperated by the conflict, especially since negotiations with the court had cast doubt on the legality of their own measures.[48]

Health officials also encountered opposition in their efforts to subject streetwalkers to regular controls for VD. In September 1927, Frankfurt prostitutes organized picket lines to protest the health office's order that they resume their regular checkups at the municipal hospital.[49] After consultations with their lawyer, the women declared that they were determined to oppose the measure, which in their eyes constituted an "illegal continuation of police control." They believed that "the new law with its provisions for compulsory medical treatment is only applicable to diseased prostitutes refusing to consult a physician" and emphasized their right to a doctor of their own choice.[50] The prostitutes' collective protest forced the health office to issue a statement defending its policy and led to a public debate about the issue. Even if ultimately most of the women accepted the health checks, their organization had put considerable pressure on Frankfurt officials.

Prostitutes' resistance to public authorities was a crucial factor in the backlash against liberal prostitution reforms during the early 1930s. In many cities, the police intensified crackdowns on streetwalkers and tightened regulations for the protection of "public decency." Prostitutes started to reach out to progressive organizations to gain support in their struggles with the police. Thus, in the spring of 1930, a group of twenty-four Cologne prostitutes appealed to the German League for Human Rights (Deutsche Liga für Menschenrechte) for help. In a letter reprinted in the left-wing journal *Die Weltbühne*, the women described how the Cologne police "hunted them down."[51] A large contingent of plainclothes policemen constantly were engaged in identifying streetwalkers; if a woman addressed one of them, she was immediately arrested and taken into custody. Conditions in the police prison were so primitive and unhygienic that one detainee had caught pneumonia there. The prostitutes urged the league to take up their case as "ostracized human beings ... [who] also have a right to live" and stressed that they too were "people's comrades" (*Volksgenossen*) whose "barbarian treatment" through police officials had to be stopped.[52]

Similarly, Berlin prostitutes protested against intensified repression through the police. In April 1930, Maria Schneider petitioned Prussia's minister of the interior "on behalf of a larger group of prostitutes residing in Berlin's working-class neighborhood."[53] The women, who solicited in the area surrounding Alexanderplatz, objected "that a veritable hunt is organized against us ... so that we no longer can enter the lodging houses." They criticized the class bias of this measure: "In the elegant neighborhoods, the same thing [i.e., prostitution] is done on a much grander scale than in our working-class neighborhood." However, no measures were taken against upper-class prostitutes because their clientele included only "better gentlemen." The Alexanderplatz prostitutes maintained that their lower-class customers had the same right to sexual gratification as the elites: "You, *Herr Minister*, have to admit that a man with a lower income also once in a while wants and needs to consort with a woman without worrying about impregnating her." If the minister could not act on their behalf, the women considered hiring a lawyer and approaching members of the Reichstag.

As the Cologne and Berlin examples show, even under conditions of increasing repression, Weimar-era *Kontrollmädchen* continued to organize in defense of their rights and professional interests. Recent gains in prostitutes' legal status significantly strengthened women's ability to challenge the continuation of certain regulationist practices such as arbitrary arrests and required medical exams for VD. In this way, *rights* became a major facilitator in enabling prostitutes to challenge predominant sexual discourse in new ways and to formulate a professional identity breaking more decisively with key elements of state-regulated prostitution.

Conclusion

To what extent does Foucault's conception of resistance help us understand the specific features and dynamics of prostitutes' political activism during the Weimar Republic? In volume 1 of *History*, Foucault emphasized the immanence of resistance to predominant sexual discourse. Resistances, he claimed, "are the odd term in relations of power; they are inscribed in the latter as an irreducible opposite."[54] This analysis captures important aspects of prostitutes' mobilization in 1920s Germany. Especially prior to 1927, prostitutes' organizations focused on ameliorating state-regulated prostitution rather than replacing the system with a radically different alternative. *Kontrollmädchen* internalized major regulationist arguments about the dangers of VD and illegal prostitution, and they justified many of their demands in conventional regulationist terms. In this sense, one could argue that a substantial portion of prostitutes' resistance took place within the parameters of predominant sexual discourse. A similar point could be made about the process by which prostitutes came to conceive of themselves as political actors. As we have seen, *Kontrollmädchen* often expressed a strong sense of their own hygienic expertise, which functioned as a major component of registered prostitutes' individual and collective professional identity. In stressing their own crucial contribution to the prevention of "venereal pollution" and "immorality," *Kontrollmädchen* at least partly reaffirmed established moral and sexual conventions.

And yet, Weimar-era prostitutes' resistance to regulationist practices also reworked predominant sexual discourse in significant ways. Based on their special expertise in sexual hygiene, prostitutes raised claims for social recognition and respect incompatible with regulationism's basic tenets and misogynist underpinnings. In the years after 1927, *Kontrollmädchen* used their recently won legal rights to launch more fundamental challenges against the authorities and to seek out alliances with progressive groups in civil society. The case of 1920s prostitutes' movements sheds new light on some of the preconditions of important qualitative shifts in the nature of resistance against predominant sexual discourse. Demands for prostitutes' rights were utterly alien to the logic of state-regulated prostitution; this also explains the viciousness of the conservative backlash against prostitution reform during the early 1930s. Prostitutes' intensified focus on claims to legal and civil rights after 1927 arguably marked a point in the development of their movement at which their resistance assumed a hitherto unprecedented measure of relative autonomy from prevailing sexual discourse. Prostitutes' new access to rights thus caused a significant rupture in the established field of strategic power relationships constitutive of the early twentieth-century German apparatus of "sexuality."

Notes

1. Petition of 1 February 1922, in Hessisches Hauptstaatsarchiv Wiesbaden, 405 (Regierungspräsident Wiesbaden)/6721, 146–94.
2. Michel Foucault, *The History of Sexuality,* vol. 1: *An Introduction,* trans. Robert Hurley (New York, 1990), 92–93.
3. Ibid., 96.
4. For the broader context of anti-venereal policies in modern Germany, see Lutz Sauerteig, *Krankheit, Sexualität, Gesellschaft: Geschlechtskrankheiten und Gesundheitspolitik in Deutschland im 19. und frühen 20. Jahrhundert* (Stuttgart, 1999).
5. On the history of state-regulated prostitution in Germany, see esp. Richard J. Evans, "Prostitution, State and Society in Imperial Germany," *Past and Present* no. 70 (1976): 106–29; Regina Schulte, *Sperrbezirke: Tugendhaftigkeit und Prostitution in der bürgerlichen Welt* (Frankfurt am Main, 1979); and Michaela Freund-Widder, *Frauen unter Kontrolle: Prostitution und ihre staatliche Bekämpfung in Hamburg vom Ende des Kaiserreichs bis zu den Anfängen der Bundesrepublik* (Münster, 2003).
6. This apt translation of *Kasernierung* is taken from Nancy Reagin, "'A True Woman Can Take Care of Herself': The Debate over Prostitution in Hanover, 1906," *Central European History* 24, no. 4 (1991): 347–80, esp. 364.
7. On the ways in which regulationism limited working-class women's choices between different social identities, see Judith R. Walkowitz and Daniel J. Walkowitz, "'We Are No Beasts of the Field': Prostitution and the Poor in Plymouth and Southampton under the Contagious Diseases Acts," in *Clio's Consciousness Raised: New Perspectives on the History of Women,* ed. Mary Hartman and Lois W. Banner (New York, 1974), 192–225, esp. 193.
8. Magnus Hirschfeld, *Geschlechtskunde,* vol. 3 (Stuttgart, 1930), 358.
9. Ibid.
10. Ibid., 359.
11. Staatsarchiv Hamburg (StAH), Senate 111-1 Cl. VII Lit. L b No. 28 a 2 Vol. 106 b, Fasc. 11, police report of 29 January 1921. For the total number of registered prostitutes at this time, see Alfred Urban, *Staat und Prostitution in Hamburg vom Beginn der Reglementierung bis zur Aufhebung der Kasernierung* (Hamburg, 1927), 98.
12. Katharina (Ketty) Guttmann and Ehrenfried Wagner both served brief terms as delegates of the Communist Party to Hamburg's parliament, the Bürgerschaft. See *Verzeichnis der Abgeordneten zur Bürgerschaft nach den Wahlen vom Februar 1921* (Hamburg, 1921.) Guttmann, a vocal critic of the KPD's growing dependence on Moscow, was expelled from the party in July 1924. See "Ausschluß aus der Partei," *Die Freiheit: Niederrheinische Tageszeitung der Kommunistischen Partei Deutschlands,* no. 7, 23 July 1924; and "Wer ist Ketty Guttmann?" *Niedersächsische Arbeiter-Zeitung,* 12 September 1924.
13. Alfred Urban, *Die Prostitution in Hamburg, zugleich die Geschichte des hamburgischen Bordellwesens von den Anfängen im Mittelalter bis zur Gegenwart,* unpublished manuscript in StAH, Handschriftensammlung 1458, part 4, 322.

14. See the detailed report on the meeting of the Vertrauensrat in the Social Democratic *Hamburger Echo*, no. 12, 8 January 1920, in StAH 135-1 I-IV (Staatliche Pressestelle), 4098.

15. According to Urban, *Prostitution in Hamburg*, 322, *Der Pranger* was published for four consecutive years between 1920 and 1924. However, I could only retrieve issues published during 1920 and 1921.

16. *Der Pranger: Organ der Hamburg-Altonaer Kontrollmädchen* 1, no. 4 (1920): 3 (emphasis in the original).

17. Ibid.

18. *Der Pranger* 2, no. 31 (1921): 2.

19. See the petition of the Jung-Bismarckbund to the Hamburg senate of 29 September 1920 in StAH (senate) 111-1-Cl. VII. Lit. Lb Nr. 28 a 2 Vol. 106 b Fasc. 10.

20. *Stenographische Berichte über die Sitzungen der Bürgerschaft zu Hamburg*, 61st session of 15 December 1920: 1789.

21. Ibid., 1790. The legal basis for this procedure was Paragraph 184 of the criminal code.

22. See StAH 376-2 (Gewerbepolizei), Gen. IX A 12 Bd.1/164–176.

23. Ibid., 169.

24. "Kontrollmädchen, unterstützt Euren Verein!," *Der Pranger* 1, no. 21 (1920): 3.

25. Ibid.

26. *Stenographische Berichte der Bürgerschaft zu Hamburg*, session on 17 June 1921 (Hamburg, n.d.), 1033–44.

27. Police report to the senate of 11 November 1921 in StAH 111-1 Cl. VII Lit. L b Nr. 28 a 2 Vol. 106 b Fasc. 10.

28. The term "underground economy" is borrowed from Timothy J. Gilfoyle, *City of Eros: New York City, Prostitution, and the Commercialization of Sex* (New York, 1992).

29. *Hamburger Echo*, 24 September 1921, in StAH 135-1 I-IV (Staatliche Pressestelle) no. 4098: "Prostitution."

30. Ibid.

31. Ibid.

32. *Hamburger Echo*, no. 447, 24 September 1921, in StAH 135-1 I-IV no. 4098.

33. Krüger's letter of 31 October 1921, in StAH 111-1 Cl. VII Lit L b Nr. 28 a 2 Vol. 106 b Fasc. 10.

34. Ibid.

35. Petition submitted by female members of the Bürgerschaft on 20 May 1925 in StAH 351-10 I (Sozialbehörde I) EF 70.15, vol. 1, 29. "Overcrowded" was defined as an apartment in which either six people shared one room with heating, or one in which twelve people shared two such rooms.

36. Petition by the League for the Reform of Criminal Justice of 5 November 1921 in StAH 111-1 Cl. VII Lis L B Nr. 28 a 2 Vol. 106 b Fasc. 10.

37. Ibid.

38. Ibid., 7.

39. Ibid.

40. See the petition to the Minister für Volkswohlfahrt of 8 June 1927 in Geheimes Staatsarchiv Preußischer Kulturbesitz [GStA-PK] Rep. 76 VIII B/3813.

41. Ibid.

42. "Gesetz zur Bekämpfung der Geschlechtskrankheiten," *Reichsgesetzblatt*, part 1, 22 February 1927, 61–63. See also the commentary by Curt Geyer and Julius Moses,

Gesetz zur Bekämpfung der Geschlechtskrankheiten nebst Erläuterungen und Kommentar (Berlin, 1927).

43. Ibid., 49–50.
44. See the various reports by local health offices in Landesarchiv Berlin (LAB) Rep. 142/1 St. B. (Deutscher/Preußischer Städtetag)/3634.
45. Report to the Reich Ministry of the Interior of 17 March 1931 in GStA-PK I. HA Rep. 84a (Justizministerium)/869, 163.
46. Health office's report of January 1932 in Staatsarchiv Bremen (StAB) Gesundheitsamt 4,130/1-R.I.1.-17.
47. See the legal brief of 29 September 1932 in StAB 4,130/1-R.I.1.-24.
48. Report about a meeting at the Bremen health office on 28 August 1928 in StAB 4,130/1-R.I.1.-24.
49. For media coverage of prostitutes' protests, see "Gesundheitskontrolle der Prostitution," *Volksstimme: Organ der Sozialdemokratie für Südwestdeutschland*, 1 October 1927; "Die Untersuchung der Prostituierten," *Volksstimme*, 5 October 1927; "Die von der Straße leben," *Volksstimme*, 2 February 1928; "Polizei und Prostituierte," *Arbeiterzeitung*, 30 September 1927; and "Polizei und Prostituierte," *Arbeiterzeitung*, 3 October 1927.
50. Cited in "Gesundheitskontrolle der Prostituierten," *Volksstimme*, 1 October 1927.
51. "Klage der Kölner Freudenmädchen," *Die Weltbühne*, no. 26, 4 February 1930, 221–22.
52. Ibid., 222.
53. See GStA -PK I. HA Rep. 77 II (Ministerium des Innern) Titel 435 Nr. 6, 239–40.
54. Foucault, *History of Sexuality*, vol. 1, 96.

CHAPTER 10

☙❦❧

Writing Love, Feeling Shame
Rethinking Respectability in the
Weimar Homosexual Women's Movement

MARTI M. LYBECK

What can a group of formulaic love stories tell us about the history of homosexuality, gender emancipation, and the demise of the Weimar Republic? The periodicals published for an audience of homosexual women in the late 1920s and early 1930s included hundreds of fictional texts in which a protagonist is rescued from lonely isolation by finding her true love.[1] The stories celebrated the love of the couple as the meaning of homosexuality. In many ways, they reproduced the standard heterosexual romance as transformed during the early decades of the twentieth century from its bourgeois origins in re-anchoring marriage and family formation to a cinematically inflected universal formula for personal happiness in a consumerist mode. The homosexual scenarios did not simply change the sex of the love object, however. Shame appeared persistently as a mediating factor in women's struggles to harmonize love and desire. A focus on the meanings and dynamics of shame suggests a number of amendments to our understanding of sexuality, subjectivity, gender, and the political affiliations that marked the Weimar period.

Die Freundin, Garçonne, and other popular periodicals produced by Weimar-era mass membership organizations constituted a print public sphere where individuals addressed the tensions and contradictions that nonelite subjects wrestled with as they engaged in defining themselves according to the "truth" of their selves harbored in their sexuality.[2] Analysis of sentimental love stories and polemical essays published in the women's periodicals reveals a tense negotiation of the new territory of love and desire open to the New Women of the post–World War I period. The sources make clear that feelings of shame accompanied sexual pleasure and desire through the Weimar period even among women pursuing nonnormative urban lifestyles. The persistence and effects of shame in the homosexual periodicals also suggests that drawing a strict binary between sexual conservatives and radicals misses an important internal dynamic among Weimar subjects coping with new opportunities in self-definition and life choices.

The trope of the heroine's struggle to choose between love and sexual desire embodied in two potential lovers was central to the novella "Bianca Torsten's Women," published in *Die Freundin*. Its depiction of the heroine's love affair with Johanna, a character who deliberately seeks out erotic adventure, explored the consequences of relationships between women whose desire was properly controlled by shame and those who seemingly enjoyed desire and pleasure without shame. The crucial role of shame was signaled in a scene at the beach. Johanna, aroused by the sight of Bianca's body, reaches out to touch her. But Bianca pushes her away with a lecture: "Not in front of other people, my dear—! Not that I care anything about people's gossip, every great person is above that. What we think of ourselves is the measure of our worth. We can live without the respect of the whole of humanity, but not without our self-respect. But to me it is an unpleasant feeling to have the exquisite fineness of our love, even if only a kiss, exposed in broad daylight."[3] The "unpleasant feeling" that Bianca could not specify was shame. The optics of shame apparent here—real or imagined exposure of one's desire to the amused, shocked, or disapproving gaze of others—repeatedly structured tensions between love and desire.

The role of shame in the conflicted attempt to define the relationship of sexual desire to love was not limited to fiction. Essays, excerpts from sexological texts, and debates carried on through letters to the magazines constitute an intertextual field for writers' confrontation with the crucial issue of desire's place in identity and homosexual politics. Connecting the lines of shame in these varied genres of homosexual movement discourse reveals the gender specificity of the struggle with desire. Although both men and women sought to represent respectability as part of their politics of emancipation, the women faced a particular need to confront the special cultural relationship between shame and femininity and to manage shame reactions conditioned by the socialization that enjoined girls to protect their innocence in relation to the sexual.[4]

This latter pedagogical use of shame as a tool to shape children's behavior can be linked with the disciplinary use of discourses of love and respectability in the periodicals under review and in the popular homosexual movement generally. The periodicals were published by the middle-class homosexual membership organizations that emerged in Berlin in the 1920s. These organizations began among men who identified as homosexual. The male-oriented organizations attempted to recruit women members by publishing separate periodicals and sponsoring clubs specifically for women. After tentative beginnings around 1924, two rival groups had become well established by 1926. One of these collapsed during the depression in 1932, but the other continued to sponsor events and publish right up until March 1933, when all such organizations were forcibly suppressed.[5] The emergence of visible female publics claiming a homosexual identity appears to be a sign of both gender and sexual liberation. But the publics of the organizations for homosexuals were oriented toward integration rather than sexual liberation for its own sake. They constructed their identities explicitly in opposition to the uncontrolled pursuit of sexual satisfaction and transgressive gender-blending associated with Weimar popular and night-club culture. By identifying with and championing bourgeois norms, homosexual advocates sought to gain tolerance or even acceptance of homosexuality from their states and societies.

It is not coincidental that many of the authors of the stories and essays that turn on the dynamics of shame were also leaders within the organizational structures of the movement. Selli Engler, author of the novella cited above, was also one of the most active figures in shaping the social space of the organizations. She saw herself as part of an intellectual and moral elite with a pedagogical and disciplinary mission that fused upward social mobility with gender emancipation. Their positioning as visible models made the issues especially urgent for them. They steered the membership away from the unrestricted pursuit of desire offered by Weimar nightlife and enforced standards of respectability they associated with class-specific social acceptability.

In urging readers to join her organization, the German League for Human Rights , Engler guaranteed the movement's respectability:

> Yes, I know why you have thus far not affiliated yourselves with any organization. In the existing circles and associations for women, one always encounters questionable elements. Because of the danger to your good reputation, you would rather avoid those places where women of our kind meet and spend your days in misery and loneliness....You respectable and impeccable (*einwandfrei*) women come to our events confidently; then certain women will no longer feel welcome and will leave on their own.[6]

Although Engler used the euphemistic "certain women," the anxiety she addressed was openly displayed desire associated with the mixed crowds in spaces of entertainment. Engler and others constantly emphasized that only "*einwandfrei*" women were welcome at organization events. The opposition between *einwandfrei* and shameless display of desire resonated with the tropes and scenarios of the love stories.

What we appear to have, then, is a straightforward case of disciplinary discourses overwhelming the emancipatory potential of sexual otherness, of self-fashioning that responds to the social norms of the dominant society, and of trivial and imitative textual production that simply mimics the ideology of the dominant culture and its sexual values. Early historians of the German homosexual movement tended to dismiss these groups as a historical dead end hopelessly mired in petty bourgeois values.[7] To the degree that this judgment holds, it meshes with a Foucauldian reading of these texts as discourses that enter into circuits of power by allowing subjects to adopt and mobilize the tools of discipline and self-management. Sexual pleasure is contained and denied, but that other pleasure of mastery and interpretation is multiplied in this operation. As Eve Sedgwick has argued, readings like this reproduce the binary opposition between liberation and repression that Foucault's deconstruction of the repressive hypothesis aimed to undo. For reasons very different from Sedgwick's, I also want to consider the repressive hypothesis and shame together in order to think beyond the conventional interpretive binaries. My contention is that texts that evoke shame and propose ways of mastering it present an extraordinary opportunity to probe the dynamics and implications of sexual emancipation in historical context. Sedgwick's insight that the enforced orthodoxies of movements are partially constituted by "highly politicized chain reaction[s] of shame dynamics" is helpful in avoiding the impulse to dismiss historical actors' strategies as deluded or regressive.[8]

Shame hardly figured at all for Foucault, yet in the stories the mechanisms for defending the self against shame fall into the same pattern of effects that Foucault associated with the confessional: "displacement, intensification, reorientation, and modification of desire itself."[9] Shame is clearly something other than legal proscription or censorship. Like pleasure, shame implies an emotional state that is highly effective in shaping behavior. Psychologists describe shame as a state of particularly painful emotions in which the self is essentially cut off from social relations and social belonging through inadequacy. The key moment of shame is exposure following the internalized sensation of seeing one's behavior through the disappointed, disapproving, or horrified eyes of others, an optics of shame that is a particularly vivid element in narratives, including the Bianca story. Shame depends on a previous state of pleasurable engagement that is interrupted by a sudden awareness of being in the wrong. Characteristics of shame relevant to my discussion include its contagious quality, spreading readily between individuals; its ability to become generalized and invade the personality as a whole; and its formative role in identity.[10] As shame prevents an "unquestioning, unaware sense of oneself," it calls into question the nature of the self, the self's relationship to its social and cultural milieu, and the values and norms of that milieu.[11] This is why psychologists and theorists have found shame central to concepts of identity and to critical theory.[12]

In the pages of the homosexual periodicals, shame was not a hidden dynamic awaiting theoretical excavation; it was part of an explicit mobilization of authorities' theories of shame in relation to gender and sexuality. These experts constructed femininity in diametrically opposed ways. One model, resonating with a Victorian mentality favored by many morality campaigners and mainstream feminists, defined women as essentially sexually innocent and non-desiring. Their destiny was love—caring and giving, rather than passionate selfish *amour*. In this variation, nakedness, physical pleasure, sexual desire, and sex acts were all assumed to be natural triggers of shame in the normal woman. An unsigned and unattributed lead article in *Die Freundin* reinforced notions of feminine sexual shame using the medical language of nineteenth-century interpreters of gender like Paolo Mantegazza.[13] Mantegazza theorized that the logic of marriage depended on the virginal woman's shame. The husband's defloration created a debt he owed his wife; in turn the wife's duty was to continue to reenact the original erotic incitement (for the male) of virginal shame through display of modesty and resistance. Visible female desire was the sign of a whore and disqualified a woman for marriage.[14] The *Die Freundin* article circulated Mantegazza's notion of feminine shame as an incitement to male desire. Originally composed as a warning to women against sexual forwardness and lack of modesty, the text is difficult to interpret in the context of a homosexual magazine. Since the warning was that wives needed this feeling of shame, it might have been printed as an example of the problematic of heterosexuality that homosexual women could thankfully avoid. It also served to advance an anti-feminist message: "There are over-excited feminists who spread and demand sex education to a degree that would eradicate a valuable treasure that we men too usually only know how to value after we have sullied it ourselves: the shame feelings of the woman."[15] This passage of the excerpt hints that masculine women could profit erotically from the enhanced pleasure of arousing the feminine lover's shame. Shame was a gendered tool of power that could be eroticized across the divide of difference.

The opposing explanation of femininity emerged in theorists like Arthur Schopenhauer and Otto Weininger.[16] They constructed "woman" as saturated with sex owing to the centrality of her reproductive role. She was defined by her need to attract and captivate a male in order to fulfill her destiny; therefore women were essentially sexually aggressive and unable to control their physical urges. In 1933, an article by a Dr. K conflated femininity and eroticism: "For women, the erotic rules the whole being—the thoughts, the deeds."[17] This statement resonated with an analogy, frequently found in texts by women authors and readers as well, that connected femininity with sensuality, laziness, greed, and prostitution in contrast to masculinity, which was intellectual, moral, and in control. Whether women were defined as shame-filled or shameless, these theories of femininity came together as a strategy appealing to homosexual women's masculine essence in order to solidify their loyalty to homosexual politics rather than feminist ideas. Movement leaders were at pains in late Weimar to associate the movement in general with masculinity.[18] As the analysis below demonstrates, within this conceptual universe, claiming masculinity could be one strategy for deflecting feelings of shame.

Similar contentions over desire and gender emerged in an angry 1931 conflict over gender roles and love relationships among the writers for *Die Freundin*'s competitor *Garçonne*. Arguments in the debate can be interpreted as two different strategies for managing sexual shame. Ilse Schwarze sharply criticized "masculine" women for arrogant attitudes that reproduced the evils of oppressive heterosexual relationships. Her arguments reveal the influence of prewar feminism. For women like Schwarze, a single-sex world represented liberation from confining gender stereotypes and limitations. The conceptions of love she argued for were compatible with the nineteenth-century model of romantic friends: "We especially have every reason to show the others how deeply and respectably we can love; we especially must consider our living together holy."[19] Schwarze was adamant that love meant mutuality rather than the attraction of opposites. The intensity of Schwarze's need to prove to the outside world that homosexual love relationships were as moral as heterosexual ones indicates the motivating presence of shame evoked by defining homosexuality in terms of erotic desire and satisfaction. Schwarze's antagonist in the debate, Thea Neumann, satirized the idealism of Schwarze's conception of love; "Well now, even if all the many angels get together in couples in order to chase after happiness together, in the course of time it almost always seems that one of these tender beings … scratches."[20] Neumann and others on her side of the debate insisted on gender difference as formative of couple relationships. For them, the shame-enforced purity of the feminine partner was necessary for maintaining erotic attraction. The arguments in the debate suggest that for some women, idealized love served as a strategy for evading the shame of unregulated desire, while others claimed a more robust masculinity in order to reject the power of shame over their sexual desires.

Many of these contributors belonged to a particular transitional generation that struggled to resolve feelings of shame internalized as part of their gendered socialization. The reading of melodramatic novels inciting love but reinforcing virtue must be seen as part of a repertoire of discipline applied to bourgeois girls' sexuality during the nineteenth century.[21] In addition to religious and family training in propriety, the figure of the prostitute and medicalized theories of shame as a biological aspect of femininity reinforced these discursive genres. Impure desires, enjoyment of sensual pleasure, and bodily enactment of either became the subject of an interpenetrating social surveillance and self-surveillance mobilizing shame. Surveillance was thematized in the stories in scenes shaped by the optics of shame described above.

A story by Ilse Schwarze, the writer who had advocated for respectable mutual love in the debate, stages the contradictory desires experienced by women in this context. The story, "From a Diary," is notable for posing a character probably meant to evoke the notorious dancer Anita Berber as the object of the protagonist's desire. In the scene described in the diary passage, set in a gambling club "years ago," desiring gazes compete with shaming ones. The diarist remembers being caught up in the excitement of gambling when she notices a famous dancer staring at her. "Her gaze fascinated me, burned into me, and I had to force myself to look away." No longer able to concentrate on her gambling, she moves off to a side table, where the two women continue their mutual staring. In the background she notices "smiling, observing glances at us; at the next table they began to whisper and laugh." Yet the magnetic woman continues to dominate her attention, finally pulling her into a passionate kiss. "I let it happen, I forgot where I was, didn't even think that we were not alone, closed my eyes and felt only her kiss on my mouth. I had never in my life felt such burning passion, passively I allowed it, lay in her arms almost unconscious. Suddenly loud laughing and talking yanked me out of it. They were standing around us and amusing themselves. I looked at them almost as if in a dream, then I realized what had happened and where I was and I turned red with shame." Her cousin hustles her away from the scene of shame.

Yet shame does not have the last word in the story. The diary reveals that the experience of passionate desire continues to haunt the narrator. The dreaming of this seminal kiss also inspires guilt feelings in the diarist. At the same time she is nurturing a more sacrificial hopeless love. Recreating desire through the memory of the kiss seems to her a "crime against the other that I loved, but who didn't want anything to do with me." Even after the dancer's death, the narrator continues to attempt to integrate the fantasy of erotic intoxication into her life, which is otherwise dedicated to hopeless love. "Probably I was only a toy to play with out of whimsy, probably she would have destroyed me. But maybe we two would have found the happiness together that both of us hunted for in vain."[22] Mutual unhappiness forms a strange bridge between the prim believer in holy love and the lascivious cabaret dancer. Poised between two impossible attractions—one spiritual, the other erotic—the diarist never has to make the choices that confronted the authors and their readers. Although Schwarze's essays prioritized respectable love and comradeship, her narratives played on the dynamics of feminine desire outside of love relationships.

Schwarze's essay and story characterized respectable love as "holy." The frequent evocation of religious language and metaphors in both essays and narratives suggests that one strategy for evading shame was transferring desire from the physical to the spiritual realm. Ikarus wrote a series of essays that situated love and desire within a binary of this kind. She claimed that eroticism meant exile from moral community; her conceptualization formed an intellectual parallel to the experience of shame as social isolation. Her essays mapped a terrain strictly divided between the space of honor, which is connected with love, modesty, historical grounding, nobility, seriousness, and eternal wisdom, and the space of shame, connected with erotic display, frivolousness, satisfaction of desire, infection, and exile. Ikarus rejected sexual eroticism: "When people say that erotic episodes bless you (*beglücken*), you can be certain that a semantic error is in play. It should be depress you (*bedrücken*), not bless you. The apparent breathing free or being satisfied is absolutely no happiness, but rather a deep breath of new anguish."[23] Women's and homosexuals' claims to freedom, happiness, and justice depended on remaining within the space of honor by explicitly renouncing desire. The obsessive reiteration of similar renunciation across many texts suggests enactment of avoiding shame by resisting temptation. But ending the analysis here reproduces the binary of repression and liberation simply changing the moral charge associated with each pole.

Niklas Luhmann has pointed out that one effect of Romanticism on the discourse of love was to intensify "seeing, experience, and enjoyment through *distance* ... in this way, the accent is relocated from fulfillment to hope, longing, and the far away."[24] The influence of Romanticism in this sense is clear in Ikarus's argumentation. For writers like Ikarus, renunciation itself had become eroticized. Religious exaltation was the proper path to satisfaction. "One grows and becomes a personality when one considers his longing holy. We certainly don't forget or lose anything when we forget fleeting and superficial love.... When one believes he 'gets something out of it,' that is nothing more than naked satisfaction of his—let's say—'feelings'! A frivolous game is played with love.... Nothing is denied to a high, fervent longing, but sensuality turns everything to dust (*den Sinnen aber wird alles nachher tot*)!"[25] Echoing Foucault's description of the effects of confession ("blissful suffering from feeling in one's body the pangs of temptation and the love that resists it"), Ikarus's elaboration of intense religious exaltation defended against the intensity of shame triggered by sexual desire, but also provided a compensation for it.[26] Seen this way, the intensity of the discourse of love was proportional to its efficacy in countering the shame triggered by desire. Many of the authors conceptualized love, therefore—according to Romantic ideas—as a kind of quasi-religious mystery entwined with the process of education and self-actualization.[27] Shame, as an emotion that shapes identity, worked in a more complex way, both disciplining and inciting embedded subjects negotiating liberation as it made sense to them.

An Elspeth Killmer story embedded shame into its plot structure. Theo Karin is established as a "knight in shining armor" to her friend, whom she has left behind in order to study art in Paris. In this exotic location—functioning like the gambling club in Schwarze's story—another artist begins to seduce her. "Wherever she went or stood this sweet poison suddenly dripped from the walls. It was not love—no—it was desire that followed her everywhere.... In her mind she enjoyed Clarissa's appetite for sensuality and burned along with her. All of a sudden she raced around Paris. How many intoxicating drinks there were to imbibe. How many women with hot eyes! She had never been aware of it." Her senses awakened by Clarissa's passion, she "became weak." Her internal monologue reflects her struggle against desire. "Will I ever free myself from what I—through her— am about to throw myself into, she thought. Will I ever be free of her, since I don't love her! Foolishness! I am going. Through this danger I will test my will and my strength."

Theo Karin does not pass the test she set for herself. "Her thirsty lips pressed themselves on those of the other. She held Clarissa in her arms and together they drained the cup to the last drop." Immediately after this scene of passion, the tone shifts abruptly from overheated to pious. In post-orgasmic bliss, Clarissa announces her intention to enter a cloister: "I am now released from the world of the flesh."[28] Just as enclosure in a cloister redeems Clarissa's sensuality, Theo Karin's reunion with her first love confirms her return to spiritual love. The double act of renunciation encloses and justifies the narrative's enactment of sexual desire and erotic satisfaction. The rapid, magical, melodramatic restoration of all three women to desirelessness evades the shame that would otherwise attach to the erotic episode. As in "Bianca Torsten's Women," Theo Karin's two lovers embody a choice between fulfillment of erotic desire and achievement of the harmonious couple through holy love.

Both "Bianca" and another novella by Selli Engler use the imagery and language of holy love to counter sexual shame. The protagonists in both perform the martyr's work of compassionate care of the former lover ruined by dissipated pursuit of desire. Bianca visualizes her love for Johanna as a desecrated altar.[29] But the second novella is notable for placing its scenes of homosexual and gendered shame in an everyday social context. The plot of "Lu and Lie" is shaped around Lu and Lie's struggle with their different experiences of shame. Lu's frequent attempts to kiss and stroke Lie in public inevitably trigger shame reactions in Lie. In the story's pivotal scene, co-workers witness a passionate embrace in the break room at their workplace. Mortified by the shame of being caught in their judgmental gazes, Lie quits her job and breaks off with Lu, who is insufficiently ashamed. Lie readily takes on the burden of bodily self-discipline that resonated in capitalist, national, and sexual registers. Delayed gratification promised health, wealth, and respect. Deprived of Lie's influence, Lu pursues her desires in bars, forfeiting all three. While the story's construction of the proper spatial, ethical, and emotional dimensions of the couple relationship is clear, hidden in the detail of the story is another fable using social relations among unmarried women in a workplace group as a metaphor for social belonging in general. The shame of exposure of both homosexuality and desire threatens to replace both characters' social integration and contribution with abjection and exile. "Lu and Lie" suggests that the protean nature of shame might also have enabled links between shame's intimate meanings for identity and sexuality, which I have been developing in this essay, and broader issues of politics, national belonging, and the post–World War I fractures that destabilized the Weimar Republic.

The complicated interface of emotion with social belonging involves not simply a single axis displacement of sexual desire onto love, but a reading of one's own shame in comparison with other sources of shame potentially experienced by other subjects. Lu and Lie's co-workers are abjected figures of ridicule and scorn. Fräulein Haase, a special target for hostility, is described from Lie's point of view: "She was almost as wide as she was tall, had little blue eyes and black hair. You could have taken her for a Jew. Oh, what did Liesbeth discover there—surely Fräulein Haase's grandmother was dead; her dirty fingernails bore sad witness of it. And, oh, how dark was her neck! If the neck was already dark, it must be eternal night in the hidden parts."[30] The doubly suspect Haase is marked as a deserving victim by her possible Jewishness and dirtiness. Within the parameters of the story, the restoration of social ties ruptured by shame requires assuming the position of the shaming observer. Every night after work, Lu torments Fräulein Haase by throwing snowballs and insults at her. "'Turn your back or else—.' Häschen did turn around and boom—there it was, not on her back, but somewhat lower.... Häschen swore. Peals of laughter answered: 'Please take a look tonight and see if you have any bruises.'"[31] Lie laughs along with Lu, her complicity justified by thoughts of Haase's dirty neck. No ethical dilemma attaches to the petty harassment and torture, subtly aimed at Haase's sexuality by references to her buttocks and "private parts," as long as it is possible to consider her unclean.

In the pivotal scene of shame, the two rejected characters are "like two hawks circling their prey."[32] Suddenly the two attractive lovers became the victims of their inferiors. For Lie, as the story's idealized heroine, the shame of being subjected to the triumphant moral judgment of dirty racial others is intolerable. The abjection of the two characters, especially the racialized Haase, serves to make homosexuality innocent in contrast, but at the same time it establishes the grounds for belonging, respect, and protection from violent persecution. Disintegrating class boundaries in the rationalized workplace are redrawn through groups of nominally equal workers. Hierarchies that could no longer be based on professional standing are reestablished on the grounds of hygiene, racial belonging, and self-control, as well as physical attractiveness. Yet another strategy for defending against shame becomes apparent in this story: projecting shame onto those who are more deserving of its painful and isolating effects. As Sedgwick's critique of identity suggests, establishment of a movement requires the dual and mixed effects of claiming innocence and shaming others; liberating one's "natural" identity while resituating pleasure and desire in the power to exclude and shame others.

For many readers, the characters Lie, Bianca, Theo Karin, and the writer of the diary must have been figures of identification. The success of these stories and essays depended on addressing those readers by giving shape and ideological substance to conflicts they recognized. The frequent evocation of shame effects suggests that constant confrontation with others' apparent freedom from the restraints of shame incited new spirals of shame rather than allowing women to discard or challenge it. Eroticizing love as religious ecstasy and claiming masculine gender were two frequently deployed strategies for translating shame into components of identity. Shame thus functioned as a productive blockage available for instrumentalization by aspiring leaders of the homosexual movement. However this mobilization does not exhaust the multiple levels of feelings, meanings, and effects associated with shame. The staging of urgent confrontations between love and desire ensured that texts would retain significant traces of the pleasures of shameless desire.

For a good majority of women confronting the potentials of same-sex (as well as opposite-sex) desire and sexual activity, shame was very likely an automatic part of the experience. Foucault's intervention disrupted the idea that the repressive content in sexual knowledge served in fact to repress that knowledge. Similarly, the isolating and abjecting content of shame responses did not simply convince individual women to repress their desires. Instead it functioned to shape desires, productively generating movements and identities, as well as individual strategies for defense against or reversal of shame. Most paradoxically, shame, like knowledge, could itself function as a generator of pleasure—especially the pleasure in renunciation and reversal.

Although it is beyond the scope of this essay to make a strong argument about shame in Weimar generally, potential connections between shame and its dense history are all too easy to imagine: war guilt and defeat, international weakness and humiliation, and impoverishment and loss of status through inflation and rationalization. Debates about censorship, another site for exploring similar dynamics, exposed the intensity of personal reactions to the sexual images and messages that were so ubiquitous in the Weimar landscape.[33] Shame's ability to shift and transform makes it likely that the many public and national occasions of shame activated intensifying connections to shame rooted in individual histories. Shame was not the cause of the collapse of the Weimar Republic, but it can be seen as part of a complex of ideology, politics, and emotion whose decisive effects included intensified valuation of masculinity, rewriting desire in the language of religious ecstasy, and displacement. The rift between the shameful and the shameless was as intimate as a conflict within individual subjectivity and identity.

Notes

1. The sources for this essay are the periodicals *Die Freundin*, published between 1924 and 1933 by the Bund für Menschenrecht, and *Frauenliebe* (1926–1930) and *Garçonne* (1930–1932), both published by the Bergmann Verlag and affiliated with the organization Deutsche Freundschaftsverband.

2. Michel Foucault, *The History of Sexuality*, vol. 1: *An Introduction*, trans. Robert Hurley (New York: Vintage, 1990), 69–70.

3. Selli Engler, "Die Frauen der Bianca Torsten," *Die Freundin*, 6 November 1929, 5.

4. A vivid fictional portrait of the inculcation and effects of girls' internalization of sexual shame can be found in Gabriele Reuter, *From a Good Family*, trans. Lynne Tatlock (Rochester, NY, 1999).

5. Little has been published on these groups in English. The most accessible discussion of the milieu is found in Claudia Schoppmann, *Days of Masquerade: Life Stories of Lesbians During the Third Reich*, trans. Alison Brown (New York, 1996). Scholarly work using these sources extensively has begun to appear in German only recently. See Heike Schader, *Virile, Vamps, und wilde Veilchen: Sexualität, Begehren und Erotik in den Zeitschriften homosexueller Frauen im Berlin der 1920er Jahre* (Königstein, 2004); Stefan Micheler, *Selbstbilder und Fremdbilder der "Anderen": Eine Geschichte männerbegehrende Männer in der Weimarer Republik und der NS-Zeit* (Constance, 2005). For a thorough analysis of the history, politics, and social functions of the organizations, see Marti M. Lybeck, "Gender, Sexuality, and Belonging: Female Homosexuality in Germany, 1890–1933" (Ph.D. diss., University of Michigan, 2007), esp. chap. 6.

6. Selli Engler, "Viele Stimmen und *ein* Ziel," *Die Freundin*, 21 May 1930, 2.

7. Two outstanding examples of this approach are James Steakley, *The Homosexual Emancipation Movement in Germany* (New York, 1975) and Hanna Hacker, *Frauen und Freundinnen: Studien zur "weiblichen Homosexualität" am Beispiel Österreich 1870–1938* (Weinheim, 1987).

8. Eve Kosofsky Sedgwick, *Touching Feeling: Affect, Pedagogy, Performativity* (Durham, NC, 2003), 11 (especially numbers 2 and 3); quote on 64. I am indebted to the audience member at the German Studies Association, where an earlier version of this essay was presented, who suggested the connections between my attempts to understand shame in a historical context and Sedgwick's theorizing of shame as central to identity politics. Although I was already thinking about these issues, Sedgwick's insights greatly sharpened my thinking.

9. Foucault, *History of Sexuality*, 23.

10. Sedgwick, *Touching Feeling*, 36; Helen Merrell Lynd, *On Shame and the Search for Identity* (London, 1958), 27–28, 34–35.

11. Lynd, *On Shame*, 30.

12. Sedgwick, *Touching Feeling*, 115–16; Lynd, *On Shame*, 57.

13. Mantegazza published several titles explaining sexual physiology. The first published in German was Paolo Mantegazza, *Die Physiologie der Liebe* (Jena, 1877).

14. My summary of Mantegazza relies on Thomas Medicus, *"Die große Liebe": Ökonomie und Konstruktion der Körper im Werke von Frank Wedekind* (Marburg, 1982), 4–16.

15. "Vom Schamgefühl der Frau," *Die Freundin*, 13 August 1930, 2.

16. Dr. Zenon, "Schopenhauer über die Frau," *Menschenrecht* 6, no. 12 (1928): 14–16; Otto Weininger, "Geschlecht und Charakter: 'Die emancipierte Frau,'" *Die Freundin*, 14 January 1931, 2–3.

17. Dr. K., "Die körperliche und seelische Struktur des Homosexuellen," *Die Freundin*, 17 February 1933, 2.

18. This masculinity strategy is discussed at much greater length in "Dancing, Struggle, and Work: The Uncertain Boundaries of the Female Homosexual Public Sphere in Weimar Berlin," chapter 6 in Lybeck, "Gender, Sexuality, and Belonging."

19. Ilse Schwarze, "Ist Männlichkeit gleichbedeutend mit Intelligenz?" *Garçonne*, no. 20 (1931): 1–2.
20. Thea Neumann, "Diskussion und Widerspruchsgeist," *Garçonne*, no. 22 (1931): 1–2, quote on 1.
21. See Irene Hardach-Pinke, "Managing Girls' Sexuality among the German Upper Classes," in *Secret Gardens, Satanic Mills: Placing Girls in European History, 1750–1960*, ed. Mary Jo Maynes, Birgitte Søland, and Christina Benninghaus (Bloomington, IN, 2005), 101–14.
22. Schwarze, "Aus einem Tagebuch," *Die Freundin*, 23 April 1930, 2–3.
23. Ikarus, "Von der Sehnsucht," *Garçonne*, no. 6 (1931): 6.
24. Niklas Luhmann, *Liebe als Passion: Zur Codierung von Intimität* (Frankfurt am Main, 1982), 172. Italics in original.
25. Ikarus, "Von der Sehnsucht," 6.
26. Foucault, *History of Sexuality*, 23.
27. See Luhmann, *Liebe als Passion*, 172. Many of the puzzling excesses of the stories are enumerated in Luhmann's description of the contribution to the semantics of love made by *Sturm und Drang* and German Romanticism—self-torture, oscillation between passion and friendship, the ideal as representative of the paradox of autonomy and submission, the important role of accident or fate in bringing the lovers together, romantic love as the privileged site of personal happiness and fulfillment (170–82).
28. E. Killmer, "Theo Karin und die Liebe," *Die Freundin*, 8 January 1930, 3–5.
29. Engler, "Die Frauen der Bianca Torsten," 3.
30. Selli Engler, "Lu und Lie," *Frauenliebe* 3, no. 50 (1928): 3.
31. Engler, "Lu und Lie," *Frauenliebe* 3, no. 51/52 (1928): 3.
32. Engler, "Lu und Lie," *Frauenliebe* 4, no. 4 (1929): 5.
33. For a close analysis of censorship struggles in the context of female homosexuality, see chapter 5, "A Public Nuisance: The Politics of Embarrassment in the German Public Sphere," in Lybeck, "Gender, Sexuality, and Belonging." For a full treatment of censorship, Klaus Petersen, *Zensur in der Weimarer Republik* (Stuttgart, 1995).

CHAPTER 11

∾ː∾

Transsexual
Herculine Barbin Meets "Liebe Marta"

PHILIPP SARASIN

E ven more than twenty-five years after Michel Foucault's death in 1984—
and longer still since his seminal *History of Sexuality*—any serious attempt
to write histories of sexualities seems necessarily to depend more or less on the
Foucauldian framework. That is not by chance, for without Foucault's work it
would have been almost impossible, or at least very difficult, not only to address the history of sexuality as an object of academic inquiry, but to do so with
a critical stance vis-à-vis the traditionally assumed "naturalness" or anthropo-
logical "universality" of sexuality. Therefore, it is no small endeavor to try to go
somehow "beyond" this conceptual framework, which today is basically our
own, and to aim at a post-Foucauldian history of sexuality.

It goes without saying that we should try to avoid falling into the well-
known lures and traps derived from a simplistic idea of sex as "nature." But
as I will argue in this chapter, the target of Foucault's critique was not primarily the *nature* of sexuality as such—not least because Foucault believed in
the possibilities of sexual *jouissance* as a corporal experience[1]—but the *symbolic
regulation* of the sex, or what is called "the Law" in the language of Lacanian
psychoanalysis.[2] It is in this sense that he dismissed all those nineteenth-century discourses that literally staged a historically specific form of sexuality, as it
eventually came to hegemonic power within bourgeois society from the end of
the eighteenth century onward, as allegedly being "natural." In a recent book, I
have shown in some detail how Foucault was not the cultural theorist opposing
"discourse" strictly to "nature" in the way in which he is frequently depicted.[3]
Rather, Foucault *did* accept the possibility of a scientific description of nature
or the body, say by biologists or geneticists.[4] What he was opposed to was,
more specifically, the pretensions of sexual pathologists and psychiatrists to
define (for other people, of course) the "true" nature and the "norms" of sexual

desire, and their aim to normalize the lust of the body within the concepts of bourgeois reproductive sexuality.

There being no doubt about that, there is hence no need to discuss this further. Much more interesting is the question of Foucault's position concerning the Law. I will argue that in seeking new possibilities for a post-Foucauldian history of sexuality, we should reconsider his rather idealistic refutation of the Law, and at the same time his "vitalistic"[5] (as Gilles Deuleuze has put it) belief that there is a space of sexual pleasure beyond any regulation by a symbolic system of cultural norms.

In what follows I will discuss these questions by examining cases of trans- and intersexuality, that is, cases in which it is difficult or impossible to assign so-called sexual identity within the framework of heterosexuality.[6] As my title suggests, I will begin by briefly recalling the famous example of the hermaphrodite Herculine Barbin, the author of a nineteenth-century diary published in 1978 by Michel Foucault, for which Foucault wrote a notable preface. Next, I will present some cases of trans- and intersexuality drawn from a large archive of 17,000 documents in Zurich that I have been working on with a research team of graduate students and a postdoctoral fellow. These documents consist of letters to the Swiss tabloid newspaper *Blick* from the 1980s—specifically, letters from readers to the *Blick* sex columnist Marta Emmenegger, which formed the basis for Emmenegger's daily advice column, "Liebe Marta" ("Dear Marta").[7] In a nutshell, I will try to contrast the case of Barbin and, especially, Foucault's commentary on it, with some observations concerning the *Blick* texts. I will argue that the difficulty in Foucault's genealogical deconstruction of a singular "sexuality"—and even "bisexuality"—is that he denies the symbolic, or at least sees it as genealogically deconstructable, even if this "Law" (I do use Lacan's term) is obviously of central importance for Herculine Barbin and for our cases. Finally, I hope to show how to avoid some difficulties posed by the Foucauldian analysis.

Herculine/Abel Barbin, Called Alexina B.

Foucault is fascinated with the life story of Alexina B., a French hermaphrodite who grew up as a girl and was educated as a woman teacher, and who was later on forced by doctors and judges to declare his/her "true" sex as a man. Foucault is expressly interested in the fact that this report allegedly describes a feminine, "intense monosexuality of religion and school life": a "world of feelings—enthusiasm, pleasure, sorrow, warmth, sweetness, bitterness—where" (and this is crucial) "the identity of the partners and above all the enigmatic character around whom everything centered," that is, Alexina B., "had no importance."[8] In this universe of pious women and adolescent girls, nobody wanted to play

"that difficult game of truth which the doctors later imposed on [Alexina's] in-
determinate anatomy."[9] Alexina's body had a fascinating vagueness, and she said
of herself: "I was born to love."[10] For Foucault, at least, Alexina is a model for
his own dream of a sexuality that transcends the medico-legal definition of sex
and the limits of a "true sex," a model for the free interplay of bodies and desire:
"The warmth that this strange presence gave to the contacts, the caresses, the
kisses that ran through the play of those adolescent girls was welcomed by ev-
erybody with a tenderness that was all the greater because no curiosity mingled
with it."[11] The text of Alexina B. (or rather Abel Barbin) is, according to Foucault, the melancholy, supremely sad reminiscence of her/his past as a creature
without a definite sex and of the "delights she experienced in not having one."[12]
Because the womanly world of convents and religious boarding schools offered
"the strange happiness, which is at the same time obligatory and forbidden, of
being acquainted with only one sex," it was possible for Alexina's sexual "non-
identity" to exist, and for "the nuances, textures, penumbrae, and dazzling hues
to be accepted as a natural part of her nature." For this reason, however, she was
"neither a woman who loved women, nor a man hidden among women … for
the inhabitants of the convent the identity-less object of a strong desire"; she
was "the cynosure of their femaleness and for their femaleness, without them
having in any way to give up their totally female world."[13]

Where Foucault is going with this argument is clear: "monosexuality" is an
alternative to a defined and determined homosexuality. Thus, as I have said,
Herculine/Abel/Alexina represents a model of sexuality that is outside sexuality, outside any sexual definition or identity. This "intense monosexuality" only
"fosters the tender pleasures that sexual non-identity discovers and provokes
when it goes astray in the midst of all those bodies."[14] The major impediment
to the free floating of bodies and desires is the sex difference itself, or more
precisely, the recognition of this difference in the context of a symbolic order
that fundamentally determines the basic patterns of sexual identity. However,
a "monosexual" context where the problem of difference does not even arise
can leave open the question of identity. In this sense, for Foucault homosexual
desire is ideally monosexual—which is exactly what fascinates him about Alexina—because only monosexual desire enables the indeterminacy of bodies and
desire, and consequently a larger range of sexual experiences, than is possible
through the hetero- or homosexual identities dictated by sexual apparatus.[15]

Unfortunately, this interpretation does an injustice to the text. Foucault
systematically suppresses Herculine's frequent expressions of "shame" and
of the "inexpressible uneasiness" that repeatedly overwhelms her, and of the
"pain" that her body, despite its obvious female appearance—as she says very
clearly—is not like the bodies of her schoolmates in the convent. Herculine has
no trouble naming the cause of her suffering: "Where would I find the strength
to declare to the world that I was usurping a place, a title, that human and di-

vine laws forbade me?"[16] It is precisely because her hermaphroditic body does not conform to these laws.

Now, to cut a long story short, I will invoke Judith Butler's critique of Foucault's interpretation. She aptly calls Barbin's pain and suffering "a metaphysical homelessness, a state of insatiable desire, and a radical solitariness."[17] Butler argues that Barbin could never have remained outside the Law: "Herculine's pleasures and desires are in no way the bucolic innocence that thrives and proliferates prior to the imposition of a juridical law. Neither does s/he fully fall outside the signifying economy of masculinity."[18] In other words, the gaps, edges, and faults of the Law are determined by the Law; they represent the limits of a given law, which Herculine realized, and which he/she could only reiterate, up to and through his/her suicide.

If I understand Butler correctly, it also means this: Herculine's tragedy was that there was no subject position for her intersexual desire, or rather, no position from which she could articulate that desire in any legitimate way. According to Butler, a heterosexual framework can accommodate Foucault's dreams of inter- or monosexual longing only at the cost of substantial suffering under the strictures of law—which Barbin also could not escape—and not only when the doctors and judges forced her to admit her "true" sex.

Gender Blurring

I would like to turn now, in the second part of this essay, to the advice column "Liebe Marta" in the popular Swiss tabloid newspaper *Blick*. To help flesh out the media logic that governed this column, and also influenced the letters, let me make three preliminary remarks:

(1) In 1980, when her column first appeared, the voice behind "Liebe Marta" quickly became an authority that the broad readership of *Blick* assumed had something to say about "everything," but especially about problems pertaining to sex and relationships with which they could identify. Judging from the many comments about her in the letters, for her correspondents she represented a genuine *sujet supposé savoir* (one who is supposed to know), as Lacan said, or more precisely, a "small big Other," to use Slavoj Žižek's term.[19] They entrusted her with their most intimate secrets and fears, often in a rough scrawl and not infrequently with spelling errors. Marta answered each letter personally and with care, regardless of whether she actually published the letters in her daily column or not.

(2) Most writers knew the rules of the medium, that is, that the letters constituted raw material for the columns. They knew that they had to formulate a "problem" and to pose a precise question. Only a minority simply described their lives and their often vague unhappiness. They knew that they probably

had a sexual problem, even when it was clear that the problem was only one manifestation of other difficulties.

(3) Marta had a very broad conception of sexuality and of sex roles. Her fundamental approach can best briefly be characterized by saying that it *included* nearly all deviant desires, that is, everything in the range of a postmodern concept of the "normal" (which she always put in quotation marks). She condemned on principle, consistently and without exception: forced sex, sex with children, and sex with animals. Her "norm" or ideal type of sexual relation was the model of "consenting adults" or of "negotiating" sex. Seen from the standpoint of such a norm of discursiveness, the only one who cannot "negotiate" accordingly are victims of force, children, and animals.

But let me focus now on a special and relatively small sample of cases of transsexuality in this extensive collection of letters. Among the total of 6,470 people seeking advice that we screened for the years 1985 to 1995, we recorded approximately thirty cases of trans- or intersexuality. Naturally, such numbers are only approximate values, because our source material has some gaps and duplications. So it is difficult, for example, to determine the exact number of advice seekers. But these are insignificant details.

I would like to begin at the textual level, that is, with letters of apparently clear-cut cases, that of "Paul," for instance (all following names are pseudonyms). A 25-year-old man, Paul writes that for sixteen years he has felt like a woman. Even as a child he hoped that one day he would wake up a girl. He describes how, with the onset of puberty, he began secretly to dress up in his mother's clothes, and then recounts: "I know that there are men who do this for sexual reasons, and who need to dress as transsexuals to be fulfilled. But for me, it had nothing to do with excitement; I never got excited. It's just that it felt right." In high school, it became clear to him "finally that I wanted to live as a real woman." He writes that he is not homosexual, but wants to love a man as a woman. Now that he is old enough and financially independent, he wants to have a sex change: "It makes no sense," he writes, "to try and talk me out of it. And I don't need any psychotherapy, either, because I have considered this step very carefully." Paul doesn't put it to Marta as a problem, but proceeds to ask precise medical and legal questions, requests articles from the medical literature, and so on.[20]

Twenty-three-year-old "Max" also reports to Marta that as an adolescent he secretly tried on his mother's clothes. Now, in the privacy of his own home, he spends "every spare minute" dressed "as a woman, but I don't go out in public [that way]." That is exactly why he decided to undergo a sex change: he wants to take hormones to develop breasts, "because only then can I go out in public looking and feeling like a woman."[21]

It is not entirely clear what the issue is here: is it "dressing up," or is it sexual "identity" (both in quotation marks)? But that is probably the wrong question, because the distinction is a false one. Whether the symbols are clothes or breasts, the real issue is always public appearance, for it is in public where the interplay of sexual identity and symbols produces the thing we call "identity." Somewhat more explicitly in this regard, although also more confusing, is another letter from a 42-year-old, twice-divorced bachelor who describes himself as a transvestite who gets sexual pleasure from dressing up as a woman and listening to women pee in ladies' rooms. Now, he writes Marta: "I know that only people with real problems come to you, and I actually have no problem because I feel very happy and don't want to change my life." He has just *one* request: he would like to have breasts so that he can go out in public as a woman, and asks about the side effects of treatment because "naturally I don't want to lose my virility." In other words, he wants a female chest in the way that one might want a sort of permanent item of attire, yet he still feels that he is a man. He asks whether the difference between his dressing as a woman and his identity as a man—all his life his name has been "Hans-Peter," and he wants officially to remain Hans-Peter—could cause him difficulties with the authorities.[22]

One final example of men who would like to have breasts and for whom it is difficult to distinguish between travesty and transsexuality: 45-year-old "Jakob," who says he is "terribly feminine," writes to Marta that he digs "real men" (and not effeminate gays), and therefore would like to "have real female breasts." He adds: "Please don't talk me out of it; I know what is in store for me." Marta, who reacts very forthrightly in such cases and always offers the names and addresses of doctors, answers: "I have no intention whatsoever of doing anything to dissuade you"—as I have said, she almost never does—but she also, as usual, recommends a psychology expert and a woman doctor as well as providing the contact information for a Ms. Bolleter from a transsexual support group, because—and here comes an extraordinary statement—"although you refer only to a female chest, Ms. Bolleter could surely give you a few references and suggestions and of course a few addresses of good male physicians." Growing breasts obviously strikes Marta as such a relatively small problem that she almost apologizes for recommending a support group. If you desperately need some hormone-induced breasts, then go get them. Hence, questioning the desire of the advice seeker for even a substantial body alteration was, already in the 1980s, inconceivable in the discourse of advice columnists in Switzerland.[23]

Already from these few cases we can see that, remarkably, both for the letter writers and for Marta, the physical borders between men and women are fairly porous. Or, put more precisely: they do not have a problem with the idea that, thanks to hormones, men can develop breasts and appear in public as "genuine women." In two cases from 1985, in which the male authors admit their homosexual desires—that is, the desire to be loved "like a woman" (i.e., to sense the force of a man on their bottom)—Marta even goes so far as to suggest in a roundabout way that they would perhaps like to "be" women and should thus at least consider a sex change! Marta thus exhibits no manifest pressure to fit in or to conform, and she repeatedly makes gentle, ironic fun of the guilty and "need to be normal" feelings of the letter writers.

Regarding all these cases, are we hence allowed to deduce that, as the old millennium rolled around, the entire question of trans- and intersexuality was no longer a problem? That would arguably be a misunderstanding. All the subjects cited up to now, perhaps even including the transvestite who feared losing his potency, suffer from the fact that, as they themselves write, they feel trapped in the wrong body.[24] As they and other similar subjects tell their stories, we can assume that in their youth they were all similarly socialized according to the "wrong" gender roles. Many men recount that they were raised by their mothers as girls, and in one case, a truly unfortunate young man wrote that his mother not only forcefully dressed and raised him as a girl but also in puberty had him treated with "hormone pills" and injected with hormones by a family doctor, so his breasts would grow and his male traits would remain minimal. Now "Markus" wanted to be "Monika," that is, he also wanted to have an operation to remove the ambiguity.[25]

There are, in addition, two or three letters in the sample we investigated that seem to suggest that their authors were sexually ambiguous in a physical sense as well. A man writes that lately his breasts had begun to grow and that his bottom was spreading; he was desperately unhappy. Another notes in a brief, anonymous letter that is more a cry for help: "My problem is that I am not sure who I am! It's like this: I am somewhere between a female and a male! I guess you'd say a 'Zwick' [hermaphrodite]." He continues, "Up to now, I have unfortunately not found a single partner who could offer me security and happiness. Please answer quickly!"[26] The tone here is strikingly different from that of other letters—but the archives provide too little data for truly comparative study. They only sound a cautionary note: a common, though oft disguised element of these stories is unhappiness. This helps us to refine our question: Why are there so many cases—indeed, a large majority—of, let us say, transsexuality, that are apparently problem-free? How can these authors speak so nonchalantly about physical sex changes? And how can the same discourse fall so easily from Marta's lips, or rather, emerge from the keys of her typewriter?

Anna's Case

I would like to take up these questions via a final case. In October 1984, following a column that dealt with a transsexual, twenty-eight-year-old "Anna" wrote to "Liebe Marta" asking that she give Anna's address to other transsexuals because she was looking for people with the same difficulties as hers. Then Anna wrote five long letters—all in the space of a month—describing her life and her ongoing sex change. Even as a child and teenager she felt very masculine: "When I was little I gave myself a nickname (Charly) because I couldn't relate to my actual name, Anna." She discusses her long-term lesbian relationships, all of which were very satisfying; she is also very happy with her current partner of several years. But she adds, "I am in the wrong body, outside a woman and inside a man; I couldn't really develop properly as either." Thus, three years previously, she began the protracted, not yet finished process of sex change. That necessitated a preliminary psychiatric assessment, which she underwent as a formality because "[I] have no problems … I have never been sick one minute of my life; I have always known and still know precisely what and who I am." The only problem, it seems, is that she cannot identify with her (female) body, and her female name, respectively. Consequently, at a very young age she chose the sex-neutral nickname "Charly" and later signed her letters with the similarly sex-neutral pseudonym "Bolle" (an expression in Swiss dialect for a sturdy boy or girl).

She obviously does not want to assume a lesbian identity—a subject position that in fact does exist and that would be more or less socially acceptable. No; she does not suffer from what might be called homosexuality, but from the difference between a female body and her male feelings. She describes her daily struggle to kiss her girlfriend in public. She says she should "suppress" this need (since she doesn't want people to take her for a lesbian)—"but not for much longer." Because, thanks to hormone injections, the hair on her face and legs is growing, her voice is deepening, and on various occasions she has already been addressed as "Mr." Why does she wish all that? Anna writes: "What I expect from my transformation is very simple: finally to be somebody…. The main thing is that I can finally circulate freely; I don't have to be forever hiding, can show and give my love when and where I wish, can kiss my girlfriend when the impulse takes us, and most important, I can marry her." What Anna wants, as we have already seen with the other cases, is to bring her outer appearance into harmony with her feeling of being a man, to the extent that she can genuinely act as a man and then marry her girlfriend. In this way, she wants to insinuate herself into the heterosexual matrix that currently, owing to her "outward" identity, marks and excludes her.

What that means, exactly, is clear if I cite a few passages that I omitted above. Specifically, Anna writes of her sex change: "I am having (only) a partial operation [that is, probably removal of her uterus] because after all I have read and heard about artificial penises, I think I will skip that. What use is it to have a penis and not really be able to do anything with it, since in recent years I have found more agreeable ways of finding pleasure … and, to tell the truth, up to now I have had no problems without one. It isn't the most important thing for me, and my girlfriend is also happy with the way things are between us. I don't run around naked." In other words, feeling like a man doesn't necessarily require having male sex organs, or obtaining surgically constructing ones. What matters most is the proper external signs. Additionally, the first transsexuals I quoted all primarily desired breasts as a comparable outward sign to be able to feel and to act as women. In contrast, no one in the sample of letters personally reported having an artificial vagina constructed as a further step.

How far this outward effect goes is evident in the final letter from "Bolle," more than a year later. Her transformation was not yet complete: she still doesn't call herself "Peter" (as she would like to be known as a man) but, she writes Marta, she wants no further contact with male transsexuals like "Monika" (formerly Markus, whom we have already encountered) because "she asked me questions that, as a man, I neither could nor wanted to answer. For example, how does it feel to be a woman? How do you get and give pleasure? I hope you understand when I say that this kind of contact isn't very useful." That is, "Bolle," with his increasingly male body (he writes of having more hair, a deeper voice, stronger muscles), who thus far has been able to satisfy his girlfriend despite his still female (penisless) sex, dismisses a male transsexual's question about female sexuality as unanswerable from the vantage of a man (or "man"). The traits and hormones make him manly enough not to be able to say what it is like to have a clitoris and a vagina—while he ("he"?) has nothing else!

Subject Positions

In order to draw a few key conclusions from the cases I have cited I would like to note first that there is obviously a decided difference between the time and the society in which Herculine lived and Switzerland in the 1980s. For Herculine, there was no symbolic repository for her sexual feelings and her physical and psychological being: there was no subject position for humans of her kind. A century later, intersexed people are commonplace in Switzerland and in the popular mass media. For people who are not sure of their so-called sexual identity, adopting this transsexual subject-position is a legitimately and relatively unproblematic option after transsexuality has indeed been socially constructed as a concept to cope with certain bodily and/or psychic phenomena.[27] Or, put more circumspectly: in the media discourse of "Liebe Marta," this subject position constitutes a possibility; to the people who write in letters, it means having a space of their own. We can even reformulate it in the Foucauldian sense: whether this possibility exists or not is solely a question of the historically alterable discursive situation in which people live. For Herculine it did not exist; for Paul, Hans-Peter, Markus, and Anna, on the other hand, it does.

The cases described here clearly show that one can take the transsexual subject-position even when the main sex organs don't obviously fit: it is possible to have a vagina and be a transsexual man or have a penis and be a transsexual woman. Or, as yet another transsexual from the "Liebe Marta" sample put it: "Disregarding reproduction and intercourse, we are very nearly the real thing." In other words, this kind of gender is—more than anything—just performance in the sense of Judith Butler: it is produced within the body by means of signs and gestures—here, in fact, "sex" always means "gender."

In all events, all these texts clearly show that this subject position functions totally *within* the heterosexual matrix. Here there is no "in between" but, rather, always only the signs for "real" women and "real" men. That is the central point: neither for intersexuality nor for "monosexuality" (to use Foucault's term) are there any subject positions. People in the sample who feel themselves to be in the wrong body or experience their body ambiguously suffer. As they express it, they will only be happy when they can bring their external appearance into harmony with their inner feelings—and indeed, as we have seen, *within* the logic of the heterosexual framework.

Beyond Foucault

No doubt it is possible to genealogically deconstruct subject positions, in the Foucauldian sense. But it does not follow—and here, I think, we have to go beyond Foucault—that people can be happy *without* discursive (that is, symbolically determined) subject positions. To imply that would lead our analysis in a false, naive-idealistic direction. Nor can one assume that deconstructing the historical contingency of subject positions—everything could always have turned out some other way—is something that a subject can do for him/herself. The meaning of "men" and "women" at any point in history is basically the Law that people must adhere to, including all our cases; further, as we have seen, this Law is at least in parts independent of their bodies. The subjects in our sample who could not fully identify either physically or emotionally with one of these two possibilities (man/woman) tried to do so via the makeshift solution of transsexuality. That is, they resorted to a somewhat unorthodox combination of, respectively, unambiguous heterosexual elements and physical traits. However, *beyond* this auxiliary solution that is transsexuality, and that complements the symbolic possibility of being "man" or "woman," there awaits no freedom for those without identity, no "monosexual" *jouissance*, but instead the horrors of the undecided and the nameless. And, we might add, there is much evidence—if not in these sources—that what overtakes many transsexuals even years after their transformation is exactly this horror of the remaining "undecided" elements of their bodily and/or psychic "identity."

This goes directly to the core of what is wrong with Foucault's history of sexuality: he ignores the obvious suffering of those who drop out of the symbolic. For us, this suffering is proof that, in our historical analysis, we must not overlook the real strength of the Law—however "historic" it might be. "Post-Foucauldian" thus means precisely this essential addition to a history of sexuality, which of course with Foucault must always proceed on the assumption that neither sexual identities nor sexualities have anything "natural" about them. In other words, "nature" is not the problem. Rather, the degree of diversity and variety of natural forms including the human body is much higher than of any conceivable symbolic system with its often very narrow and pedantic rules. And so is sex: it brings all kind of bodies and body parts into play, but it is not derived from bodily "norms" or forms and does not depend on what "the" body "is," or bodies are. Thus, again, the problems people may have with their sexualities are fundamentally and inevitably the problems of the symbolic, whereas Foucault apparently believed that there could be subjectivity and sexuality beyond any societal order, beyond any symbolic frames, structures, or norms.[28] Or perhaps Foucault only hoped or yearned for this possibility, or used the fantasy of such a possibility as a wedge against the unhappiness that the social order and the symbolic, in his observation, produced.

This is then exactly why we call Foucault a radical thinker. If you are able, as an excellent historian, to historically deconstruct any conceivable symbolic system—and let us suppose you are not a cynic—then what is the form of freedom you believe in? What is it that provides you your freedom, say your sexual freedom, beyond all these frames and norms of hetero- or homosexual desire? Perhaps the question may sound a little bit academic—in other words, all too speculative and irrelevant for practical purposes. Nevertheless, I would like to close my chapter with a short nod to Foucault's views of genetics.

It is perhaps not only by chance that in the same year 1978, when he published the diary of Herculine Barbin, he also wrote an "Introduction" to the English edition of George Canguilhem's *The Normal and the Pathological,* where he sketches his view of genetics and of man as a biological being.[29] In this highly interesting text, Foucault explores and exposes a line of thinking that, though he follows it explicitly only in a very few other texts, seems to be quite revealing of his way of thinking.[30] What is man, Foucault asks, when we take the new insights on the genetic code seriously (insights that Foucault had already taken into account in an earlier article on French geneticist François Jacob and his book *La logique du vivant* in October 1970)? His answer focuses on genetic mutation: he learned from Jacob that man is the product not only of a code that Foucault accepts as the "program" of life, but fundamentally of genetic variation, i.e., of mutation, or as he puts it, of genetic "error" and "contingency." And for Foucault, it is basically this ongoing possibility and reality of genetic contingency and "error" that is at the deepest roots of the fact that the process of evolution has led to man as a being who is not entirely "*à sa place,*" and hence decentered. In other words, genetic mutation and "error" appear as the very core, "at the root of what makes human thought and its history."[31]

Perhaps it is only due to a chronological accident that Foucault published these lines in the same year as the diary of Alexina B.; therefore, we should take care not to fall into the trap of over-interpretation … yet I doubt it is an accident. What Foucault discovers in the life story of Herculine/Abel Barbin is the freedom of a body apparently subjected to genetic "error." And he did not hesitate to look for just the possibility of a certain degree of "freedom"—baptized "monosexuality"—offered by such a bodily difference from the "normal."

Notes

1. Michel Foucault, "Michel Foucault, ein Interview: Sex, Macht und die Politik der Identität," in M. Foucault, *Schriften in vier Bänden: Dits et Ecrits*, vols. 1–4 (Frankfurt am Main, 2001–05), vol. 4, 909–924, here 909; see also Didier Eribon, *Foucault und seine Zeitgenossen* (Munich, 1998), 29–81. This chapter is based on some of my arguments in "Transgender - straight sex. Sexuelle Körper und die symbolische Ordnung bei Michel Foucault unter der 'Lieben Marta,'": in: Peter-Paul Bänziger, Stefanie Duttweiler, Philipp Sarasin, Annika Wellmann (Hg.), *Fragen Sie Dr. Sex! Ratgeberkommunikation und die mediale Konstruktion des Sexuellen* (Frankfurt am Main, 2010) 346–374.
2. See Michel Foucault, *History of Sexuality*, vol. 1: *An Introduction* (New York, 1978).
3. Philipp Sarasin, *Darwin und Foucault: Genealogie und Geschichte im Zeitalter der Biologie* (Frankfurt am Main, 2009).
4. See for instance Michel Foucault, "Introduction," in Georges Canguilhem, *On the Normal and the Pathological; with an Introduction by Michel Foucault*, trans. Carolyn R. Fawcett (Dordrecht, Boston, and London, 1978), ix–xx.
5. Gilles Deleuze, *Foucault* (Frankfurt am Main, 1992), 129.
6. From a large amount of literature covering this broad field see esp. Annette Runte, *Biographische Operationen: Diskurse der Transsexualität* (Munich, 1996).
7. See Peter-Paul Bänziger, *Sex als Problem. Körper und Intimbeziehungen in Briefen an die "Liebe Marta"* (Frankfurt am Main, 2010); Annika Wellmann, *Beziehungssex. Medien und Beratung im 20. Jahrhundert* (Köln, 2012).
8. Michel Foucault, ed., *Herculine Barbin: Being the Recently Discovered Memoirs of a Nineteenth-Century French Hermaphrodite*, trans. Richard McDougall (New York, 1980), xiv and xiii.
9. Ibid., xii.
10. Ibid., 27.
11. Ibid., xii.
12. Ibid., xiii.
13. Translated from the French version of the text in *Schriften in vier Bänden*, vol. 4: *1954–1988*, p. 120, missing in the American original version.
14. Foucault, *Herculine Barbin*, xiv.
15. Cf. Judith Butler, *Gender Trouble: Feminism and the Subversion of Identity* (New York, 1990), 135–37.
16. Foucault, *Herculine Barbin*, 52.
17. Butler, *Gender Trouble*, 132.
18. Ibid., 144.
19. Slavoj Žižek, *The Ticklish Subject* (London, 2000), 334.

20. LM-Dok. #6270.
21. LM-Dok. #1530.
22. LM-Dok. #8078.
23. LM-Dok. #8242–8243.
24. See to this point the account of Alexina B.'s case by Andreas Hartmann: "Im falschen Geschlecht. Männliche Scheinzwitter um 1900," in *Der falsche Körper: Beiträge zu einer Geschichte der Monstrositäten*, ed. Michael Hagner (Göttingen, 1995), 187–220, esp. 216.
25. LM-Dok. #292.
26. LM-Dok. s.n. (File 58/6).
27. See Stefan Hirschauer, *Die soziale Konstruktion der Transsexualität: Über die Medizin und den Geschlechtswechsel* (Frankfurt am Main, 1993).
28. See Philipp Sarasin, *Michel Foucault zur Einführung*, 5th ed. (Hamburg, 2012), chap. 8.
29. Foucault, "Introduction," ix–xx.
30. For all that follows see my *Darwin und Foucault*, chap. 10.
31. Foucault, "Introduction," xix.

SECTION III

~:~

The Politics of Sexual Ethics

Foucault consistently taught his readers and listeners to be skeptical of programs for emancipation. He pointed out that struggles styling themselves as liberatory frequently set up new norms and ideals; incitements, he noted, could also be strictures. For those uncomfortable with the sexual revolution that swept the West from the 1960s and 1970s on, it became easy to invoke Foucault for moral authority when one did not want to sound like an old-fashioned stuffy moralist who simply had qualms about other people's freedom (or one's own). By the turn of the millennium, advocates for sexual freedom—whether they were proponents of reproductive rights or the civil liberties of gays and lesbians or of the rights of the disabled or of adolescents—could count on being put on the defensive in a wholly new way. No longer was it only critics from the right complaining that hedonism was selfish and shallow and freedom was dangerous and destructive—or, in the more sophisticated variant, borrowing from feminism to declare that the sexual revolution had been sexist. Now also left-leaning or politically moderate intellectuals, wielding Foucault, delighted in accusing sexual rights advocates of participating—either naively or coercively—in the same ever-spreading "sexualization" of society that the sexual revolution had set in motion.

Revisiting the development of conflicts over sexual rights and sexual free-doms in twentieth-century Germany provides a salutary corrective to reductive accusations that the notions of rights and freedoms are not only hopelessly imbricated with relations of power but thus somehow also dispensable. All of the essays gathered in this section take Foucault's cue in carefully historicizing ethical problems rather than assuming that ethics are time-transcending; all concern themselves with the work of either experts or activists. All are centrally concerned with investigating the multiplicity of rhizomatic interconnections between sex and power, and between the personal and the political. Some work to explicate the remarkable effectiveness of the opponents of sexual rights and sexual freedoms; some grapple with the difficulties encountered by those seek-ing to make ethical arguments on behalf of sexual rights and sexual freedoms. All use Foucault but also reach beyond him to borrow and adapt insights from other theorists of sexual culture, politics, and ethics—whether returning to Freud or moving sideways to Gilles Deleuze or forward to Bruno Latour. Yet while remaining firmly grounded in their respective past moments, all the es-says deal with ethical problems in and around the topic of sex that also have resonance in our present—whether those ethical problems have to do with efforts to separate sex from reproduction (Matysik, Huneke) or with issues of gender-role behavior and sexual orientation (Pretzel, Mildenberger, Perinelli), whether they deal with questions about the relationships (or lack thereof) be-tween sex and love (Matysik, Huneke, Perinelli) or with the relationships (or lack thereof) between the pursuits of sexual happiness and social justice (Ma-tysik, Pretzel, Perinelli).

Two of the essays do emphasize the normativity potentially implicit also in liberalizing projects (Huneke, Perinelli); three analyze the writings of ei-ther medical or juridical authorities bent in some way on restricting sexual expression (Pretzel, Mildenberger, Huneke); and three explore the impasses encountered and imaginative efforts undertaken by advocates for sexual rights (Matysik, Pretzel, Perinelli). Read with and against each other, these essays spanning the twentieth century remind us both how extraordinarily vulnerable sexual rights and freedoms have been and yet also how stubbornly their impor-tance has reasserted itself. All the essays gathered here also provide warnings and resources for future struggles; they make inescapably clear that developing and defending sexual ethics will be an ongoing project. As Matysik notes in her opening essay for this section, it was Foucault himself who pointed out shortly before his death (in his commentary on Immanuel Kant's "What Is Enlighten-ment?") that there can never be any ethics without freedom. Freedom is the very condition in which ethics become possible.

Dagmar Herzog

CHAPTER 12

~ː·~

Beyond Freedom
A Return to Subjectivity in the History of Sexuality

TRACIE MATYSIK

Recent years have seen an important development in the history of sexuality in central Europe and beyond, a development that could be described as a modification of the Foucauldian project. As early as 2005, Edward Ross Dickinson and Richard Wetzell identified a shift underway in their review essay in *German History*. According to Dickinson and Wetzell, Foucault's influence, which once inspired historians to detect the disciplinary mechanisms that worked on and shaped—even "colonized," in their words—the modern subject, has given way to a focus on the wiggle room that subjects have had in their negotiation of those disciplinary mechanisms.[1] In their assessment of the field, they gave considerable attention to Harry Oosterhuis's work, *Stepchildren of Nature*, as an example of the new emphasis, highlighting its attention to the narratives that the patients of the famous sexologist Richard von Krafft-Ebing told of their own experiences. While Foucault had seen sexologists such as Krafft-Ebing as quintessential practitioners of the taxological methods that enabled disciplined identity formation, Oosterhuis's return to the patients and their narratives was supposed to depict the ways in which subjects' desires and self-formations could not be contained entirely by disciplinary mechanisms. As Oosterhuis notes: "The historian should be cautious in accepting medical rhetoric at face value, in privileging medical theory over practice, and placing the scientific enterprise of doctors above the actual treatment and the existential experience of patients. Life as concrete experience will inevitably be trapped within the contradictions of constraint and choice, similarity and diversity."[2]

Yet as Foucault and his readers have long maintained, the distinctive element of modern forms of discipline is not their ability to control or manipulate their subjects, but rather the *participation* of subjects in the regulatory framework. Indeed, one could say that the shift from *Discipline and Punish* to volume 1 of *The History of Sexuality* was marked precisely by Foucault's shift of interest from a Nietzschean focus on the subject as a product of internalized discourses and mechanisms of social regulation to a focus on the importance of individuals' desires in the production and reinforcement of regulatory practices—the source of their effectiveness, so to speak. Many in German historiography have drawn attention precisely to this dimension of inciting and mobilizing sexual desire, including most prominently Dagmar Herzog in her work on National Socialism and its memory, Scott Spector's attention to sexual self-formation in *fin-de-siècle* Vienna, and Philipp Sarasin's work on the eighteenth and nineteenth centuries (although these contributions are by no means limited to the working out of a Foucauldian paradigm).[3]

With all this attention to subjects and their desires, however, it is worth dwelling for a bit on just what kind of subject we historians might be talking about when we talk about the history of sexuality, and what dimensions of subjectivity we might be well served to reconsider in a new light. Indeed, Foucault himself became somewhat weary of his own insights shortly after he completed volume 1 of *The History of Sexuality*, in which he seemed to have painted the desiring individual into a corner that, if accurate, left little room for self-determination. Signs of his theoretical self-criticism began to emerge in the second and third volumes of his study in the history of sexuality, in which he began exploring ideas of the "care of the self" and creative ethical practices.[4]

One of his more lucid articulations of his own shift came in an interview entitled "The Ethics of the Concern of the Self as a Practice of Freedom." In this interview he did not renounce his earlier understanding of the subject as a product of discursive disciplinary networks. Rather, he explained, he was simply shifting emphasis from the passive subject as the entity on whom those disciplinary mechanisms work, or whom they produce, to the active subject who reflects on and negotiates those mechanisms. Yet he now stressed that the active subject—again, still a product of discursive mechanisms—can nevertheless make choices about how the self will situate itself in relationship to any particular disciplinary practice. While the subject cannot remove itself from a network of disciplinary practices, it can choose to affirm or reject specific practices as meaningful for the self. In this regard, Foucault strongly insisted on a rhetoric of freedom over liberation or emancipation, noting that the ontological condition of ethics is freedom.[5] Indeed, it is not surprising that Foucault was also returning to Kant in this period of his work, most notably in his essay "What Is Enlightenment?" While that essay focused on the modern subject's capacity for self-reflexiveness, one could see the moral argument forming along Kantian lines as well. Where Kant would understand moral freedom as the ability to do other than follow natural desires, or to do something other than obey the laws of nature, Foucault would seem to be understanding moral freedom as the ability to do other than simply follow the laws of disciplinary expectations. A free subject for Kant is a part of nature and yet demonstrates the ability to be more than nature, and a free subject for Foucault is a product of discourse and yet bespeaks something more than discourse—the ability to reflect on and negotiate discursive demands.[6]

In the next few pages I want to turn to a historical figure whose work might be said to be anticipating the Foucauldian practice of ethical freedom while also going beyond it. The figure in question is Helene Stöcker, a leading sexual-emancipationist active from the 1890s into the 1930s. She became most famous for her role in the 1904–05 founding of the League for the Protection of Mothers, an organization through which she advocated for women's reproductive rights on all fronts: the right to reproduce within and outside of marriage, and the right not to reproduce—including the right to sexual education, contraception, and abortion. With the outbreak of war in 1914, she turned her energies to internationalist pacifism. Throughout the 1920s she continued to concentrate on internationalist pacifism, fusing her understanding of international relations to her support for individuals' sexual autonomy. In 1933 she had to flee Nazi Germany, migrating through Switzerland, Sweden, and Russia to the United States, where she finally died in exile in 1943.

Stöcker is a particularly interesting figure for thinking about subjectivity in the history of sexuality in large part because she was engaged with so many of the turn-of-the-century discourses on those matters that subsequently became important for later twentieth-century theories of both subjectivity and sexuality. At the same time, we can see her as something of a case study about the workings of a desiring subject in a specific context. On this front, my focus on her formulation of a "New Ethic" as a concept that shifted over the decades should illustrate what it might have meant in the early twentieth century to practice a Foucauldian version of ethical freedom. At the same time, we can witness how her negotiation of discourses, moralities, regulations, crises, and catastrophes—and even some slippages in her own writing—might suggest a historiographical need to move beyond Foucauldian freedom and toward alternative understandings of human subjectivity.[7] Or, as I will suggest below, her work might suggest a need to take seriously the challenge psychoanalysis has long posed to the Foucauldian (both mid- and late-career) framework, and to recognize something of the subject that is not explainable either through discursive mechanisms or historical interpretation.

Helene Stöcker: The New Ethic and Its Vicissitudes

Stöcker began formulating the New Ethic in the years surrounding the turn of the nineteenth century to the twentieth, a time when she was immersed in reading works from the German Romantics and Friedrich Nietzsche. She understood the New Ethic first and foremost as an alternative to the "old ethic," a form of Christian asceticism that she took to be the dominant form of social morality in her era. Drawing especially on Nietzsche, she painted the old ethic as "gloomy life renunciation and negation," a perspective that saw individuals as "disobedient sinners" and the sex drive as "evil in itself."[8] She also followed Nietzsche in suggesting that Christianity was not alone in denigrating the flesh, but that residues of Christian asceticism had made their way into science, art, and politics—any realm of activity that sought "God" or "the 'absolute truth,' the 'absolute' in general" as outside or beyond human desire.[9] Indeed, she saw asceticism and any pursuit of a transcendent absolute as the basis of social hostility, *ressentiment*, and slave morality.

In contrast, Stöcker asserted, the New Ethic would seek to "establish this life, our life, as if it were valuable."[10] In particular, it would affirm the individual's physical and sexual existence. Although she emphasized that all individuals suffer under the reign of the ascetic ideal—"we all suffer under it, whether we have made this clear to ourselves or not"— she explained that women had traditionally been its main target.[11] In popular discussion, women were at once prescriptively condemned to asceticism and descriptively assumed to have little sexual desire other than for reproduction. Stöcker countered both by asserting that women *do* have sexual desires outside of reproduction: "She is actually born to love with every fiber of her being, with mind, heart, and sense, with every nerve, because she is in the noble sense … much more sexually desirous than the man."[12] She thus found medical and scientific accounts to the contrary to be inscrutable: "How men who as doctors and physiologists should have at the very least superficial knowledge of the nervous system of women; how physiologists dare simply to deny to women the senses and the desire for union with a beloved man, that will meanwhile remain a psychological riddle. I must confess that each time when I attempt to comprehend this claim, I am disconcerted and dumbfounded as if one had said that women in general are lacking eyes or hands."[13]

In the language of ethics, Stöcker further insisted that women *should* express their sexual desires. The New Ethic in fact presumed that an affirmative stance toward physicality *coincided with* ethics for both men and women. It removed the *ressentiment* associated with asceticism, enabling genuine love of the other—both neighbor and object of erotic interest. In this regard, Stöcker presented the New Ethic as fundamentally synthetic. If the old ethic was analytical, dividing the subject into mind and matter and setting the two components of the subject at odds with one another, the synthetic presupposed a fundamental compatibility between mind and matter. Casting the synthetic in the feminine mode, she noted of those who embody it: "To us everything purely analytical is the greatest offense and a passionate pain. To separate the intellect from the life of emotions or drive would seem base to us, contemptuous, immoral. Complete unity, complete desire, feeling, thinking, agreement, harmony—all of these things are what, according to our taste, make us human. To us an analysis without an ensuing synthesis is the enemy, contrariety in itself, that which kills, that which has to be fought eternally. Our will to life, our life itself, is the drive towards synthesis."[14] At other times, but in a similar vein, Stöcker flirted explicitly with the idea of a monist subject, a subject in whom mind and matter are simply two attributes or representations of a single substance, or a subject in whom mind and matter are not intrinsically at odds.[15]

Against accusations that the New Ethic was simply alternately individualistic or a new form of eudaemonism, Stöcker protested that it rather offered a more certain route to social responsibility. Drawing on her long interest in the German Romantics, she turned to Friedrich Schleiermacher as a means to illustrate how inherently social the New Ethic must be, or rather, to explain what it meant to articulate a socially responsible individualistic ethics. According to Stöcker, the key to the extension of an individual ethics to a social ethics lay in the moral ambition to love the other. She heralded Schleiermacher's claim that an individual seeking "to cultivate himself as a determinate being must be open to all that he is not," or to affirm rather than reject or annihilate the other's difference.[16] Stöcker further clarified that one can only do this if one first practices self-definition, i.e., self-articulation rather than an understanding of the self through differentiation from the other. Accordingly, self-articulation *precedes* the potential for responsibility to the other and makes a genuine love for the other possible. As a result, an ethic of social responsibility begins with a love of self, both body and soul.

In her argument for sexual emancipation and sexual autonomy, Stöcker was by no means making a case against the value of responsibilities in individual and social life, nor was she arguing for any sort of total liberation from social norms. Indeed, she suggested that norms and values should be revised rather than dismissed: "Nothing is more foolish and false than the idea that when one pursues the New Ethic, one wants to abolish morality in general. We could never do without a measure of values for our behavior. It is a question only of how values are measured."[17] Rather, in Stöcker's terminology, she was arguing for the New Ethic as an alternative to reigning conceptions of *Sittlichkeit*, which she understood to imply uncritically inherited moral norms.[18] The terminological distinction between *Ethik* and *Sittlichkeit* is not inherently a philosophically meaningful one, but contextually it resonated with complementary claims that *Ethik* (ethics) served as a meta-ethical practice of reflection on *Sittlichkeit* (morality) or moral norms.[19] But the New Ethic retained many features attributed to *Sittlichkeit*, most notably ideas of social responsibility and love for one's neighbor. Stöcker simply found the New Ethic to be a more comprehensive and meaningful way to conceptualize such moral ideals.

Taking a signal from her regular appropriation of Nietzsche's call for the "re-valuation of values," we could say that she was not arguing for complete eman-cipation from the material and cultural constraints that individuals face, but rather for a more effective and self-determined negotiation of those constraints. The New Ethic would thus affirm self-articulation, including pursuit of sexual desire, as the basis of love and concern for the neighbor, while challenging the ascetic ideal and the moral norm of monogamy. Moreover, through participa-tion in the discursive practices of her environment, Stöcker could subtly re-define the terms of moral regulation. Both *Sittlichkeit* and *Ethik* circulated in German culture, but Stöcker chose to attach her project to *Ethik*, the term that connoted a slightly more academic meaning and was slightly less tied to regula-tory ambitions. In doing so, she could create a recognizable language, a moral language, with which to argue for political and cultural change—be it access to contraception and sexual education or state support for single mothers. In her appeal to the New Ethic, then, she was neither advocating absolute liberation of the subject nor creating a new regulatory discourse, but rather making avail-able to herself and others a range of *choices* in moral comportment.

Arguably Stöcker produced her most creative intellectual work, at least on matters of ethics and sexuality, during the Kaiserreich. Yet the new valences that entered her writings in the Weimar and National Socialist years, though perhaps intellectually less weighty or consistent, raise important retrospective questions also about the sexual and moral subject before World War I. It is thus worth a brief glance at some of those new valences here.

Like several of the more radical and socialist activists of the Kaiserreich, she turned to pacifist internationalism in the wake of national hostilities. After the war she continued to focus on the importance of subjective desires—now, how-ever, fusing them to campaigns for international cooperation. "One can hope," she wrote in her book *Erotics and Altruism*, "that perhaps through the horrible experiences of the war we have learned something about relations between na-tions as about personal love," adding "that just as in relations between man and woman, also in international relations the love of the neighbor provides the best opportunity for self-satisfaction."[20] In this period she began to emphasize ever more the problem of violent instincts in the individual and their competi-tion with more nurturing or "life-preserving" instincts. At this point, however, she considered these two tendencies—the destructive and life-preserving—at once to persist across time but also to be educable:

> We now believe neither with Rousseau that in the beginning of humanity there was "paradise," i.e., the absolute good of humans, nor that we will in foresee-able time be transformed into "angels." We may however assume that we can take care to create a new spirit through an appropriate education, that the lower and destructive instincts in people remain ever more latent, while the helpful,

constructive, mutual cooperation can be developed with the knowledge of the advantages they offer humanity. Then man will be freed from barbarism, from the self-destruction of mutual murder that is at bottom nothing more than a sign of mental weakness and helplessness.[21]

The historically specific experience of the war, she argued, had caused people to forget the power of the life-preserving instinct, such that the destructive instinct seemed to dominate. But the instincts altogether *could* be reoriented with careful attention to individual development.

Stöcker's premise that the instincts might be open to reeducation derived not least from the gendered way in which she understood them. Drawing on the work of the sexologist Mathilde Vaerting, Stöcker aligned the life-creating (sexual) and life-preserving instincts with the feminine and maternal, and the life-destroying instincts with the masculine.[22] Reaching back to turn-of-the-century thinkers such as Wilhelm Fliess and Otto Weininger, however, she insisted that the masculine and feminine principles do not belong to men and women, respectively, but rather are distributed variously across all individuals.[23] In part because of their role in reproduction and in part because they had historically been spared the task of fighting in war, women were more easily attuned to the feminine, life-preserving principle. As a consequence, they were historically especially well situated to further its influence: "It is as educator to the good, not to death and killing, as educator to life that the woman fulfills her calling in the world."[24] A comparison to Sigmund Freud's discussion of life and death instincts is helpful by way of contrast. Freud maintained that the death drive only ever manifests itself indirectly, but always coupled with the life or sex drives—indeed, the former taking its energy and pleasure from the latter. If Stöcker did not emphasize the fusion of violence and pleasure, she nonetheless saw the life-preserving and life-destroying instincts as closely tied to one another, feeding off the same energy. Where Freud's death drive remained impervious to training, however, Stöcker's instincts could be directed with social effort and historical development.[25]

In this turn to instincts, we see Stöcker quite clearly shifting gears, responding to a set of discourses different from those motivating her turn-of-the-century work. In the Weimar period she was speaking much less about sexual emancipation, which explicitly engaged the language of morality, and more about subjective sources for international conflict. Yet her turn to instincts and their relation to national and international politics engaged bodily desires and pleasures even more directly than her sexual-emancipationist work in the Kaiserreich had done. Moreover, by concentrating on the educability of the instincts at this point, she was more pointedly speaking to the ways in which individuals and communities can choose—at least partially—to harness their desires to specific discursive meanings, rather than merely passively accepting the dominant biological or cultural pressures. The sexuality of body and mind became, for Stöcker, both enduring *and* open to social organization—with individuals and groups capable of shaping the meaning of desirous attachments. Nevertheless, an important continuity persisted, by which she associated sexuality and affirmation of the body with social responsibility. As the title of her book, *Erotics and Altruism*, would suggest, the pursuit of sexual desire—now understood as life-creating and life-preserving—was to enhance social flourishing, the preserver of "the most elementary and innate right of each person, the right to life."[26]

Yet a shift of still another kind occurred in Stöcker's writings after her forced exile in 1933—a shift that called into question the project of freedom that could be seen to have underlain her work throughout the Kaiserreich and the Weimar periods. Writing her never-to-be-published autobiography from exile in the United States, she began to grapple more thoroughly with Freudian psychoanalysis than she had hitherto done. In addition to fond reminiscences about her correspondence with Freud and her visit to Vienna, she recalled her participation at the famous Munich Congress, at which the falling-out between Freud and his student Carl Jung dominated. In retrospect, she found Jung's efforts to insist on non-sexual drives—and specifically on a moral drive, or a drive to participate in cultural ideals—to have been more valuable and acceptable than Freud had allowed.[27] Nevertheless, as she continued with her reflections, she revealed her own doubts about moral drives and their ability to counter innate tendencies toward violence, acknowledging that because of events in recent decades, "the Rousseauian belief in the original good of human nature had been fundamentally driven out." Moreover, she added: "The observation of people and of individuals, much like the experience of great individuals, the state, and nations since the beginning of the world wars, appears to justify Freud's doubt about the cultural capacity of humans."[28] Reflecting on Freud's question as to how long it would take until others became pacifists, she noted that the question "is now more justified and unanswerable than ever."[29]

At this point Stöcker was acknowledging most directly the idea that humans might be motivated by a violent drive that could not be redirected or re-educated for productive social purposes. But perhaps at a more significant level, she was also for the first time in her career acknowledging that there might be something about human subjectivity that cannot be made entirely good, that cannot be reconciled with moral explanation or possibility, or that might be resistant to social education or discipline. Certainly her status in exile, her horror at the violence on the European continent, and her resulting doubts about modern civilization seemed to push Stöcker to this utterance, or to her willingness to grant to human subjectivity a dimension of unaccountability.

Yet her prose had in fact betrayed her in earlier years as well, albeit laden then with promises of exulted transcendence rather than with threats of primal violence. Even as she was articulating the New Ethic, for instance, she had spoken often of a dimension of the feminine subject that always "wants to be so much more" than the recognizable, masculine subject.[30] In that case, she celebrated the element of the feminine that exceeded the heterosexual matrix and the ascetic-rational model of the liberal citizen-subject. But the feminine subject that "goes beyond" was always one that could not be articulated in existing discourse, even as Stöcker perceived its presence in the women around her: it was something, she said, that "unites the ununifiable."[31] Further, in her Weimar writings, even as Stöcker argued for the educability of the drives, there were moments when those drives seemed to take on a life of their own. For instance, she noted in *Erotics and Altruism* that, "more certainly than ever before we are able to recognize how closely death and life, killing and producing, national hatred and sexual love are wound together." While she tried at this point to tame the destructive instincts by asserting that history leads to androgyny, a condition in which the feminine, life-preserving instinct is always present to counter its opposite, she seemed already here to be reluctantly acknowledging that the destructive instinct might never be fully eradicated or educated away.[32] Stöcker's open acknowledgment in her autobiography of a dimension of subjectivity that could not be accounted for or made good in discursive terms—could not necessarily be negotiated reflectively by the free subject—thus marked more of a continuity in her thought than even she might have wanted to admit.

Given these tensions in Stöcker's work—her manipulation of discourses but also her reluctant suggestion that something of subjectivity may exceed discursive capture—it is not surprising that she has been an object of interest to historians as they work through and beyond Foucauldian paradigms. Christl Wickert's intellectual biography of Stöcker, for instance, focused on her unconventional lifestyle and whether it was as nonnormative as she envisioned.[33] In addition, much work has concentrated on Stöcker's attention to reproductive rights and its relationship to eugenics and biopolitics.[34] Moving away from matters of discipline, normativity, and biopolitics, Edward Ross Dickinson has recently thrown paradigms to the wind, interested more in the unpredictability of discourses in the early twentieth century. He has consequently highlighted the way in which Stöcker and her circle around the New Ethic and the League for the Protection of Mothers stood apart from the majority of writers on sexual morality at the turn of the century, in that her group almost uniquely presented women as having sexual desires beyond motherhood. Yet he has also pointed to the irony that Stöcker's project ultimately became the sexological norm by the 1920s, a turn that demonstrates the unpredictable shifts that intellectual claims might undergo.[35]

From quite a different angle, but still focused on challenges to dominant paradigms of passions and desire while considering both Stöcker's intellectual work and unconventional lifestyle, Caroline Arni has found in Stöcker a radical rethinking of love and its articulation.[36] Perhaps closest to my own approach here is Kristin McGuire's dissertation, "Activism, Intimacy, and the Politics of Selfhood: The Gendered Terms of Citizenship in Poland and Germany, 1890–1918," which returned to the intimacy of politics that Stöcker had advocated, emphasizing in particular how Stöcker infused the intimate into the political. To this extent, McGuire's work builds on recent studies that have overturned the paradigm that once saw the *Lebensreform* movements in fin-de-siècle Germany as apolitical, now casting them instead in a light that views the personal—or, in some cases, the civil-societal—*as* political. Yet McGuire also sees in Stöcker one whose emphasis on intimacy also suggests that subjectivity and citizenship are never fully "saturated" by the political—or that something about subjectivity in particular resists full mobilization for political or social projects.[37]

Indebted to the work of these and other historians, I want to suggest yet another path of exploration that Stöcker's work makes possible, one that takes a cue from, but is not devoted to, the psychoanalytic tradition with which Stöcker herself had flirted. Specifically, if Stöcker's lifelong project of ethics reform seems to have anticipated in many ways a late-Foucauldian ethical practice of freedom, it might also seem to point beyond Foucault altogether—and toward, as noted, the challenge that psychoanalytic theory long posed to the Foucauldian paradigm (both early and late). On this front the Lacanian theorist Joan Copjec has articulated better than perhaps anyone the standoff between psychoanalysis and what she calls "historicism."

According to Copjec, historicism assumes that discourse can account entirely for the subject: it brings the subject into being and shapes the choices the subject confronts. Conversely, in psychoanalysis, she claims, the subject exceeds discourse, or creates itself as inaccessible in discourse, using discourse not so much to reveal itself as to cover itself up. To understand what Copjec means, it might help to think of the working of the subject in comparison with the "Freudian slip." One understands the "Freudian slip" as the indirect manifestation of a repressed desire, the effort by the subject to cover up a desire through alternative or indirect representation. With analysis, so the logic goes, such a repressed desire might reveal itself more directly. Similarly, the subject uses discourse for purposes of deflection. But in its formation, the movement that brings it into being and continues to mark its uniqueness, it enacts a more radical form of repression (foreclosure, in Lacanian terminology), creating "a loss that can never be made good."[38] This subject can never return, in the sense of the repressed, except "*in* its very effacement."[39] Yet in its effacement—in its distancing itself always from its own statements and acts—it makes itself felt as subject. "To state it somewhat differently," Copjec argues, "in psychoanalysis the subject is not hypostatized, but hypothesized—that is, it is only ever *supposed*: we never actually encounter it face to face."[40] One could think of this subject in terms of radical privacy: the idea that the subject is inaccessible not only to the historian or observer but to itself as well.

Insofar as the subject uses discourse to cover itself up, to create sites of inaccessibility or radical privacy in discourse, Copjec further maintains, it epitomizes a challenge to the historian: "For the incomplete—and permanently so—accessibility of any moment to itself, its partial absence from itself, forbids historicism's motivating premise: that the past must be understood in its own terms. This is a simple impossibility: *no historical moment can be comprehended in its own terms*; the circuit of self-recognition or coincidence with itself which would enable such comprehension is deflected by an investment that cannot be recuperated for self-knowledge." Referring to the role of the historical reader, she adds: "Historicity is what issues from this inevitable and constitutive misapprehension of ourselves—from what Freud would call the latency of historical time with regard to its own comprehension. This notion of latency must not be positivized, as though something lay dormant but already formed in the past, and simply waited to emerge at some future time; this would indeed be a continuist notion. Instead, latency designates our inaccessibility to ourselves, and hence our dependence on others—on other times as well as other subjects."[41] In other words, if subjects of the past cannot be redeemed or captured fully and made present to us as researchers, it is in part because we as subjects are not fully present to ourselves. We do not make ourselves whole by recovering fully formed lost subjects from the past (what Copjec would call a "continuist" premise), but we do perform a moral task when we *engage* the subjects of the past who are dependent on us because of their latency, while remaining open to and respecting their inaccessibility or radical privacy. Whereas ethical practice for Foucault consisted in the free negotiation of discursive frameworks, for Copjec it is the engagement of the subject that refuses our grasp or our historical explanation.

Of course one need not turn to psychoanalysis to speak of subjectivity or other historical phenomena that cannot be fully explained. Dominick LaCapra, for instance, has long pointed to the "work-like" dimension of cultural products in a complementary manner. "Significant cultural artifacts," he explains, "offer in a particularly accentuated manner a variable articulation or combination of critical and transformative work (or play) on pertinent contexts, along with a strangeness, alterity, or opaque and enigmatic dimension that is in excess both of contexts and of the delimited sociopolitical work on them."[42] These "significant cultural artifacts"—be they artworks, literature, music, or something else—are "work-like" insofar as they bring together dimensions of their social, political, cultural contexts in uncanny ways that do more than merely reflect or reproduce those contexts, and insofar as they radically transform our understanding of those contexts in ways hitherto inconceivable. In short, one cannot account for them merely by adding up elements of existing discourse. Such "work," he notes, prompts feelings of the sublime or the traumatic, as it exceeds the limits of understanding in the sense of calculation.[43] While LaCapra finds this quality only in rare cultural artifacts, one could arguably assert that subjectivity is *inherently* work-like, and that to be a subject is to do this kind of transformative work—or play—in culture, even if in simple ways that may not draw the attention of the historian. Thus what LaCapra sees as transcendent or sublime could just as easily describe a quotidian element of subjective life. Similarly, resisting any theoretical orientation, Nick Mansfield has defined subjectivity in his brief textbook on the topic as something that "remains permanently open to inconsistency, contradiction, and unselfconsciousness. Our experience of ourselves remains forever prone to surprising disjunctions that only the fierce light of ideology or theoretical dogma convinces us can be homogenized into a single consistent thing."[44]

If there is then nothing unique to psychoanalysis in the idea of a work-like subjectivity, or of a subjectivity that is neither fully explained by its historical context nor manifest fully or identifiably in discourse, there is also nothing unique about the turn to this work-like character of subjectivity in the history of sexuality. Indeed, historians of memory and trauma have been particularly attentive to aspects of subjectivity that evade direct representation. In her writing about the sexologist Charlotte Wolff, for instance, Darcy Buerkle narrates Wolff's return to Berlin decades after her exile during the Third Reich. Focusing on the gaps in Wolff's autobiographies, and emphasizing the abstractions and obfuscations with which Wolff presented her own life, Buerkle importantly does not retreat into interiority or to a fetishizing of the inaccessible. Rather, almost enacting the ethical practice regarding latency that Copjec suggests, Buerkle turns Wolff's interiority over to the reader, who is left to grapple with the traces: "If she [Wolff] craved directness and projected it, too, she was also guarded, trepidatious, injured and proud. She lived with enormous gaps in her story; so too, she seems to indicate, will her readers and interpreters."[45] Similarly, in his treatment of Edith Stein, a Carmelite nun murdered at Auschwitz for her Jewish heritage and ultimately canonized by the Vatican, Scott Spector focuses on her "unruly self-representation," which works at least in part as a form of "passing," creating a relationship to multiple identities (Jewish, Catholic, female, scholar) that can "disturb assumptions of authentic, irrevocable and unexchangeable identity." He approaches her life and work as a form of "intimate history" that "is not a sub-genus of History as much as it is a challenge to it." Quoting Michel Beaujour, Spector finds in Stein's case a set of "fragments that do not conform to the stereotype and out of which the subject can fashion an idiosyncratic ensemble of metaphors where he will find himself (again) or get lost."[46]

Within the history of gender and sexuality, Suzanne Stewart-Steinberg's study of the formation of Italian citizens as "post-liberal subjects" is a particularly noteworthy undertaking, one that at least partially mediates the stand-off between the Foucault-inspired approach to constructed subjects and the psychoanalytic model that Copjec endorses. Tracing the evolution of sexed subjects—and especially the masculine subject—in post-unification Italy, Stewart-Steinberg identifies a paradox in what she describes as the "Pinocchio Effect," in which the masculine subject embodies an anxiety about its own existence, "self-conscious of its own fictional status."[47] Yet Stewart-Steinberg finds in ideology—understood as the social mechanisms that produce subjects both as free agents who choose to respond to the call of those mechanisms, and as subjects mastered by their law or their call— the best means to think about this self-consciously fictional subject. Ideology in this sense, she explains, relies on the pleasure that the subject experiences in its relationship to social norms—a pleasure that controls or drives the subject but that "is not reducible to the effects of ideology," or is not merely the subject's joy in meeting social norms.[48] In a sense, while Stewart-Steinberg ultimately continues to understand the subject as a discursive product, thus enabling her to re-create historically the process of modern masculine subject-formation, her approach to ideology allows her to thematize how subjects get produced in historically specific ways so as to make them inaccessible to full discursive disclosure. Stewart-Steinberg is thus not making transhistorical claims about the makeup of subjectivity, but rather is attuned to the historically specific ways in which "post-liberal" subjects of Italian modernity function. Akin to the psychoanalytic prompt, however, she is sensitive to the kinds of historical methods that researchers might use if they want to understand their subjects as not fully open to discursive demonstration.

Conclusion

Recent years have seen the history of sexuality moving away from its once strong focus on such matters as population politics, hygiene, and normative constructions of sexual identities, and toward seemingly more "subjective" matters such as emotions, intimacy, self-determination, and memory. Accordingly, it behooves us to be attentive to our presuppositions about the constitution of subjects and subjectivity. My discussion of Helene Stöcker above is intended to provide one example of the range of questions about these matters we might confront. She herself seemed to move from a Nietzschean "revaluation of values" (that might be seen as a Foucauldian practice of ethical freedom, avant la lettre) to a stronger focus on biological drives and finally to an openness to psychoanalysis. In tracing Stöcker's evolution, however, my point is not to suggest that any one of these approaches to subjects and subjectivity—or any combination therein—is a preferred or correct approach. Rather, my point is simply to suggest that we not inadvertently foreclose conceptions of the subject that may be philosophically valid but that do not easily fit our standard disciplinary practices.

The disciplinary focus of the Foucauldian framework provided a form of legitimacy to the study of the history of sexuality, offering an answer to the "who cares" question. But its focus on discourse in particular also corresponded well to documentary norms of the historical profession, even as it advanced—and continues to advance—the range of questions historians ask. The same can also be said of any turn to a practice of ethical freedom, or to a focus on emotions and their public formation. The attention to subjectivity as that which only gets *indirectly* represented in discourse, however—whether we are talking about a psychoanalytic reading or not—poses more documentary challenge. In this regard it is noteworthy that several of the examples of "historiography" I cite above were not written in standard historiographical contexts. Darcy Buerkle's essay accompanied an art exhibit; Scott Spector's essay on Edith Stein appeared in a journal of German studies; and Suzanne Stewart-Steinberg works properly in the field of literary theory and analysis—albeit historically informed.

My point is also not to suggest that a turn to indirect manifestations of subjectivity replace more macroscopic studies. The more comprehensive studies of bodily practices, structures of emotions, and regulatory—and emancipatory—politics continue to link the history of sexuality in meaningful ways to other crucial problematics in social, cultural, and political history. My suggestion is only that, alongside these more comprehensive studies, we retain attention to subjectivity and its *inconclusive* nature. By allowing questions of subjectivity to ripple into the present without having to be captured in the past—by exposing ourselves to its latency—we can continue to pose questions to more comprehensive contextual studies and to remind ourselves of the complex lives and desires of the individual subjects living amidst and shaping those contexts. Moreover, as we move slowly through, and perhaps just beyond, the Foucauldian moment in the history of sexuality, it seems we can only benefit from opening ourselves to non-Foucauldian conceptions of the subject as well.

Notes

1. Edward R. Dickinson and Richard Wetzell, "The Historiography of Sexuality in Modern Germany," in "Sexuality in Modern German History," ed. Edward R. Dickinson and Richard Wetzell, special issue, *German History* 23, no. 3 (2005): 297. For a very good discussion of the importance of the "Copernican turn" that Foucault's intervention in the historiography of sexuality made, see Franz Eder, *Kultur der Begierde: eine Geschichte der Sexualität* (Munich, 2002). I am grateful to the Institute for Historical Studies at the University of Texas at Austin for the time and funds that enabled me to complete this essay.

2. Harry Oosterhuis, *Stepchildren of Nature: Krafft-Ebing, Psychiatry, and the Making of Sexual Identity* (Chicago, 2000), 12. For additional examples of historiographical ef-

forts to think beyond the Foucauldian framework, see Claudia Bruns and Tilman Walter, eds., *Von Lust und Schmerz: Eine Historische Anthropologie der Sexualität* (Cologne, Weimar, and Vienna, 2004); and the collection of essays in "Sexuality in Modern German History," the special edition of *German History* edited by Wetzell and Dickinson, 23, no. 3 (2005).

3. Dagmar Herzog, *Sex After Fascism: Memory and Morality in Twentieth-Century Germany* (Princeton, NJ, 2005); Scott Spector, "The Wrath of the 'Countess Merviola': Tabloid Exposé and the Emergence of Homosexual Subjects in Vienna in 1907," *Contemporary Austrian Studies* 15 (2007): 31–47; Philipp Sarasin, *Reizbare Maschinen: Eine Geschichte des Körpers 1765–1914* (Frankfurt am Main, 2001). Outside German historiography, good examples include Judith Surkis, *Sexing the Citizen: Morality and Masculinity in Third Republic France* (Ithaca, NY, 2006); Carolyn Dean, *The Frail Social Body: Pornography, Homosexuality, and Other Fantasies in Interwar France* (Berkeley, CA, 2000); Judith Walkowitz, *City of Dreadful Delight: Narratives of Sexual Danger in Late-Victorian London* (Chicago, 1992). Provocative studies of non-European contexts include Afsaneh Najmabadi, *Women with Mustaches and Men without Beards: Gender and Sexual Anxieties of Iranian Modernity* (Berkeley, CA, 2005); Ann Laura Stoler, *Carnal Knowledge and Imperial Power: Race and the Intimate in Colonial Rule* (Berkeley, CA, 2002).

4. Michel Foucault, *The Use of Pleasure: The History of Sexuality*, vol. 2, trans. Robert Hurley (New York, 1985) and *The Care of the Self: The History of Sexuality*, vol. 3, trans. Robert Hurley (New York, 1986).

5. See Foucault's interview with H. Becker, R. Fornet-Betancourt, and A. Gomez-Müller entitled "The Ethics of the Concern of the Self as a Practice of Freedom," trans. P. Aranov and D. McGrawth, in Michel Foucault, *Ethics, Subjectivity and Truth: Vol. I of the Essential Works of Foucault, 1954–1984*, ed. Paul Rabinow (New York, 1997), 281–301.

6. Michel Foucault, "What Is Enlightenment," trans. Catherine Porter, in *The Foucault Reader*, ed. Paul Rabinow (New York, 1984), 32–50. For further elaboration on this overall move, see "An Aesthetics of Existence," and "The Art of Telling the Truth," trans. Alan Sheridan, in *Michel Foucault: Politics, Philosophy, Culture: Interviews and Other Writings 1977–1984*, ed. Lawrence Kritzman (New York, 1990). Efforts to synthesize Foucault's ethics include: John Rajchman, *Michel Foucault: The Freedom of Philosophy* (New York, 1985); John Rajchman, *Truth and Eros: Foucault, Lacan, and the Question of Ethics* (New York, 1991); Timothy O'Leary, *Foucault: The Art of Ethics* (London and New York, 2002); Arnold Davidson, "Ethics as Ascetics: Foucault, the History of Ethics, and Ancient Thought," in *The Cambridge Companion to Foucault*, ed. Gary Guttman (Cambridge, 1995).

7. There is now a substantial literature on Stöcker's life and work. Some of the most prominent examples include Edward Ross Dickinson, "Reflections on Feminism and Monism in the Kaiserreich, 1900–1913," *Central European History* 34, 2 (2001), 191–230; Ann Taylor Allen, "Mothers of the New Generation: Adele Schreiber, Helene Stöcker, and the Evolution of a German Idea of Motherhood," *Signs* 10, no. 3 (1995): 418–38; Gudrun Hamelmann, *Helene Stöcker, der 'Bund für Mutterschutz' und 'Die neue Generation'* (Frankfurt am Main, 1992); Christl Wickert, *Helene Stöcker, 1869–1943: Frauenrechtlerin, Sexualreformerin und Pazifistin. Eine Biographie* (Bonn, 1991); Rolf von Bockel, *Philosophin einer "neuen Ethik": Helene Stöcker (1869–1943)* (Hamburg, 1991); Amy Hackett, "Helene Stöcker: Left-Wing Intellectual and Sex

Reformer," in *When Biology Became Destiny: Women in Weimar and Nazi Germany*, ed. Renate Bridenthal, Atina Grossman, and Marion Kaplan (New York, 1984), 64–83; Bernd Nowacki, *Der Bund für Mutterschutz (1905–1933)* (Husum, 1983). My own reading of Stöcker is especially indebted to Ann Taylor Allen, *Feminism and Motherhood in Germany, 1800–1914* (New Brunswick, NJ, 1991) and Heide Schluppmann, "Die Radikalisierung der Philosophie: Die Nietzsche-Rezeption und die sexualpolitische Publizistik Helene Stöcker's," *Feministische Studien* 3 (1984): 10–38.

8. Helene Stöcker, "Zur Reform der sexuellen Ethik," *Mutterschutz* 1, no. 1 (1905): 3–12, here 4–6.
9. Helene Stöcker, "Unsere Umwertung der Werte," in H. Stöcker, *Die Liebe und die Frauen* (Minden, 1906), 15.
10. Stöcker, "Zur Reform der sexuellen Ethik," 8.
11. Ibid., 3–4.
12. Helene Stöcker, "Die Moderne Frau," in Stöcker, *Die Liebe und die Frauen*, 20.
13. Helene Stöcker, "Frauenbewegung und Mutterlichkeit," in Stöcker, *Die Liebe und die Frauen*, 99.
14. Stöcker, "Unsere Umwertung," 16.
15. On her small but enthusiastic encounter with Spinozist monism, see The Swarthmore Peace Collection, DG 035, Box 1, File 2. For an effort to read the centrality of Monism in the League for the Protection of Mothers, and to understand it—quite contrary to my claim here—as typical of nineteenth-century liberalism, see Dickinson, "Reflections on Feminism," esp. 222.
16. Helene Stöcker, "Neue Ethik in der Kunst," *Mutterschutz* 1, no. 8 (1905): 302.
17. Stöcker, "Von neuer Ethik," *Mutterschutz* 2, no. 1 (1906): 3–11, here 3.
18. Stöcker, "Zur Reform der sexuellen Ethik," 3. See also Stöcker, "Von neuer Ethik," 5–11; Helene Stöcker, "Das Werden der sexuellen Reform seit hundert Jahren," in Hedwig Dohm et al., *Ehe? Zur Reform der sexuellen Moral* (Berlin, 1911), 38.
19. See for instance entries for "Ethik," "Sittlichkeit," and "Moral," in Rudolf Eisler, *Wörterbuch der philosophischen Begriffe*, 3rd ed. (Berlin, 1910). Additional examples that keep roughly to the distinction include: Friedrich Paulsen, *Einleitung in die Philosophie*, 9th ed. (Stuttgart and Berlin, 1903); Oswald Külpe, *Einleitung in die Philosophie*, 7th ed. (Leipzig, 1915); Friedrich Kirchner, *Wörterbuch der philosophischen Grundbegriffe*, 4th ed., ed. Carl Michaëlis (Leipzig, 1903); Heinrich Schmidt, *Philosophische Wörterbuch*, 4th ed. (Leipzig, 1919); Christian von Ehrenfels, *Grundbegriffe der Ethik* (Wiesbaden, 1907).
20. Helene Stöcker, *Erotik und Altruismus* (Leipzig, 1924), 72–73.
21. Helene Stöcker, *Die Frau und die Heiligkeit des Lebens* (Leipzig, 1921), 8.
22. Ibid., 2–3.
23. Stöcker, *Erotik und Altruismus*, 67–68.
24. Ibid., 3.
25. See Sigmund Freud, *Jenseits des Lustprinzips* in *Gesammelte Werke, chronologisch geordnet*, ed. Anna Freud et al., 18 vols. (London, 1940), vol. 13.
26. Stöcker, *Frau und Heiligkeit*, 9.
27. Helene Stöcker, "Psychoanalyse 1911/1912," in the Swarthmore Peace Collection, DG 035 Box 1, Folder 5, pages 3–5. See also Ludger M. Hermanns, "Helene Stöckers autobiographisches Fragment zur Psychoanalyse," *Luzifer-Amor* 4, no. 8 (1991): 177–80.
28. Stöcker, "Psychoanalyse," 10.
29. Ibid., 12.

30. Stöcker, "Unsere Umwertung," 11.
31. Ibid., 14.
32. Stöcker, *Erotik und Altruismus*, 15–16, 69.
33. Wickert, *Helene Stöcker*.
34. Richard Evans, *The Feminist Movement in Germany 1894–1933* (London, 1976): 130–39; Marie-Luise Janssen-Jurreit, "Nationalbiologie, Sexualreform und Gebürten-rückgang—Über die Zusammenhänge von Bevölkerungspolitik und Frauenbewegung um die Jahrhundertwende," in *Die Überwindung der Sprachlosigkeit*, ed. Gabriele Dietz (Darmstadt and Neuwied, 1978), 139–75; Rosemarie Schumann, "Helene Stöcker: Verkünderin und Verwirklicherin," in *Alternativen: Schicksale deutsche Bürger*, ed. Olaf Graf (Berlin, 1987), 163–95; Paul Weindling, *Health, Race, and German Politics Between National Unification and Nazism 1870–1945* (Cambridge, 1989), esp. 250–57; Cornelia Usborne, *The Politics of the Body in Weimar Germany: Women's Reproductive Rights and Duties* (Ann Arbor, 1992), esp. 7–8; Ann Taylor Allen, "German Radical Feminism and Eugenics, 1900–1908," *German Studies Review* 11 (1988): 31–56; Ann Taylor Allen, *Feminism and Motherhood in Germany*, 173–205.
35. Edward Ross Dickinson, "'A Dark, Impenetrable Wall of Complete Incomprehension': The Impossibility of Heterosexual Love in Imperial Germany," *Central European History* 40 (2007): 467–97.
36. Caroline Arni, "Simultaneous Love: An Argument on Love, Modernity, and the Feminist Subject at the Beginning of the Twentieth Century," *European Review of History—Revue européene d'Histoire* 11, no. 2 (2004): 185–205.
37. Kristin McGuire, "Activism, Intimacy, and the Politics of Selfhood: The Gendered Terms of Citizenship in Poland and Germany, 1890–1918" (Ph.D. Dissertation, University of Michigan, 2004).
38. Joan Copjec, "Introduction," in Copjec, ed., *Supposing the Subject* (New York, 1994), ix.
39. Ibid., xi.
40. Ibid., xi. An interesting non-Lacanian psychiatric parallel to the subject as a constructed fantasy can be found in Robert Michels, "Overview of an Evaluation," in *Approach to the Psychiatric Patient: Case-Based Essays*, ed. John W. Barnhill (Washington, DC, and London, 2009), 434–37.
41. Copjec, "Introduction," ix.
42. Dominick LaCapra, *History in Transit: Experience, Identity, Critical Theory* (Ithaca, 2004), 10–11.
43. Ibid., 11.
44. Nick Mansfield, *Subjectivity: Theories of the Self from Freud to Haraway* (New York, 2000), 6–7.
45. Darcy Buerkle, "Points of Departure," in *Everything I Need*, ed. Matthew Buckingham (London, 2007), 26.
46. Scott Spector, "Edith Stein's Passing Gestures: Intimate Histories, Empathic Portraits," *New German Critique* 75 (1998): 32; citing Michel Beaujour, *Poetics of the Literary Self-Portrait*, trans. Yara Milos (New York, 1991), 197.
47. Suzanne Stewart-Steinberg, *The Pinocchio Effect: On Making Italians (1860–1920)* (Chicago, 2007), 5.
48. Ibid., 9.

~:~

CHAPTER 13

Homosexuality in the Sexual Ethics of the 1930s

A Values Debate in the Culture Wars between Conservatism, Liberalism, and Moral-National Renewal

ANDREAS PRETZEL

At the beginning of the 1930s, a shift toward a more authoritarian, conservative social and cultural politics took place in Germany. Accompanied by an economic crisis, political turbulence, and the rise of the National Socialists, the political aspect of this change has been described in many different ways.[1] Its cultural dimension, however, has received only cursory attention.

A pathbreaking study entitled *Berlin Alexanderplatz: Radio, Film, and the Death of Weimar Culture* was published in 2006 by Peter Jelavich. He did not interpret Hitler's seizure of power as the decisive turning point for cultural politics, but rather dates the end of pluralistic cultural production at the 1930/31 New Year. Jelavich analyzes the cultural shift on the basis of debates surrounding the film and radio versions of Alfred Döblin's famous novel *Berlin Alexanderplatz*. Jelavich elucidates the political anxieties of the time and increasing attempts at censorship, which marked a creeping process of adaptation to the increasingly powerful conservative *Zeitgeist* that eventually culminated in self-censorship. He characterizes his study as "a cautionary tale about how fear of outspoken right-wing politicians can cause cultural production to be curbed and eventually eliminated as a critical counterforce to politics."[2] For the radio play and film versions, Döblin had tellingly removed those portions in which homosexuality was positively represented.[3]

The topic had had crucial significance for the novel, but by 1930 it was no longer deemed portrayable in the mass media of the Weimar Republic. Yet that is not to say that homosexuality was no longer talked about from that point forward. To the contrary, in scholarly discourse as well as the mass media homosexuality remained an ever-present topic. In the humanities, the study of homosexuality as an ethical problem can even be said to have experienced something of a heyday. In the remarkably numerous publications on "sexual ethics," homosexuality was a topic of great significance. What catalyzed this torrent of publications?

Homosexuality and the Reform of Criminal Law

On the 16 October 1929, the Reichstag committee on criminal law ruled with a slim, one-vote majority in favor of a partial decriminalization of homosexuality, which had been criminalized since 1871.[4] To be sure, this was only the back-room decision of a committee of the German Reichstag, and the entire parliament would have had to confirm or reject it. But this committee's preliminary resolution was so decisive in terms of setting the course of the debate that it made headlines and prompted press releases. In particular, it unsettled the conservative critics of Weimar liberalism and motivated them to launch a comprehensive counterattack.

The decision concerning the criminality of homosexuality was used as a rallying cry for taking stock of Weimar culture by condemning its excesses and searching for new, modern forms of propriety and morality.[5] "Sexual ethics" became one component of a debate in the cultural struggle between conservatism, liberalism, and what came to be known as a movement for "moral-national renewal."

It was indeed the case that complaints about a supposed "chaotic state of moral concepts" or "discontent with civilization"—to borrow Sigmund Freud's terminology from his psychoanalytic diagnosis of his era in 1930—were very wide-ranging.[6] Familial and marital life, along with nonmarital relationships and intergenerational dynamics, had all changed radically with the modernization of urban life during the 1920s. Traditional values and a sense of attachment to a particular locale yielded to new ways of life that were shaped by the mass media, consumer culture, sports, the pursuit of enjoyment and self-fulfillment, and new social movements like the women's and youth movements.

The homosexual movement had also attracted public attention and recognition. The movement's occasional coalitions with like-minded groups seeking the reform of the criminal code, its self-confident pursuit of publicity, and its political contacts and demands were interpreted in conservative circles as threatening, disruptive maneuvers and criticized as "homosexual propaganda." Nonetheless, advocates of reform found a supporter of decriminalization in the chairman of the criminal code committee. Professor Wilhelm Kahl (1849–1932) had found an audience for the movement's demands through his work as the former director of the Prussian Evangelical General Synod and as the rector of Berlin University; it was his vote that had made the difference in the Reichstag committee's decision to reform the law on homosexuality. His authority had even led—to name just one example—to conservatives' support for a partial liberalization of the law, even if that support came in the hope that homosexual propaganda would thus come to an end. After all, as far as they were concerned, the only thing worse than what homosexuals practiced in private was what they achieved with their public self-assertion and their visibility. Kahl, who adhered to a strategy of "suppressing by making invisible" (Bourdieu), shared this opinion as well.[7]

Despite Kahl's clout, the close outcome of the preliminary vote in the criminal code committee was vehemently criticized; many who had traditionally considered themselves to be authorities on the issue of homosexuality felt they had been bypassed by the committee when it reached this decision. Bavaria's former justice minister, Ernst Müller-Meiningen (1866–1944), registered his veto in the press. Disapproval was also registered by the Center Party delegate Gustav Trunk (1871–1936), whose long tenure as Baden's justice minister and three terms as state president placed him among the most influential politicians in the state of Baden, and who was one of the supporters of a rightward trend in the politics of the Center Party. Finally, the three-term Chancellor of the Weimar Republic Wilhelm Marx (1863–1946), who had led the Catholic Center Party from 1920 until 1928, was publicly critical of the committee's decision as well.[8]

Psychiatrists and forensic experts at German university clinics also weighed in at the prompting of the *Deutsche Medizinische Wochenschrift* (*German Medical Weekly*).[9] From the viewpoint of a homophobia-inspired psychology of the individual, Alfred Adler expressed his objection in an updated edition of *The Problem of Homosexuality*, which was published in 1930. His work was frequently referred to in the sexual ethics literature of the 1930s.

To be sure, the reform proposition had already been politically defeated in March of 1930. The government turned the reform of the criminal code over to the interparliamentary committee for the coordination of criminal codes between Germany and Austria, and reform of the law on homosexuality did not enjoy majority support among the members of this committee. Despite this development, the debate about the relationship between morality and society became more intense, and the newly installed conservative government made this debate an important part of a political and religious culture war. In the humanities, this culture war was waged on the battlefield of ethics.

Catholic Interventions

As early as 1929, the pastoral ethicist Rudolf Geis (1892–1958) published a tract, *Catholic Sexual Ethics*, that he intended to serve as a categorical defense of an endangered system of values. Geis's piece aimed to mobilize readers to participate in a social conflict perceived as a "decisive battle." It claimed to offer a manifesto of contemporary Catholic sexual ethics in the form of a metaphysics of sexual life. For him, the question of homosexuality was a particularly pressing issue; he even addressed it in the foreword and warned of "pathological attempts in our time to valorize sexual disorder and even to defend diseased inversions of the sexual drive as unproblematic varieties of the enjoyment of life."[10] This book was an effective form of protest expressed on behalf of the Catholic clergy. And homosexuality did indeed present the Catholic fortress of values with a challenge. It was perceived as a threat to the fundamental dogma of the relationship between the sexes, an attack on the sacrament of reproductive marriage, and a disavowal of the plan of the holy Creator.

Geis's *Sexual Ethics* was at its core a marriage manual that inveighed against every form of departure from the norm in gender relations and anticipated what the head of the Catholic Church would decree one year later. The dogmatics and systematics of his sexual ethics follow to the greatest possible extent the line that would be presented officially in the Marriage Encyclical of December 1930, which was issued by Pope Pius XI. The papal pronouncement in defense of "healthy marriage" was directed against the liberal *Zeitgeist* of the Weimar republic. The circular simultaneously offered missionary support for a religious moral offensive, waged by the Association of Catholic Intellectuals, that conceived of itself as a movement for reform and renewal. At the behest of the pope, who blessed the association's meetings with his approval, the association was to take action against positions "which the foundations of German *Kultur*, being Catholic through-and-through, cannot accept."[11] At the 1928 and 1930 meetings of the association, sexuality was the only topic discussed. In 1928, when the debate over the general reform of the criminal code shifted its focus to the decriminalization of homosexuality, the putative endangerment of youth by homosexuals was placed on the agenda, and the director of the Berlin police's Department of Homosexuality (*Homosexuellendezernat*), Bernhard Strewe (1881–1957), was invited as a principal witness. One year later, Strewe was called as an expert police witness by the Reichstag's committee on criminal law, before which he again invoked the bogeyman of the endangerment of youth by homosexuals.[12]

In 1930, the Vienna philosopher Aurel Kolnai (1900–1973) published his own *Sexual Ethics*, a comprehensive, humanistic defense of Catholic positions. Kolnai replaced the standard ethics of duty with a phenomenologically based ethics of values such as the one Max Scheler (1874-1928), the philosophical standard-bearer of an intellectual movement of religious renewal within the Catholic tradition, had proposed. Kolnai's *Sexual Ethics* clearly distinguished itself from the preacherly style of Geis's *Sexual Ethics*, which presented itself as asserting revealed truth as it expounded articles of the faith. Kolnai's text, by contrast, contained an extensive engagement with liberal understandings of society and moral concepts.

Kolnai—who had once been an advocate of psychoanalysis and then devoted himself to Catholicism at the same time as he distanced himself from sexology[13]—condemned homosexuality in the name of Catholicism, and with a philosophical verve similar to that of the philosopher Otto Weininger (1880–1903). His stances on homosexuality developed in critical dialogue with the theories advanced by representatives of the homosexual liberation movement, and in particular with the writings of Magnus Hirschfeld (1868–1935) and Hans Blüher (1888–1955). Kolnai not only attempted with his sexual ethics to classify homosexuality as a moral perversion and the "gravest sin," but also warned of a danger to society that would emerge with the recognition of homosexual relationships.[14]

Kolnai's disquisitions on homosexuality relied on an assumption of a life-determining fixation that makes homosexuality appear to be unchangeable. This reference to Hirschfeld's thesis of a biologically conditioned homosexuality, which therefore had to be recognized as a natural right, was inverted by Kolnai so that it reemerged as its opposite: precisely because it constituted a life-determining and immutable fixation, homosexuality was—in comparison with other perversions—marked by such a "deep-rooted inversion" and a "uniquely categorical, existence-determining [condition]" that a "bridge to normality" for homosexuals was therefore fundamentally lacking. Kolnai thus rejected a priori the possibility of a comparison with heterosexual relationships and denied homosexuality any meaning or value. Homosexuality was entirely excluded from the heteronormative world order that Kolnai prescribed "for the purpose of healing" (in the sense of Catholic principle and natural rights) the ills he saw wrought by liberal conceptions of the state.[15]

Kolnai's determination to ostracize homosexuals referred, however, only to male homosexuals. Along with the majority of sexual ethicists, psychiatrists, and criminologists of his time, he viewed lesbian desire as harmless and in no way as threatening, since "acts of pleasure and in particular tenderness" were "for women more a universal possibility." Contrary to his view of the lifelong, immutable fixation of homosexuality in men, in the case of lesbian behavior "the transition to normality" was "an unremarkable" one.[16]

In order to prove the particular danger posed by male homosexuality, Kolnai drew upon Hans Blüher's theory of the male society (*Männerbundtheorie*). Blüher's valuation and defense of homosexuality diverged from Magnus Hirschfeld's by relying not on biological-natural, but rather sociopolitical arguments. Blüher felt the homoerotic male fraternity or society—the *Männerbund*—played an important role in perpetuating the state.[17] As he did with Hirschfeld's theory, Kolnai turned this argument around, into its opposite: he saw in mutual desire between men an endangerment of the ordinary social structure of heteronormative, hegemonic power relations. If "man as the bearer of ethics and reason" were to dissipate his "sexual value" in homosexual relationships, and if his relationships were to become dependent upon the logic of homosexual desire and thus undermine rather than sustain society, a "thoroughgoing transformation of the categorical structure of the world" would take place.[18] Kolnai also assigned homosexual desire its own essential logic, which consisted of "perspectives determined by lust" and "sexual intentions" that bore "antisocial," "world-destroying," and "world-overturning" aspects. Strengthened by male promiscuity, the establishment of homosexual groups, and homosexual propaganda, an existential danger to society would emerge, as homosexuals would build "a state within the state, their own 'club' in the lap of the society."[19] Kolnai's homophobic construction of this picture of the "enemy" employs a vocabulary conspicuously similar to anti-Semitism, replete with notions of a foreign body, an infiltration, and an endangerment of the *Volk*. It was a seemingly engaging and plausible argument, and one indicative of the radical mentalities of the time—even if, as in this case, it was advanced by a Catholic of Jewish origin against homosexuals.

Protestant Stances

By comparison with Catholic verdicts, Protestant positions seem at first glance somewhat more flexible; however, upon closer observation they leave no doubt as to their similarly strict rejection of and particular fixation on homosexuality. In 1930, Theodor Haug, the pastor of the seminary church in Tübingen, published a comprehensive work on sexual ethics intended to provide the Christian community with a modern, practically oriented Protestant casuistry. Haug performed a balancing act with his remarks on homosexuality: while he supported a planned reform of the elements of the criminal code that concerned homosexuality, at the same time he held fast to homophobic prejudices fueled by fear of seduction and the attribution of a sickness to homosexuals.

For Haug, the "uncanny spread" of homosexuality was principally due to "longing for enjoyment," "seduction," and "habit-formation."[20] Against these influences, Haug looked to mobilize the powers of resistance through belief in God and the care of the soul. His sexual ethics aimed at being an ethics of the will—looking to inspire homosexuals to find healing through faith—and, should the Christian conversion program fail, threatened to "exclude" incorrigible homosexuals "as presenting a danger for all (one thinks of the forsaken and the possessed of the New Testament!)." Haug made very clear that the "struggle of Christians against the unnaturalness of same-sex love [must] be conducted with undiminished power, and indeed with new strength."[21] The Protestant sexual ethics of Theodor Haug reveals a partial, albeit begrudging, acceptance of homosexuality against the backdrop of reformist intentions. However, the Protestants' political representatives in the German National People's Party (Deutsch-Nationale Volkspartei, or DNVP) left no doubt as to their opposition to a decriminalization of homosexuality.

Evidently, homosexuality did not meet with favorable recognition in the sexual ethics put forward by either of the Christian churches. Insofar as particularly *reproductive*—i.e., procreative—marriage (not so much heterosexuality in and of itself) was canonized and held up as the privileged site of normal and healthy sexuality, homosexuality necessarily appeared to be abnormal and worthless and was classified as pathological and sinful. This ethics' estimation of homosexuality was not focused on same-sex love, i.e., on an ethic of love and sexual relationships. Rather, it was based on a hierarchy of values that elevated reproduction and the gender order to the level of a supernatural purpose. Christian positions, however, constituted only a portion of the debate on values.

Liberal Positions

In 1931, August Messer (1867–1937), a professor of philosophy at the University of Giessen, published yet another *Sexual Ethics*, which advertised itself as a non-religious and liberal response to Christian sexual ethics. Messer's ethics of value placed freedom and responsibility at the center of his philosophical grounding of sexual ethics. His plea for a more painstaking, "thoughtful evaluation" took "the homosexuals" as its exemplary case.[22]

Messer's foundational ethical imperative was without question an extraordinary innovation in ethical treatments of sexuality, as Messer conceived of society and state in a secular way and connected ethics to responsibility and the freedom of the individual. However, Messer did not elaborate much beyond this gesture to a new perspective on values. His plea for the decriminalization of consensual same-sex sexual relationships between adult men, as envisioned by the reform proposal in the Reichstag, instead depended primarily on publications of the liberal Giessen-based legal scholar Wolfgang Mittermaier and the Berlin-based sexologist and cofounder of the homosexual movement, Magnus Hirschfeld.[23] Messer did not provide a philosophically novel evaluation of homosexuality itself; this remained a lacuna in liberal thinking of the time. For the humanities, this meant that at the beginning of the 1930s, there was no ethically based defense of homosexuality. Those who were attracted to the same sex remained—from the viewpoint of ethics—"dispossessed of happiness in love,"[24] to recall the title of one of the first informational tracts that had, at the turn of the century, dared to assert homosexuals' claim to a life of dignity and societal acceptance.[25]

Before the publication of his *Sexual Ethics* in 1930, August Messer had conducted a debate on the question of abolishing Paragraph 175 (the law regarding homosexuality) from 1927 to 1929 in *Philosophie und Leben* (*Philosophy and Life*), a journal he himself edited.[26] The inspiration for the debate had been a letter from a reader, Adolf Brand (1874–1945), who (along with Hirschfeld) was among the cofounders of the homosexual movement. Brand was infuriated by slander that governmental attorneys directed at Hirschfeld and the cosigners of an anti–Paragraph 175 petition that had been circulated by the Wissenschaftlich-humanitäres Komitee (Scientific Humanitarian Committee, or WhK). The debate Messer led in response demonstrated the enmities and objections to which liberal stances on homosexuality were subject and the kinds of emotional outbursts they provoked. When Adolf Brand self-confidently announced, "the noble love of a man is entirely equal to the noble love of a woman," a Dr. Rudolf Leinen responded with the following: "The man who is not depraved can only hold that sodomitic sacrilege must be atoned for by the most fearful punishment his imagination can find: immolation by fire and brimstone from heaven! The Catholic Church holds this view in counting the sodomite's sin among the ones most offensive to Heaven, and I place my hope regarding this issue, too, on the Center [Party]."[27] It bears emphasis that these remarks appeared in a philosophy journal. They are no different from the aggressive rhetoric of the National Socialists.

Indeed, it is possible that these vehement reactions by his journal's readers gave August Messer one more reason to exercise self-censorship in his *Sexual Ethics* by leaving a philosophically innovative assessment of homosexuality's value undeveloped. In light of the change in public opinion, the positions held by right-wing politicians in the Weimar Republic, the campaigns of religious groups, and the enmity experienced by proponents of decriminalization, from 1930 onward a positive valuation of homosexuality seemed hardly feasible. The window of opportunity for altering societal attitudes and legal provisions regarding sexuality had thus already closed in 1930, not with the National Socialist seizure of power in 1933. As a result, August Messer kept to a juridically (rather than philosophically) based argument.

In the field of conflict constituted by the debate over the reform of the criminal code, the thematization of homosexuality and ethics led to a mobilization of anti-homosexual prejudice that doomed nonreligious ethical attempts to develop a defense of homosexuality. The churches collaborated with moral philosophers to advance the promulgation of conservative social values, and the sociopolitical influence held by the churches only lent further weight to their interpretative claims.

Crisis and Cultural Reaction

The debates over sexual ethics reflected a crisis emerging from the changing character of gender roles and relationships between the sexes at the end of the

1920s. The particular status and argumentative use-value that the topic of homosexuality acquired in this context can be interpreted not least as a response
to anxieties regarding a hegemonic conception of masculinity that was felt to
be eroding.[28] In the face of destabilization, conservative and religious sexual
ethics reacted by formulating and promoting heteronormative notions of masculinity and homophobic constructions of the enemy.

In this context, the obsession with seduction scenarios needs also to be read
as part of this perceived crisis of hegemonic masculinity.[29] Marriage, family,
and youth were held to be particularly vulnerable. While Catholic opinions
insisted upon an all-encompassing rejection of homosexuality, both Protestant
and liberal positions distinguished between homosexuality involving adult men
on the one hand and man-boy relationships on the other, and thereby abided
by contemporary reform proposals aimed at decriminalizing the former and
harshly punishing the latter. It is notable that the proponents of sexual ethics
paid very little attention to male prostitution, which was likewise to be subject
to harsh punishment according to the reform proposals.[30] In the media, as in
the homosexual movement, the topos of the danger posed by male prostitution
played an important role, as it was linked to seduction scenarios and to the
blackmailing of homosexuals.[31] Though parts of the homosexual movement,
and in particular the League for Human Rights (Bund für Menschenrecht)
led by Friedrich Radszuweit (1876–1932), demanded the punishment of male
prostitutes and sought to distance themselves from prostitution and prostitutes, opponents of the decriminalization of homosexuality did not distinguish
between prostitutes and homosexuals; instead, they equated them with one
another as "riff-raff," "scum," and "the most dangerous type of criminal," as Bavaria's former Justice Minister Müller-Meiningen put it.[32]

In this situation, hope for the decriminalization of male-male sexual relationships dwindled in the rising chorus of a conservative-religious mobilization strengthened by a rightward political shift. Liberal objections drew
increasingly little attention or fell silent in the face of the witch hunt loosed
against homosexuality. As early as 1930, resigned voices were audible in the
homosexual movement. Friedrich Radszuweit, who led the group with the
largest membership, declared that in the wake of the political reversal that resulted from the outcome of the Reichstag election, "now our cause to eliminate
Paragraph 175 has become almost hopeless."[33] Just as desperate and hopeless
was the call of his successor, Paul Weber, for the Alliance for Human Rights to
"combat the strongly escalating cultural reaction led by ecclesiastical authorities" in the wake of the Prussian coup (*Preussenschlag*) in 1932.[34] The commis-
sary government of Prussia under the former Center Party politician Franz
Bracht (1877–1933), installed by emergency decree, had indeed inaugurated
a reactionary transition in moral politics. Weber felt it to be "the beginning of
a new era" that would involve intrusion "into the private life of the homosexual

person," not least due to threats to close homosexual establishments by police decree.[35]

The Catholic Center Party played an important and pace-setting role during the course of the reactionary turn, which in contemporary usage had tellingly come to be called the "cultural reaction" (*Kulturreaktion*). A member in all governments of the Weimar Republic, the party had been able to strengthen its influence in the constellations of political power at the end of the 1920s. After its rightward shift in 1928, which was inaugurated with the assumption of party leadership by the archconservative prelate Ludwig Kaas (1881–1952), the party pursued a politics of moral-religious renewal in the right-wing-conservative and reactionary governments from 1930 onward.

The National Socialist German Workers' Party (Nationalsozialistische Deutsche Arbeiterpartei, or NSDAP) strengthened this aggressive moral politics against the plurality and liberality of the Weimar Republic. Beginning in 1930, they gained increasing political influence through their targeted provocations (*Aktionismus*), hateful tirades, and campaign rallying cries. Their goal of a moral-*völkisch* renewal went hand in hand with a politics of moral-religious renewal. After the Nazis' ascent to power in 1933, this unified goal-setting remained an important precondition for the coalition between the Nazis and—despite all their differences—the conservative politicians close to the Center Party, and for the "moral-national renewal" introduced by their campaigns and intensifications of laws.

Yet from 1931 onward, the Nazis did not mention homosexuality, at least for the time being. To be sure, during the debates over the reform of the criminal code in 1929 and 1930 they had left no doubt regarding their homophobia and had ethically condemned and fundamentally repudiated homosexuality, but public statements on the matter vanished by the end of 1930.[36] The reason for this was a homophobic slander campaign by the Nazis' political opponents, which embarrassed the party and put it on the defensive.

By early 1931, Social Democrats and Communists had initiated a press campaign against homosexual storm trooper (Sturmabteilung, or SA) leaders that drew attention across Germany.[37] The campaign was intended to reveal the hypocrisy and dishonesty of the National Socialist movement, but it discredited a cause the leftist parties had championed only a few years prior—namely, the prevention of discrimination against homosexuality and a fight on behalf of its reevaluation.

Given this situation in the 1930s, it had become unrealistic to continue thinking about a reform of the criminal code provision pertaining to homosexuality, let alone an ethical valuation of homosexuality. By 1930, Magnus Hirschfeld—surely the best-known sexual reformer of the Weimar Republic, who had made it his life's work to fight for the reevaluation and decriminalization of homosexuality—saw no possibility of further success in Germany

212 ᙍ *Andreas Pretzel*

because of pressure from National Socialists and conservative Center Party members. He therefore began traveling to deliver lectures around the world. In November of 1931, in a card he sent home to Germany from India, he wrote of his progressive activism: "as this is now more or less closed off for me in Germany, I am very happy to be able to continue my work as a 'cosmopolitan.' When I write 'closed off,' I mean only to say that I feel somewhat paralyzed between the Scylla of Nazism and the Charybdis of the Center Party."[38]

This threatening situation, along with an atmosphere of powerlessness but also a desire for self-assertion, serves to convey what homosexuals felt in Germany at the beginning of the 1930s. The homosexual movement, too, ended up in a dangerous situation between Scylla and Charybdis. A phase of increasing repression and oppression had begun. The visibility of homosexuals—to the general public and to each other—would be made to disappear and wither. From their position on the offensive, homosexuals and their supporters were pushed back on the defensive.

One further indicator of this defensive stance, and of increasing self-censorship, is offered by the *Moral History of the Post-War Era* (published in 1931/32), an impressive summary, written from the viewpoint of liberal authors, of the problems, progress, and transformations of the Weimar period. Though the women's and youth movements, for example, are described as achievements, a chapter on the homosexual movement is missing entirely; even its mere existence remains unmentioned.[39] This is all the more conspicuous, given that the main editor of the work, Magnus Hirschfeld, was one of the leading representatives of the homosexual movement—and indeed, one of its cofounders.

Implications for the Genealogy of Discourse

The developments at the beginning of the 1930s call the usual periodization, according to which 1933 and the National Socialists' accession to power represented a turning point, into question. There is no doubt that the year 1933 constituted a caesura as far as domestic policy was concerned. With respect to sexual politics and the history of morality, however, it is more appropriate to designate a much earlier turning point in 1930. Occurring with the political shift toward conservatism, this turn manifested itself in cultural developments and in moral and sexual politics alike. New power relations led to a displacement of the discourse: liberal positions were increasingly marginalized, and religiously conservative and reactionary voices took precedence. The turn in sexual and moral politics at the beginning of the 1930s was part of a transition between different kinds of political systems and was a legacy of the Weimar period—not, as it has mistakenly been assumed, purely an effect of the Nazis' seizure of power.

The homophobic battle over morals can be interpreted as an expression of a hegemonic yet crisis-prone masculinity and as a homophobic modernization of hegemonic masculinity. At the same time, the battle can be understood as part of a discourse of normalization, as Jürgen Link describes with reference to Foucault.[40] This qualitative shift in sexual politics was set in motion by religious communities, the Catholic Center Party, and Protestant groups who looked to the DNVP for political representation of their interests. The rise of the National Socialists attended, and succeeded, the efforts of these groups.

Conclusion

In his introduction to *Sex, Politics, and Society*, Jeffrey Weeks reminds us that Foucault's famous "repressive hypothesis" so effectively rebuts our customary ways of thinking about the Victorian treatment of sexuality that an inquiry into the nature and kinds of "repression" that might be exercised on sexuality is obviated. But "it seems clear," Weeks writes, "that at certain times some political and social regimes are more 'repressive,' both ideologically and physically (as in the case of Nazi Germany) than others."[41]

The shift in the discourse(s) of sexuality discussed in this essay offers an opportunity to analyze whether Foucault's rejection of the notion of a true "repression"—however accurate and useful it may be in the case of the Victorians—can remain tenable when presented with a case in which a "repressive" discourse complex could be, and was, rearranged and supplemented in order to justify forced sterilization, deportation, and murder. The central question, then, would concern whether the repressive hypothesis requires revision, or at least expansion, to include "repression" as a positive ensemble of practices with its own (historically conditioned) degrees of severity, and with its own discursive corroborants in ethics, politics, and religion.

Translated by William Seth Howes and Erik Huneke

Notes

1. See Heinrich August Winkler, *Weimar 1918–1933: Die Geschichte der ersten deutschen Demokratie* (Munich, 1998).
2. Peter Jelavich, *Berlin Alexanderplatz: Radio, Film, and the Death of Weimar Culture* (Berkeley, CA, 2006), xii.
3. Ibid., 17, 101, 140f., 213.
4. On the debate surrounding the criminal code, see Kai Sommer, *Die Strafbarkeit der Homosexualität von der Kaiserzeit bis zum Nationalsozialismus* (Frankfurt am Main, 1998), 276–93.

5. See Magnus Hirschfeld, *Sittengeschichte der Nachkriegszeit*, vols. 1–2 (Leipzig and Vienna, 1931–32).
6. Hermann Hass, *Sitte und Kultur im Nachkriegsdeutschland* (Hamburg, 1932), 10.
7. Reichstag, IV. Wahlperiode 1928, 21. Ausschuss (Reichsstrafgesetzbuch), 85. Sitzung, verhandelt Berlin, den 16. Oktober, 7f.; Pierre Bourdieu, *Die männliche Herrschaft* (Frankfurt am Main, 2005), 202.
8. See Friedrich Radszuweit, "Bourgeoisie und Homosexualität," *Das Freundschaftsblatt* 8, no. 33 (14 August 1930), Bl. 1-2, here Bl. 1.
9. See *Deutsche Medizinische Wochenschrift* 55 (October 1929): 811f.; *Deutsche Medizinische Wochenschrift* 56 (January 1930): 85–8, 128–30.
10. Rudolph Geis, *Katholische Sexualethik*, 2nd ed. (Paderborn, 1929), 1.
11. "Pius XI," in *Religion und Seelenleiden: Vorträge der V. Sondertagung des Katholischen Akademikerverbandes in Kevelar*, ed. Wilhelm Bergmann (Augsburg, 1930), 9f.
12. See Jens Dobler, *Zwischen Duldungspolitik und Verbrechensbekämpfung* (Frankfurt am Main, 2008), 541f.
13. See Francis Dunlop, *The Life and Thought of Aurel Kolnai* (Aldershot, 2002).
14. Aurel Kolnai, *Sexualethik: Sinn und Grundlagen der Geschlechtsmoral* (Paderborn, 1930), 260–72.
15. Ibid., 261f., 265.
16. Ibid., 268.
17. Claudia Bruns, *Politik des Eros* (Cologne, 2008).
18. Kolnai, *Sexualethik*, 266f.
19. Ibid., 269f.
20. Theodor Haug, *Im Ringen um Reinheit und Reife: Tatsachen und Richtlinien für eine evangelische Sexualethik* (Stuttgart, 1930), 192–97.
21. Ibid., 376.
22. August Messer, *Sexualethik* (Berlin, 1931), 16.
23. Ibid., 244–51.
24. Otto de Joux (i.e., Otto Rudolf Podjukl), *Die Enterbten des Liebesglückes: Ein Beitrag zur Seelenkunde* (Leipzig, 1893).
25. Mark Lehmstedt, *Bücher für das „dritte Geschlecht": Der Max Spohr Verlag in Leipzig* (Wiesbaden, 2002), 44–53.
26. *Philosophie und Leben*, 3 (1927): 338–39; 4 (1928), 292–97; 5 (1929), 113–16.
27. *Philosophie und Leben*, 4 (1928): 292–97.
28. R. W. Connell, *Masculinities* (Berkeley, CA, 1995).
29. See Martin Lücke, *Männlichkeit in Unordnung* (Frankfurt am Main, 2008), 326.
30. See Kolnai, *Sexualethik*, 217n1; Messer, *Sexualethik*, 152.
31. See Lücke, *Männlichkeit in Unordnung*.
32. Ernst Müller-Meiningen, "Die Reform des Strafrechts," *Münchener Neueste Nachrichten*, no. 32 (2 February 1930), quoted in "Friedrich Radszuweit: Pfui Herr Justizminister A.D. Dr. Ernst Müller-Meiningen," *Das Freundschaftsblatt* 8, no. 8 (20 February 1930), Bl. 1-2, cited Bl. 1.
33. Friedrich Radszuweit, in *Freundschaft 8.*, no. 41 (9 October 1930).
34. Paul Weber, in *Freundschaftsblatt* 10, no. 20 (19 May 1932).
35. Paul Weber, "Wettlauf um die Sittlichkeit," *Freundschaftsblatt* 10, no. 36 (8 September 1932).
36. See *Völkischer Beobachter*, Reichsausgabe, 2 August 1930.

37. Susanne zur Nieden, ed., *Homosexualität und Staatsräson: Männlichkeit, Homophobie und Politik in Deutschland 1900–1945* (Frankfurt am Main, 2005), 147–92.
38. Magnus Hirschfeld, Postcard sent to Maria Krische, 20 November 1931, Private Archive of Beat Frischknecht, Zurich.
39. See Hirschfeld, *Sittengeschichte der Nachkriegszeit*.
40. Jürgen Link, *Versuch über den Normalismus: Wie Normalität produziert wird* (Wiesbaden, 1999), 49.
41. Jeffrey Weeks, *Sex, Politics, and Society: The Regulation of Sexuality since 1800* (London, 1989), 9.

~:~

CHAPTER 14

Socialist Eugenics and Homosexuality in the GDR
The Case of Günter Dörner

FLORIAN G. MILDENBERGER

The German Democratic Republic (GDR) was an outlier in the otherwise ostensibly unified cluster of states that comprised the now defunct Eastern bloc. East German leaders might have claimed that they were moving shoulder to shoulder with their "big brother" in Moscow. But they allowed for a plethora of social reforms that to some extent have not yet been achieved even in today's Russia, such as the depathologization of homosexuality and legalization of abortion.[1] At the same time, however, and as something of a countervailing tendency to these reforms, the government allowed doctors and scientists to pursue "socialist eugenics"—in other words, a prophylactic health-care system with a eugenic basis. Soon research was underway that counteracted the liberal impulses in the legislative domain. A prominent example of such research is the work of the endocrinologist Günter Dörner.

Unlike the principles of National Socialist racial hygiene, which are more familiar to the general public and historians alike, socialist eugenics' tenets were never entirely realized in practice. While the basic principle of socialist eugenics was based upon the concept of neo-Lamarckianism, which stipulated that acquired characteristics could be inherited by the next generation,[2] National Socialist racial hygiene was based upon an exaggerated form of Mendelism and the notion of the immutability of one's genetic predisposition. Depending on the practitioners involved, the ideal of rigorous scientific inquiry was sacrificed in both instances to a supposedly higher ideal—a dictatorship based on either race or class.

Those deemed to be "fit" (*Geeignete*) because of their genetic disposition and their lifestyle as "high-value" proletarians and servants of the socialist cause were supposed to be privy to comprehensive financial and sociopolitical support coupled with socialist indoctrination. As a result of such efforts, children would be devoted communists from birth—or at the very least they would be more amenable to being raised as communists. Such policies were tested in the USSR during the 1920s, and German doctors—among them the sexual researcher Magnus Hirschfeld—became intrigued by them.[3] There were, however, also severe setbacks in the development of socialist eugenic thinking. The concept of neo-Lamarckianism came to be debunked, and after Stalin's rise to power, the eugenic impulse grew weak in the Soviet Union. In Germany, those socialist eugenicists who were not compelled to leave the country, such as Karl Valentin Müller and his followers, wound up pledging their loyalty to the National Socialists.

After 1945, there was a revival of eugenic tendencies, albeit only in the GDR. National elites were generally suspected—and not without justification—of having cooperated with the National Socialists, and this suspicion applied particularly to doctors. But these same doctors were now being enticed with the basic principles of socialist eugenics and allowed to rise again as the custodians of a new social order—in other words, to play the same role that had been conceived for them under National Socialism. The vague orientation of "red racial hygiene" made it possible for the former opponents of neo-Lamarckianism and the promoters of National Socialist racial hygiene to take part in the new configuration of power. After the definitive rejection of neo-Lamarckianism—which was by then known as Lysenkoism—during the 1960s, the former National Socialist racial hygienists and their allies actually rose to become the advocates of new political and scientific principles for the health-care system. This was particularly significant for the GDR in the aftermath of 1961. After the construction of the Berlin Wall, which hermetically sealed the GDR from the West, the government needed to devise forms of relief that would provide inexpensive diversion for the populace. At the same time, however, the populace needed to be controlled; for this reason, liberalizing legislative tendencies and eugenic thought went hand in hand in the socialist state that was the GDR.

The proponents of socialist eugenics sought to achieve good health for all members of the working class. State guidelines left it up to individual researchers to decide what constituted good health. During the 1920s, socialist eugenicists did not consider homosexuality to be a form of mental illness. Magnus Hirschfeld and his Scientific Humanitarian Committee (Wissenschaftlich-humanitäres Komitee, or WhK) were comrades-in-arms for the general cause of socialist health policy. But the new advocates of socialist eugenics after 1945 had not been immune to the influence of years of National Socialist rule. Many of them had never been adherents of neo-Lamarckianism and instead abided by National Socialist policies regarding "genetic health" (*Erbgesundheitspolitik*) during the 1930s and 1940s. In their capacity as agents of National Socialist

policy, they approved castrations and sent mentally ill homosexuals to institutions that carried out "euthanasia." Under the GDR's "real existing" socialism,
homosexual intercourse was punishable by the same law (Paragraph 175) that
had been valid during the Weimar Republic. It thus should come as no surprise
that homosexuality was pathologized in medical advice books of the 1950s and
1960s.[4]

At the same time, doctors during the 1960s were also trying to overcome
societal inhibitions about discussing sexuality. These reformers were concentrated in the Section for Marriage and Family in the German Society for
Overall Hygiene (Sektion Ehe und Familie der Deutschen Gesellschaft für die
gesamte Hygiene—see the essay by Erik Huneke in this volume). Their goal
was not sexual reform, but instead social hygiene. Their methodological tool-
box included sexual education, abortion, contraception, and the protection of
youth—all courtesy of the provident political party that could then fully concentrate on core tasks such as addressing the sluggish economic growth under
communism. Anything that did not constitute a compelling state interest—
such as sex among minors or even homosexual intercourse among adults—was
to be legalized. Considering that consensual adult male homosexuality was
decriminalized in 1968 in the GDR, all research regarding homosexuality was
supposed to be prophylactic in nature, apply to future social conditions, and be
inexpensive to boot, since financial resources were in short supply.

The endocrinologist Günter Dörner was a leading figure in this endeavor.
Born on 13 July 1929 in Hindenburg (a town in Silesia), he graduated from
the secondary school (*Gymnasium*) in Halberstadt (a town in Thuringia) and
studied medicine at the Humboldt University in Berlin from 1948 to 1953.
His interest in endocrinology arose in the course of his studies, and in 1953
he completed a doctoral thesis entitled "The Desensitization to Estrogens of
the Hypothalamus-Pituitary System" under the direction of Walter Hohlweg.
Hohlweg was a student of the Viennese professor Eugen Steinach, who during
the 1920s had been something of a celebrity in German-speaking hormone
research circles. Steinach had promised older men "eternal youth" by manip-
ulating the spermatic duct, and together with Magnus Hirschfeld he hoped
to be able to "cure" male homosexuality with testicle transplants. By pursuing
these aims, he believed that he had furnished proof of the congenital basis for
sexual deviance.[5] Steinach also collaborated with Walter Hohlweg to develop
hormone preparations for Schering-Kahlbaum AG in Berlin.

In 1928, Hohlweg transferred from Vienna to the main Schering laboratory in Berlin. Along with Adolf Butenandt (who would later win the Nobel
Prize) and Butenandt's colleague Hans Herloff Inhoffen, Hohlweg conducted
research in the years leading up to 1945 on the effects of hormones (and above
all of female hormones) on the male organism. In 1932, Hohlweg identified a
hormonal differentiation between men and women, the so-called "Hohlweg

effect." According to this principle, women (but not men) produce the pituitary hormone LH after being administered estrogen.[6] When Schering's production facilities in Berlin were dismantled in late May 1945 as a form of reparation to the Soviet occupation authorities, many researchers left the city. A few, among them Hohlweg, became professors at the University of Berlin or the Charité. In 1951, Hohlweg established the Institute for Experimental Endocrinology, which collaborated closely with such East German pharmaceutical companies as VEB Jenapharm and Arzneimittelwerk Dresden. He also attracted to his laboratory a number of younger researchers, one of whom was Dörner.

After completing his doctoral research, Dörner at first worked as an assistant doctor (*Assistent*) in gynecology at the hospital in Fürstenwalde, then later transferred to the Institute of Pathology in Berlin-Buch. Only in 1957 did he return to serve as Hohlweg's loyal assistant professor (*Assistent*). He completed his *Habilitation*, "The Function of Stilbestrol Diphosphate in the Treatment of Prostate Carcinoma," in 1959 and was appointed instructor a year later. After the construction of the Berlin Wall in 1961, the Austrian Hohlweg left the GDR, and Dörner succeeded his mentor as the institute's director. He intended for his own research to be the consummation of Hohlweg's and Steinach's teachings, and later on he characterized his work as building upon Hirschfeld's research. He took advantage of the financial resources and political possibilities (such as the elimination of dissenting voices) under real existing socialism and was of service to the regime in many ways. Dörner did not wage an isolated one-man campaign; instead, he was the founder of an entire school of medical thought. Many of his students (including Wolfgang Rohde, Franziska Götz, Fritz Stahl, and Lothar Krell) held endocrinology professorships in the GDR and outlasted the political turn (*Wende*) of 1990.

Dörner hoped to make use of cybernetics, which was effectively elevated to the level of state doctrine by leading socialist theoreticians of the time, as the theoretical framework and methodological approach for his research. In 1962, Dörner claimed to be able to classify the circulation of hormones according to mechanical, always identical, and consequently supra-individual pathways.[7] He consistently used rats as the subjects of his research on sexual physiology and sexual psychology, following in the footsteps of Eugen Steinach, who had pioneered the use of rats (instead of guinea pigs) since they were easy to keep and never experienced procreative difficulties.

As of the beginning of the 1960s, Dörner believed that the research methods and studies of hormonal research in the English-speaking world resonated with his own, and he strove to bring his own research findings into line with the outcomes of those studies. This was the case, for example, when he first publicly presented his findings regarding the etiology of homosexuality in 1967. Dörner based his research on the earlier studies of his American colleagues Milton Diamond and William C. Young, who like Dörner studied the effects of administering specific hormones to pregnant research animals.[8] But Dörner "forgot" to take into account some of the observations of these colleagues, such as the fact that the results of such tests could hardly be applied directly to humans, and that the rat was completely unsuitable as a research animal for hormonal studies: "Pregnancy is so short in the rat that, even though progesterone probably is secreted by the placenta ... this species is believed unsuitable for an investigation such as we have conducted on the guinea pig."[9] Thus, from the very outset of Dörner's research, the way in which he drew upon the studies of other endocrinologists was controvertible.

Dörner emphasized—ostensibly based upon the observations of Diamond and Young—that an endocrine explanation for human homosexuality was the logical conclusion of his research on rats.[10] Dörner had castrated newborn male rats during their first day of life and administered androgens to them after they had lived for three months. The animals immediately manifested "feminine"—in other words, "passive"—sexual behavior, and Dörner concluded that the cause of this behavior was "hormonally induced true homosexuality."[11] Since gonadal development is genetically determined, Dörner suspected that the brain harbored an "eroticization center" that took on a feminine tenor due to the lack of exposure to androgens. He noted that humans could undergo hormonal fluctuations after the ninetieth day of pregnancy. By 1967, he had come to suspect that such fluctuations were the cause of male homosexuality in humans.

In 1968, Dörner announced that he had injected newborn female rats with androgens and thereby artificially caused them to engage in masculine behavior, which he deemed to be "female homosexuality."[12] The title of the resulting article, "Hormonal Induction and Prevention of Female Homosexuality," allows one to discern the nature of his intentions, and indeed, Dörner conducted many studies on rats as he sought to find a way to prevent homosexuality. In 1968, he arrived at the conclusion that he could induce and then prevent homosexuality by engaging in stereotactic brain surgery, during which he would create "bilateral electrolytic lesions in the central hypothalamus."[13] Dörner thus exerted a lasting influence over supporters of stereotactic brain surgery in the Federal Republic of Germany (FRG) who sought to "cure" pedophiles by performing lobotomies.[14]

But in order to position himself as a genuine socialist eugenicist, Dörner needed to find a way to prevent homosexuality from coming into being before birth. Beyond this, he felt compelled to find a way to identify homosexual men according to their endocrinological profiles. This was especially the case since the methods that had been proposed to distinguish homosexuals from heterosexuals—whether simple psychiatric tests, Kretschmer's theory of bodily structure, or the theory that male homosexuals had female chromosomal profiles—had all proven to be false leads. Beginning in the late 1960s, Dörner concentrated on applying the research of his mentor Hohlweg to his own studies. In 1968, Dörner claimed that he had produced the "Hohlweg effect," or estrogen feedback effect, in male rats in which "homosexuality" had been hormonally induced. With recourse to his observations about the role of hormonal fluctuations during the course of pregnancy, he now declared that:

> On the basis of this animal experiment, the following finding could explain the hormonal pathogenesis of male homosexuality: an intrauterine androgen deficit experienced by the male fetus during the critical period during which the eroticization center develops leads to a bisexual or even purely feminine determination of a person's psycho-sexual orientation, depending on the extent of the deficit and the susceptibility of the eroticization center. The extrauterine onset of testicular testosterone production during puberty has a stimulating "sexundifferentiated" effect on the bisexual or purely femininely inclined eroticization center. The result is female sexual behavior in an organism that is genotypically and phenotypically male.[15]

Having studied about 1,000 rats (according to his own account), in 1969 Dörner ventured to extend his research to include human subjects. He maintained that he had observed the positive estrogen feedback effect not only in rats, but also in homosexual men.[16] On this basis he explained that he could prevent homosexuality in an unborn child by administering androgens once the sex of a fetus had been determined. In 1970, after conducting a comprehensive review of the existing literature, Dörner came to the conclusion that the organizational center for sexual development must be found in the area of the hypothalamus, although the location differed depending on a person's sex. Dörner believed that he could precisely define this differentiation by using rats' developmental process as an analogy for that of humans. According to Dörner, the "hypothalamic organizational phase" occurred between the fourth and seventh month of fetal development. Dörner conducted tests of pregnant women's amniotic fluid to determine hormonal concentrations and thereby set standard values for the range of normal hormonal levels. He also emphasized that he had observed the positive estrogen feedback effect in six homosexual men between the ages of twenty-four and thirty-seven, but that he was not able to generate the same effect in their heterosexual counterparts. Consequently, in Dörner's opinion, homosexual men did not behave any differently than did female rats. He did not divulge how he secured the cooperation of his research subjects. In 1971, before the legalization of abortion in the GDR, Dörner claimed to have measured the release of testosterone and androstenedione by twenty-nine women who were between the seventh and twelfth weeks of their pregnancies. He wrote, "After aborting these fetuses, we were able to ascertain their gonadal and/or gonosomal sex."[17]

In other, highly ethically dubious studies, Dörner provided no indication of the origin of his human research subjects, as when, for instance, he noted:

> After using coal gas to kill the mother and newborn rat between the sixteenth day of fetal development and the sixteenth day of life in 304 cases, we removed their brains and suspended them in formaline 1:10 (as done by Stieve) or a buinic solution.... In a parallel study, we performed a histological examination of the hypothalami of thirty-four human fetuses between the fourteenth and thirtieth weeks of development with the aforementioned techniques.[18]

It must be emphasized here that Dörner was by no means alone in pursuing such a methodology. He behaved no differently than did countless colleagues in the United States and the FRG, though of course this does not diminish the ethical dubiousness of his actions. He might have provided a few new interpretations of the views of his colleagues Diamond and Young, but Dörner still spoke only in terms of theories, without claiming to have produced incontestable findings. After all, at that time he was not a fanatic completely blinded by ideology but instead a scientist who absolutely wanted to be taken seriously.

The debate moved to the international realm in 1972. Dörner organized an international conference on hormone research in Berlin from 20 to 23 September where, along with his team, he presented the findings of his long-standing research projects. This move to the international realm was facilitated by the high regard in which hormone research was held in medical circles during the 1970s. A considerable number of internationally renowned researchers hoped that hormone research would yield key insights about human behavior. Numerous U.S. researchers too felt that the characteristics of precisely the kind of "male" hormones studied by Dörner would be able to provide a comprehensive explanation of the causes of sexual deviance, aggressiveness, and other behavior that diverged from the norm.

At this time, Dörner left behind cybernetics, which had fallen out of favor in the West, and aligned his research findings with those of teratology—the theory of deformities (*Missbildungen*). Homosexuality was thus classified as a deformity that needed to be identified and eradicated.[19] Dörner had already explained how he sought to identify homosexuality—an evaluation of a pregnant woman's amniotic fluid would suffice. In 1976, he proposed a concept of prophylactic heterosexualization: "However, an important preventive therapy of sexual differentiation disturbances might become possible in the future by administration of androgens in gonosomal male foetuses with androgen deficiency during the critical differentiation periods of genital organs and, in particular, of the brain."[20] He discounted the possibility that administering androgens to an unborn child might cause its mother to acquire masculine features.[21]

This defensive stance was all the more controversial because in 1969 Dörner—following the work of U.S. hormone researcher John Money—had declared that administering androgens to pregnant female rats could induce "homosexuality" in their female offspring.[22] Money had referred to studies of young girls who manifested ostensibly "masculine" behavior and whose mothers had been treated with hormones while pregnant.[23] Dörner was apparently so completely convinced of the differentiation between the male and female sex and between male and female hormones that he considered hormone therapy to be an appropriate method for ensuring the heterosexualization of socialist society, despite the known risks that the administration of hormones posed to pregnant women. There was not even the slightest bit of room in his thinking for "intermediate sexual stages (*sexuelle Zwischenstufen*)," intersex identity, or transgender identity, and even today he betrays no familiarity with the concept of gender as a historically and culturally variable social construct. In accordance with his biologically based logic, Dörner extrapolated from his studies to claim that transsexual men would react to the estrogen feedback test in a manner analogous to that of women. Not long thereafter, he compared the results for transsexuals with those for homosexual men and concluded that, from the standpoint of their hormonal physiology, transsexuals could be considered comparable to homosexuals.[24]

In the years leading up to 1978, Dörner elaborated a conceptual framework by which he sought to identify and eradicate homosexuality. It only remained for him to move from theory to practice and to provide an answer to the question as to why homosexuality still existed at all under socialism. Dörner's answer was that the stress of pregnancy disrupted a woman's hormonal circulation and thus catalyzed the development of homosexuality.[25] To support this contention, he alluded to the impact of World War II but declined—perhaps just to be on the safe side?—to ascertain whether it also applied to younger gay men and lesbians who had been born under the auspices of the GDR. Dörner thereby definitively left the solid ground of scientific methodology and anointed himself the preceptor of a new form of annihilation through health policy. Instead of performing comprehensive cohort studies, he relied upon platitudinous analogies from questionable experiments with animals and interpretation of animal behavior, which he applied to small-scale studies involving a limited number of people that yielded nothing in the way of reliable findings. It is apparent that Dörner's assessment of the etiology of homosexuality constituted an intentional rejection of any kind of scientific methodology. At the same time, he amalgamated what he had previously posited as being only theories into a unitary doctrine.

By 1978 or 1979, Dörner was on the cusp of making the leap to an active form of eugenics. A number of opponents consequently came onto the scene, particularly in the West. Leading figures in the German Society for Sexual Research (Deutsche Gesellschaft für Sexualforschung) had tried in vain for years to compel Dörner to participate in public discussions at international conferences, but he consistently evaded their pressure. In 1981, Martin Dan-necker, Gunter Schmidt, Eberhard Schorsch, and Volkmar Sigusch wrote a strongly worded critical assessment of Dörner's research (one that has since been frequently reprinted).[26] They emphasized that they were not surprised to see hypotheses gleaned from experiments on animals being applied to the practice of medicine on humans. But as far as Dörner's "crude socio-biologism" was concerned, they believed that "[h]is goal is to eradicate homosexuality by means of radical endocrinological interventions during human embryonic de-velopment."[27] They viewed the typecasting undertaken by Dörner to be non-sensical, and they concluded by imputing to their antagonist a plan for the "endocrinological euthanasia of homosexuality."[28] While their words met with deafening silence in the GDR, many in the West concurred with this critique. The conservative West German newspaper *Die Welt*, for instance, described Dörner's proposal to alter sex hormones in utero so as to affect sexual orienta-tion "a horrible vision of the future." Even American newspapers reported that Dörner's "incredible idea has drawn a storm of protest in West Germany," as the tabloid *Weekly World News* reported in 1985.[29] The *Orlando Sentinel* too informed readers that Dörner's claim that—as the paper paraphrased it—"par-ents in the future may be able to determine whether their children are het-erosexual or homosexual" had provoked "harsh criticism from West German newspapers."[30]

Dörner suffered a severe loss of influence and simultaneously came to the realization that his research had fallen out of sync with the recent evolution of social values in the GDR as well. Numerous teachers, psychologists, and even medical colleagues in East Germany had come to regard homosexuality as a normal form of behavior—indeed, one that could be fully realized under so-cialism.[31] At the same time, the GDR during the early 1980s was characterized by an extreme scarcity of financial resources and a consequent change of course in the health-care system. Part of this change entailed the de facto disempow-erment of all advocates of expensive prophylactic medicine. Moreover, when the immunodeficiency disease AIDS began to spread in the early 1980s, there was—even in the GDR—a broad expression of solidarity with, rather than discrimination against, homosexuals.[32] Dörner was faced with the wreckage of his life's work. He must have felt like a mountain climber who realized only after an agonizing ascent to the summit that he had climbed the wrong moun-tain. It was time for him to change course. Should he migrate immediately to the eugenicist camp? A single failure, newly born homosexual, fatality, or an-drogenized child would have been sufficient to end his career. Since endearing himself to the government was a highly dubious option, he chose to undertake a complete change of course instead.

In 1989, to the amazement of his antagonists and at almost the same time as the complete overturning of the GDR's law on homosexuality (Paragraph

151, which had been largely predicated upon the supposed need to prevent the "seduction" of youths by adults of the same sex), Dörner made a dramatic about-face and claimed that his research had proven that homosexuality was a congenital trait.[33] On this basis, Dörner maintained not only that he had always advocated the decriminalization of homosexuality because homosexuals could not be held legally accountable for their congenital predisposition, but also that he was the true heir to the sexual researcher Magnus Hirschfeld.

From then on, Dörner delighted in the frequent repetition of this new self-portrayal. Among other things, in March 1989 he submitted to the World Health Organization a proposal for depathologizing homosexuality in which he also, however, eagerly continued to promote as cutting-edge research his own prior work on how hormone supplementation in utero could affect gender role-behavior (and to his mind therefore also sexual orientation). Thus the proposal begins with the declaration "Bisexuality and homosexuality should be recognized as natural sexual variations." But it went on to claim that prenatal stress could raise androgen levels in utero and thus produce in a female fetus a "more male-type sexual brain organization (i.e., female homosexuality)," while androgen deficiency "can predispose males to a more female-type sexual brain organization (i.e., male homosexuality)."[34]

Dörner was not pleased that his new self-portrayal was winning him not just followers but enemies as well. This was in part because he never tired of mentioning—in the same breath as his statements about depathologizing homosexuality—that he could nonetheless prevent transsexuality from developing before birth by administering hormones to pregnant women.[35] And it was not least because he continued, also in his purportedly now homosexual-friendly statements, to make utterly reductive and scientifically untenable assertions about homosexuality that positioned it preeminently as a form of gender deviance. He had not really learned from his earlier mistakes after all. But thanks to his new research project on the genetic consequences of environmental poisons, Dörner weathered the evaluation to which all academic employees were subjected after reunification and remained the director of the Institute for Experimental Endocrinology until 1997.

Dörner's long track record certainly did not go unnoticed after 1990, but—in a bizarre twist—he was honored rather than excoriated. In the fall of 2002, then President Johannes Rau, a Social Democrat, awarded the Great Cross of Merit of the FRG's Federal Order of Merit (Großes Verdienstkreuz des Bundesverdienstordens der BRD) to honor Günter Dörner for his life's work in the field of endocrinology. Implicitly, Dörner was being honored for his efforts to establish a prophylactic, socialist community of values (*Wertegemeinschaft*) with a heterosexual foundation. News of the award sparked protests and criticisms from sexuality researchers and journalists.[36] A letter signed by dozens of prominent scholars and activists emphasized that Dörner's goal was and remained "the elimination of homosexuality via hormonal intervention during pregnancy"—an aim, they asserted, that "contradicts utterly the ethos of scientific research." And the protesters concluded that the very idea of "the endocrinological prophylaxis of homosexuality is not only an extraordinary insult to homosexual men and women. What is also damaged is the reputation of the Federal Republic itself, as it honors a man, with one of the highest honors it can give, for having openly and publicly promoted the possibility of an endocrinological euthanasia of homosexuality."[37]

The outcry was to no avail. Rau's presidential office rebuked the protesters, accusing them of misrepresenting the breadth and international significance of Dörner's work and of verging on defamation of the president himself. In the wake of the conferral of the honor, the Berlin gay scene was briefly animated by debate, but it quickly petered out. After all, during the same ceremony in which Dörner was honored, Volker Beck, the head of the Lesbian and Gay Federation in Germany (Lesben- und Schwulenverband in Deutschland), had received a Federal Cross of Merit on a Ribbon (Bundesverdienstkreuz am Bande). The award was of a less exalted class than Dörner's, but the honoring of Beck nonetheless received more attention in the press and public discussion than the Dörner problem. The progressive newspaper *taz* did, however, let itself get sarcastic about the peculiar political conjuncture in which the self-styled representative of Germany's homosexual community could stand side by side on a podium and allow himself to be feted together with a "proven homo-enemy."[38] In the years since, Dörner's preferred self-representation has succeeded. At the moment of this printing, the Wikipedia page devoted to Dörner mentions (and links to) the protesters' letter, but its overall tone and message support an interpretation of Dörner as a longtime supporter of homosexual rights.[39]

The Puzzle of Dörner's Success

The work of Michel Foucault helps us understand many things, but not does entirely help us in the case of Günter Dörner. Why was Dörner's science—which in hindsight appears manifestly sloppy—taken seriously in the context of 1970s communist East Germany? How was it possible for him to be honored in 2002? All told, the answers lie neither in some backward state of the field of endocrinology more generally in the 1970s, nor in a grasp of how hormones function that remains insufficient to this day. The answers lie in politics as much as in science.

Foucault does help, in that he taught us that everything that counts as knowledge or truth is actually imbricated with power. So it is not just Dörner's proposal that same-sex object choice could be altered by endocrinological intervention that demonstrates the value of this Foucauldian insight. More telling is the very fact of Dörner's founding premise that there existed such a category of persons as "homosexuals," persons best understood as gender-transitive—an assumption that should already have been critically interrogated and historicized. The puzzle is why that did not happen. Here we may need to supplement Foucault with the work of Bruno Latour to find a more subtle explanation for the complex mechanisms by which politics recurrently enters into laboratories—and also the mechanisms by which laboratory research results are disseminated back into the public realm.[40] Yet ultimately, it is not just the instability of truth or its imbrications with power that need to be considered. It is the stubbornness also of patent absurdity—the apparent impossibility of dislodging Dörner's status despite the unmistakable flaws in his theories and propositions—that requires further reflection.

A partial explanation for Dörner's success in the 1970s may lie in the wider context of disdain for homosexuality that transcended the communist-capitalist divide in that era. More mundanely, the answer may lie in the strong confusion reigning in that decade (as it does to this day), in the popular and scientific communities alike, about the etiology of homosexual orientation (and the relationship, or lack thereof, between gender role and object choice). That someone back in the 1970s had claimed that someday he might be able to prevent homosexuality in utero could seem merely symptomatic of the times—a forgivable lapse in a long career, all the more so since American scholars at the time also found Dörner's work with rats interesting, even if they did not believe it could or should be transferred to humans.

Yet in the end, it is the ongoing generally positive reception of Dörner's work that remains the real riddle—and the fact that he was ostentatiously honored despite articulate protests from his critics, and even as Germany, after unification, moved ever more toward an officially "homo-friendly" stance. Was this strictly a matter of governmental bureaucratic banality or incompetence? After all, former Easterners were hard to come by as potential Bundesverdienstkreuz recipients.[41] A history of entanglement with the communist government or work that had been inadequately recognized internationally could create obstacles for a proposed honoree. Dörner seemed to have passed muster on both counts—and Rau, as president, was a special advocate for East-West reconciliation. Or was it that the history of eugenics criss-crosses other political and ethical divides in complex ways? The history of eugenics has yet to be fully researched in its implications for thinking about race or disability; it has certainly not been scrutinized thoroughly for its potential repercussions for thinking about same-sex object choice. Here the story gets stickier, since there is in fact some (problematic but nonetheless conceivable) plausibility in Dörner's effort to position himself as heir to Magnus Hirschfeld. Hirschfeld too evinced an interest in hormonal treatments for same-sex orientation—and some of his homosexual patients sought these of their own volition.

Finally, however, there remains the painful irony that among some gay rights activists, a search for a biologistic basis for same-sex object choice continues into the twenty-first century. What this tells us about ongoing ambivalence about "homosexuality," even within that unstably bounded category of persons to whom that term has come to refer, tells us something—something unpleasant but important—about the durability of anti-homosexual ugliness in our supposedly emancipated and tolerant present.

Translated by Erik Huneke

Notes

1. See Sophia Kishkovsky, "Russia Enacts Law Opposing Abortion," July 15, 2011. *New York Times*, http://www.nytimes.com/2011/07/15/world/europe/15iht-russia15.html. Accessed March 16, 2012.
2. Michael Schwarz, *Sozialistische Eugenik: Eugenische Sozialtechnologien in Debatten und Politik der deutschen Sozialdemokratie 1890–1933* (Berlin, 1995); Peter Weingart, Jürgen Kroll, and Kurt Bayertz, *Rasse, Blut und Gene: Geschichte der Eugenik und Rassenhygiene in Deutschland*, 3rd ed. (Frankfurt am Main, 2005).
3. Magnus Hirschfeld, "Das russische Sexualstrafrecht," *Die Aufklärung: Monatsschrift für Sexual- und Lebensreform* 1 (1929): 225f.
4. Joachim S. Hohmann, "Geschichte, Ziele, Leistungen und Perspektiven der Sexuologie in der DDR," in *Sexuologie in der DDR*, ed. Joachim S. Hohmann (Berlin, 1991), 9–50, here 15.
5. Florian Mildenberger, "'Verjüngung' und 'Heilung' der Homosexualität: Eugen Steinach in seiner Zeit," *Zeitschrift für Sexualforschung* 15 (2002): 302–22; H. Stoff, "Ewige Jugend": *Konzepte der Verjüngung vom späten 19. Jahrhundert bis ins Dritte Reich* (Cologne, 2004): 30–87.
6. W. Hohlweg and K. Junkmann, "Die hormonal-nervöse Regulierung der Funktion des Hypophysenvorderlappens," *Klinische Wochenschrift* 11 (1932): 321–23.
7. Günter Dörner, "Kybernetische Wirkungsmechanismen bei endokrinen Regulationen," *Zeitschrift für die gesamte innere Medizin und ihre Grenzgebiete* 17 (1962): 574–80, here 577.
8. M. Diamond and W. C. Young, "Differential Responsiveness of Pregnant and Nonpregnant Guinea Pigs to the Masculinizing Action of Testosterone Propionate," *Endocrinology* 72 (1963): 429–38.
9. Ibid., 437.
10. Günter Dörner, "Tierexperimentelle Untersuchungen zur Frage einer hormonellen Pathogenese der Homosexualität," *Acta biologica et medica Germanica* 19 (1967): 569–84, 570.
11. Ibid., 572. At first glance, it might seem odd that the "masculine" hormone androgen would induce "feminine" sexual behavior in castrated male rats, but the logic of Dörner's experiment was as follows: when male rats were castrated, they effectively became female, physiologically speaking. Thus whenever the endocrine system was stimulated, it would release only female hormones—and Dörner believed that he had induced such a release by administering androgens. What Dörner did not take into account was that

the rats were already sexually mature by the time he administered androgens and were thus releasing hormones whenever the possibility of copulation arose. But since the male rats had no testicles and produced only female hormones, they expressed their desire for copulation by behaving like female rats. If Dörner had chosen to administer androgens before the rats had reached sexual maturity, he very well might have caused the rats to exhibit masculine behavior, albeit still without the ability to copulate. At this earlier stage in their life, these rats would likely not have endured the fate of being stigmatized as "homosexuals" by endocrinologists, but would instead have suffered the ignominy of being bitten to death by other rats that would have viewed these gender-nonconformist rats as alien entities within their kinship system.

12. Günter Dörner, "Hormonal Induction and Prevention of Female Homosexuality," *Journal of Endocrinology* 42 (1968): 163f.

13. G. Dörner, F. Döcke, and G. Hinz, "Entwicklung und Rückbildung neuroendokrin bedingter männlicher Homosexualität," *Acta biologica et medica Germanica* 21 (1968): 577–80, here 578.

14. F. Roeder and D. Müller, "Zur stereotaktischen Heilung der pädophilen Homosexualität," *Deutsche medizinische Wochenschrift* 94 (1969): 409–15; H. Orthner et al., *Zur Therapie sexueller Perversionen: Heilung einer homosexuell-pädophilen Triebabweichung durch einseitigen stereotaktischen Eingriff im Tuber cinereum* (Beiträge zur Sexualforschung 46) (Stuttgart, 1969).

15. Günter Dörner, "Die Entwicklung der Gonadotropin- und Sexualhormonforschung an der Charité," *Zentralblatt für Gynäkologie* 90 (1968): 62–72, 69.

16. Günter Dörner, "Zur Frage einer neuroendokrinen Pathogenese, Prophylaxe und Therapie angeborener Sexualdeviationen," *Deutsche medizinische Wochenschrift* 94 (1969): 390–96, here 391.

17. G. Dörner, F. Stahl, F. Götz, P. Rößner, and H. Halle, "Der Einfluss des fötalen Geschlechts auf den Androgengehalt im Frühschwangerenharn," *Endokrinologie* 58 (1971): 264–68, here 264.

18. G. Dörner and J. Staudt, "Vergleichende morphologische Untersuchungen der Hypothalamusdifferenzierung bei Ratte und Mensch," *Endokrinologie* 59 (1972): 152–55, here 152–54.

19. Günter Dörner, "Problems and Terminology of Functional Teratology," *Acta biologica et medica Germanica* 34 (1975): 1093–95, here 1094.

20. Günter Dörner, *Hormones and Brain Differentiation* (Amsterdam, 1976), 229.

21. Ibid.

22. Dörner, "Zur Frage eines neuroendokrinen Pathogenese," 392.

23. A. A. Ehrhardt and J. Money, "Progestin-Induced Hermaphroditism: IQ and Psychosexual Identity in a Study of Ten Girls," *Journal of Sex Research* 3 (1967): 83–100, 83.

24. G. Dörner, W. Rohde, K. Seidel, W. Haas and G. Schott, "On the Evocability of a Positive Oestrogen Feedback Action on LH Secretion in Transsexual Men and Women," *Endokrinologie* 67 (1976): 20–25.

25. G. Dörner, Th. Geier, L. Ahrens, L. Krell, G. Münx, H. Stieler, E. Kittner, and H. Müller, "Prenatal Stress as a Possible Aetiogenetic Factor of Homosexuality in Human Males," *Endocrinology* 75 (1980): 365–68.

26. M. Dannecker, G. Schmidt, E. Schorsch, and V. Sigusch, "Stellungnahme zu den Forschungen des Endokrinologen Prof. Dr. Günter Dörner zum Thema Homosexualität," *Sexualmedizin* 10 (1981): 110–11.

27. Ibid., 110.
28. Ibid., 111.
29. *Die Welt* quoted and the "storm of protest" discussed in "Select Your Kids' Sexual Preferences," *Weekly World News* 6, no. 49 (17 September 1985): 24.
30. "Sexual Preference by Order," *Orlando Sentinel*, 31 July 1985, http://articles.orland osentinel.com/1985-07-31/news/0320020200_1_endocrinology-masculine-or-fem inine-horrible-vision. Accessed March 16, 2012.
31. O. Brühl, "Sozialistisch und schwul: Eine subjektive Chronologie," in *Homosexualität in der DDR: Materialien und Meinungen*, ed. Wolfram Setz (Hamburg, 2006), 89–152, here 127.
32. Dagmar Herzog, *Sex after Fascism: Memory and Morality in Twentieth-Century Germany* (Princeton, NJ, 2005), 252; Michael Bochow, *Schwule Männer, AIDS und Safer Sex* (Berlin, 2001). Dörner remained less sympathetic. See Günter Dörner, "Hormonabhängige Gehirnentwicklung und Homosexualität," in R. Werner, ed., *Homosexualität: Herausforderung an Wissen und Toleranz* (Berlin, 1987), 175–80.
33. F. Pfäfflin, "Neuroendokrine Forschungsergebnisse und Sexualwissenschaft: Zur Vorgeschichte eines Konflikts," *Zeitschrift für Sexualforschung* 3 (1990): 54–74, 61.
34. Günter Dörner, "Proposal for Changing the Status of Homosexuality Under the W.H.O.'s Classification of Diseases," available at http://www.nel.edu/22_6/ NEL220601R02a_Dorner_.htm. Accessed March 16, 2012.
35. G. Dörner, I. Poppe, F. Stahl, J. Kölzsch, and R. Uebelhack, "Gene- and Environmental-Dependent Neuroendocrine Etiogenesis of Homosexuality and Transsexualism," *Experimental and Clinical Endocrinology* 98 (1991): 141–50, 149.
36. See especially Florian Mildenberger, "Rattenfänger auf Schloss Bellevue," *Gigi*, accessed March 16, 2012, http://www.gigi-online.de/Rattenf%E4nger23.html; and Elmar Kraushaar, "Der homosexuelle Mann...," *taz*, 11 June 2003, p. 20.
37. Protestbrief von Dr. Günter Grau, 3 December 2002, http://www.hirschfeld.in-berlin.de/frame.html?http://www.hirschfeld.in-berlin.de/aktuell/bundespraesident_doerner.html.
38. Kraushaar, "Der homosexuelle Mann...."
39. http://de.wikipedia.org/wiki/Günter_Dörner, accessed March 16, 2012.
40. B. Latour and S. Woolgar, *Laboratory Life: The Social Construction of Scientific Facts* (Los Angeles, 1979); Bruno Latour, *We Were Never Modern*, trans. Catherine Porter (Cambridge, MA, 1993).
41. See "Im Osten kaum Orden," *taz*, 4 March 1997, p. 4.

CHAPTER 15

~:~

Sex, Sentiment, and Socialism
Relationship Counseling in the GDR in the Wake of the 1965 Family Law Code

ERIK HUNEKE

The building of the Berlin Wall in 1961 was, among other things, the product of a government that had serious reservations about the ongoing demographic viability of the German Democratic Republic (GDR). Yet the Wall did not prove to be a panacea in this regard, since the GDR witnessed a declining marriage rate and an increase in the number of illicit abortions performed on younger women during the 1960s. During the first Continuing Education Conference for Problems Pertaining to Marital and Sexual Counseling, which was held in Rostock in October 1965, a certain Dr. Lungwitz projected that over the coming years the GDR's population would increase only incrementally—from 17.25 million in 1970 to 17.67 million in 1980—and that not until after 1980 would East Germany have a "normal population structure."[1] These demographic concerns spawned a number of governmental measures, first implemented during the 1950s but later expanded, especially after Erich Honecker assumed the mantle of leadership as general secretary of the Central Committee of the Socialist Unity Party (Sozialistische Einheitspartei Deutschlands, or SED) in 1971. These included financial incentives for childbearing coupled with the legalization, on 9 March 1972, of first-trimester abortion for any reason and the increasing availability of contraception (especially in the form of the Pill). These measures met with some degree of success, given that the number of live births in the GDR rose from 180,336 in 1973 to 245,132 in 1980.[2]

Another facet of the GDR's response to its demographic woes was the ambitious plan to establish a dense network of marital and sexual counseling centers (*Ehe- und Sexualberatungsstellen*, or ESBs) under the auspices of the Ministry of Health and of marital and familial counseling centers (*Ehe- und Familien-*

beratungsstellen, or EFBs) under the auspices of the Ministry of Justice beginning in the mid 1960s.[3] Relationship counseling centers had originally emerged
from the ferment accompanying the development of the sciences of the self at
the fin de siècle and the concomitant rise of the welfare state; the profession of
social work; feminist activism around questions of motherhood; debates about
contraception, abortion, demographic concerns, eugenics, social hygiene, and
sex reform; and advice literature published by such internationally renowned
figures as Ellen Key, Marie Stopes, and Theodor van de Velde. This potent
cocktail of phenomena has rightly attracted its fair share of scholarly attention.[4] Much of this scholarship has focused on the imbrication of marital counseling with the demographic and eugenic concerns of state population policy,
and on the ways in which such counseling provided a vector for the welfare
state's exertion of social control along Foucauldian lines.[5]

But, as Dagmar Herzog has argued,

> in the early 1970s the regime shifted and began enthusiastically promoting the
> very ubiquity of uncommitted youth heterosexuality which 1960s empirical
> studies had forced it reluctantly to acknowledge. This was read at the time by
> Western observers as a clearly desperate measure to raise birthrates in the wake
> of the introduction of the pill and the legalization of first-trimester abortions.
> But the East German context suggests that even more important than demog-
> raphy was the regime's abiding anxious desire to bind young people emotionally
> to the socialist project.[6]

The emotional dimension of the socialist project is also in evidence in Dorothee Wierling's "collective biography" of an East German generational cohort,
in which she found that a number of her interviewees, who were socialized in
the GDR during the 1950s and 1960s, tended to conflate, at least in retrospect, memories of familial relationships with their relationship to the GDR,
and that the common denominator in both cases was a language of love.[7] The
mapping of personal emotions onto those elicited by notions of belonging to
a state is certainly not a phenomenon that was unique to the GDR.[8] But the
role of marital and sexual counseling in potentially cementing or undermining
this emotional conflation of personal and political relationships points to the
constitutive ambivalence of at least one aspect of the educational dictatorship
(*Erziehungsdiktatur*) that Wierling sees as having taken shape in the GDR during the 1960s.[9]

The network of marital counseling centers constituted an effort to forge an
emotional bond not only with the young, but also with East Germans of older
generations, on the basis of a more candid discussion of sexual and marital
life. But the success of this project was contingent upon a number of factors
that proved to be beyond the control of high-level government officials. While
some counseling centers, like those of Dr. Siegfried Schnabl in Erlabrunn and

Dr. Lykke Aresin in Leipzig, were wildly popular in large part because of their role as providers of contraception and treatment for sexual dysfunction, many other counseling centers attracted a negligible number of visitors.[10] Youthful visitors were in particularly short supply.[11] Rural residents often feared becoming fodder for the local gossip mill and consequently visited counseling centers in more densely populated areas, if at all.[12] There was an incessant refrain in governmental reports at the local, regional, and national levels that not enough was being done to publicize the existence and methodologies of counseling centers, but in the case of the city of Erfurt—to provide but one example—publicity apparently was not enough. Despite announcements in the local press, the Erfurt EFB, which had been founded in July 1964 (prior to the promulgation of the mandate to establish such centers in the 1965 Family Law Code), had attracted no more than ten visitors during its initial year of operation—and some of these visitors had problems that could not be addressed by an EFB. The Erfurt center shut down as a result, only to be reopened later because of the legal requirement that every district have its own EFB.[13]

This did not diminish the central authorities' conviction that a comprehensive, uniform network of counseling centers was necessary, but their exhortations often ran up against bureaucratic recalcitrance—what one might consider a form of *Eigensinn* in the sense pioneered by Alf Lüdtke—on the part of local authorities and prospective counselors who did not see the point of putting much effort into something for which there seemed to be little or no popular demand.[1414] Even as high-level authorities remained committed to marital counseling, they also often hoped that East Germans would want advice on the socialist configuration of familial life that was not restricted to the domain of sexuality. But the contours of marital counseling were far from immune to popular pressure. As Donna Harsch has argued,

> [o]ver time, East German "healthcare consumers" drove marriage counseling toward greater individualization, professionalization, and specialization than the regime originally envisioned. Though the mix of methods used to "fix" troubled marriages remained more communal, traditional, and state-directed than in the West, the state's understanding of marital conflict became less ideological, moralistic, and social, and more pragmatic, individual, and psychological.[15]

Exploring the affective dimension of the interaction between citizen and state in the context of marital counseling can provide a new perspective on what one might call the "primacy of demographic concerns" in understandings of East German history.[16]

The network of counseling centers that emerged in the GDR during the mid 1960s did not constitute a mere palimpsest of its predecessors on German soil. The Weimar era had witnessed a proliferation of marital counseling offered by sex reformers like Magnus Hirschfeld, ardent socialist advocates of birth control like Max Hodann, and Social Darwinist eugenicists like Anne-Marie Durand-Wever.[17] In an effort to counteract the rapid spread of venereal disease during the tumultuous aftermath of World War II, military authorities directed German health officials in the Soviet zone of occupation to establish marital and sexual counseling centers, many of which ceased operation during the early 1950s due to the rapidly declining demand for their services.[18] One could also say that the SED, which had been largely allergic to the remnants of the pre–World War II sex reform movement, was suddenly poised to revive one of its most salient legacies.

Expert voices considered trust (*Vertrauen*) to be an important emotional basis for both "socialist" love relationships and a successful dynamic between marital counselors and the advice seekers who came to them. As Lykke Aresin emphasized in the very title of her book on matters pertaining to sexual and marital counseling, *Consultation Hour of Trust* (*Sprechstunde des Vertrauens*), it was imperative that counselors have not only impeccable professional credentials, but also the life experience and community respect that would enable them to earn the trust of the general population. If confronted with a confession of "abnormal" sexual behavior, for example, the counselor was not to engage in moralizing pontification, but instead lend an understanding ear and recommend a dispassionate, medically informed course of action.[19]

But the basis for establishing such trust was, on any number of levels, a rather shaky one. For one thing, many East German relationship manual authors in the years leading up to and following 1965 bewailed the resilience of atavistic notions about intimate life—an inheritance of the bourgeois era that continued to have deleterious consequences for educating a new generation of socialist youth.[20] Aresin explicitly invoked the lingering influence of conceptions of sexual shame, gender inequality, and prudishness as reasons why otherwise thoroughly modern East Germans would need an outlet to discuss problems related to their intimate lives.[21] Indeed, the tenor of many relationship advice manuals betrayed a fundamental distrust of East Germans' ability to internalize socialist moral norms regarding marriage, family, and sexuality. After all, why else would the need to establish a comprehensive network of counseling centers have seemed so pressing?[22] In this book *Jugend und Liebe*, for instance, Rolf Borrmann echoed other GDR advice manual authors in saying that intimate life had not yet received sufficient attention in socialist society, and that interpersonal relationships informed by socialist principles would not develop on their own. For him and many other purveyors of relationship advice in the GDR, attitudes toward love, sexuality, marriage, and family were inextricably intertwined with the development of socialist convictions, character traits, and behavioral patterns.[23] Even as late as 1988, Lykke Aresin and Erwin Günther (a professor and director of the dermatological clinic at the Friedrich

Schiller University in Jena) reiterated the frequent call for the "education of the educators" (*Erziehung der Erzieher*).[24] Aresin and Günther noted:

> Parents, teachers, university instructors, and other educators have still not overcome their hostility [toward sexuality]; some apparently think that since everyone can speak freely about sexuality, they need not do so themselves. But more than 100 years ago Friedrich Engels opposed prudishness and two-faced morality by writing, "It is about time that at least German workers become accustomed to speaking dispassionately about activities in which they themselves are engaging on a daily or nightly basis—about natural, indispensable, and particularly pleasurable matters.[25]

If Friedrich Engels could not provide sufficient incitement to sexual discourse, who could?

But the problem turned out to be less the purported unwillingness of East Germans to discuss sexual matters than their frustration at how difficult it was to find trustworthy individuals with whom to do so. To be sure, a press campaign and surveys of potential visitors to counseling centers were intended to reveal and debunk the hesitations the general population might have had about seeking counseling, most of which stemmed from reluctance to have the state or mass organizations intervene in private matters. A draft of an article that was to appear in *Armee-Rundschau* in March 1965 opined that "[t]here are probably a whole series of reservations about having other people 'lecturing' someone about marital problems that need to be overcome. The organization of marital counseling centers needs to address such concerns so that an atmosphere of trust reigns in the counseling offered."[26] But relationship advice manual author Rudolf Neubert noted again and again in his book *Fragen und Antworten* that his epistolary correspondents complained that they had no one else to consult about their sexual travails.

Once the SED saw fit to provide opportunities for GDR citizens to seek out counseling services on a broader scale, the populace, in turn, proved itself to be quite selective in according trust to marital counselors. Report after report pointed to the fact that most counseling centers suffered from a dearth of visitors, contrary to Herzog's assertion that East Germans "flocked to" them.[27] In areas marked by a particularly strong allegiance to the Catholic Church, such as the town of Heiligenstadt, whose EFB no one visited during the course of 1966, Justice Ministry officials speculated as to whether or not a priest should be invited as a member of the counseling collective, provided that a suitable candidate could be found who would not seek to place the EFB under the orbit of ecclesiastical control.[28] The most popular counseling centers tended to be those that were known for dispensing advice regarding sexual dysfunction and contraception, including Aresin's own ESB at the Gynecological Clinic of the

Karl Marx University in Leipzig, which attracted more than 800 visitors in 1964.[29] This was bound to discomfort officials and nonmedical experts who were reluctant to accord too much importance to the "sexual question."[30]

Indeed, the question of whether or not to include the word "sexual" in the name of the expanded network of marital counseling centers provoked a fair amount of controversy among officials, since numerous officials believed that using "Marital and Family Counseling Centers" (those overseen by the Ministry of Justice) as opposed to "Marital and Sexual Counseling Centers" (those overseen by the Ministry of Health) would dissuade the unmarried from seeking counsel. These concerns were particularly pronounced among those who saw relationship counseling centers as falling primarily under the purview of medical experts. The authors of one report noted that "we have some reservations about the term 'Marital and Family Counseling Center' deployed in the Family Law Code draft, since a) 'marriage' of course falls under the rubric of 'family' and b) not all problems having to do with the elimination of sexual disorders and contraception should be seen in connection with the concepts of 'marriage' or family.'"[31] And like the call for greater deployment of psychological knowledge in counseling centers, the debates surrounding their naming also seeped into the press. A 1965 interview with Berlin gynecologist Dr. Lothar Obgartel quoted him as saying that "'[w]e consciously strive for the term marital and sexual counseling in contrast to the often declared marital and family counseling. This is not merely a play on words ... the naming should indicate that the counseling is not limited to those who are married or engaged.'"[32]

The Ministry of Justice adopted a decidedly different stance. A 1965 report advocated the use of the term "marital and family counseling center" to assuage the populace's misgivings about seeking out counseling that touched upon intimate matters:

> As far as the name is concerned, it seems as if the term used in the law's draft—"Marital and Family Counseling Centers"—is the most advantageous one. To be sure, this term does not encompass the full range of counseling offered, since it does not include premarital sexual relationships. This would be the case with the term "sexual counseling." The survey regarding marriage counseling has already revealed quite clearly, however, that the strongest reservations exist about counseling in sexual-erotic matters—a finding that stands in stark contrast to the prevailing practices of counseling centers. The name should not only aim to be as precise as possible, it must also provide the best strategy for overcoming existing reservations [on the part of the general populace]. For this reason the term suggested by doctors, "Counseling Center for Generational Questions," must unreservedly be rejected.[33]

Thus the very naming of the counseling centers was emotionally charged at the highest levels of decision making, even if the nuance of the terminology used might have been lost on the population at large. Ultimately, the Health

Ministry issued Decree 3/68 stipulating that ESBs were to be just the medical branch of the more comprehensive, multidisciplinary counseling offered by
EFBs.[34] This resulted in many calls from officials for EFBs to merge officially
with ESBs to become marital, family, and sexual counseling centers (*Ehe-,
Familien- und Sexualberatungsstellen*, abbreviated as EFSBs or EF-SBs).[35] The
EFSB in Berlin-Lichtenberg, a pioneer in this regard, was among the most successful counseling centers in the GDR, with an average of 80 to 120 visitors
per month in 1968, about half of whom came for "medical" reasons.[36] The proliferation of acronyms caused a certain amount of confusion among some regional officials: the regional court (*Bezirksgericht*, or BG) of Gera, for instance,
reported the existence of *either* 10 EFBs, 10 ESBs, and 1 EF-SB *or* 1 EFB, 1
ESB, and 10 EF-SBs in early 1969.[37]

The problematic groundwork for building relationships of trust surrounding
the promulgation of socialist sexual norms also extended to the relationship between the SED and the professionals who were to serve as counselors. The SED
had harbored significant mistrust of psychological professionals during the 1950s,
as exemplified by the Pavlov campaign waged by Walter Hollitscher, Alexander
Mette, and Dietfried Müller-Hegemann to discredit "bourgeois" explanations for
human behavior.[38] This campaign was predicated on the notion that social factors, rather than intrinsic characteristics, were determinative of the conditioned
reflexes that governed many behavioral patterns. It also entailed a rejection of
Sigmund Freud's allegedly inappropriate reification of sexuality (and the libido in
particular) as an animalistic force that shaped much of human behavior.[39]

But the shift from a loose, uncoordinated web of counseling centers (i.e., the
few that survived after the "mass extinction" of ESBs during the early 1950s) to
a centralized system mandated by the Ministries of Justice and Health stemmed
to a significant extent from what Greg Eghigian has called the "psychologization of the socialist self" that began in the GDR during the late 1950s. After
having been discredited as a capitalist relic by many in the SED during the first
decade of the GDR's existence, psychology came to be seen as a useful tool for
defining the parameters of the "socialist personality" and the forms of deviance
that threatened its development. Indeed, Eghigian argues that "the SED's obsession with policing conformity lies in its vision of the self not simply as a political, but as a psychopedagogical, project."[40] The rehabilitation of psychology
went hand in hand with a recrudescence of social scientific inquiry more generally, and concerns about the family and sexuality provided a particularly salient rationale for this development. During a discussion in 1965 that included
doctors, nurses, and community members, Siegfried Schnabl noted that other
countries' experience demonstrated the usefulness of relationship counseling,
and that "[h]is psychotherapeutic practice convinced him of the need for such
centers. Two-thirds of the cases he dealt with concerned disturbances in marital life, and particularly in the domain of sexuality."[41]

While Harsch has argued that it was East German "'healthcare consumers'" who pushed marital counseling away from collective and toward "individualizing" methods, to a significant extent this "individualization" also reflected the intentions of high-level officials. While counselors were referred to as being members of a collective, counseling sessions themselves were typically supposed to be one-on-one, unless a spouse came as well or the expertise of a second counseling collective member was required.[42] Rather than presenting a clear dichotomy between "individualized" and "collective" approaches to marital counseling, however, many ESBs and EFBs strove to combine both kinds of methods. The importance of confidentiality of counseling sessions was repeatedly emphasized (so as to win over the populace's trust), but this was hard to maintain when social forces (*gesellschaftliche Kräfte*) were also supposed to be called upon to intervene in marital disputes. In one noteworthy case, a counselor at a center in Sömmerda met with a woman whose husband was having an adulterous affair with a female colleague. The husband said that he would not be able to tear himself away from his lover as long as they worked in the same place, so the Sömmerda EFB obtained another job for the husband, who thereupon returned to his family.[43] Aside from the rather pat treatment of the emotional dynamics of this adulterous situation (which was rather typical of written documentation about the practice of ESBs and EFBs, which was not exactly raw material for bodice rippers), the counselor did not see any contradiction between upholding the principle of confidential counseling and intervening in such a way that would make it difficult to hide the wife's involvement. He was also rather naive in his belief that the key to dissolving a sexually charged emotional attachment was changing one's working environment, although he was not alone in this belief as workplace transfers were a not-infrequent response to illicit affairs between colleagues.

In the GDR, it was thus not the case that "modern," individualizing courses of treatment usurped "traditional," communal forms of intervention, as Harsch has argued, but instead that a specifically East German conception of the psychological expert's professional role in mediating relationships—between the sexes, within the family, and among members of a collective—was emerging. Collective efforts at intervention were not always deemed to be the most successful ones, but they were never dispensed with entirely.[44] The role of the psychological professional in the GDR was thus paradoxically to draw upon (at least implicitly) a "bourgeois" legacy of expert knowledge about sexual behavior with the ostensible goal of weaning the populace away from what were deemed outdated "bourgeois" attitudes about, and emotions associated with, sexual behavior.[45] But that professional was to do so in a way that cultivated East German laypersons' trust in both a seemingly non-ideological form of expertise and the providence of socialist humanism courtesy of the SED.

Official concerns about East Germans' unwillingness to accept the intervention of state institutions in their intimate lives were tempered by ambivalence about the extent to which the populace seemed to crave an outlet for sexual discourse. Even as the state was creating an infrastructure that enabled such discourse, officials and professionals remained divided as to whether helping to constitute emotionally satisfying sexual relationships for East Germans would translate into an emotionally satisfying relationship between ordinary citizens and the polity in which they resided. The relative unpopularity of many EFBs in particular (the counseling centers that did not have "sexual" in their name), with the exception of those with counselors who addressed citizens' pressing emotional and sexual needs, served as a litmus test for the populace's willingness to render the personal political, and to sanction state intervention in their intimate and emotional lives.

One of the biggest frustrations engendered by the process of creating a network of EFBs and ESBs was the sluggishness with which many district councils (*Räte der Kreise*) followed the regional courts' and Berlin-based authorities' exhortations to establish them. Time and time again, regional court (*Bezirksgericht*) officials who were responsible for reporting to the MdJ on the status of EFB development bemoaned local officials' failure to take any initiative at all in finding appropriate space and staff for counseling centers—what I have called bureaucratic *Eigensinn*. Some observers alleged that this resulted from the fact that the 17 February 1966 Implementation Directive for the Family Law Code did not stipulate which agency of local government was responsible for EFB formation.[46] Given the apparently widespread confusion about the distinction between ESBs and EFBs, many local officials might have assumed that local health officials would take care of the matter.

Numerous counseling centers experienced difficulty in recruiting appropriate medical personnel, as many smaller municipalities lacked a plethora of medical specialists well-versed in marital counseling and work in an EFB was on a mostly voluntary basis (only social workers were typically on salary; other counselors received a small honorarium). By contrast, medical and psychiatric professionals who worked in ESBs received compensation for their efforts from the Ministry of Health.[47] Thus, a medical professional who agreed to work as part of an EFB's counseling collective had to be motivated by something other than money—loyalty to her or his patients, but also a sufficient emotional connection of loyalty to the state on whose behalf she or he would be offering her or his professional expertise. Counting on such loyalty was potentially quite a leap of faith for the government, since there was evidence of disgruntlement among medical personnel at polyclinics (which were not infrequently the institutional homes of counseling centers): in 1971, the popular medical advice periodical *Deine Gesundheit* noted that 260 of its readers had complained about doctors' arrogance, tactlessness, poor listening skills, failure to explain the nature of an illness, excessive haste in conducting medical exams that more often than not consisted only of writing a prescription, and failure to model appropriate behavior for their patients.[48]

Despite the many internal admissions of the failure to establish a fully operational marital counseling center in every district of the GDR, in public pronouncements, by contrast, the centers were a point of pride. The flagship counseling centers attracted visitors from other (mostly socialist) countries—the head of a Warsaw polyclinic visited the Berlin-Lichtenberg EFSB, jurists and doctors from Chile, Bulgaria, and Hungary consulted with the EFB in Mitte, and Africans of unspecified nationality paid a visit to the EFB in Prenzlauer Berg.[49] Professor Gerhard Misgeld, editor of *Deine Gesundheit*, noted in 1971 that the GDR's Working Group on Marriage and Family (Arbeitsgemeinschaft Ehe und Familie) had been established in 1964 and since then had helped to set up 200 ESBs throughout the GDR. By contrast, the working group's counterpart in the Federal Republic of Germany, which had been founded in 1952 (Misgeld did not attempt to explain why it predated its equivalent in the GDR by twelve years), had established only twenty-three ESBs, despite West Germany's considerably larger population.[50] This was one arena of inter-German competition in which the East Germans appeared to be "winning."

During the waning years of the GDR, however, the often precarious longevity of individual counseling centers became even more pronounced as the total number of ESBs, EFBs, and EFSBs dropped from 274 in 1977 to 230 in 1985 and 189 in 1987.[51] In a belated attempt to curry favor with every elusive youthful advice-seeker, a legal adviser and SED party member at the VEB *Dienstleistungskombinat* Dresden sought to establish what might very well have become the match.com of the GDR—a matchmaking computer program whose title roughly translates as "Boy Meets Girl through the Computer" (*Sie und Er per Computer*). While the comrade (*Genossin*) might not have been a consummate wordsmith, she did not lack for ambition: she hoped that her idea for a computer-mediated "relationship counseling center" (*Partnerberatungsstelle*) would soon be adopted throughout the GDR.[52]

Conclusion

Edward Ross Dickinson has diagnosed the emergence of "the outlines for a new master narrative of modern German history" that

> draws heavily on the theoretical and historical works of Michel Foucault and Detlev J. K. Peukert, and on the earlier work of the Frankfurt School, Max Weber, and the French theorists of postmodernism. In it, rationalization and

science, and specifically the extended discursive field of "biopolitics" (the whole complex of disciplines and practices addressing issues of health, reproduction, and welfare) play a key role as the marker and most important content of modernization.[53]

Dickinson provides a two-pronged critique of this master narrative: he contends that, like the *Sonderweg* thesis that alleges that Germany's unique societal characteristics were what led it to embrace National Socialism, this interpretative vantage point all too easily conflates German biopolitics with totalitarianism. He also seeks to alter the prevailing understanding of the term "biopolitics" more generally by characterizing it "not only as a project of elites and experts, but as a complex social and cultural transformation."[54] By explicitly equating the social welfare approach of the German Democratic Republic with that of Germany during the Nazi period and thereby upholding an altogether too clear-cut dichotomy between "democratic" and "totalitarian" biopolitical motivations and policies, Dickinson detracts from his otherwise very astute argument.[55] For instance, he contends that "scientific 'fact' is democracy's substitute for revealed truth, expertise its substitute for authority. The age of democracy is the age of professionalization."[56] But a major impetus behind the SED's unflagging devotion to the concept of marital counseling from 1965 onward was precisely the desire to harness professional expertise in the interest of imparting a "socialist" imprimatur to family life.

But as in democratic polities, the marshaling of professional expertise for political ends did not occur without friction or ambivalence. National and regional officials harangued recalcitrant local authorities about their reluctance or failure to establish counseling centers. Jurists, teachers, and Democratic Women's League (Demokratischer Frauenbund Deutschlands) members (some of whom also served as EFB counselors) resented the fact that their expertise was often superfluous, given that in many clinics the majority of visitors sought out medical, psychological, or psychotherapeutic counseling instead. While proud of the propagandistic value of the comprehensive network of counseling centers for the GDR's image abroad, officials at the Ministries of Justice and Health were not necessarily thrilled that so much of the work of marital counseling centers revolved around contraceptive advice, the treatment of sexual dysfunction, or attempts to mediate in marital conflicts that had progressed too far to be resolved.[57] Even experts who advocated more candid discussion of sexual matters emphatically emphasized that relationships and marriages could not be reduced to their sexual component.[58]

Unlike many marital counseling centers established during the Weimar era, the period of National Socialist rule, and the immediate aftermath of World War II, the GDR's EFBs and ESBs of the 1960s and thereafter did not (at least as far as the archival trail reveals) focus on performing premarital health exams, but instead on providing counseling that would address the emotional causes of sexual dysfunction, marital conflict, and childrearing difficulties. The tendency to combine individualized, professional counseling with collective, ideologically informed intervention by socialist collectives reflected a realization of the need to respect the emotional integrity of those who sought advice. Counselors and officials did not want anyone to think, after all, that advice seekers were being "pumped for information" (*ausgehorcht*)—even though they did not explicitly acknowledge why East Germans would have had good reason to fear being spied upon by a state-run entity, given the pervasive presence of Secret Police (Stasi) informants. From this perspective, the ardor with which officials hoped for the viability of marital counseling in the GDR reflected an effort to (re)gain citizens' trust by setting up a benevolent form of biopolitics against the regime's pernicious system of police surveillance. The marital counseling center as an institution both reflected and fostered shifting understandings about the relationship between sexuality, procreation, and pleasure, but its role in societal transformation could be construed even more broadly: in attempting to cement an emotional bond between East Germans and their polity, the "clinic" sought to transform itself from a "panopticon" into a haven for a *Sprechstunde des Vertrauens*.

Notes

1. Bundesarchiv Berlin-Lichterfelde (BArch), DP1 VA 1445, Band 2, Dr. Beyer, Vermerk betr. 1. Rostocker Fortbildungstage über Probleme der Ehe- und Sexualberatung vom 22. bis 24. Oktober 1965, Ministerium der Justiz (MdJ), Hauptabteilung (HA) Recht, Berlin, 27 October 1965, 3 (119 of archival file).
2. Mary Fulbrook, *The People's State: East German Society from Hitler to Honecker* (New Haven, 2005), 150–54. While the GDR had lagged behind other socialist countries in decriminalizing abortion, largely out of fear about the birthrate and the purported concern to "protect" women from the deleterious health consequences of abortion, by 1972 the SED had come to see the provision of the Pill and relatively unfettered access to first-trimester abortion as actually fostering rather than undermining women's motivation to bear children resulting from planned pregnancies. Whereas before 1972, the SED did not view family planning as a constitutive element of the equality (*Gleichberechtigung*) of men and women, it now maintained that providing women with the means to determine the timing and number of births was integral to their equality in domestic, educational, and vocational life—although abortion was to remain the method of last resort. Moreover, Health Minister Ludwig Mecklinger maintained that unlike in bourgeois society, where women were subject to "transcendental powers or the workings of nature" and thus were consigned to more or less compulsory motherhood, the legalization of abortion was another way in which socialism implemented the findings of science and medicine to improve human life. See Gerhard Misgeld, "Ein weiterer Schritt," *Deine Gesundheit* 4 (April 1972): 100–104, here 101. In response to the question "Should we be afraid that our state is 'dying out'?" Dr. Rayner of the

Health Ministry noted that while the 9 March 1972 law was initially accompanied by a precipitous decline in the birthrate, this decline had long been underway in other countries as well (regardless of the nature of their respective abortion laws), and that since October 1973 the GDR's birthrate had begun increasing for the first time in years. See "Das Interview: Bilanz der Familienplanung," interview conducted by Burghild Fertig with Dr. Rayner of the Ministry of Health, *Deine Gesundheit* 3 (March 1974): 68–69, here 69.

3. Paragraph 7 of the 17 February 1966 Implementation Directive (Durchführungsbestimmung) for Paragraph 4 of the 20 December 1965 Family Law Code (Familiengesetzbuch, or FGB) called for the establishment of EFBs in every district (*Kreis*) of the GDR; the Ministry of Health had already planned on creating ESBs in every district in 1964, and this was codified in Paragraph 11 of the March 1965 Law for the Protection of the Working Mother (Gesetz zum Schutz der erwerbstätigen Mutter).

4. Some key works include Atina Grossmann, *Reforming Sex: The German Movement for Birth Control and Abortion Reform, 1920–1950* (New York, 1995); Cornelia Usborne, *The Politics of the Body in Weimar Germany: Women's Reproductive Rights and Duties* (Ann Arbor, 1992); Alfons Lapisch, "'Hygiene ist Moral—Moral ist Hygiene': Soziale Disziplinierung durch Ärzte und Medizin," in *Soziale Sicherheit und soziale Disziplinierung: Beiträge zu einer historischen Theorie der Sozialpolitik*, ed. Christoph Sachße and Florian Tennstedt (Frankfurt am Main, 1986); Young-Sun Hong, *Welfare, Modernity, and the Weimar State, 1919–1933* (Princeton, 1998); Paul Weindling, *Health, Race, and German Politics between National Unification and Nazism, 1870–1945* (Cambridge, 1989); and Michelle Mouton, *From Nurturing the Nation to Purifying the Volk: Weimar and Nazi Family Policy, 1918–1945* (Washington, DC, and New York, 2007).

5. See Michel Foucault, *The Birth of the Clinic: An Archaeology of Medical Perception*, trans. A. M. Sheridan Smith (New York, 1973) and Detlev J. K. Peukert, *Grenzen der Sozialdisziplinierung: Aufstieg und Krise der deutschen Jugendfürsorge von 1878 bis 1932* (Cologne, 1986).

6. Dagmar Herzog, *Sex after Fascism: Memory and Morality in Twentieth-Century Germany* (Princeton, NJ, 2005), 187.

7. Dorothee Wierling, *Geboren im Jahr Eins: Der Jahrgang 1949 in der DDR: Versuch einer Kollektivbiographie* (Berlin, 2002), 103–13.

8. See, for example, Mrinalini Sinha, "Nations in an Imperial Crucible," in *Gender and Empire*, ed. Philippa Levine (New York, 2004), 181–202.

9. Wierling, *Geboren im Jahr Eins*, 559.

10. Norbert and Lykke Aresin's ESB was formally established in 1963, but it built upon a fifteen-year-long tradition of providing marital and sexual counseling at the gynecological clinic of the University of Leipzig. Of the 838 visitors to Norbert and Lykke Aresin's ESB in 1964, a number of whom came from other parts of the GDR, 47.8 percent came seeking contraceptive advice and 36.2 percent sought treatment for sexual dysfunction; see BArch, DP1 VA 1445, volume 3, untitled and unpaginated document about the Aresins' ESB. Edward Ross Dickinson has pointed out that the aims of a 1926 Prussian decree regarding voluntary premarital eugenic counseling were thwarted because the majority of those who sought counseling were motivated by the desire for birth control rather than concern about "the quality of their prospective offspring." East Germans, along similar lines, opted for contraceptive advice over ideological indoctrination. See Edward Ross Dickinson, "Biopolitics, Fascism, Democracy: Some Reflec-

tions on Our Discourse about 'Modernity,'" *Central European History* 37 (2004): 1–48, here 14.

11. For one of many complaints about the lack of youthful visitors to counseling centers, see BArch, DP1 VA 1757, volume 5, Bericht über den Erfahrungsaustausch der in den Ehe- und Familienberatungsstellen tätigen juristischen Mitarbeiter aus den Bezirken Frankfurt/Oder, Halle und Karl-Marx-Stadt, July 1970, 8.

12. BArch, DP1 VA 1446, Protokoll über die Fachtagung der Familienrichter (in Erfurt) am 22. November 1966 zu dem Thema: Erfahrungsaustausch über Ehe- und Familienberatungsstellen, 9 (132 of archival file); BArch, DP1 VA 3007, Band 1.3561, Silbernagel of BG Halle (Saale), Überblick über Stand der Bildung und der Tätigkeit der Ehe- und Familienberatungsstellen und der dabei aufgetretenen Probleme, 1 (75 of archival file).

13. BArch DP1 VA 1445, Band 2, Bericht über die Struktur und Arbeitsweise der bisher tätigen Eheberatungsstellen, 19 August 1965, 5 (36 of archival file).

14. BArch, DP1 VA 1446, Bericht über den Stand der Bildung und der Tätigkeit der Ehe- und Familienberatungsstellen in der DDR, MdJ in Berlin, 7 March 1967, 5 (151 of archival file). This report, like many others, noted that EFBs *were* necessary as evidenced by the fact that many people went to their local courts' legal information office (*Rechtsauskunft*) with their marital and familial problems—but in many cases, they did so instead of going to the EFB since the *Rechtsauskunft*'s hours were more convenient and because in many cases EFB visitors with legal problems would likely be referred to the court anyway. For more on the concept of *Eigensinn*, see Alf Lüdtke, ed., *The History of Everyday Life: Reconstructing Historical Experiences and Ways of Life*, trans. William Templer (Princeton, NJ, 1995).

15. Donna Harsch, *Revenge of the Domestic: Women, the Family, and Communism in the German Democratic Republic* (Princeton, 2007), 290.

16. The term "primacy of demography" is inspired by Timothy Mason's coinage "the primacy of politics." See Timothy Mason, *Nazism, Fascism and the Working Class*, ed. Jane Caplan (Cambridge, 1995).

17. Kristine von Soden, *Die Sexualberatungsstellen der Weimarer Republik 1919–1933* (Berlin, 1988).

18. Annette F. Timm, "The Legacy of *Bevölkerungspolitik*: Venereal Disease Control and Marriage Counselling in Post-WWII Berlin," *Canadian Journal of History/Annales canadiennes d'histoire* 33 (1998): 173–214. On 26 January 1952, Käthe Kern, director of the Department for Mothers and Children at the Ministry of Health, instructed all regional authorities not to establish any new ESBs given the lack of demand for their services. See BArch, DQ1 5144, letter from Käthe Kern, Leiterin der HA Mutter und Kind, Ministerium für Gesundheitswesen (MfG), an alle 5 Länder, 26 January 1952, 141 of archival file.

19. Lykke Aresin, *Sprechstunde des Vertrauens: Fragen der Sexual-, Ehe- und Familienberatung*, 2nd ed. (Rudolstadt, 1968), 23–25, 73.

20. One example among many of this genre is Rudolf Neubert, *Fragen und Antworten zum "Neuen Ehebuch" und zur "Geschlechterfrage"* (Rudolstadt, 1961).

21. Aresin, *Sprechstunde des Vertrauens*, 8.

22. Rudolf Neubert noted that his books *Das neue Ehebuch* and *Die Geschlechterfrage*, published in the 1950s, had elicited about 500 letters from readers. He frequently wondered why the advice seekers had turned to an author they did not know rather than to family or collective members, and indeed thought that the very genre of the book

that he wrote was a symptom of the transitional period (*Übergangszeit*) that would become superfluous once socialist conceptions of sexual and married life had been fully absorbed by East Germans. But he also saw the establishment of a comprehensive network of ESBs as one potential antidote to this situation. See Neubert, *Fragen und Antworten*, 158, 223.

23. Rolf Borrmann, *Jugend und Liebe: Die Beziehungen der Jugendlichen zum anderen Geschlecht*, 3rd rev. ed. (Leipzig, Jena, and Berlin, 1966), 5.

24. This phrase stems from, among other manuals, Borrmann, *Jugend und Liebe*, 163.

25. Lykke Aresin and Erwin Günther, "Einleitung," in *Sexualmedizin: Ein Leitfaden für Medizinstudenten*, ed. Lykke Aresin and Erwin Günther, 3rd rev. ed. (Berlin, 1988), 11–12, here 11.

26. BArch, DP1 VA 1445, vol. 1, Entwurf eines Artikels für die *Armee-Rundschau* über Eheberatung, 18 March 1965, 2 of article, 62 of archival file.

27. Herzog, *Sex after Fascism*, 203. The reports can be found in BArch, DP 1 VA 1445 and 1446, among other files.

28. BArch, DP1 VA 1446, Krutzsch, Bericht über den Erfahrungsaustausch der im Bezirk Erfurt in den Ehe- und Familienberatungsstellen tätigen Richter vom 22. November 1966, 1 (118b of file).

29. BArch, DP1 VA 1445, vol. 2, Bericht über die Struktur und Arbeitsweise der bisher tätigen Eheberatungsstellen, 19 August 1965, 1, 7 (34 and 37 of archival file). At this clinic, 47.8 percent of visitors came to inquire about contraception, 10.7 percent about female sexual disorders, 9.8 percent about general sexual disorders, 9.3 percent about marital conflicts that stemmed from sexual disorders, 6.4 percent about male sexual disorders, and 5.3 percent about pregnancy counseling; 4.3 percent brought up other problems. See BArch, DP1 VA 1445, vol. 2, unpaginated part of archival file, report on the Leipzig Eheberatungsstelle.

30. Borrmann, *Jugend und Liebe*, 6.

31. BArch, DP1 VA 1445, vol. 1, Stellungnahme des Ministeriums für Gesundheitswesen zur Schaffung von Ehe- und Familienberatungsstellen im Sinne des Entwurfes des Familiengesetzbuches der Deutschen Demokratischen Republik von Obermedizinalrat Dr. Oerter, Abteilung Organisation des Gesundheitswesens, Berlin, 13 May 1965, 2 (98 of archival file).

32. BArch, DP1 VA 1445, vol. 2: "Gut beraten in die Ehe. Zu Familien- und Sexualproblemen—Tagung in Rostock," an article in *Neue Zeit* by Karl-Georg Eickenjäger, 95 of archival file.

33. BArch, DP1 VA 1445, vol. 2, Bericht über die Struktur und Arbeitsweise der bisher tätigen Eheberatungsstellen, 19 August 1965, 12–13 (back of 39 and 40 of archival file).

34. BArch, DP1 VA 1446, volume 4, Aus der Wochenmeldung des Bezirks Neubrandenburg, undated but presumably from 1968, 1–2 (37–38 of archival file).

35. See, for example, BArch, DP1 VA 1757, letter from Judge Naumann, Stadtgericht von Groß-Berlin, 3. Zivilsenat, to MdJ, HA IV, 13 September 1968, 6 (98 of archival file); BArch, DP1 VA 1446, unnumbered volume would be 5 in terms of sequence, letter from MdJ, HA Gesetzgebung, to Rolf Borrmann, 26 July 1967.

36. BArch, DP1 VA 1757, Protokoll der Beratung mit Mitarbeitern der Ehe- und Familienberatungsstellen in der Hauptstadt der DDR am 14. August 1968, Judge Naumann, Stadtgericht von Groß-Berlin, 3. Zivilsenat, 1 September 1968, 2–3 (41–42 of archival file).

37. BArch, DP1 VA 1756, Gera subsection, Gera: Stand: 1. März 1969 vs. letter from Siegert, Direktor des BG Gera, to MdJ in Berlin, HA IV, 11 February 1969.

38. Heike Bernhardt, "Mit Sigmund Freud und Iwan Petrowitsch Pawlow im Kalten Krieg: Walter Hollitscher, Alexander Mette und Dietfried Müller-Hegemann in der DDR," in *Mit ohne Freud: Zur Geschichte der Psychoanalyse in Ostdeutschland*, ed. Heike Bernhardt and Regine Lockot (Gießen, 2000), 172–203; Sabine Hanrath, "Strukturkrise und Reformbeginn: Die Anstaltspsychiatrie in der DDR und der Bundesrepublik bis zu den 60er Jahren," in *Psychiatriereform als Gesellschaftsreform: Die Hypothek des Nationalsozialismus und der Aufbruch der sechziger Jahre*, ed. Franz-Werner Kersting (Paderborn, Munich, Vienna, and Zurich, 2003), 31–61, here 45.

39. Borrmann, *Jugend und Liebe*, 39; Neubert, *Fragen und Antworten*, 34.

40. Greg Eghigian, "The Psychologization of the Socialist Self: East German Forensic Psychology and Its Deviants, 1945–1975," *German History* 22 (2004): 181–205, here 203.

41. BArch, DP1 VA 1445, vol. 2, Vermerk über die Veranstaltung des Ministers im Bergarbeiterkrankenhaus "Dr. Georg Benjamin" Erlabrunn, 29 July 1965, not paginated.

42. BArch, DP1 VA 1446, Entwurf von Richtlinien über die Arbeitsweise und die Organisation von Ehe- und Sexualberatungsstellen in der Deutschen Demokratischen Republik, Arbeitsgemeinschaft Ehe und Familie in der Sektion Hygiene und Gesundheitsschutz der Frau der Gesellschaft für Gesundheitsschutz in der Deutschen Gesellschaft für die gesamte Hygiene, 26 September 1966, 7 (196 of archival file).

43. BArch, DP 1 VA 1446, Protokoll über die Fachtagung der Familienrichter [from Erfurt] am 22. November 1966 zu dem Thema: Erfahrungsaustausch über Ehe- und Familienberatungsstellen, 11 (134 of archival file).

44. BArch, DP1 VA 1757, volume 5, Bericht über den Erfahrungsaustausch der in den Ehe- und Familienberatungsstellen tätigen juristischen Mitarbeiter aus den Bezirken Frankfurt/Oder, Halle und Karl-Marx-Stadt, July 1970, 10 (198 of archival file).

45. For another example of an East German tendency to put "bourgeois" or "petty-bourgeois" wine into socialist bottles, see Anna-Sabine Ernst, "Vom 'Du' zum 'Sie': Die Rezeption der bürgerlichen Anstandsregeln in der DDR der 50er Jahre," *Mitteilungen aus der kulturwissenschaftlichen Forschung* 33 (1993): 190–209.

46. BArch, DP1 VA 1757, Einschätzung zum Stand der Arbeit mit den Ehe- und Familienberatungsstellen im Bezirk Neubrandenburg, sent by Barwinsky, BG Neubrandenburg, to MdJ in Berlin, HA IV, 10 September 1968.

47. BArch, DP1 VA 1446, Bericht über den Stand der Bildung und der Tätigkeit der Ehe- und Familienberatungsstellen in der DDR, MdJ in Berlin, 7 March 1967, 2 (148 of archival file).

48. Gerhard Misgeld, "Die Leser hatten das Wort," *Deine Gesundheit* 10 (October 1971): 312–14, here 314.

49. BArch, DP1 VA 1757, Protokoll der Beratung mit Mitarbeitern der Ehe- und Familienberatungsstellen in der Hauptstadt der DDR am 14. August 1968, Judge Naumann, Stadtgericht von Groß-Berlin, 3. Zivilsenat, 1 September 1968, 3 (42 of archival file).

50. Gerhard Misgeld, untitled editor's foreword, *Deine Gesundheit* 10 (October 1971): 290.

51. BArch, DP1 VA 3007, Band 1.3561, Entwurf: Information über die Entwicklung und die Arbeit der Ehe- und Familienberatungsstellen im Jahre 1977, 31 October 1977, 1 (209 of archival file) for 1977 figure; BArch, DP1 SE 2144, volume 3, untitled chart with EFB and ESB breakdown for all regions in the GDR, unpaginated archival file

for 1985 and 1987 figures. The author of the 1977 report claims that the number of marital counseling centers in the GDR had remained unchanged between 1969 and 1977, but given the frequent openings and closings of these institutions, this contention strikes me as implausible.

52. BArch, DP1 SE 2144, volume 3, letter from Lindner, stellvertretender Direktor des BG Dresden, to Genosse Eichhorn, MdJ in Berlin, HA III, 4 July 1988, 3.
53. Dickinson, "Biopolitics, Fascism, Democracy," 1.
54. Ibid.
55. Ibid., 44.
56. Ibid., 46.
57. BArch, DP1 VA 1757, letter from Kohlbach, Stadtbezirksgericht Berlin-Weissensee, to Judge Naumann, Stadtgericht von Groß-Berlin, 10. September 1968, Betr. Tätigkeit der Ehe- und Familienberatungsstelle Weissensee, 2 (45 of archival file).
58. Borrmann, *Jugend und Liebe*, 56.

CHAPTER 16

~:~

Longing, Lust, Violence, Liberation

Discourses on Sexuality on the Radical Left in West Germany, 1969–1972

MASSIMO PERINELLI

The present essay hopes to complicate an apparent certitude about the New Left sexual revolution of the 1960s. From the viewpoint of the 1990s, the slogan of sexual liberation was used in 1968 only as leverage against female comrades, in order to make it harder for them to say "no." Furthermore, the later left-wing analysis of the '68ers correlates strikingly with the bourgeois, anti–left-wing reception of 1968 with respect to sexuality. A more precise look into the tangle of voices, practices, theories, and actions should reveal that the line of contention was drawn not between compulsory bourgeois morality and liberating sexuality, but rather between heteronormative-genital, repressive-desublimated sexuality on one side, and a polymorphously perverse, partial-drive-accepting stance on the other—a line that ran right *through* the so-called sexual revolution.

What is today referred to as the sexual revolution of 1968 assumed that new forms of sexuality presented an opportunity to attack the Fordist logic of the factory in the industrialized West, along with its imperialistic war policy. Theoretically schooled by the Marxist-psychoanalytic writings of Wilhelm Reich and Herbert Marcuse, and in Germany primarily by Reimut Reiche and Fritz Haug,[1] it was thought that Western culture was predicated upon subli-mation, i.e., a suppression of sexual drives and their translation into cultural achievements. What Freud still conceived of positively was now understood as a genuine problem of repression, from which emancipation ought to be sought. Freedom under the conditions of capitalism could only ever be freedom in the willingness to sublimate, in the productive compulsion to repress one's drives. It would always be a repressive freedom. While according to Marx, the development of domination (*Herrschaft*) through the organization of labor was, as a process of political economy, primary, it was now emphasized that the precondition for this process was a psychological one: namely, the establishment of an authoritarian character through the suppression of (above all) child sexuality. The organization of drives was therefore called the process of sexual economy. According to this logic, it became important to talk about sexuality, to analyze its functional interconnections, and finally to free oneself from the repressive prohibitions of bourgeois morality. Sexual liberation in the 1960s was therefore, at least at the theoretical level, much more than a simple serendipitous opportunity to increase the number of one's sexual partners. Imagining the longed-for liberation drew on the concept of "nonrepressive desublimation"— that is, the transgression of the numerous reigning sexual-moral commandments and proscriptions. In fact, true liberation was conditional upon these transgressions being truly lived, rather than merely consumed in the context of a permitted and temporarily controlled border-crossing (i.e., a repressive desublimation) that would do nothing but enable the transgressor all the better to once again bear the weight of authoritarian structures.

Foucault's concept of heterotopia is crucial for his consideration of the need to expand what counts as political. The question that holds the thesis of this chapter concerns the attempts back then to create a multiplicity of spaces, arrangements, and assemblages within which an other, a completely different, sexuality could be developed. Could these attempts be understood as "counterpositions" or "counterforces" in the sexual-political dispositive,[2] and as ones pointing toward a possible reality that differed entirely from the present-day neoliberalization of the sexual economy and its hidden concomitant, fundamentalist-religious sex-hatred? Were there, then, practices or debates that did not lead to a "discursification of Sex"[3]—a lesson from Foucault according to which all speech about sex could only ever be a building block of the dominant sexual dispositive, i.e., of sexist circumstances—but that instead de-discursified sexuality?

A Note on Sources

For a closer investigation of the different positions and practices of what we today label the sexual revolution, alternative and left-wing print media from the 1960s and early 1970s are especially useful. In these, all possible actors find their voices: the organized political groups and communes, prominent individual representatives of the movement, students and apprentices, alternative businesses and restaurants, and even the letters and personal ads of the readers themselves. Furthermore, alongside print contributions, newsletters and magazines also presented visual material—photos, collages, and cartoons—that often was less vigorously vetted before publication and therefore offers deeper insight into the emotional conditions and imagination of the era. Thus *Der Spiegel*, *konkret*, *Kursbuch*, *Das Da*, *Pardon*, *Charlie Kaputt*, *Linkeck*, and *St. Pauli Nachrichten* were considered in the preparation of this essay. The richest source, however, is the West Berlin "underground" newspaper *Agit 883*, which was published during the phase most decisive for our analysis, the years from 1969 to 1972.

In comparison with other sources, *Agit 883* has the advantage of having been the most-read organ of the nondogmatic left in West Berlin and the old Federal Republic—and, with its weekly circulation of up to 6,000 copies, the most widely circulated leftist paper that was also noticed outside Berlin. All substantive debates within the left-wing alternative and radical-oppositional scene played out in the pages of *Agit 883*. Given the collective character of many households and structures, it can be assumed that each copy was read by a number of people. The consciously open framework of the paper also meant that up to a hundred activists attended the public editorial meetings. *Agit 883* thus constitutes a privileged point of entry into the discourses within the West German New Left during the transition into the 1970s; it will be the main focus in the following discussion.[4]

Heterotopic Assemblages

The reading of the periodicals listed above intends primarily to differentiate and sort out the many varieties of "talking about sex," and to ask who was talking, what was said, and whether what was said necessarily functioned to foster a dispositive of domination, or whether there were also longings expressed therein that could undermine the prevailing discourses of sexuality and enable the construction of entirely different forms of association. To be sure, we will need to stay with Foucault in understanding every form of acting and speaking as inevitably productive and having effects of power. But not all that was produced was necessarily connectable to existing systems of order. In pursuing this consideration, I articulate a critique of Foucault's thought that was already evident in the argument Gilles Deleuze and Félix Guattari had with Foucault about the concept of the assemblage. In a footnote, Deleuze and Guattari formulate a central objection that is also decisive for my exploration:

> Our only points of disagreement with Foucault are the following: (1) to us the assemblages seem fundamentally to be assemblages not of power but of desire

(desire is always assembled), and power seems to be a stratified dimension of the assemblage; (2) the diagram and abstract machine have lines of flight that are primary, which are not phenomena of resistance or counterattack in an assemblage, but cutting edges of creation and deterritorialization.[5]

Deleuze and Guattari here distinguish a classical form and understanding of resistance from a "creation" that does not emerge through a "counterattack," but rather through a flight, a desertion of existing circumstances. Thus this essay, too, distinguishes between the "militant porno wing"[6]—which looked to shock and challenge bourgeois morals with as constant and provocative a thematization and practice of sex as possible—and the quieter voices in the debate, which, while only too easily drowned out amidst the often disturbing sexism of the time, spoke unceasingly of a real utopia, a heterotopia.

Sexpol

It was precisely heterotopia that was on the agenda of the *Sexpolgruppen*, for it was not only the university student movement that rediscovered Wilhelm Reich's theoretical writings on sexual economy from the 1930s through Herbert Marcuse's works of the mid and late 1960s. The group Sexpol-Nord (West Berlin), which comprised mainly apprentices and secondary school students, was founded in the fall of 1968. From their discussions emerged the often-cited *Sexpol Protocols*, which were first published in *konkret* with the cooperation of Ulrike Meinhof and Peter Homann. The *Sexpol Protocols* were to "make class consciousness clear—even when sexuality is being talked about."[7] In the protocols, young male and female comrades discuss their experience with sex, love, and gender relations.

Underlying the discussion was the conviction that the capitalist system depended upon an authoritarian character that was primarily inculcated through the repression of child sexuality. Because their sexual desire was forbidden and taboo, children were compelled to seek gratification in alternate activities, which would themselves be socially preconfigured and regulated. The theory that sexuality was repressed in bourgeois society in order to shape human beings within that society in an authoritarian mold was discussed in countless reading groups, political circles, and publications. Sexual liberation meant developing a revolutionary desire and pleasure out of sexual-economical "frustration." Initially, Sexpol-Nord advertised in *Agit 883* to tout its reading group and the texts associated with it. The Sexpol movement's formulations bore a strong resemblance to Foucault's concept of the emergence of a biopolitical dispositive primarily operative at the level of the body and its sexuality:

Those familiar with Marx's theory of reproduction know that we are dealing with a biologization of the capitalist reproduction process. A reproduction of repression and its system of values is the inevitable outcome of the reproduction of the relations of capital. And just as the last word in Marxist reproduction theory is the social revolution, so too is the last word of this Freudian/Marcusian theory the bio-psychic revolution.[8]

Although the author engages Marcuse critically, he nevertheless sketches with marked precision the political intervention of sexual liberation, which is to be understood less as a classical uprising than as—according to Marcuse—a "great refusal," as a "no-longer-participating in oppression under the sign of the pleasure principle."[9] Also explicitly emphasized was that the mere sexualization of society was by no means a real liberation: in "the bourgeois sex-wave of our times ... the old sexual taboos are replaced by an increasing manipulation of consciousness."[10]

Dagmar Herzog justifiably emphasizes the problematic nature of the equation of sexual liberation and antifascism within the revolt of 1968, for it was precisely National Socialism that had been characterized by aggressive sexual rhetoric and practice that had little to do with the staid morality of the 1950s against which young leftists rebelled. The anti-authoritarian revolt against the apparently inhibited—and *therefore* fascist—parental generation overlooked, according to Herzog's decisive thesis, the aggressive pro-sex politics of the Nazi period, and was therefore incapable of historicizing the postwar retreat of the philistine middle class into the nuclear family as the way in which the perpetrator generation distanced itself from its guilty past.[11] For this reason, a critical analysis of the various opinions regarding sexual politics of the New Left movement—like a critique of views of sexuality under National Socialism—must clearly distinguish the authoritarian "functionaries of truth" from struggles for a new, anti-authoritarian "art of living," as Foucault puts it.

In the context of the 1968 revolt, it is important to look more closely at those who did not fit the concepts of social order represented by the often all-too-authoritarian bureaucrats of the Socialist German Student Federation (Sozialistischer Deutscher Studentenbund, or SDS) or by other, mainly male, leaders of the movement. The *Sexpol Protocols* joined the profusion of voices concerned with "not being a fascist, even (and especially) when one considers oneself a revolutionary militant."[12] Drawing inaccurate and denunciatory parallels between the New Left of the 1960s and the Nazis has become a favorite activity among early twenty-first-century historians, often themselves former New Leftists.[13] In this situation, it is even more pressing to emphasize the complexity within the sexual politics of each era. While parallels could thus possibly be drawn between the phallic heterosexism and fantasy of control of National Socialism and some behaviors among the '68ers, such attitudes and behaviors must be distinguished from attempts to engage in nonnormative sexual practices unfettered by racist, capitalist, or patriarchal baggage as part of a critique of authority.

The Cacophony of *Agit 883*

Roughly speaking, six perspectives on the realm of the sexual can be identified in the pages of *Agit 883*, though this categorization must necessarily remain inexact as there were more than a few overlaps between groups. A first, distinct perspective was that of the editorship of *Agit 883* itself, which ultimately se- lected the texts and consistently made its own stance clear. Next, some quieter voices from communes and anti-authoritarian projects beyond Kommune 1 and 2, which had an important place in the newspaper. Third and fourth, there were the so-called Hashish Rebels, later militants, and the Marxist-Leninist parties that subsequently competed with them. In addition, and mainly in the interstices between utterances by other groups, one can find the first autono- mous women's groups—in particular the Women's Liberation Front, which was allied with the militant Tupamaros West Berlin. The topic of sexuality was most clearly brought into the journal, however, by the sixth group: its readers. Countless letters and especially personal ads reveal the significance the topic had for the scene.

These six groups found themselves engaged in an implicit argument about the importance and meaning of sexuality for a revolutionary liberation, an argument within which the balance of power shifted decisively during the publication's three-year run. Whereas in 1969 the contributions of the Sexpol movement carried significant weight and the personal ads concerned them- selves with the possibility of experimenting with new kinds of relationships, by 1972 the militaristic and dogmatic party voices had grown louder in de- riding (and eventually openly opposing) sexual experiments as involving sec- ondary contradictions or bourgeois distractions from the main lines of battle. The initial challenges to the macho posturing (*Mackergehabe*) of the so-called comrades-in-chief (*Obergenossen*), along with the thematization of relations of power within the collective, were thereby effectively silenced.

Sexpol Movements: The Early Years

In the 1969 *Agit 883*, the calendar of events of the Republican Club located in the district of Charlottenburg, which was the center of the undogmatic left movement in West Berlin, holds a number of reading recommendations—for example, *Sexuality and Class Struggle* by SDS leader Reimut Reiche—or invitations to discussions on such topics as "The power question in the anti-authoritarian patriarchy of the Republicans and its mirror image in the patriarchy of the mass media and the scripts of television shows and the inability of underprivileged broads (*Weiber*) finally to open their mouths."[14] Eventually, a Sexpol working group took shape within the Republican Club.

One thread of discussion in the newspaper involved an attack on the leader of the Falken (Falcons, an organization of Socialist Youth of Germany) by the bourgeois press and the Berlin prosecutors' office. It was sparked by an episode during which male and female youths deliberately slept together in tents at the organization's campground and were furthermore encouraged to explore their sexuality by Falken chaperones.[15] The case was reported upon in several issues of the publication, and the Falken themselves offered a statement: "They want to smash the Falken, because they rattled one of the chains that bind humans to capitalist society: sexual morality."[16] Also noteworthy is how seamlessly the editorial staff of *Agit 883* translated criticism of the repressive compulsory character of sexuality into an attack on political opponents. One manifestation of this tendency can be found in the many caricatures of violent cops or fathers who clearly derived sexual pleasure from giving someone a thrashing (fig. 16.1).

Meanwhile, the flyers of Kommune 1 present the idea of sex as a valve through which pent-up frustration could be vented. A flyer put out by the commune on the occasion of a "protest while strolling" ("*Spaziergangsdemonstration*") in the Kurfürstendamm shopping district read, "We demand for the police: a 35-hour work week, so that they might have more time, more leisure for their girlfriends and wives and thus be able to lose their aggressions in loveplay," and went on to say, "if we uncork the red wine / the billy club stays pocketed / the policemen need a muse / we're thinking of Beate Uhse." (Uhse was the premier purveyor of sex toys, pornography, aphrodisiacs, and sex advice to the West German populace.)

Particularly in the linkage of political violence and sexual pleasure, the flyers' portrayal of the anti-authoritarians' enemies—fascists, cops, fathers, judges—and the portrayal of their own scene is uncannily identical. Although anti-authoritarian authors attributed the violence of fathers to authoritarian child-rearing and the authoritarian and violent state, they deemed the sexual titillation that they derived from their own militancy as something positive. It is thus unsurprising to find instructions for the assembly of a Molotov cocktail juxtaposed with a depiction of an erect penis with a speech bubble emerging from its tip that says: "The penis is the appropriate instrument for the smashing of bourgeois sexual morality" (fig. 16.2). Another issue imagines an anti-authoritarian commune, represented as a woman, being brutally penetrated from behind by the justice system (fig. 16.3).

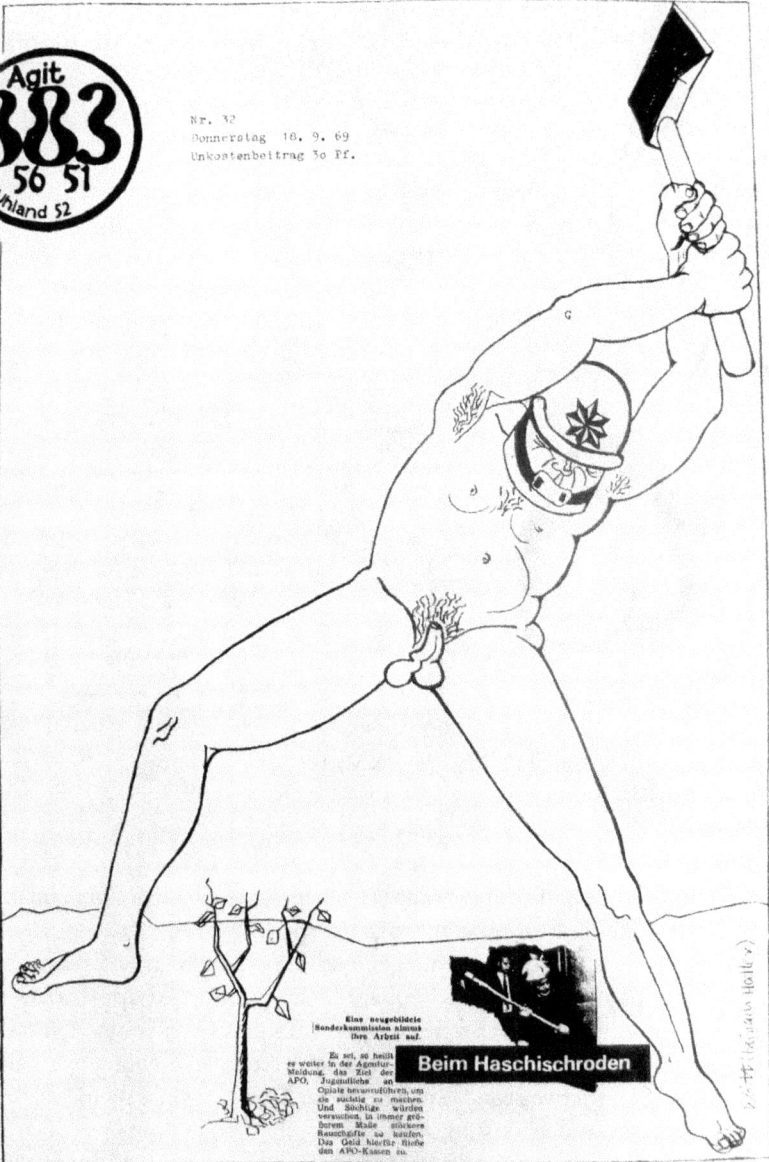

Figure 16.1. *Agit 883*, no. 32, 15 September 1969, cover. Markus Mohr and Hartmut Rübner (rotaprint 25), eds., *Agit 883: Bewegung, Revolte, Underground in Westberlin 1969–1972* (Berlin and Hamburg, 2006).

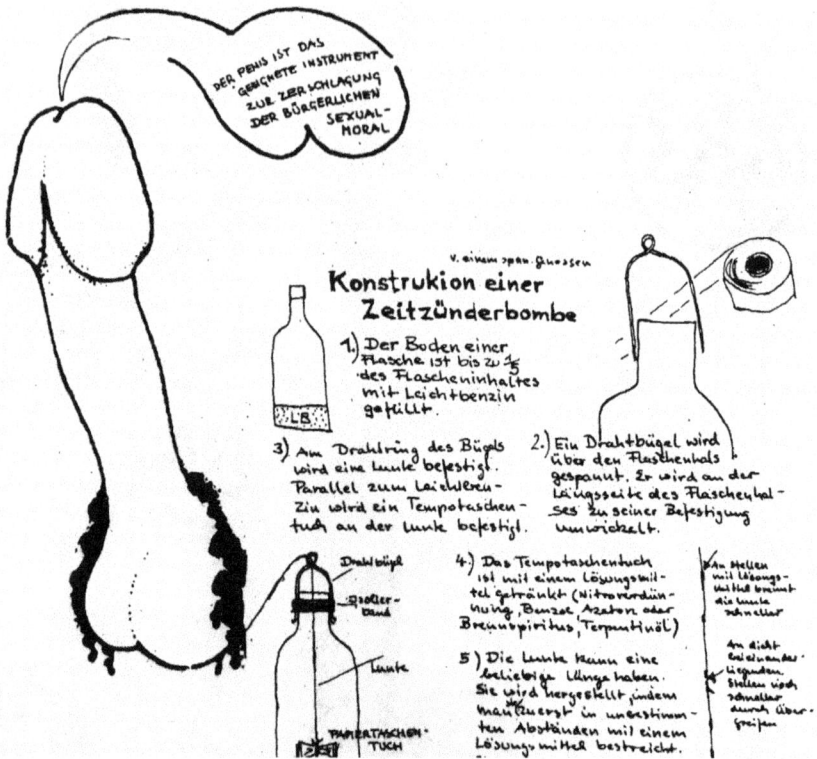

Figure 16.2. *Agit 883*, no. 13, 8 May 1969, 2. Markus Mohr and Hartmut Rübner (rotaprint 25), eds., *Agit 883: Bewegung, Revolte, Underground in Westberlin 1969–1972* (Berlin and Hamburg, 2006).

In short, phallic sexuality appears as an impetus of repressive state apparatuses and, at the same time, of resistance against them.

In contrast, some of the younger authors—rebellious girls from group homes, groups of secondary school students, pupils, and apprentices—presented a very different perspective in their numerous articles in *Agit 883*. For example, the paper documented the successful struggle of young "women from Eichenhof [a restrictive group home in Berlin Tegel]" against their "fascist" warden, Kaltwasser, and against, more generally, the "group home terror."[17] Sexual demands, in particular, were in the foreground of the political campaign. The girls called for, among other things, "an overnight vacation every weekend," "the distribution of the birth control Pill and other forms of contraception to all girls," "a thorough explanation of sexually transmitted diseases," and much more.[18] Another group of youth more humorously demanded the "centralization of sexual-political schoolwork."[19]

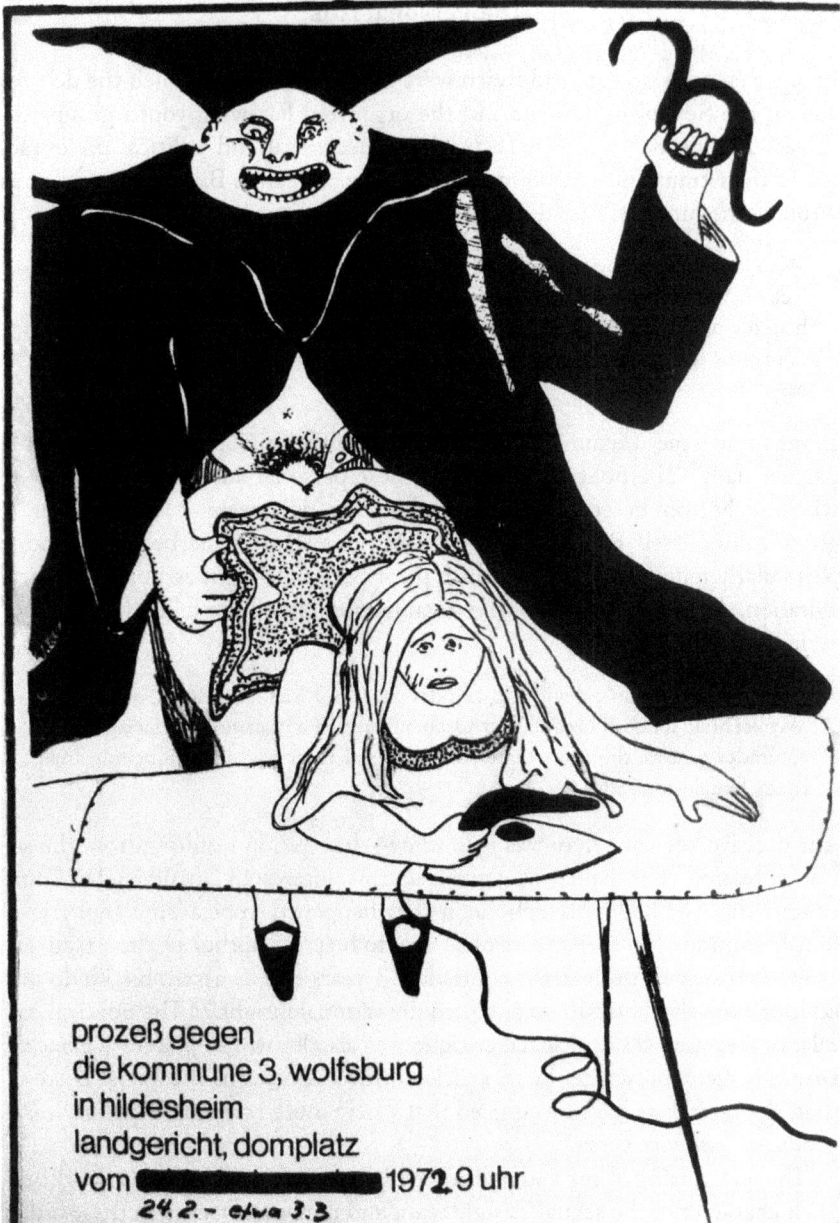

Figure 16.3. *Rote Hilfe*, no. 2, 14 February 1972, cover. Barnbule, ed., *Prinzip Solidarität* (Hamburg, 2012).

The Personal Ads

Haug, Reiche, Marcuse, and Reich were the names around which the debates among the Sexpol movement and the organized left-wing youth groups revolved. In *Agit 883's* personal ads, these theoretical and political discourses found their translation into everyday practice. A reader, B. Schibrowski, thus wrote in the June 1969 issue of *Agit 883*:

> Who knows a psychoanalyst who adheres to the analytical theory of Wilhelm Reich? Which patient, politically aware woman (17–20 yrs.) is prepared to help me out of my sexual distress and thereby help me overcome the repressive bourgeois fetters of my environment. The attempt to do so will not be entirely easy.[20]

In the same issue, a "young man with orgasm difficulties" sought "a new female partner daily." The political valence of these personal ads, which come overwhelmingly from heterosexual men seeking sex, does seem at best a veneer. A group calling itself Red Construction Workers (Rote Bauarbeiter) provided particularly telling examples of this type of personal ad gussied up as political agitation. At the end of 1969, the organization placed the following personal ad in *Agit 883*:

> Away with the wank-devil! On Sunday at 11:00 A.M. the Red Construction Workers had a liquid breakfast at Oranienplatz 15 and came to a decision: Two comrades require the immediate restoration of their sexual equilibrium. Help them, female comrades.[21]

The decisive keyword here was *frustration*—frustration resulting from the social repression of sexuality. To counteract this, interested female readers could contact the *Agit 883* by telephone, if they happened to be a "slim (not frigid) female comrade (up to 30 years old)" able to help the author of the ad, an "all-around frustrated proletarian comrade, 33 years old … assess his libido and educate himself politically so as to acquire rational insight."[22] The political correlation between sex and social critique was also known to jailbird ("*Knacki*") Bruno Kalle, who wrote, in an article entitled "Coitus in the Penal System," that "the capitalists have recognized that where more screwing happens, less is produced, and vice versa."[23]

The intermixing of sex and political enlightenment, and in particular the explicit character of the sexual, is significant and noteworthy even in these rather pathetic texts. If it was not simply pure cynicism in play, a personal ad in which a male comrade sought a "female comrade who also knows to converse with the lower half of the body"[24] did clearly express the widely held notion that sexuality and politics could not be thematized separately from one another. A similar move is made by another male comrade in issue 52: "30 y.o. seeking female comrade who can debate hotly with both sets of lips. With child or in a living collective is A-OK."[25] Another issue contained one of the few personal ads by women in which the political and the intimate were similarly intertwined with one another: "Not yet completely emancipated female student of German literature seeks male comrades to mediate between theory and practice through the expansion of experience and consciousness. Warning: needs love, but is aggressive!"[26] And, finally, "two comrades" sought one female comrade each "for ongoing discussion of the topic, causes and effects of social frustration." The women should be prepared to "participate decisively, actively and working from the social basis upwards in the exploration of this thematic complex."[27] Regardless of how transparent or superimposed the argument for political liberation via sex may appear in hindsight, it is nevertheless notable how intimately the two spheres were connected in almost every one of the personal ads (see fig. 16.4).

In this vein as well, then, prison inmates looked for a female comrade who, "directly upon their release," could help "heal" them from "their here acquired complexes towards girls," while a "student couple frustrated by its surroundings" sought "other couples for conversation and mutual pleasure."[28]

Frequently sought were "repression-free spaces" in which cohabitation and sexuality mixed freely. "Repression-free" was a buzzword of the classifieds, regardless of whether they concerned a job, living arrangements, sex, or child-rearing. The desire or decision to create spaces in which a non-repressive desublimation of the kind Marcuse propagated could take place permeated each page of classified advertisements. The page was like the object to which it referred—a heterotopic space that placed itself in opposition to the increasing severity and militancy in the political articles. In the middle of 1970, the editors put an end to personal ads with a brief announcement in the classified section: "Bourgeois requests for a lay (*Bummsgesuche*) will no longer be accepted. 883."[29]

It was only three issues later that a short explanation came from 883's new editorship, which wanted to make the former "bar newsletter" (*Kneipenblatt*) into a "paper fighting on behalf (*Kampfblatt*) of the Communist rebels." The

Genosse sucht Mädchen zwecks Unterhaltung, Saufereien usw. evtl. auch für's Bett. Bude vorhanden, K. Heinrich, 1-61, Urbanstr. 25D

Figure 16.4. *Agit 883*, no. 33, 25 September 1969, 3, example of a classified ad. Markus Mohr and Hartmut Rübner (rotaprint 25), eds., *Agit 883: Bewegung, Revolte, Underground in Westberlin 1969–1972* (Berlin and Hamburg, 2006).

explanation announced the discontinuation of personal ads, as the classifieds were now "only [to foster] connection (*Verbindung*) among comrades." Although the personal ads in particular would after all have been quite conducive to promoting "connection among comrades," they did not appear again for the remainder of the paper's lifespan, although an advertisement in which "cheerful people (male and female) are sought as models for pornographic photos with a progressive bent" was apparently unaffected by this measure.[30] Here the contested line was drawn separating the polymorphic experiments of many male and female comrades from the genital reterritorialization discourses within the movement.[31]

Pornography

Agit 883's editors appear to have had a thoroughly muddled attitude toward pornography. All possible discourses were freely mixed up, ranging from anti-repressive political activism directed against anti-pimping laws (often used against parents or hotel owners who permitted unmarried couples to sleep together) and against laws regarding same-sex sexual practices, to sexual denunciations of political enemies and the symbolic rape of same by the hyper-potent comrade, to crude sexist statements about women. The feminist critique of pornographic representation, or of correspondingly brutal and sexually charged utterances—a critique that by 1969 had already been underway for some time—was almost completely lacking in *Agit 883*. The editorship also failed to make any truly positive references to this form of critique. Instead, indecision reigned with respect to the issue of pornography. While in the first issue the editors exhorted their readers: "Comrades! Send contributions, news, porn, pictures, ideas, suggestions, critique, information, caricatures, agitprop, inspiration, announcements, etc.,"[32] porn had been removed from the list by the third issue. For the pornography industry, however, the first call had been enough. Already in the second issue "*young slim girls* [sic underline]" were sought as "nude models for amateur photography. 10–40 DM hrly."[33] These commercial want ads were a staple throughout all three years of *Agit 883*, even if they were usually more explicitly political, as in issue 54, where a Comrade Wolf looked for a "chick for 24 Polit-Pop-Pornos (the take will be split 50-50) who can also 'gab' intellectually."[34]

Along related lines, left-wing publishers placed ads in left-wing papers, as in this one from the Verlag Klaus Bär: "Politics and Pornography: Let's create conditions for porn in the Federal Republic like those in Denmark! Let's force the rulers to abolish Paragraph 184 by mass-circulating porn! Let's fight against all forms of sexual oppression!" Only after these pugnacious demands did the titles of the actual products make their appearance in small print. The advertising strategy assumed that porn by its very nature had an anti-authoritarian aspect and thus that mass-scale purchase of porn was in itself transgressive and rebellious; the actual objects being proffered—"150 Love Positions," "Fuck in Gotham City," or "Hookers in St. Pauli"—seemed, by comparison, almost beside the point.[35] The idea that with pornography one could explode the social mechanisms of compulsion was widely held within the New Left at the time, and could be found in numerous publications. Thus, for instance, the 1969 issue of the left-wing Frankfurt paper *StreitZeitSchrift* on the topic "Pornography" could just as easily have been published in *Agit 883*:

> In the pornographically spurred-on fantasy the subject can not only try out socially taboo partial drives (*Partialtriebe*), i.e., perversions, but in addition, as Susan Sontag demonstrated with respect to the "History of O," the subject can begin to explore heretofore inaccessible spaces of consciousness, and come to an expansion of the Ego into the visionary that is even bigger than an explosion of the chains laid on the Ego by the Superego.[36]

The erotic and political ambiguity of the term "explosion" (*Sprengung*) was also used in *konkret* by the Becker-Versand to advertise its third-rate sex literature: "Explosives for connoisseurs!" (*Sprengstoff für Kenner!*)[37] Moreover, the in-house production of erotic material was heralded by prominent figures, e.g. Horst Mahler, as itself a politically oppositional activity.

Indeed, though pornography was deployed as a successful provocation against the repressive philistinism of bourgeois society, and often mobilized in the struggle against legislation involving sexual practices—like the anti-pimping law, Paragraph 175 (criminalizing homosexuality), or Paragraph 218 (criminalizing abortion)—relatively few political statements addressed what exactly pornography could contribute to liberation. The issue of *StreitZeitSchrift* constitutes an exception to this rule. But even *Pardon* had dedicated an issue to the topic and come to the conclusion that "pornography is not what is supposed to be affected by intervention into private life, but rather that which it is standing in for in the judges' eyes: sexuality. Frustration, after all, is considered moral."[38]

Otherwise, the statement that pornography was political was neither contradicted nor thematically elaborated. Instead, there were silly treatments of the topic, as with the editors' little joke in designating *Agit 883* a "Mickey Mouse Pop and Porn Paper."[39] The editors first thematized pornography in December of 1970, after a reader's letter challenged them to "bring on the porn." Instead of taking a stance themselves, the editors asked readers for "a barrage of opinions." One issue later, the only letter that was ever published on this "problem" appeared. "Uwe, et al." wrote:

> You wanted opinions about the problem of porn: just look at the sexually inhibited faces in the subway, on the construction site, at the office. Almost all

pleasure themselves or masturbate instead of asking one another if they'd like to fuck. Or they compensate for their horniness by obsessing about fashion, listening to underground music, and consuming hashish and/or alcohol. Therefore: open a "Fuck Corner" in 883, in which readers can report on their sexual experiences as well as on why only so few of them can have a proper orgasm. You could also reissue something by Wilhelm Reiche [sic]![40]

The letter effectively fused the (primarily Weimar-era) sexologist Wilhelm Reich and the 1960s SDS leader Reimut Reiche into one person, and hence touched upon a theoretical lacuna of the project to overcome sexual taboos. Predictably, there was to be no "Fuck Corner" in *Agit 883*, just as there was no further statement made by the editors.

Only in the spring of 1971 was pornography mentioned again. This statement made clear the editors' completely unreflective and myopic treatment of the topic of pornography—a treatment that could not, or did not want to, distinguish between liberating and violent sexuality. The Election-Fuck Political Fest ("Wahlbums Polit-fete"), which was organized by the Black Cells (Schwarze Zellen)[41] and supported by *Agit 883*, was advertised with a sketch consisting of an opened vagina, penetrated by an enormous penis, through which the face of a happy young man is visible (fig. 16.5).

The slogan "Fuck the System" acquired a clear gendered aspect with drawings like these; in *Agit 883* and elsewhere it became obvious who the "System" was, and who was fucking it. With the paper's increasing self-positioning vis-à-vis the militaristic aspects of the nascent anti-imperialist scene surrounding the emerging Red Army Faction, a violent rhetoric appeared that also crosscut with the realm of sexuality. Adjacent to the Wahlbums image there was already a report on the party:

> The WAHLFETE was really swell. Why? For the first time, there were more apprentices, young workers, and schoolkids. Both bands banged it out real nice, people smoked grass and drank. The porn flick they showed—well—if the chicks hadn't had any teeth in their mouths, the guy probably could have spent fifteen more hours with a hard-on. The movie about the Cambodia demonstration was very good.[42]

A few pages later in the same issue, the topic of pornography was topped off with yet another drawing (see fig. 16.6). A grinning stick figure with an outsized erect penis, umbrella in hand, stood above the caption "Our 883-Porno!" With the sarcastic suggestion of an intent to emulate *Charlie Kaputt*, the paper associated with the Socialist Unity Party of West Berlin (Sozialistische Einheitspartei Westberlin, or SEW), which featured numerous pornographic pictures, the *Agit 883* editorial staff was herewith publishing the porn that had been promised for so long—for "[a]fter all, we too approve of the pleasure principle!"

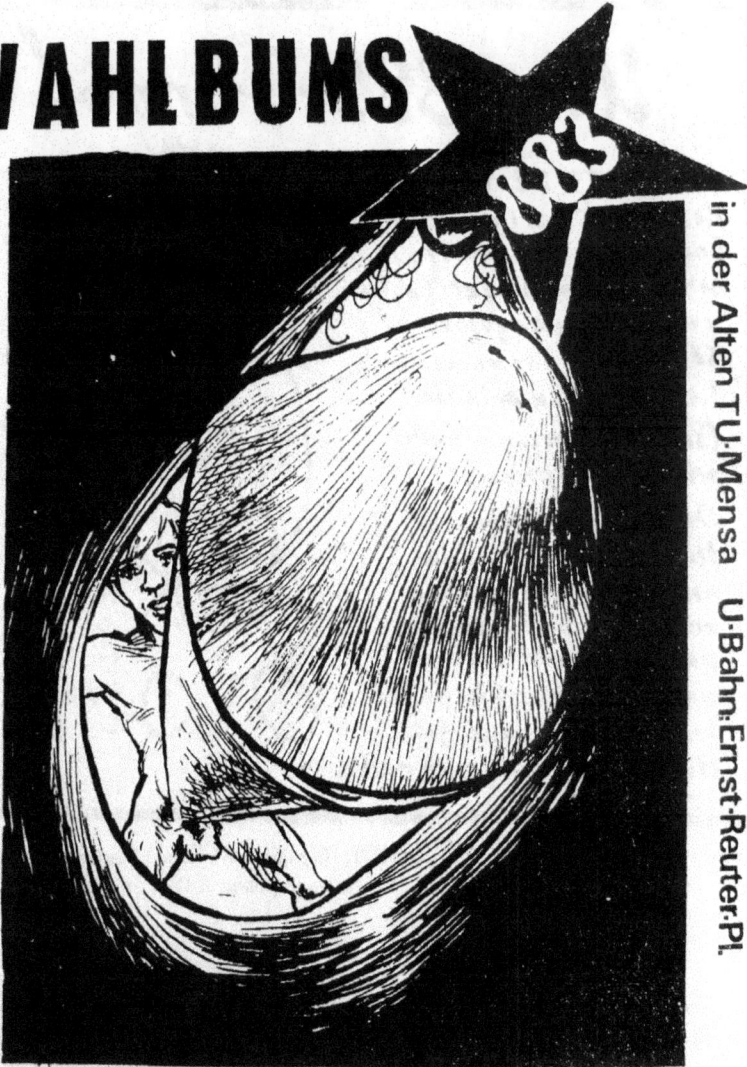

Figure 16.5. *Agit 883*, no. 77, 19 March 1971, 5. Markus Mohr and Hartmut Rübner (rota-print 25), eds., *Agit 883: Bewegung, Revolte, Underground in Westberlin 1969–1972* (Berlin and Hamburg, 2006).

Figure 16.6. *Agit 883*, no. 77, 19 March 1971, 10. Markus Mohr and Hartmut Rübner (rotaprint 25), eds., *Agit 883: Bewegung, Revolte, Underground in Westberlin 1969–1972* (Berlin and Hamburg, 2006).

The ironic reference to the pleasure principle and thereby the mockery of the Sexpol movement crossed directly over into the denigration of the women's movement: "Since the women in our fine society take precedence [*haben Vortritt*, a pun on entering buildings first] and some female comrades of emancipated consciousness feel disadvantaged, now here's something for them: Semmler, naked." Besides veiling with humor the attacks on the SEW (the initials in German are pronounced "es-ee-we"), the Sexpol movement, and the emancipation of women, the drawing also subjected the stick figure of Christian Semmler to a homophobic attack. An arrow pointing to the umbrella in his hand was accompanied by the following advice: "Umbrella; stick it in the rear and open slowly for a colossal increase in pleasure!"

Gays

Political opponents were denounced (and not only in *Agit 883*) through the questioning of their sexual potency. The image of the impotent man was connected to that of the gay man: as someone who lacked sexual prowess with women, he thus connoted effeminacy and homosexuality. The image of the violent father or policeman aroused by his own sadism—implying something of a critical perspective on male sexuality—was countered by the image of one's own phallic potency and of the genital deficiencies of the enemy (see fig. 16.7). Although the drawings came in part from the same individual contributors, their political statements were categorically self-contradictory. The homophobic image of the political enemy was also to be found in many statements of the early women's movement. In many of these pronouncements, the man of the Establishment was assumed to be incapable of pleasing his wife. For example, after an argument about the sale of *Agit 883* in the music club Park, the Women's Liberation Front considered the club's owners to be "impotent limp-dicks" whose "Zionist boss—the pig—paid thousands of Marks" from their earnings "to Israel."[43]

Once again it was in the classified section that other, less contemptuous voices of the movement let themselves be heard. Gay personal ads were certainly more circumspect and, in contrast to all other ads, were almost always kept anonymous. In one, a gay man admitted that "I suffer greatly from loneliness."[44] In another ad, a "homosexual comrade [sought] contact with like-minded comrades."[45] And yet another ad from two men looking for "bed-partners" gently mocked the notion that they might only be seeking sex by declaring that "conversations are not off limits."[46]

That homosexuality was recurrently politically integrated and accepted into the primarily heterosexual scene as nonconforming activity even as blatant homophobia set the scene's overall tone seems simply paradoxical. Two final examples make this incoherence clear. In an August 1969 article that criticized a comrade of the Kreuzberg Basisgruppe, sexual denunciation established the basic tenor of the attack: "Gussied up in a white babydoll blouse which could very well have come from Selbach's fairy-fag shop (*Tuntenshop*), our pal sits—looking rail-thin from behind—at a table by the window and talks far too loudly." In short, the despised comrade was not a real man; he was only assigned the masculine gender in quotation marks: "'He' is named *JOHANNES* ... [and] has bad luck with the ladies." After this double sexual insult came an (also sexually charged) call to the rest of the group for violence against this unmanly comrade: "Think of something nice to do with your Johannes-dolly, but quickly, if I might make that request, because otherwise I'll have to think of something!"[47]

Figure 16.7. *Agit 883*, no. 67, September 1970, 10. Markus Mohr and Hartmut Rübner (rotaprint 25), eds., *Agit 883: Bewegung, Revolte, Underground in Westberlin 1969–1972* (Berlin and Hamburg, 2006).

Yet on the opposite page, *Agit 883* printed the Black Panther Huey Newton's explicitly anti-homophobic speech to the "revolutionary brothers and sisters of the liberation front of women and homosexuals"—even though the speech was neither introduced nor annotated nor, in subsequent issues, explicitly discussed.[48] The racist stereotype of the exceedingly virile black male intersected with the latent homophobia of the German heterosexual comrades, and they effectively negated each other. Newton's reconciliatory words to the gay community did not appear to detract from his virility and therefore his radicalism, though in Germany of course this was already known:

> The Negro fucks superbly
> And can also thrash the cops [*pigs* in original]
> And on top of all that
> He is a good bomb-layer.
> Hurray for internationalism![49]

Children

In the articles, letters from readers, and personal ads of the communes and collectives, child-rearing and the prevention of the development of an authoritarian character through the liberation of child sexuality played an important role. While the editorial board did not express its views on the topic—or at least not earnestly—the large number of requests in the classified section conveyed a very different impression of the topic's relevance. A substantial portion of the ads were devoted to child care arrangements, whether on an individual basis or in the form of an attempt to locate or organize a *Kinderladen*. At the end of the 1970s, and certainly by the 1980s, the West German left had abandoned sexuality as a politicized terrain of happiness and liberation, and, as Dagmar Herzog has argued, a conception contrary to that of the earlier '68ers took hold. The new mantra was "Sex and politics never did work."[50] Herzog has characterized Klaus Theweleit's book *Male Fantasies* (*Männerphantasien*) as "an energetic and imaginative last-ditch attempt at an optimistic reading of the relationship between the personal and the political."[51]

With regard to child sexuality, this position was further strengthened in the decades that followed: children disappeared completely from the now barely perceptible talk about sexuality, eroticism, and lust. By the same token, they reappeared with increasing frequency in the growing debate concerning violence and abuse. The broad conceits of the 1960s that a revolutionary transformation of the human being might be effected through a permissive approach to the sexual desires of adolescents and children were retrospectively denounced as pedophilic (male) fantasy and rendered scandalous and taboo.

From today's perspective, it is striking that the associative short-circuit of the liberation of child sexuality to pedophilia had not yet taken place. In an *Agit 883* article, to be sure, a warning was issued concerning a supposed comrade who, in his capacity as a social worker, housed underage male street children in his home, slept with them, and prostituted them. The outrage and political line of attack were directed almost exclusively against the profit this man made and did not explicitly engage his sexual relations with boys. On the contrary, such relationships were accepted as another manifestation of the liberation of child sexuality and were not questioned politically. "Homosexuality has always existed, and always will. No argument, no commentary. We are understanding and broad-minded enough to tolerate even homosexual acts with minors, since ten- to 14-year-old boys finally want to find out, after all their inhibited upbringing, all the things one can do with that thing below the belly." It was only because the social worker in question "sent out boys to make money for him as streetwalkers" that he was, in the eyes of the heterosexual comrades who judged him, no longer a "'normal' homosexual," but rather "quite simply" a "criminal pimp."[52]

The candor with which sexual curiosity in children was discussed is the most conspicuous aspect of the left-wing treatment of child-rearing. In the late 1960s, the creation of *Kinderläden* and their anti-authoritarian, pro-pleasure education were of central importance to the revolutionary process. As early as 1965 Ursula Schmiederer had written in *Das Argument* that since (according to Wilhelm Reich) the tightly knit nuclear family rejected the sexuality of children, one had to consider whether more of children's upbringing should occur outside the family.[53] As the "Proletarian *Kinderladen*" in the Brehlostraße in Bochum formulated it in 1970, "[t]he occasional separation of children from families [was] a strategic measure undertaken to break the chain of the production of market-appropriate personalities."[54]

The first *Kinderladen* initiative, however, had another point of origin. During the Vietnam Congress in February of 1968, women spontaneously organized the first experimental alternative kindergarten in order to afford themselves enough time to participate in the political debates and activities. The problems of the so-called student marriages were already being discussed during the mid 1960s, when freshly married women would end their studies, take a job, and finance their husbands' education while also taking care of their living expenses. If that was not enough to end their academic careers, the arrival of the first child would usually deal the final blow. Female comrades from the Action Council for the Liberation of Women organized the first *Kinderladen* after the Vietnam Congress and united as the Action Council of Socialist Kinderläden (Aktionsrat der sozialistischen Kinderläden). The justification was initially the liberation of women from the time- and energy-consuming sphere of reproduction, which along with exclusion from political work often gave rise to loneliness in stagnant relationships:

The repressiveness of the society at large continues to take its toll on women, who for their part pass the aggression they receive from the rest of society on to their children. Given time constraints, women are unable to contemplate their situation and deduce its consequences. There is an acute need for an institution that relieves mothers of childcare responsibilities during a certain number of hours of the day so that they can work. This need cannot be satisfied for two main reasons: a) there are too few kindergartens, and b) those which do exist are managed in an authoritarian way, so that it would be damaging to the children to send them to such a facility. Consequently, kindergartens must be founded as soon as possible.[55]

Groups from the Extra-Parliamentary Opposition (Außerparlamentarische Opposition, or APO) quickly took over the *Aktionsrat* and supplied the *Kinderläden* with a concept of the politicization of children that was theoretically informed by Reich's and Marcuse's sublimation theory. The repressive, authoritarian building of character—which was held to lead to one's subsumption under structures of domination and capitalist social relations in adulthood—was to be prevented through the strict affirmation of children's sexuality. As members of Kommune 2 formulated it: "For us, a positive attitude toward child sexuality does not merely entail candidly explaining sexual functions to children, but rather also involves affectively affirming the feelings of pleasure which come from children's genitals."[56]

In *Agit 883*, countless postings were placed by parents seeking openings in *Kinderläden* or by young people in student marriages attempting to organize collective day care arrangements for their children. The sheer magnitude of these readers' voices gives a sense of the relevance of the topic "child care" at the time, and of what, from the perspective of today, could seem like a rather peculiarly vigorous effort to break down boundaries between private and public and to live the putatively private spheres of family and reproduction in collective arrangements.

Women's Liberation

The new women's movement that arose at the end of the 1960s left little trace of itself in radical left-wing papers like *Agit 883*. To be sure, the critique of the Alpha Comrades was documented, for instance in the famous November 1968 flyer issued by the Frankfurt Broads' Council (*Frankfurter Weiberrat*), which read, "Liberate the socialist pricks from their bourgeois dicks" (see fig. 16.8). However, it found only limited entry into political debates.

With the increasing militancy and militarization of left-wing discourse during the transition to the 1970s, the issue of sex clearly decreased in importance and was crowded out by debates about armed struggle and increasing repression by the state. At this historical turning point, the movement broke into

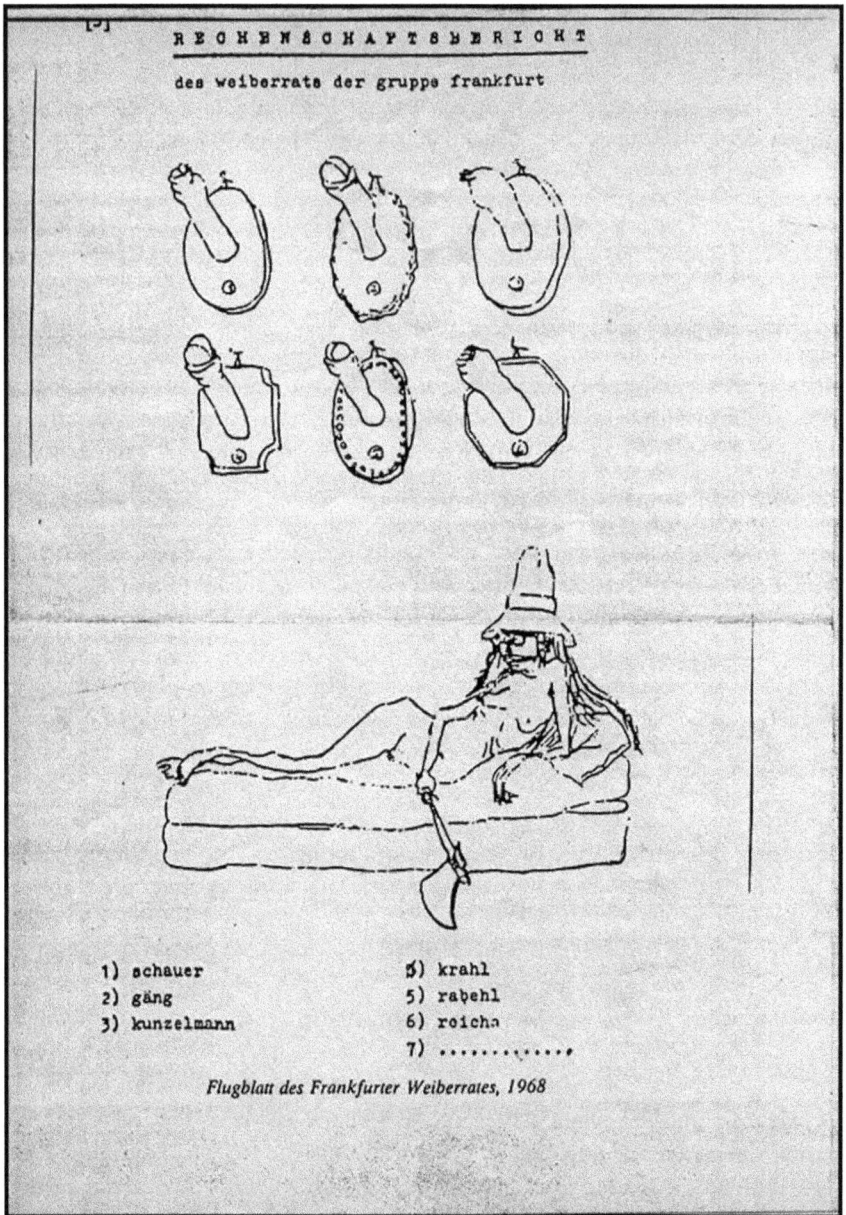

RECHENSCHAFTSBERICHT

des weiberrats der gruppe frankfurt

1) schauer   5̸) krahl
2) gäng   5) rabehl
3) kunzelmann   6) reicha
                 7) ....

Flugblatt des Frankfurter Weiberrates, 1968

Figure 16.8. Political leaflet distributed by Frankfurter Weiberrat, November 1968.

miniature sub-movements like those for squatting, ecology, armed struggle, gay and lesbian rights, women's liberation, or the *Kinderläden*. Only in *Agit 883*'s final issue in early 1972 did an article appear on gender relations in the productive and reproductive spheres, questioning the theory of primary and second-ary contradictions[57]—a theory that, to be sure, had already been called into question by the Sexpol movement but had, by dint of the advance of orthodox Marxist-Leninist thought, once again become a guiding thread of radical left-wing thought.

Nevertheless, it remains important to emphasize that sexuality also had positive connotations for the feminist groups of the era. For feminists, laws prohibiting pimping, abortion, and pornography were all instruments of the Establishment's oppression of free sexuality. Based on Reimut Reiche's *Sexual-ity and Class Struggle*, liberating sexuality could be distinguished from its repres-sive counterpart within the movement. Reiche's text, which sharply criticized the "braggadocio" (*Großprotze*) of some Kommune 1 members and labeled the behavior of other communards as "Stalinist," also criticized the "brutalizing attitude of control" (*Verfügungscharakter*) that existed with respect to female residents in the commune. An Alpha Comrade's remarks about the "breaking-in" of girls like horses,[58] for example, were often later repeated as indicative of a typical position held by '68er men. Even though the brutal attitude of some communards was indeed effectively captured in these remarks, this often-in-voked phrase has functioned primarily as a means by which smug and voy-euristic anti-leftists can condemn the entirety of the '68ers' attempt at sexual liberation. After all, at the time a great deal was said, but only very little of it survived. It bears remembering, however, that Reiche and the women's move-ment pioneers who were associated with him most definitely did not denounce the practice of all "free" sexuality, but rather only the phallus-fixated carryings-on of some prominent comrades that, sadly, have become infamous.

Nevertheless, and contrary to the popular teachings of Wilhelm Reich, the partial drives (i.e., oral and anal desires, tenderness, warmth, etc.) were also emphasized by many at the time and posited against the genitality—the dick-fixatedness—of many left-wing men. Sexuality remained, in the early days of the women's movement, a positive point of reference. And some men too were able to criticize the restricted sexual imaginations of their peers. In the mid 1960s, *Das Argument* wrote in its special issue on "Sexuality and Authority," with reference to Adorno, that any (pseudo-)sexualization that was accompa-nied by de-eroticization simply could not be emancipatory, for with an increas-ing tabooization of the partial drives, the sexual act would become nothing but a sterile "act of hygiene."[59]

By the beginning of the 1970s, little of this at once critical and apprecia-tive thinking about sex was registered in the pages of *Agit 883* any more. In a few other places, discomfort was announced. In the June 1969 issue of *Kurs-buch*, for instance, feminist Heide Berndt vehemently criticized the sexuality in many communes but particularly in Kommune 1, noting that "[t]he initiation of 'sexual cross-connections' … is … often the result of a conflict stemming from contradictory emotions: jealousy, separation anxiety, longing for security, trumping another individual, proving one's own irresistibility, etc." and was by no means a "harmless game of musical chairs."[60] And by 1973 at the latest, Ulrike Meinhof and a number of other female readers did begin writing in *konkret* to complain about sexist portrayals.

At the beginning of 1968, the Action Council for the Liberation of Women had already commented critically on the "sex-wave" (*Sexwelle*)—a term from mainstream journalism that was disdained by all affiliated with the left—in no uncertain terms. The council's members remarked on the widespread assumption that the "sex-wave," even with all of its negative consequences, nevertheless had contributed to a liberation of sexuality from its bourgeois taboo status. The council agreed that it was positive that sexuality was being thematized and also saw benefits in the practice of premarital intercourse, distribution of birth control, rising divorce rates, and even partner swaps and group sex. However, the women also recognized a double standard in the mainstream sex-wave's justification of "deviant" practices mainly as a means of preserving marriages and families; in other words, they saw the "sex-wave" primarily as just another instantiation of repressive desublimation. Indicative of this line of analysis is the argument that "[e]ven if there's ten times as much screwing as before, that wouldn't be a real liberation of sexuality. For merely to amass orgasms, even if man and woman arrive at them simultaneously, cannot yet be seen as a satisfying form of sexuality."[61] The genitally oriented sexual behavior of many communards as well as other citizens was hereby described—and rejected—in a very apposite manner, and quite early on. Yet in the pages of *Agit 883*, there were increasingly fewer traces of such perspectives.

Marxist-Leninist Parties and the Militant Left

Although these two camps within the New Left—the Marxist-Leninists and the militants—were opposed to one another at the turn to the 1970s (an outcome of their differences on the topics of organization and direct action), their contemptuous attitudes toward the attempts during the 1960s to politicize sexuality were similar. For both groups, the "real" business of politics, i.e., the state and its repression, was in the foreground, while they had only disdain for the Sexpol movement, the organization of private life in the communes and the *Kinderladen* movement, or the women's movement's criticisms of the political machos.

The Marxist-Leninist (M-L) groups and parties justified this unequivocally with reference to the primary antagonistic relation of capital and labor, from which everything else could be derived. Thus, according to a 1969 piece in *Agit 883*, "a completely false assessment of the most important tasks which

lie before us" would result if one "were to begin reading the writings that concern themselves with the secondary contradiction." After all, "specifically sexual
conflicts arise out of the class structure of society and are derived from the
main contradiction."[62] Two issues later, the writers made clear who had been
responsible for the wrong turn: they singled out for censure Herbert Marcuse,
"who has already planted a number of counterrevolutionary theories in our
heads."[63] This particular emphatic rejection of the anti-authoritarian movement was subsequently criticized by the editors of *Agit 883* as "a few polemical
comments by the M-L group," and in the next issue, the "historical accomplish-
ments of the anti-authoritarian movement" were enumerated in an article that
emphasized the "productive processing of experience" and praised the anti-
authoritarians' spontaneity in all kinds of areas—whether in wildcat strikes,
women's struggles, or direct action against police, to name a few. The editors
defended these more spontaneous battles as particularly characteristic of the
1968 revolt and the sources of its dynamism.[64] In short, despite being defensive
on the level of theory in the face of the authoritarian conduct of the dogmatic
M-L groups, it was at the time still known all too well that it was precisely the
"counter-activities" of tens of thousands of activists that had created the true
oppositional spaces within society and produced the most wonderful moments
in the struggle for a different life: genuinely heterotopic experiences.

Although there no doubt existed a consciousness of the significance of the
polymorphic struggles and experiments that had taken place outside of party-
political or avant-gardist fantasies, the editorial staff of *Agit 883* and the
militant groups allied with it increasingly availed themselves of more harshly
sexualized language. Ignorance of feminists' demands for a confrontation with
violence in gender relations was everywhere evident. Sex showed up only in the
context of nastiness. One random but typical example of the mixture of militancy, sexism, and puerile jargon can be found in Red Army Faction member
Thorwald Proll's letter from "exile," in which he described in stream-of-con-
sciousness how an "american [sic lowercase] journalist who can lick her own
cunt, on whose wall was a photo of daniel cohn bendit [sic lowercase] at the
spot where he drank a glass of red wine, and who will travel to vietnam [sic
lowercase] shortly,"[65] had given him five pounds.

Conclusion

The source materials consulted for this essay confirm the dominant historiographical consensus about sexuality in West Germany at the end of the 1960s
even as they also contradict that consensus fundamentally. Put briefly, even
before the oft-invoked infamous tomato-pelting of pompous prominent New
Left men by enraged New Left women in Frankfurt in 1968,[66] there had been

pitched battles about the sexist marketing of naked female bodies in the left-wing papers, an extremely incisive critique of the sexual politics of many communes (particularly of Kommune 1 and its hung-up and sexually limited machos-in-chief), and clear recognition that the longed-for New Human Being could not be created, or lived, out of thin air. The debate within the left at the time contained a number of warnings that the lifting of bourgeois repression could easily bring new constellations that would be no less repressive. And at whose cost the predominantly male discourse about sex was being conducted, and who was being excluded from it, were also specified in these texts with remarkable acuity and consistency. It is thus all the more astounding that these critical and thoughtful voices were so thoroughly erased in subsequent accounts of the era.

In the first decade of the new women's movement, sexuality definitely remained a positive point of reference. The liberation of children from the authoritarian character through an affirmation of their sexuality, various attempts to break apart the bourgeois property relations inherent in monogamous dyadic relationships, the mockery of political opponents as impotent or at the very least sexually inhibited—all these remained topics for the feminist movement. What that meant concretely was that despite the criticism of widespread sexism within the radical left, sex was not abandoned as a potentially revolutionary force—at least, not at first. Only at the end of the 1970s, with the general conservative backlash in West Germany and the collapse of the '68ers, did the leftist discourse on sex tip back the other way, falling into its puritanical opposite.

In *Agit 883*, those other voices—the at once critical and pro-sex side of sexual liberation—were rarely heard. If one reads the paper from its inception in 1969 until its demise in 1972, the reason for the "tough" treatment of sex seems to be the movement's increasing militarization, whose development can be traced in the pages of the paper and which was accompanied by a growing contempt and derision for everything soft and tender—everything that was not in tune with a "Fuck the System" attitude. It is this disdain for tenderness that most precisely demarcates the line between the anti-authoritarian and the radically militant wings of the New Left. The articles in *Agit 883*, like those in other papers of the era, were dominated by radicals' and militants' conceptions of politics and of what should be considered "really" important. But the readers and their contributions—in the form of housing requests, the arrangement of child-rearing, double entendre requests for ride-sharing, and (above all) the many personal ads indicate the utter centrality of the topic of sexuality for the wider New Left scene.

The contempt for the sexual that became dominant with the creation of the Red Army Faction and its anti-imperialist pose meant the end of fragile attempts to experience sexuality beyond hard comrade penises on the one hand and bourgeois sexual morality on the other. This contempt persisted into the

1980s, leading to a complete expulsion of the realm of sex from the horizon of liberation.

The (re)reading of Michel Foucault's *History of Sexuality*, which had a far-reaching impact on the (academic) left during the poststructuralist wave at the beginning of the 1990s, did not change anything either. On the contrary, it helped to legitimate the impulse to expel the subject of sex from the movement. After all, according to Foucault there was no repressed sexuality that could become visible and mutable through speech, but instead a constant discussion of sex since the eighteenth century that had led to the production of a normalized sexuality as well as to the creation of the perverse practices that were excluded from it. In the 1990s, however, these pathbreaking theoretical insights were reduced to a justification for censoring any discussion of the sexual in political debate. This translated into a silence resembling that of the conservative camp: no one, in short, had any idea how what happened under the covers at home could possibly have anything to do with social change.

At the same time, paradoxically—and in this case in complete disregard of Foucault's theories—there was an extraordinary explosion of speech and writing about the violent character of heterosexual practices and, furthermore, about the supposedly almost compulsorily abusive relationship between men and children. The denunciation of the "child molester" worked just as well in radical left-wing scenes as in anti-leftist circles—a fact illustrated by the case of Bettina Röhl, who stumbled across a 1976 article by Daniel Cohn-Bendit in the left-wing men's magazine *Das Da* in which he had written "that certain children [in the anti-authoritarian kindergarten in which Cohn-Bendit had worked] unzipped my fly and began to tickle me."[67] Röhl was not alone in trying to cross historical swords with the erstwhile leftist protagonist.

With the benefit of historical and political hindsight, it is surely a difficult task to refrain from repudiating entirely the whole complex of representations of sexuality, pornography, relationships, communes, sexist utterances and images, personal testimonies, and analyses, along with the propagation of anti-authoritarian models for child-rearing, that one finds in the articles, editorial commentaries, letters from readers, and in particular the imagery in the New Left papers. A phrase coined by Italian feminists in 1975, "Compagni di lotta, fascisti a letto,"[68] became a slogan that circulated in the German left of the 1980s and 1990s: "Comrades in the street, fascists in bed." In this post–New Left discourse, the machos of yesteryear had done nothing but shoot porn films and abuse children under the guise of the liberation of child sexuality, meanwhile pressuring "their" female comrades to sleep with them if they wanted to avoid being categorized as part of the odious Establishment (and at the same time preventing the women from engaging in any political activity of their own).

Indeed, as shown here, one can find much evidence of such attitudes. In the manner and style of the sexualized representations of the rebellion against the "system run by pigs" (*Schweinesystem*), there was not much difference between left-wing papers like *Charlie Kaputt*, the successor to the *Linkeck* in Berlin, and the widely circulated publications like *konkret*, *Das Da*, or even the *St. Pauli Nachrichten*. Magazines directed also at a broader mainstream audience differed from the self-proclaimed uncompromisingly revolutionary publications only in the professionalism of the pinup girls on their cover pages and in their photo galleries. The revolutionary publications criticized the high-quality, glossy photos in *konkret* as a form of bourgeois commercialization. *Linkeck* called the pinups in *konkret* "hygienic sex" and "idiotic eye-whoring," while *Agit 883* demanded, "Smash *konkret!*" and described its publisher, Röhl, as an "impotent publisher of the German *Playboy*."[69] Instead of depicting polished girls in cheesecake poses, *Linkeck* and *Agit 883* reinforced a different sexist dynamic by deploying mostly naked women as symbols of the state who, in photomontages and drawings, were often fucked by the revolutionary fighters. In short, the suspicion with which the post–New Left leftist movements of the 1980s and 1990s regarded 1968 seems always to be reconfirmed—namely, that sexuality was necessarily inflected by sexism and violence and thus could never be an instrument for possible liberation. As a result, sexuality came to find itself once again on the side of authority—at least as far as opposite-sex sexuality was concerned.

In the wake of the poststructuralist feminist theoretical innovations of the late 1990s, attempts to return the topic of sexuality to left-wing debate, and to tap it for its critical potential—as was done in the special issue on "the correlation between sexual morality and repression"[70] put out by *Arranca!*—ended with a boycott of the journal by the radical leftist scene, or at the very least with the blacking out of entire journal sections of the issue. This time, however, in contradistinction to the situation in the 1960s and 1970s, the censorship received the energetic support of "anti-patriarchal" men's groups. The women of Hamburg's leftist infoshop Black Market (*Schwarzmarkt*) also explicitly justified the censorship of *Arranca!* by invoking what they too summarily called the "sexual revolution of the '68ers":

> [In an *Arranca!* article] it is claimed that, among other things, the "sexual revolution" that began in 1967 was impelled by the "feminist and anti-authoritarian" portions of the movement. This is sheer **historical revisionism** [sic bold] at the cost of a women's movement which first developed some years later, as this movement formed precisely out of the necessity to defend itself *against* [sic underline] the "sexual revolution," in which men wanted to grant themselves penetration-oriented access to as many women's bodies as possible![71]

This "historical" analysis is empirically wrong, but for many it seemed persuasive. In this version, the so-called sexual revolution of the 1960s was thus not a (tragically failed) attempt to counter with a new social reality the patriarchal and authoritarian family relationships of the parental generation that had been formed in the time of National Socialism and during the conservative postwar era of the 1950s. On the contrary, it was maintained that the new feminist movement had become necessary because of the need to combat and liberate oneself from the movements of the 1960s. Notably, not only were countless sexual-political experiments and ideas of the 1960s overlooked by this account, but the female agents of 1968 were rendered invisible and demoted to the status of victims.

What is interesting about this position is the marked analogy between the radical leftist historiography of the last quarter-century and the historiography of bourgeois conservative groups. Both directed—and continue to direct— their gaze at the sexual aspect of the student movement, but in doing so they focus exclusively on those voices from within the scene that did, in fact, attempt to achieve liberation through sexuality, mostly in the form of brutal male pornographic fantasy.

In other words, the generation of radical leftists that succeeded the '68ers assessed bourgeois society's prurient interest in the sexual practices of the 1960s New Left as complicity: the leftist men who lived out pornographic fantasies or made pornography were in cahoots with the bourgeois men who got off on it and marketed it. In publications like *Radikal* and *Interim*, which cast themselves as the spiritual successors of *Agit 883*, and in the numerous local scene papers, one can find no mention of pleasurable sexual acts, but instead quite a bit about rape. At forums and group meetings in the 1980s and 1990s, it was sexism—not sex—that was on the agenda. One thing is certain: writing the recent sexual history of the left would be far more complicated than writing that of the 1960s, and would probably be limited to a documentation of the numerous debates about sexism.

Instead of seeing the '68ers' sexual revolt as nothing but violence, once again suppressing and silencing the critical voices within the '68er movement, and consigning to obscurity the numerous attempts people made then to change their own lives, including within sexual relationships, it seems more promising to observe the lines of conflict running *through* the sexual-political discussions of the time. For one thing, it is historically imprecise to characterize the emergence of the new women's movement as merely a reaction against male-dominated movements. Women did not begin with a move to separatism—that was seen as a last resort. Instead, a mutual debate was demanded. Helke Sanders's famous speech representing the Action Council for the Liberation of Women before the September 1968 SDS delegates' conference in Frankfurt makes this complexity clear. What Sander called for was, above all, the abolition of the division between the private and the political, and, at long last, the thematization of sexuality in political debate: "Why do you all buy [the books of Wilhelm] Reich? Why do you talk about class struggle here, but about orgasm difficulties

278 ~: Massimo Perinelli

only at home? Is that not a topic for the SDS to discuss? We do not want to participate anymore in this repression (*Verdrängung*)." Similarly, Heide Berndt in *Kursbuch* did not just criticize the male communards' fantasies of access to "all girls," but rather wanted complicated feelings like "jealousy, separation anxiety, [and the] longing for security" to be brought into more open discussion.[72]

The heterogeneous and precarious experiments that also existed in the 1960s did their part to shape that generation and marked an important historical stage, but they have found little purchase in the subsequent journalistic discourse–machine. The "oppositional behavior" in the realm of the sexual—the flight-paths out of the existing circumstances—could not easily be turned into discourse. After all, as Foucault remarked about the sexual liberation and homosexual movement of the 1960s, "it is not so much about uncovering the real truth of sexual life, as it is about using one's sexuality for the construction of manifold relationships."[73] The "coming-into-being" of a "polysexuality"[74] that Foucault propagated took place as a real experience—as a way of living—in the counter-spaces of society. But by that time, it was the more sensational stories from below the belt that were being marketed, as for example in the 1966 *Spiegel* issue "Sex in Germany," or in *konkret* in the voyeuristic 1969 report on communes in "Love in the LivingBathKitchen (*WohnKloKüche*)."[75] For the unprogrammatic, noncommercial, and nonlurid voices, we need to look behind the shrill sloganeering of the headlines of the day. *Agit 883* and other leftist magazines are important historical documents that indicate how revolutionary ideals that sought to link pleasure and liberation, and to reclaim sexuality as positive and crucial, could be reterritorialized by those who held opposing ideals. Today, we still await the debate that might be able draw emancipatory conclusions from this history.

Translated by William Seth Howes and Erik Huneke

Notes

1. See Wilhelm Reich, *Die sexuelle Revolution* (Frankfurt am Main, 2004 [1936]); Wilhelm Reich, Erich Fromm, and Siegfried Bernfeld, *Dialektischer Materialismus und Psychoanalyse* (pirated copy from the 1960s [1934]); Herbert Marcuse, *Psychoanalyse und Politik* (Frankfurt am Main, 1968), especially the 1956 lecture "Trieblehre und Freiheit"; Reimut Reiche, *Sexualität und Klassenkampf: Zur Abwehr repressiver Entsublimierung* (Frankfurt am Main, 1968), and *Das Argument*, a newspaper published by Wolfgang Fritz Haug.
2. Michel Foucault, *Die Ordnung der Dinge: Eine Archäologie der Humanwissenschaften* (Frankfurt am Main, 1971), 20.
3. Ibid., 10.
4. Despite its wide circulation and important position on the leftist scene, *Agit 883* has almost been forgotten in recent years. Only the volume by rotaprint 25, *agit 883. Be-*

wegung, Revolte, Underground in Westberlin 1969–1972, which digitized all of its issues on a CD-ROM in 2006, made it possible to have access to the entire print run of this valuable source. The publication is accessible in its entirety at http://plakat.nadir .org/883/index.html.

5. Gilles Deleuze and Félix Guattari, *A Thousand Plateaus: Capitalism and Schizophrenia*, trans. Brian Massumi (Minneapolis, 1987), 531n39.

6. *konkret*, no. 10, 5 May 1969, 16.

7. Hans-Peter Gente, ed., *Marxismus Psychoanalyse Sexpol*, vol. 2, *Aktuelle Diskussion* (Frankfurt am Main, 1972), 11.

8. Robert Steigerwald, "Eine Kritik an Herbert Marcuses Schrift: 'Triebstruktur und Gesellschaft,'" in Gente, *Marxismus Psychoanalyse Sexpol*, 223–40, here 226.

9. Ibid., 232.

10. Ibid., 233.

11. Dagmar Herzog, *Sex after Fascism: Memory and Morality in Twentieth-Century Germany* (Princeton, NJ, 2005), 175ff.

12. Michel Foucault: "Der 'Anti-Ödipus'—Eine Einführung in eine neue Lebenskunst," in M. Foucault, *Dispositive der Macht: Über Sexualität, Wissen und Wahrheit* (Berlin, 1978), 225–230, here 228.

13. The tendency is widespread, but see especially recent works by the historians Götz Aly and Wolfgang Kraushaar.

14. *Agit 883*, no. 2, 20 February 1969, 3.

15. See *Agit 883*, nos. 27, 28, 29, and 34.

16. *Agit 883*, no. 27, 14 August 1969, 3.

17. *Agit 883*, no. 57, 24 April 1970, 4.

18. *Agit 883*, no. 54, 26 March 1970, 10.

19. *Agit 883*, no. 42, 27 November 1969, 2.

20. *Agit 883*, no. 19, 19 June 1969, 3.

21. *Agit 883*, no. 41, 20 November 1969, 3.

22. *Agit 883*, no. 43, 4 December 1969, 3.

23. *Agit 883*, no. 24, 24 July 1969, 5.

24. *Agit 883*, no. 44, 11 December 1969, 3.

25. *Agit 883*, no. 52, 26 February 1970, 10.

26. *Agit 883*, no. 45, 18 December 1969, 3.

27. *Agit 883*, no. 55, 3 April 1970, 3.

28. *Agit 883*, no. 58, 1 May 1970, 3.

29. *Agit 883*, no. 60, 14 May 1970, 4.

30. *Agit 883*, no. 62, 5 June 1970, 12.

31. See Henning Schmidgen, *Das Unbewußte der Maschinen: Konzeptionen des Psychischen bei Guattari, Deleuze und Lacan* (Munich, 1997), 33f.

32. *Agit 883*, no. 1, 13 February 1969, 3.

33. *Agit 883*, no. 2, 20 February 1969, 2.

34. *Agit 883*, no. 54, 26 April 1970, 3.

35. *Agit 883*, no. 54, 26 March 1970, 4.

36. *StreitZeitSchrift: Pornografie: Dokumente, Analysen, Fotos, Comics*, 7, no. 1 (1969): 89.

37. *konkret*, no. 5, 24 February 1969, 45.

38. "Wem schadet eigentlich Pornografie?" *Pardon*, no. 10, October 1967, 36–38, here 38.

39. *Agit 883*, no. 48, 5 February 1970, 3.

40. *Agit 883*, no. 73, 24 December 1970, 12.

41. The Schwarzen Zellen, a young proletarian group in Berlin, based itself in 1970 and 1971 on the strict militancy and community concept of the Black Panther Party and on the concept of armed struggle in urban environments.

42. *Agit 883*, no. 77, 19 March 1971, 5.

43. *Agit 883*, no. 59, 7 May 1970, 4.

44. *Agit 883*, no. 32, 18 September 1969, 3.

45. *Agit 883*, no. 72, 4 December 1970, 11.

46. *Agit 883*, no. 21, 3 July 1969, 3.

47. *Agit 883*, no. 27, 14 August 1969, 5.

48. *Agit 883*, no. 75, 5 February 1971, 9.

49. *Agit 883*, no. 57, 24 April 1970, 5.

50. Herzog, *Sex after Fascism*, 234. Cf. Klaus Theweleit, *Männerphantasien* (Basel and Frankfurt am Main, 1986).

51. Herzog, *Sex after Fascism*, 241.

52. *Agit 883*, no. 77, 13 March 1971, 9.

53. Ursula Schmiederer, "Emanzipation der Frauen. Anmerkungen zu den Argument-Heften," *Das Argument: Sexualität und Herrschaft* 4, no. 7 (December 1965): 41–46, here 44.

54. Projektgruppe Brelohstraße, *Hi ha ho—die Bonzen komm'n ins Klo: Bericht über zwei Jahre proletarische Vorschulerziehung* (Bochum, 1973), 39.

55. Berliner Kinderläden, *Antiautoritäre Erziehung und sozialistischer Kampf* (Cologne and Berlin, 1970), 75f.

56. Kommune 2 (Christel Bookhagen, Eike Hemmer, Jan Raspe, Eberhard Schultz), "Kindererziehung in der Kommune," *Kursbuch: Frau, Familie, Gesellschaft* 17 (June 1969): 147–78, here 166.

57. *Agit 883*, no. 87, 22 January 1972, 16.

58. "Erobern Kommunen Deutschlands Betten? Mehr Sex mit Marx und Mao," *Pardon*, no. 8, August 1967, 16–23, here 22.

59. Schmiederer, *Das Argument*, 45.

60. Heide Berndt, "Kommune und Familie," *Kursbuch: Frau, Familie, Gesellschaft* 17 (June 1969): 129–46, here 132.

61. Some remarks on the *Sexwelle* in Berliner Kinderläden, *Antiautoritäre Erziehung*, 107–112, here 108.

62. *Agit 883*, no. 33, 25 September 1969, 4.

63. *Agit 883*, no. 35, 9 October 1969, 6.

64. *Agit 883*, no. 36, 16 October 1969, 4.

65. *Agit 883*, no. 52, 5 March 1970, 10.

66. At a conference of SDS delegates, Helke Sander gave a speech that formulated a feminist critique of the leftist movement. Because the SDS higher-ups on the dais ignored the speech completely, Sigrid Rüger, a female activist, pelted them with tomatoes. This act served as a founding myth of the new women's movement in Germany.

67. Daniel Cohn-Bendit. "Damals im Kinderladen…," *Das da*. no. 8, August 1976.

68. Italien, "Männer raus!" *Der Spiegel*, no. 53, 29 December 1975, 58.

69. *Agit 883*, no. 70, 28 October 1970, 11.

70. *Arranca! Schwerpunkt: SEXualmoralischer Verdrängungszusammenhang*, no. 8 (1996).

71. FrauenLesbenTag im Infoladen Schwarzmarkt und die Frauen aus der gemischten Ladengruppe des Schwarzmarkt, "Transparenz in der Zensur oder Warum wir die Arranca no. 8 nicht verkaufen," *Interim*, no. 374, 2 May 1996, 12–15, here 13.

72. Berndt, "Kommune und Familie," 133.
73. Michel Foucault, *Von der Freundschaft als Lebensweise: Michel Foucault im Gespräch* (Berlin, 1984), 86.
74. Ibid., 86 and 90.
75. See "Sex in Deutschland," *Der Spiegel*, no. 19 (2 May 1966): 50–69; "Liebe in der WohnKloKüche. Subkultur Berlin," *konkret*, no. 14, June 1969.

~:~

Tomorrow Sex Will Be Good Again

DAGMAR HERZOG

> By creating the imaginary element that is "sex," the deployment
> of sexuality established one of its most essential internal operating
> principles: the desire for sex—the desire to have it, to have access
> to it, to discover it, to liberate it, to articulate it in discourse, to for-
> mulate it in truth. It constituted "sex" itself as something desirable.
> —Michel Foucault, *The History of Sexuality*

Germany in the first decade of the twenty-first century has returned to its early twentieth-century status as one of the most—if not *the* most—liberal and "sex-positive" cultures in the world. In some ways, Germany is more progressive now than it was a hundred years ago. The core trend is toward broad tolerance of diversity and strong defense of the ethical value of individual self-determination. This is evident in such phenomena as the nonchalance with which openly gay and lesbian politicians and cultural figures are accepted across the political spectrum while gay bathhouses, Christopher Street Day parades, and gay and lesbian civil unions are treated as unremarkable. In 2001 the "life-partner law" (*Lebenspartnerschaftsgesetz*) for same-sex couples went into effect, and in 2005 its benefits were further expanded. Lesbian couples are still barred from using sperm donor banks in Germany and must find volunteers or go outside the country, and skirmishes over adoption are ongoing. But there is no question that the trajectory is toward equalization of heterosexual and homosexual partnerships.

This expansive mentality is also, if more prosaically nonetheless significantly, noticeable in such phenomena as the photos of fully naked male and female teenagers in the bestselling teen magazine *Bravo*—along with tips for gentle caressing and accounts of what it feels like to have intercourse "for the first time," as well as in the government-sponsored anti-HIV public health campaigns replete with consistently witty and explicit condom ads on billboards dotting the nation in train stations, city streets, and rural fields alike. The broad-minded liberality is additionally evident in the 2002 decision to decriminalize prostitution—a striking contrast to such stereotypically sexually progressive cultures as the Netherlands (where Amsterdam has launched an effort to "clean up" the city's red light district) and Sweden (which since 1999 prosecutes not prostitutes but their johns—on the argument that any impersonal exchange of sex for money is shameful and perverse and not to be tolerated by the state).

Moreover, it bears pointing out that the affirmative atmosphere and enumerated freedoms represent an achievement of long years of activist struggle and arduous post-fascist learning processes. A complicated interplay of transnational pressures and intra-national conflicts over sexual mores and sex-related laws led first, in the Cold War 1950s, to the consolidation of a conservative sexual culture in the Federal Republic of Germany. Church and political leaders interpreted Nazism's barbarism as intrinsically connected to its frank promotion not only of sublime marital pleasures but also of pre- and extramarital libertinism for all those racially and ideologically approved by the regime to have sex (i.e., the majority of the population), and they avidly promoted the restoration of "family values" as an anti-Nazi imperative. In fact, "tidying up" German sexual mores recommended itself as an effective way to overcome the genocidal past as a massive displacement of moral discourse occurred, away from the issue of popular complicity in expropriation and mass murder and toward a narrowed conception of morality as majorly concerned with sex.

At the same time, the European Court of Human Rights, which began its work in 1959, grew out of a transnational commitment to secure the rights of the individual against an arbitrary and violent state, with several articles explicitly formulated in reaction to the experiences of Nazism's brutal invasions into bodies and relationships alike—among them the rights to found a family through marriage, to a private life free from state scrutiny, and to nondiscrimination. The court, as of the early twenty-first century, has come to understand its task as not only protecting individuals against sexual violence and abuse, but also protecting the right to *desired* sexual activity (whether homo- or hetero-) as well as the right to the freely chosen formation of intimate partnerships. The process of political reunification with the former German Democratic Republic in the wake of the fall of communism, and the integration of the former East Germans with their generally strong commitment to the defense of sexual rights as human rights and pride in the culture of sexual freedom and romance they had been able to develop despite political repression, contributed important impulses to the maintenance and further development of ongoing progressive legislation.

Yet in the last few years, conservatism has been returning, in a roundabout way. The complex of issues surrounding European identities and citizenships—with all the accompanying assumptions about appropriate inclusions and exclusions—now rests with remarkable frequency on sex-related concerns. Germany, along with the rest of Western Europe, is increasingly defining itself as the defender of "sexual democracy" against what is taken to be a constitutively homophobic and misogynistically repressive European Islam. Sensationalist public and media discussion rivets on such issues as honor killings, demands for bridal virginity, female genital cutting, and arranged or "forced" marriages. But the lines of conflict are fractured and contradictory, for—in odd counterpoint to the effusive and aggressive defenses specifically of women's sexual rights against the disrespect of those rights purportedly evinced by Islam—ambivalences about self-determined female sexuality are evident in a number of areas in public policy development and media and popular debate. The debates have become thoroughly garbled, even as the endless commentary propping up the cultural consensus about the purported demerits of Islam keeps these contradictions from becoming too easy to decode. (For instance, in a 2009 flurry of upbeat government and media pronouncements due to a study showing a recent uptick in the notoriously low German birthrate, from 1.33 to 1.37, it became clear not only that sometimes immigrant women are counted and sometimes not, but that when Muslim women stay at home with young children, this is deemed a sign of awful patriarchalism; when non-Muslim women do so, the Christian Democratic party congratulates itself for having developed improved family policies.)[1] In the animus against Islam, support for female sexual independence is central. In the distress over a declining German birthrate, by contrast, female sexual independence is perceived as a problem, and a backlash against feminism is evident, replete with criticisms of German women's lamentable reliance on contraception.

In the constant exhortations to native-born German women to be more avidly reproductive, and even while the growth of a native-born population that is both Muslim and German is variously either bemoaned or disavowed, there is a recurrent rehearsal of a (faulty but nonetheless strategically effective) historical argument: in the pre-pill 1950s, it is asserted, German women had more children and stayed home happily, but the sexual revolution ruined all that. Now people just selfishly seek sexual pleasure, which only spreads anomie— so the argument goes. It has become quite popular in the early twenty-first century to slam the 1960s and 1970s for encouraging meaningless hedonism. This may appear gender-neutral in some versions, but it inevitably is meant as preeminently an attack on female self-determination. In Germany—with its long-standing dearth of child care facilities and lack of all-day schooling—it is especially difficult to combine career and motherhood (in contrast with, say, France or Scandinavia); these are some practical reasons for the lower birthrate. But what is inescapably evident in the last several years is the return, with a vengeance, of unabashedly forthright hostility to feminism and a surprisingly uninhibited articulation of longing for a "little woman at the stove" (*Heimchen am Herd*) who will repair the ego of the husband when he comes home from his stressful day at work.

✦ ✦ ✦

Can Michel Foucault's observations from the 1970s in any way help us decipher the impasses and peculiarities of the current cultural-political juncture? *The History of Sexuality* was, after all, written as the sexual revolution was unfolding across the Western world. And this was, it bears remembering, a world before HIV, before the fall of communism, and before the rise of European Islam. It was also a world before a conservative backlash against the sexual revolution was anywhere in evidence (a backlash, it should be noted, that was ascendant even before HIV and then used the arrival of this terrifying pandemic—and not without grim pleasure—to make the case for a return to sexual moderation instead of promiscuity. However, a reconstruction of the historical record suggests that this backlash was not unrelated to anger about the feminist movement and women's demands for better treatment in bed). And—not least— it was a world before there was any hint of the alarmism that would become rampant across Europe in the 1990s over what was purportedly a massive plunge in women's *and* men's experiences of themselves as having the urge (supposedly so unruly, though apparently more elusive) for aroused connection and physical entanglement with another human that is called, for want of a better term, libido.

Writing in the midst of the revolution, Foucault poked fun at the inflated self-importance of those many individuals who vociferously and grandiloquently denounced sexual repression and called for liberation. He pointed out that one "must not think that by saying yes to sex, one says no to power," for power works not only (though also) through restrictions. Power works as well by stimulating aspirations, by dangling hope. The message of the optimism peddlers of the 1970s, in Foucault's mocking summary, was: "Tomorrow sex will be good again."[2]

Foucault's scathing skepticism was certainly appropriate for his historical moment, even as his scoffing reminds us that already then the constant promises of spectacular happiness barely hid an anxiety that hopes might be disappointed. And Foucault's skepticism also remains warranted today, although it needs to be updated. It certainly remains salutary for contemporary readers of Foucault to continue to feel a bit chagrined when using terms like *individual rights* or *sexual self-determination*. Foucault did more than anyone to teach us to be dubious *both* about the notion of an autonomous individual subject *and*— maybe even more importantly—about the very idea that there is any such thing as "sex." Foucault was quite right to point out that "sex" was nothing but a "fictitious unity" that artificially grouped together "anatomical elements, biological functions, conducts, sensations, and pleasures," and that it should give us pause to "ponder all the ruses that were employed for centuries to make us love sex, to make knowledge of it desirable and everything said about it precious."[3] Already in the 1970s, Foucault wondered whether people even liked sex, or what they had been taught to think sex was. "Pleasure," as Foucault once remarked, "is a very difficult behavior."[4]

Now we live on the other side of that sexual revolution, in its melancholic, conflicted, ennui-ridden aftermath. Now the real challenge, we are informed, is no longer orgasm (in any event quite easily available via masturbation, sex toys, Internet porn, and/or Viagra, as the occasion demands). Now, according to the ever-ready advice-givers, the Holy Grail is *love*. The confusion about how to bring together thoughts and bodies, performance and intimacy, is palpable and pervasive.

Foucault noted in *The History of Sexuality*: "What sustains our eagerness to speak of sex in terms of repression is doubtless this opportunity to speak out against the powers that be, to utter truths and promise bliss, to link together enlightenment, liberation, and manifold pleasures; to pronounce a discourse that combines the fervor of knowledge, the determination to change the laws, and the longing for the garden of earthly delights."[5] While a traditional Freudian interpretation of the conflicts between post-Christian secularism and Islamic neo-fundamentalism might speculate that *sex* is always what is going on beneath the surface of other conflicts, a Foucauldian interpretation might instead say that what is at stake may actually be a desperate effort to keep "sex" desirable. As we struggle to come to terms with the apparently inevitable imperfections of "sex," then, there may be some way in which continually talking about the sexual specter of Islam reassures us about the value of the Western system, even though we sense that "the garden of earthly delights" is no longer just around the corner. The chatter becomes a means to keep hope alive in our jaundiced, jaded age. Maybe tomorrow sex will be good again.

Notes

1. For a concise summary, see E.S., "Ein Hoch auf Geburtenraten und Hausfrauenquoten," *JurBlog.de*, 18 February 2009, http://www.jurblog.de/2009/02/18/ein-hoch-auf-geburtenraten-und-hausfrauenquoten/.
2. Michel Foucault, *History of Sexuality*, vol. 1, *An Introduction*, trans. Robert Hurley (New York, 1978), 157, 7.
3. Ibid., 154, 159.
4. Michel Foucault in conversation with Stephen Riggins, "The Minimalist Self," first published in *Ethos* (Fall 1983), reprinted in Lawrence D. Kritzman, ed., *Michel Foucault: Politics, Philosophy, Culture: Interviews and Other Writings 1977–1984* (New York, 1988), 12.
5. Foucault, *The History of Sexuality*, 7.

❧ SELECT BIBLIOGRAPHY ☙

Adam, Barry D. "Structural Foundations of the Gay World." *Comparative Studies in Society and History* 27 (1985): 658–71.

Aldrich, Robert, ed. *Gay Life and Culture: A World History*. London, 2006.

Allen, Ann Taylor. *Feminism and Motherhood in Germany, 1800–1914*. New Brunswick, NJ, 1991.

Babayan, Kathryn, and Afsaneh Najmabadi, eds. *Islamicate Sexualities: Translations across Temporal Geographies of Desire*. Cambridge, MA, 2008.

Babka, Anna, and Susanne Hochreiter. *Queer Reading in den Philologien: Modelle und Anwendungen*. Göttingen, 2008.

Bérubé, Allan. *Coming Out under Fire: The History of Gay Men and Women in World War Two*. New York, 1990.

Bland, Lucy, and Laura Doan. *Sexology in Culture: Labeling Bodies and Desires*. Chicago, 1998.

———. *Sexology Uncensored: The Documents of Sexual Science*. Chicago, 1998.

Bloch, Iwan. *The Sexual Life of Our Time*. New York, 1937.

Bochow, Michael. *Schwule Männer, AIDS und Safer Sex*. Berlin, 2001.

Bray, Alan. *The Friend*. Chicago, 2003.

Breitenberg, Mark. *Anxious Masculinity in Early Modern England*. Cambridge, 1996.

Bridenthal, Renate, Atina Grossman, and Marion Kaplan. *When Biology Became Destiny; Women in Weimar and Nazi Germany*. New York, 1984.

Brown, Peter. *The Body and Society: Men, Women, and Sexual Renunciation in Early Christianity*. New York, 1988.

Bruns, Claudia. *Politik des Eros*. Cologne, 2008.

Bruns, Claudia, and Tilman Walter, eds. *Von Lust und Schmerz: Eine Historische Anthropologie der Sexualität*. Cologne, Weimar, and Vienna, 2004.

Burger, Glenn, and Steven F. Kruger, eds. *Queering the Middle Ages*. Minneapolis, 2001.

Burghartz, Susanna. *Zeiten der Reinheit, Orte der Unzucht: Ehe und Sexualität in Basel während der Frühen Neuzeit*. Paderborn, 1999.

Butler, Judith. *Bodies That Matter: On the Discursive Limits of "Sex."* New York, 1993.

———. *Gender Trouble: Feminism and the Subversion of Identity*. New York, 1990.

———. *Undoing Gender*. New York, 2004.

Canguilhem, Georges. *The Normal and the Pathological*. New York, 1989.

Canning, Kathleen. *Gender History in Practice: Historical Perspectives on Bodies, Class, and Citizenship*. Ithaca, NY, 2006.

Carter, Philip. *Men and the Emergence of Polite Society in Britain 1660–1800*. London, 2001.

Chauncey, George Jr. "Christian Brotherhood or Sexual Perversion? Homosexual Identities and the Construction of Sexual Boundaries in the World War I Era." In *Hidden from History: Reclaiming the Gay and Lesbian Past*, edited by Martin Bauml Duberman, Martha Vicinus, and George Chauncey, Jr. New York, 1989.

———. *Gay New York: The Making of the Gay Male World, 1890–1940.* New York, 1995.

Clark, Anna. *Desire: A History of European Sexuality.* New York, 2008.

Connell, R. W. *Masculinities.* Berkeley, CA, 1995.

Copjec, Joan, ed. *Supposing the Subject.* New York, 1994.

Corbin, Alain. *L'harmonie des plaisirs: Les manières de jouir du siècle des Lumières à l'avènement de la sexologie.* Paris, 2008.

Crawford, Katharine. *European Sexualities, 1400–1800.* Cambridge, 2007.

Crompton, Louis. *Homosexuality and Civilization.* Cambridge, MA, 2003.

Cuncun, Wu. *Homoerotic Sensibilities in Late Imperial China.* London, 2004.

Davidson, Arnold. *The Emergence of Sexuality: Historical Epistemology and the Formation of Concepts.* Cambridge, MA, 2001.

Dean, Carolyn. *The Frail Social Body: Pornography, Homosexuality, and Other Fantasies in Interwar France.* Berkeley, CA, 2000.

Deleuze, Gilles. *Foucault.* Translated by Sean Hand. Minneapolis, 1988.

Deleuze, Gilles, and Félix Guattari. *A Thousand Plateaus: Capitalism and Schizophrenia.* Translated by Brian Massumi. Minneapolis, 1987.

Dickinson, Edward Ross. "'A Dark, Impenetrable Wall of Complete Incomprehension': The Impossibility of Heterosexual Love in Imperial Germany." *Central European History* 40 (2007): 467–97.

———. "Policing Sex in Germany, 1882–1982: A Preliminary Statistical Analysis." *Journal of the History of Sexuality* 16, no. 2 (2007): 204–50.

Dickinson, Edward Ross, and Richard Wetzell, "The Historiography of Sexuality in Modern Germany." *German History* 23, no. 3 (2005): 291–305.

Dinges, Martin. *Hausväter, Priester, Kastraten: Zur Konstruktion von Männlichkeit in Spätmittelalter und früher Neuzeit.* Göttingen, 1999.

———. *Männer-Macht-Körper: Hegemonial Männlichkeit von Mittelalter bis heute.* Frankfurt am Main, 2005.

Dinshaw, Carolyn. *Sexualities and Communities, Pre- and Postmodern.* Durham, 1999.

Dürr, Renate. *Mägde in der Stadt: Das Beispiel Schwäbisch-Hall in der Frühen Neuzeit.* Frankfurt am Main, 1995.

Duttweiler, Stefanie. "Subjektivierung im Modus medialisierter Sexualberatung." *Schweizerisches Archiv für Volkskunde* 104 (2008): 45–65.

Duttweiler, Stefanie, and Peter-Paul Bänziger. "'Chère Marta, j'ai un problème': La mise en mots du malaise sexuel dans le courrier du cœur." *Revue des Sciences Sociales* 36 (2006): 108–15.

Eder, Franz. *Kultur der Begierde: Eine Geschichte der Sexualität.* Munich, 2002.

Eghigian, Greg. "The Psychologization of the Socialist Self: East German Forensic Psychology and Its Deviants, 1945–1975." *German History* 22 (2004): 181–205.

Ellis, Havelock, and John Addington Symonds. *Sexual Inversion.* London, 1897.

El-Rouayheb, Khaled. *Before Homosexuality in the Arab-Islamic World, 1500–1800.* Chicago, 2005.

Eribon, Didier. *Foucault.* Translated by Betsy Wing. Cambridge, MA, 1992.

Ernst, Anna-Sabine. "Vom 'Du' zum 'Sie': Die Rezeption der bürgerlichen Anstandsregeln in der DDR der 50er Jahre." *Mitteilungen aus der kulturwissenschaftlichen Forschung* 33 (1993): 190–209.

Evans, Richard. *The Feminist Movement in Germany 1894–1933.* London, 1976.

———. "Prostitution, State and Society in Imperial Germany." *Past and Present* 70 (1976): 106–29.

Ferdinand, Ursula, et al., eds. *Verqueere Wissenschaft? Zum Verhältnis von Sexualwissenschaft und Sexualreformbewegung in Geschichte und Gegenwart*. Münster, 1998.

Foucault, Michel. *The Birth of the Clinic: An Archaeology of Medical Perception*. Translated by A. M. Sheridan Smith. New York, 1973.

———. *Discipline and Punish: The Birth of the Prison*. Translated by Alan Sheridan. New York, 1977.

———. *Ethics, Subjectivity and Truth: Vol. I of the Essential Works of Foucault, 1954–1984*. Edited by Paul Rabinow. New York, 1997.

———. *The Hermeneutics of the Subject: Lectures at the Collège de France 1981–82*. Edited by Frédéric Gros. General Editors: François Ewald and Alessandro Fontana. English Series Editor: Arnold I. Davidson. Translated by Graham Burchell. New York, 2005.

———. *The History of Sexuality*, vol. 1, *An Introduction*. Translated by Robert Hurley. New York, 1978.

———. *The History of Sexuality*, vol. 2, *The Use of Pleasure*. Translated by Robert Hurley. New York, 1985.

———. *The History of Sexuality*, vol. 3, *The Care of the Self*. Translated by Robert Hurley. New York, 1986.

———. "Introduction." In Georges Canguilhem, *On the Normal and the Pathological*. Translated by Carolyn R. Fawcett. Dordrecht, Boston, and London, 1978.

———. "Nietzsche, Genealogy, History." In *Language, Counter-Memory, Practice: Selected Essays and Interviews*, edited by D. F. Bouchard. Translated by D. F. Bouchard and Sherry Simon. Ithaca, NY, 1977.

———. *Politics, Philosophy, Culture: Interviews and Other Writings 1977–1984*. Edited by Lawrence D. Kritzman. New York, 1988.

———. "What Is Enlightenment." Translated by Catherine Porter. In M. Foucault, *The Foucault Reader*. Edited by Paul Rabinow. New York, 1984.

———. "Der 'Anti-Ödipus'—Eine Einführung in eine neue Lebenskunst." In M. Foucault, *Dispositive der Macht. Über Sexualität, Wissen und Wahrheit*. Berlin, 1978.

———. *Die Ordnung der Dinge: Eine Archäologie der Humanwissenschaften*. Frankfurt am Main, 1971.

———. *Schriften in vier Bänden: Dits et Ecrits*, vols. 1–4. Frankfurt am Main, 2001–05.

———. *Von der Freundschaft als Lebensweise: Michel Foucault im Gespräch*. Berlin, 1984.

———, ed. *Herculine Barbin: Being the Recently Discovered Memoirs of a Nineteenth-Century French Hermaphrodite*. Translated by Richard McDougall. New York, 1980.

Foyster, Elizabeth. *Manhood in Early Modern England: Honour, Sex and Marriage*. London, 1999.

Freccero, Carla. *Queer / Early / Modern*. Durham, 2006.

Freud, Sigmund. *Gesammelte Werke, chronologisch geordnet*. Edited by Anna Freud et al. London, 1940.

Frevert, Ute. *A Nation in Barracks: Conscription, Military Service and Civil Society in Modern Germany*. Translated by Andrew Boreham and Daniel Brückenhaus. New York, 2004.

Fritzsche, Peter. *Reading Berlin 1900*. Cambridge, MA, 1996.

———. "Vagabond in the Fugitive City: Hans Ostwald, Imperial Berlin and the Grossstadt-Dokumente." *Journal of Contemporary History* 29, no. 3 (1994): 385–402.

Gilfoyle, Timothy J. *City of Eros: New York City, Prostitution, and the Commercialization of Sex*. New York, 1992.

Gleixner, Ulrike. *"Das Mensch" und "der Kerl": Die Konstruktion von Geschlecht in Unzuchts-verfahren der Frühen Neuzeit (1700–1760)*. Frankfurt am Main, 1994.

Goldberg, Jonathan. *Queering the Renaissance*. Durham, 1993.

Goldberg, Jonathan, and Madhavi Menon. "Queering History." *Publications of the Modern Language Association of America* 120 (2005): 1608–17.

Greenberg, David F. *The Construction of Homosexuality*. Chicago, 1988.

Grossmann, Atina. *Reforming Sex: The German Movement for Birth Control and Abortion Reform, 1920–1950*. New York, 1995.

Gustafson, Susan E. *Men Desiring Men: The Poetry of Same-Sex Identity and Desire in German Classicism*. Detroit, 2002.

Gary Guttman, ed. *The Cambridge Companion to Foucault*. Cambridge, 1995.

Hacker, Hanna. *Frauen und Freundinnen: Studien zur "weiblichen Homosexualität" am Beispiel Österreich 1870–1938*. Weinheim, 1987.

Haggerty, George E. *Men in Love: Masculinity and Sexuality in the Eighteenth Century*. New York, 1999.

Halperin, David M. *How to Do the History of Homosexuality*. Chicago, 2002.

———. "Is There a History of Sexuality?" In *The Lesbian and Gay Studies Reader*, edited by Henry Abelove. New York, 1993.

Hamelmann, Gudrun. *Helene Stöcker, der 'Bund für Mutterschutz' und 'Die neue Generation.'* Frankfurt am Main, 1992.

Harrington, Joel F. "*Hausvater* and *Landesvater*: Paternalism and Marriage Reform in Sixteenth-Century Germany." *Central European History* 25 (1992): 52–75.

———. *Reordering Marriage and Society in Reformation Germany*. Cambridge, 1995.

Harsch, Donna. *Revenge of the Domestic: Women, the Family, and Communism in the German Democratic Republic*. Princeton, NJ, 2007.

Hartmann, Andreas. "Im falschen Geschlecht: Männliche Scheinzwitter um 1900." In *Der falsche Körper: Beiträge zu einer Geschichte der Monstrositäten*, edited by Michael Hagner. Göttingen, 1995.

Hauser, Walter. *Der Justizmord an Anna Göldi: Neue Recherchen zum letzten Hexenprozess in Europa*. Zurich, 2007.

Healey, Dan. *Homosexual Desire in Revolutionary Russia: The Regulation of Sexual and Gender Dissent*. Chicago, 2001.

———. "Masculine Purity and 'Gentlemen's Mischief': Sexual Exchange and Prostitution between Russian Men, 1861–1941." *Slavic Review* 60, no. 2 (2001): 233–65.

Hekma, Gert. "Homosexual Behavior in the Nineteenth-Century Dutch Army." *Journal of the History of Sexuality* 2 (1991): 266–88.

Hendrix, Scott, and Susan Karant-Nunn, eds. *Masculinity in the Reformation Era*. Kirksville, MO, 2008.

Hergemöller, Bernd-Ulrich. *Mann für Mann: Biographisches Lexikon zur Geschichte von Freundesliebe und mann-männlicher Sexualität im deutschen Sprachraum*. Hamburg, 1998.

———. *Männer, 'die mit Männern handeln,' in der Augsburger Reformationszeit*. Munich, 2000.

———. "Sodomiter: Schuldzubeschreibungen und Repressionsformen im späten Mittelalters." In B.-U. Hergemöller, *Randgruppen der spätmittelalterlichen Gesellschaft*. Warendorf, 1990.

Hermanns, Ludger M. "Helene Stöckers autobiographisches Fragment zur Psychoanalyse." *Luzifer-Amor* 4, no. 8 (1991): 177–80.

Hershatter, Gail. *Dangerous Pleasures: Prostitution and Modernity in Twentieth-Century Shanghai.* Berkeley, CA, 1997.

Herzer, Manfred. "Zastrow – Ulrichs – Kertbeny: Erfundene Identitäten im 19. Jahrhundert." In *Männerliebe im alten Deutschland,* edited by Rüdiger Lautmann. Berlin, 1992.

Herzog, Dagmar. *Sex after Fascism: Memory and Morality in Twentieth-Century Germany.* Princeton, NJ, 2005.

———. *Sex in Crisis: The New Sexual Revolution and the Future of American Politics.* New York, 2008.

———. "Sexuality in the Postwar West." *Journal of Modern History* 78 (2006): 144–71.

Hewitt, Andrew. *Political Inversions: Homosexuality, Fascism, and the Modernist Imaginary.* Stanford, CA, 1996.

Hirschauer, Stefan. *Die soziale Konstruktion der Transsexualität: Über die Medizin und den Geschlechtswechsel.* Frankfurt am Main, 1993.

Hirschfeld, Magnus. *Berlins Drittes Geschlecht.* Edited by Manfred Herzer. Berlin, 1991 [1904].

———. "Das russische Sexualstrafrecht." *Die Aufklärung: Monatsschrift für Sexual- und Lebensreform* 1 (1929): 225–26.

———. *Die Homosexualität des Mannes und des Weibes.* Berlin, 1914.

———. *Geschlechtskunde,* vol. 3. Stuttgart, 1930.

———. *Sittengeschichte der Nachkriegszeit,* vols. 1–2. Leipzig and Vienna, 1931–32.

Hitchcock, Tim, and Michele Cohen, eds. *English Masculinities.* London, 1999.

Hohmann, Joachim S., ed. *Sexuologie in der DDR.* Berlin, 1991.

Hong, Young-Sun. *Welfare, Modernity, and the Weimar State, 1919–1933.* Princeton, NJ, 1998.

Hössli, Heinrich. *Eros: Die Männerliebe der Griechen, ihre Beziehung zur Geschichte, Erziehung, Literatur und Gesetzgebung aller Zeiten.* Berlin, 1996.

Houlbrook, Matt. "Soldier Heroes and Rent Boys: Homosex, Masculinities, and Britishness in the Brigade of Guards, circa 1900–1960." *Journal of British Studies* 42 (July 2003): 351–88.

Hull, Isabel. *Sex, State and Civil Society in Germany, 1700–1815.* Ithaca, NY, 1996.

Jagose, Annmarie. *Queer Theory: An Introduction.* New York, 1997.

Janssen-Jurreit, Marie-Luise. "Nationalbiologie, Sexualreform und Gebürtenrückgang— Über die Zusammenhänge von Bevölkerungspolitik und Frauenbewegung um die Jahrhundertwende." In *Die Überwindung der Sprachlosigkeit,* edited by Gabriele Dietz. Darmstadt and Neuwied, 1978.

Jazbinsek, Dietmar, Bernward Joerges, and Ralf Thies. "The Berlin 'Großstadt-Dokumente': A Forgotten Precursor of the Chicago School of Sociology." Wissenschaftszentrum Berlin für Sozialforschung. Berlin 2001. http://bibliothek.wzb.eu/pdf/2001/ii01-502.pdf

Karant-Nunn, Susan C. "'Fragrant Wedding Roses': Lutheran Wedding Sermons and Gender Definition in Early Modern Germany." *German History* 1 (1999): 25–41.

Karant-Nunn, Susan C., and Merry E. Wiesner-Hanks, eds. *Luther on Women: A Sourcebook.* Cambridge, 2003.

Karras, Ruth. "Prostitution and the Question of Sexual Identity in Medieval Europe." *Journal of Women's History* 11 (1999): 159–77.

Katz, Jonathan Ned. "Coming to Terms: Conceptualizing Men's Erotic and Affectional Relations with Men in the United States, 1820–1892." In *A Queer World,* edited by Martin Duberman. New York, 1997.

————. *The Invention of Heterosexuality.* New York, 1996.

Kennedy, Hubert. *The Life and Works of Karl Heinrich Ulrichs, Pioneer of the Gay Movement.* Boston, 1988.

Kolnai, Aurel. *Sexualethik: Sinn und Grundlagen der Geschlechtsmoral.* Paderborn, 1930.

Kord, Susanne. "Ancient Fears and the New Order: Witch Beliefs and Physiognomy in the Age of Reason." *German Life and Letters* 61, no. 1 (2008): 61–78.

Kounine, Laura. *Witch-Hunting and Attitudes to Gender in Counter-Reformation Würzburg.* M.Phil. diss., Cambridge University, 2007.

Krafft, Sybille. *Zucht und Unzucht: Prostitution und Sittenpolizei im München der Jahrhundertwende.* Munich, 1996.

Krah, Hans. "Freundschaft oder Männerliebe?" In *Forum Vormärz Forschung: Jahrbuch 1999*, vol. 5: *"Emancipation des Fleisches": Erotik und Sexualität im Vormärz*, edited by Gustav Frank and Detlev Kopp. Bielefeld, 1999.

Krass, Andreas. "Queer lesen: Literaturgeschichte und Queer Theory." In *Gender Studies: Wissenschaftstheorien und Gesellschaftskritik*, edited by Caroline Rosenthal, Therese Frey Steffen, and Anke Väth. Würzburg, 2004.

————. *Queer Studies in Deutschland: Interdisziplinäre Beiträge zur kritischen Heteronormativitätsforschung.* Berlin, 2009.

Kuchta, David. *The Three-Piece Suit and Modern Masculinity: England, 1550–1850.* Berkeley, CA, 2002.

Lange, Konrad. *Der Papstesel: Ein Beitrag zur Kultur-und Kunstgeschichte des Reformationszeitalters.* Göttingen, 1891.

Lapisch, Alfons. "'Hygiene ist Moral—Moral ist Hygiene': Soziale Disziplinierung durch Ärzte und Medizin." In *Soziale Sicherheit und soziale Disziplinierung: Beiträge zu einer historischen Theorie der Sozialpolitik*, edited by Christoph Sachße and Florian Tennstedt. Frankfurt am Main, 1986.

Laqueur, Thomas. *Making Sex: Body and Gender from the Greeks to Freud.* Cambridge, MA, 1990.

————. "Orgasm, Generation, and the Politics of Reproduction Biology." In *The Gender/ Sexuality Reader*, edited by Roger N. Lancaster and Micaela di Leonardo. New York, 1997.

Lehmstedt, Mark. *Bücher für das „dritte Geschlecht": Der Max Spohr Verlag in Leipzig.* Wiesbaden, 2002.

Link, Jürgen. *Versuch über den Normalismus: Wie Normalität produziert wird.* Wiesbaden, 1999.

Lochrie, Karma. *Heterosyncrasies: Female Sexuality When Normal Wasn't.* Minneapolis, 2005.

Lorey, Christoph, and John Plews. *Queering the Canon: Defying Sights in German Literature and Culture.* Rochester, 1998.

Lücke, Martin. *Männlichkeit in Unordnung.* Frankfurt am Main, 2008.

Lüdtke, Alf, ed. *The History of Everyday Life: Reconstructing Historical Experiences and Ways of Life.* Translated by William Templer. Princeton, NJ, 1995.

Luhmann, Niklas. *Liebe als Passion: Zur Codierung von Intimität.* Frankfurt am Main, 1982.

Lutz, Alexandra. *Ehepaare vor Gericht: Konflikte und Lebenswelten in der Frühen Neuzeit.* Frankfurt am Main and New York, 2006.

Lybeck, Marti M. "Gender, Sexuality, and Belonging: Female Homosexuality in Germany, 1890–1933." Ph.D. diss., University of Michigan, 2007.

Lynd, Helen Merrell. *On Shame and the Search for Identity*. London, 1958.

Mansfield, Nick. *Subjectivity: Theories of the Self from Freud to Haraway*. New York, 2000.

Mantegazza, Paolo. *Physiology of Love and Other Writings*. Translated by Nicoletta Pireddu. Toronto, 2008.

Marcuse, Herbert. *Psychoanalyse und Politik*. Frankfurt am Main, 1968.

Mason, Timothy. *Nazism, Fascism and the Working Class*. Edited by Jane Caplan. Cambridge, 1995.

Matysik, Tracie. "In the Name of the Law: The 'Female Homosexual' and the Criminal Code in Fin de Siècle Germany." *Journal of the History of Sexuality* 13, no. 1 (2004): 26–48.

Maynes, Mary Jo, Birgitte Søland, and Christina Benninghaus, eds. *Secret Gardens, Satanic Mills: Placing Girls in European History, 1750–1960*. Bloomington, IN, 2005.

McGuire, Kristin. "Activism, Intimacy, and the Politics of Selfhood: The Gendered Terms of Citizenship in Poland and Germany, 1890–1918." Ph.D. diss., University of Michigan, 2004.

Medick, Hans, and Anne-Charlotte Trepp, eds. *Geschlechtergeschichte und Allgemeine Geschichte: Herausforderungen und Persektiven*. Göttingen, 1998.

Medicus, Thomas. *"Die große Liebe": Ökonomie und Konstruktion der Körper im Werke von Frank Wedekind*. Marburg, 1982.

Merrick, Jeffrey. "Chaussons in the Streets: Sodomy in Seventeenth-Century Paris." *Journal of the History of Sexuality* 15 (May 2006): 167–203.

———. "Sodomitical Scandals and Subcultures in the 1720s." *Men and Masculinities* 1 (1999): 365–84.

Micheler, Stefan. *Selbstbilder und Fremdbilder der "Anderen": Eine Geschichte männerbegehrende Männer in der Weimarer Republik und in der NS-Zeit*. Constance, 2005.

Mildenberger, Florian. "'Verjüngung' und 'Heilung' der Homosexualität: Eugen Steinach in seiner Zeit." *Zeitschrift für Sexualforschung* 15 (2002): 302–22.

Mouton, Michelle. *From Nurturing the Nation to Purifying the Volk: Weimar and Nazi Family Policy, 1918–1945*. Washington, DC, and New York, 2007.

Müller, Klaus. *Aber in meinem Herzen sprach eine Stimme so laut: Homosexuelle Autobiographien und medizinische Pathographien im neunzehnten Jahrhundert*. Berlin, 1991.

Murray, Jacqueline, and Konrad Eisenbichler. *Desire and Discipline: Sex and Sexuality in the Premodern West*. Toronto, 1996.

Najmabadi, Afsaneh. *Women with Mustaches and Men without Beards: Gender and Sexual Anxieties of Iranian Modernity*. Berkeley, CA, 2005.

Naphy, William. *Born to Be Gay: A History of Homosexuality*. Stroud, 2004.

Nowacki, Bernd. *Der Bund für Mutterschutz (1905–1933)*. Husum, 1983.

O'Leary, Timothy. *Foucault: The Art of Ethics*. London and New York, 2002.

Oosterhuis, Harry. *Stepchildren of Nature: Krafft-Ebing, Psychiatry, and the Making of Sexual Identity*. Chicago, 2000.

Ostwald, Hans. *Männliche Prostitution*. Leipzig, 1906. Repr. *Männliche Prostitution im kaiserlichen Berlin*. Berlin, 1991.

Peukert, Detlev J. K. *Grenzen der Sozialdisziplinierung: Aufstieg und Krise der deutschen Jugendfürsorge von 1878 bis 1932*. Cologne, 1986.

Phillips, Kim M., and Barry Reay, eds. *Sexuality in History: A Reader*. New York, 2002.

Puff, Helmut. "Localizing Sodomy: The 'Priest and Sodomite' in Pre-Reformation Germany and Switzerland." *Journal of the History of Sexuality* 8 (1997): 165–95.

———. *Sodomy in Reformation Germany and Switzerland, 1400–1600*. Chicago, 2003.

Rajchman, John. *Michel Foucault: The Freedom of Philosophy.* New York, 1985.

———. *Truth and Eros: Foucault, Lacan, and the Question of Ethics.* New York, 1991.

Reagin, Nancy. "'A True Woman Can Take Care of Herself': The Debate over Prostitution in Hanover, 1906." *Central European History* 24, no. 4 (1991): 347–80.

Roper, Lyndal. "'The Common Man,' 'The Common Good,' 'Common Women': Reflections on Gender and Meaning in the Reformation German Commune." *Social History* 12 (1987): 1–21.

———. "Gender and the Reformation." *Archiv für Reformationsgeschichte* 92 (2001): 290–302.

———. *The Holy Household: Women and Morals in Reformation Augsburg.* Oxford, 1989.

———. "Jenseits des Linguistic Turn." *Historische Anthropologie* 3 (1999): 452–66.

———. *Oedipus and the Devil: Witchcraft, Sexuality, and Religion in Early Modern Europe.* London, 1994.

———. *Witch Craze: Terror and Fantasy in Baroque Germany.* New Haven, 2004.

Rubin, Gayle. "Thinking Sex: Notes for a Radical Theory of the Politics of Sexuality." In *Pleasure and Danger: Exploring Female Sexuality,* edited by Carole Vance. London, 1984.

Rublack, Ulinka. *The Crimes of Women in Early Modern Germany.* Oxford, 1999.

———. "Fluxes: The Early Modern Body and the Emotions." *History Workshop Journal* 53 (2002): 1–16.

———. "Pregnancy, Childbirth and the Female Body in Early Modern Germany." *Past and Present* 150 (1996): 84–100.

———. "Wench and Maiden: Women, War and the Pictorial Function of the Feminine in German Cities in the Early Modern Period." *History Workshop Journal* 44 (1997): 1–22.

———, ed. *Gender in Early Modern German History.* Cambridge, 2002.

Rüling, Anna. "Welches Interesse hat die Frauenbewegung an der Lösung des homosexuellen Problems?" *Jahrbuch für sexuelle Zwischenstufen* 7 (1905): 131–51.

Runte, Annette. *Biographische Operationen: Diskurse der Transsexualität.* Munich, 1996.

Sarasin, Philipp. *Foucault und Darwin: Genealogie und Geschichte im Zeitalter der Biologie.* Frankfurt am Main, 2009.

———. *Michel Foucault zur Einführung.* 3rd ed. Hamburg, 2008.

———. *Reizbare Maschinen: Eine Geschichte des Körpers 1765–1914.* Frankfurt am Main, 2001.

Schader, Heike. *Virile, Vamps, und wilde Veilchen: Sexualität, Begehren und Erotik in den Zeitschriften homosexueller Frauen im Berlin der 1920er Jahre.* Königstein, 2004.

Schmidgen, Henning. *Das Unbewußte der Maschinen: Konzeptionen des Psychischen bei Guattari, Deleuze und Lacan.* Munich, 1997.

Schnell, Rüdiger. *Frauendiskurs, Männerdiskurs, Ehediskurs: Textsorten und Geschlechterkonzepte in Mittelalter und Früher Neuzeit.* Frankfurt am Main, 1998.

———. *Geschlechterbeziehungen und Textfunktionen: Studien zu Eheschriften der Frühen Neuzeit.* Tübingen, 1998.

———. *Text und Geschlecht: Mann und Frau in Eheschriften der frühen Neuzeit.* Frankfurt am Main, 1997.

Schoppmann, Claudia. *Days of Masquerade: Life Stories of Lesbians During the Third Reich.* Translated by Alison Brown. New York, 1996.

Schulte, Regina. *Sperrbezirke: Tugendhaftigkeit und Prostitution in der bürgerlichen Welt.* Frankfurt am Main, 1979.

———. *The Village in Court: Arson, Infanticide and Poaching in the Court Records of Upper Bavaria, 1848–1910.* Translated by Barrie Selman. Cambridge, 1994.

Schultz, James. *Courtly Love, the Love of Courtliness, and the History of Sexuality.* Chicago, 2006.

———. "Love without Desire in *Mären* of the Thirteenth and Fourteenth Centuries." In *Mittelalterliche Novellistik im europäischen Kontext: Kulturwissenschaftliche Perspektiven,* edited by Mark Chinca, Timo-Reuvekamp-Felber, and Christopher Young. *Beihefte zur Zeitschrift für deutsche Philologie* 13. Berlin, 2006.

Schumann, Rosemarie. "Helene Stöcker: Verkünderin und Verwirklicherin." In *Alternativen: Schicksale deutsche Bürger,* edited by Olaf Graf. Berlin, 1987.

Schuster, Beate. *Das Frauenhaus: Städtische Bordelle in Deutschland 1350–1600.* Paderborn, 1992.

———. *Die freien Frauen: Dirnen und Frauenhäuser im 15. und 16. Jahrhundert.* Frankfurt am Main, 1995.

Schwarz, Michael. *Sozialistische Eugenik: Eugenische Sozialtechnologien in Debatten und Politik der deutschen Sozialdemokratie 1890–1933.* Berlin, 1995.

Schwitter, Beatrice. "Sexualaufklärung als biographisches Element in brieflichen Narrationen." *Schweizerisches Archiv für Volkskunde* 104 (2008): 83–100.

Schwules Museum and Berlin Akademie der Künste, eds. *Goodbye to Berlin? 100 Jahre Schwulenbewegung. Eine Ausstellung.* Berlin, 1997.

Scribner, Robert W. *For the Sake of the Simple Folk: Popular Propaganda for the German Reformation.* Cambridge, 1981.

Sedgwick, Eve Kosofsky. *Epistemology of the Closet.* Berkeley, CA, 1990.

———. *Novel Gazing: Queer Reading in Fiction.* Durham, NC, 1997.

———. *Touching Feeling: Affect, Pedagogy, Performativity.* Durham, NC, 2003.

Setz, Wolfram, ed. *Homosexualität in der DDR: Materialien und Meinungen.* Hamburg, 2006.

Shepard, Alexandra. *Meanings of Manhood in Early Modern England.* Oxford, 2003.

Shephardson, Charles. "History and the Real: Foucault with Lacan." *Postmodern Culture* 5 no. 2 (1995), doi: 10.1353/pmc.1995.0015.

Sigusch, Volkmar. *Geschichte der Sexualwissenschaft.* Frankfurt am Main, 2008.

Sommer, Kai. *Die Strafbarkeit der Homosexualität von der Kaiserzeit bis zum Nationalsozialismus.* Frankfurt am Main, 1998.

Spector, Scott. "The Wrath of the 'Countess Merviola': Tabloid Exposé and the Emergence of Homosexual Subjects in Vienna in 1907." *Contemporary Austrian Studies* 15 (2007): 31–47.

Starn, Randolph. "The Early Modern Muddle." *Journal of Early Modern History* 6 (2002): 296–307.

Steakley, James. *The Homosexual Emancipation Movement in Germany.* New York, 1975.

Steidele, Angela. *In Männerkleidern: Das verwegene Leben der Catharina Margaretha Linck alias Anastasius Lagrantinus Rosenstengel, hingerichtete 1721.* Cologne, 2004.

Stieber, Wilhelm, and Hans Schneikert. *Praktische Lehrbuch der Kriminalpolizei.* Potsdam, 1921.

Stöcker, Helene. "Das Werden der sexuellen Reform seit hundert Jahren." *Ehe? Zur Reform der sexuellen Moral.* Berlin, 1911.

———. *Die Frau und die Heiligkeit des Lebens.* Leipzig, 1921.

———. *Die Liebe und die Frauen.* Minden, 1906.

———. *Erotik und Altruismus.* Leipzig, 1924.

———. "Zur Reform der sexuellen Ethik." *Mutterschutz* 1, no. 1 (1905): 4–6.

Stolberg, Michael. "A Woman Down to Her Bones: The Anatomy of Sexual Difference in the Sixteenth and Early Seventeenth Centuries." *Isis* 94 (2003): 274–99.

Stoler, Ann Laura. *Carnal Knowledge and Imperial Power: Race and the Intimate in Colonial Rule.* Berkeley, CA, 2002.

———. *Race and the Education of Desire: Foucault's History of Sexuality and the Colonial Order of Things.* Durham, 1995.

Strasser, Ulrike. *State of Virginity: Gender, Religion, and Politics in an Early Modern Catholic State.* Ann Arbor, 2004.

Surkis, Judith. *Sexing the Citizen: Morality and Masculinity in Third Republic France.* Ithaca, NY, 2006.

Theweleit, Klaus. *Männerphantasien.* Basel and Frankfurt am Main, 1986. English: *Male Fantasies: Women, Floods, Bodies in History.* Translated by Stephen Conway in collaboration with Erica Carter and Chris Turner. 2 vols. Minneapolis, 1987.

Thies, Ralph. *Ethnograph des dunklen Berlin: Hans Ostwald und die "Großstadt-Dokument" (1904–1908).* Cologne, 2006.

Timm, Annette F. "The Legacy of *Bevölkerungspolitik*: Venereal Disease Control and Marriage Counselling in Post–WW II Berlin." *Canadian Journal of History / Annales canadiennes d'histoire* 33 (1998): 173–214.

Tobin, Robert. *Warm Brothers: Queer Theory and the Age of Goethe.* Philadelphia, 2000.

Traub, Valerie. "The Present Future of Lesbian Historiography." In *A Companion to Lesbian, Gay, Bisexual, Transgender, and Queer Studies,* edited by George E. Haggerty and Molly McGarry. Oxford, 2007.

———. *The Renaissance of Lesbianism in Early Modern England.* Cambridge, 2002.

Trumbach, Randolph. "Blackmail for Sodomy in Eighteenth-Century London." In "Eighteenth-Century Homosexuality in Global Perspective," edited by Bryant T. Ragan Jr. and Jeffrey Merrick. Special issue, *Historical Reflections / Réflexions Historiques* 33 (Spring 2007): 23–39.

———. *Sex and the Gender Revolution,* vol. 1, *Heterosexuality and the Third Gender in Enlightenment London.* Chicago, 1999.

Ulrichs, Karl Heinrich. *The Riddle of 'Man-Manly' Love: The Pioneering Work on Male Homosexuality,* vol. 1. Translated by Michael A. Lombardi-Nash. Buffalo, 1994.

Usborne, Cornelia. *The Politics of the Body in Weimar Germany: Women's Reproductive Rights and Duties.* Ann Arbor, 1992.

Vicinus, Martha. "Lesbian History: All Theory and No Facts or All Facts and No Theory?" *Radical History Review* 60 (1994): 57–75.

von Bockel, Rolf. *Philosophin einer "neuen Ethik": Helene Stöcker (1869–1943).* Hamburg, 1991.

von Ehrenfels, Christian. *Grundbegriffe der Ethik.* Wiesbaden, 1907.

von Krafft-Ebing, Richard. *Psychopathia Sexualis.* 8th ed. Stuttgart, 1893.

von Soden, Kristine. *Die Sexualberatungsstellen der Weimarer Republik 1919–1933.* Berlin, 1988.

Walkowitz, Judith. *City of Dreadful Delight: Narraties of Sexual Danger in Late-Victorian London.* Chicago, 1992.

Weeks, Jeffrey. *Against Nature: Essays on History, Sexuality, and Identity.* London, 1991.

———. *Sex, Politics, and Society: The Regulation of Sexuality since 1800.* London, 1989.

———. *Sexuality.* 2nd ed. New York, 2003.

Wegert, Karl. *Popular Culture, Crime and Social Control in 18ᵗʰ Century Württemberg.* Stuttgart, 1994.

Weindling, Paul. *Health, Race and German Politics between National Unification and Nazism, 1870–1945.* Cambridge, 1989.

Weingart, Peter, Jürgen Kroll, and Kurt Bayertz. *Rasse, Blut und Gene: Geschichte der Eugenik und Rassenhygiene in Deutschland.* 3rd ed. Frankfurt am Main, 2005.

Wickert, Christl. *Helene Stöcker, 1869–1943: Frauenrechtlerin, Sexualreformerin und Pazifistin. Eine Biographie.* Bonn, 1991.

Widder, Michaela. *Frauen unter Kontrolle: Prostitution und ihre staatliche Bekämpfung in Hamburg vom Ende des Kaiserreichs bis zu den Anfängen der Bundesrepublik.* Münster, 2003.

Wiesner-Hanks, Merry E. *Christianity and Sexuality in the Early Modern World: Regulating Desire, Reforming Practise.* London, 2000.

Wunder, Heide. *He Is the Sun, She Is the Moon: Women in Early Modern Germany.* Translated by Thomas Cunlap. Cambridge, MA, 1998.

Zeeland, Steven. *Military Trade.* New York, 1999.

Ze'evi, Dror. *Producing Desire: Changing Sexual Discourse in the Ottoman Middle East, 1500–1900.* Berkeley, CA, 2006.

Žižek, Slavoj. "The Seven Veils of Fantasy." In S. Žižek, *The Plague of Fantasies.* London, 1997.

———. *The Sublime Object of Ideology.* London, 1989.

———. *The Ticklish Subject: The Absent Centre of Political Ontology.* London, 1999.

zur Nieden, Susanne, ed. *Homosexualität und Staatsräson: Männlichkeit, Homophobie und Politik in Deutschland 1900–1945.* Frankfurt am Main, 2005.

∻ CONTRIBUTORS ∽

Robert Beachy is Associate Professor of History at Goucher College. He received his doctorate from the University of Chicago in 1998 and is the author of *German Civil Wars: Nation Building and Historical Memory, 1756–1914*, with James Retallack (under contract with Oxford UP 2014), and *The Soul of Commerce: Credit, Property and Politics in Leipzig, 1750–1840* (Brill 2005). He has also edited a number of essay collections. His current project is *Gay Berlin and the Origins of Homosexuality, 1852–1933* (in preparation).

Dagmar Herzog is Professor of History and Daniel Rose Faculty Scholar at the Graduate Center, City University of New York. She is the author of *Sex in Crisis: The New Sexual Revolution and the Future of American* Politics (2009), *Sex after Fascism: Memory and Morality in Twentieth-Century Germany* (2005), and *Intimacy and Exclusion: Religious Politics in Pre-Revolutionary Baden* (1996) and the editor of *Lessons and Legacies VII: The Holocaust in International Perspective* (2006). She is currently writing a history of sexuality in twentieth-century Europe for Cambridge University Press.

Erik Huneke is a Ph.D. candidate in history at the University of Michigan, Ann Arbor. His dissertation is entitled "The Sexual Valence of Socialist Morality: Defining Normalcy and Deviance in the German Democratic Republic, 1949–1989." His research has been supported by grants from the Berlin Program for Advanced German and European Studies and the Academic Foundation of the Berlin State Parliament.

Andreas Krass is Professor of Medieval German Literature at the Goethe University in Frankfurt am Main. He is author of *Meerjungfrauen: Geschichten einer unmöglichen Liebe* (2010), *Geschriebene Kleider: Höfische Identität als literarisches Spiel* (2006), and *Stabat mater dolorosa: Lateinische Überlieferung und volkssprachliche Übertragungen im deutschen Mittelalter* (1998) and the editor of *Queer Studies in Deutschland: Interdisziplinäre Beiträge zur Kritischen Heteronormativitätsforschung* (2009) and *Queer denken: Gegen die Ordnung der Sexualität* (2003). He is also the co-editor of *Tinte und Blut: Politik, Erotik und Poetik des Martyriums* (2008) and *Bündnis und Begehren: Ein Symposium über die Liebe* (2002). He is currently writing a book on the literary history of male friendship (*Männerfreundschaft: Geschichten einer Passion*) for S. Fischer Verlag, Frankfurt am Main.

Kirsten Leng completed her Ph.D. in the joint doctoral program in history and women's studies at the University of Michigan in 2011 and is currently a postdoctoral fellow in sexuality studies at Northwestern University. She has received support and prizes from the Social Sciences and Humanities Research Council (Canada), the German Academic Exchange Service, and the International Institute at the University of Michigan, among others. Her contribution is related to her dissertation, which was nominated for a Pro-Quest Distinguished Dissertation Award, titled "Contesting the Laws of Life: Feminism, Sexual Science, and Sexual Governance in Germany and Britain c. 1880–1914."

Marti M. Lybeck is Assistant Professor of History at the University of Wisconsin, La Crosse. Her dissertation was selected as 2009 best first manuscript in queer studies by SUNY Press and won the Fritz Stern Dissertation Prize of the German Historical Association. She is currently finishing a book manuscript titled *Desiring Emancipation: New Women and Homosexuality in Germany, 1890–1933*.

Tracie Matysik is Associate Professor in the Department of History at the University of Texas, Austin, where she teaches courses in European intellectual history. She is the author of *Reforming the Moral Subject: Ethics and Sexuality in Central Europe, 1890–1930* (Ithaca: Cornell University Press, 2008) and is currently writing a book on the history of Spinozism in modern German thought.

Florian G. Mildenberger is an independent scholar who lives in Berlin. His main interests are the history of sexuality and discourses about Darwinism and creationism in Germany. His *Habilitation* thesis, *Umwelt als Vision: Leben und Werk von Jakob v. Uexküll, 1864–1944*, was published in 2007 (Franz Steiner Verlag, Stuttgart). He is also the author of *...In der Richtung der Homosexualität verdorben: Psychiater, Kriminalpsychologen und Gerichtsmediziner über männliche Homosexualität 1850–1970* (2002) and *Allein unter Männern: Helene Stourzh-Anderle in ihrer Zeit (1890–1966)* (2004).

Massimo Perinelli is a research assistant at the University of Cologne, where he teaches American history as well as film and history, and where he received his doctorate in 2008. He is the author of *Liebe 47—Gesellschaft '49: Geschlechterverhältnisse in der deutschen Nachkriegszeit* (Hamburg 1999) and of *Fluchtlinien des Neorealismus: Der organlose Körper der italienischen Nachkriegszeit 1943–1949* (2009). He is also the co-editor of the series *Geschlecht – Kultur – Gesellschaft* (LIT-Verlag). In 2006 he co-organized and actively participated in the international conference *Animals in Film—a History of Mankind* in Cologne and is co-editor of the forthcoming book. He is currently working on a new project on governmentality and biopolitics in the progressive era.

Andreas Pretzel has been a researcher at the Research Unit for the History of Sexual Science in Berlin since 1992. He has led and guided many research projects on the persecution of homosexuals during the Holocaust and the fate of persecuted postwar homosexuals. Pretzel is one of the cofounders of the "Initiative Queer Nations," which aims to establish an institute for the study of homosexualities past and present in remembrance of the famous institute of Magnus Hirschfeld in Berlin, destroyed by the Nazis. His publications include *Wegen der zu erwartenden hohen Strafe* (2000) and *NS-Opfer unter Vorbehalt: Homosexuelle Männer in Berlin nach 1945* (2002).

Helmut Puff, Professor at the Department of History and the Department of Germanic Languages at the University of Michigan, Ann Arbor, works and publishes on history, literature, culture, gender, and sexuality in the late medieval and early modern periods, primarily in German-speaking Europe. His publications include *Sodomy in Reformation Germany and Switzerland, 1400–1600* (2003) and *Zwischen den Disziplinen? Perspektiven der Frühneuzeitforschung* (co-edited with Christopher Wild, 2003).

Julia Roos is Associate Professor of History at Indiana University, Bloomington. Her research focuses on the history of gender and sexuality in twentieth-century Germany, and she has published on prostitutes' movements and the conservative backlash against liberal prostitution reforms in the Weimar Republic. She is the author of *Weimar through the Lens of Gender: Prostitution Reform, Woman's Emancipation, and German Democracy, 1919–33* (Ann Arbor: University of Michigan Press, 2010). Her current research project examines the role of gender, nationalism, and propaganda in the 1920s campaign against France's colonial occupation troops in the Rhineland.

Ulinka Rublack is Reader of St. John's College and Lecturer in History at Cambridge University. Her work explores the social and cultural history of early modern Europe and the early modern German lands with a particular focus on issues of gender. Among her many publications are *The Crimes of Women in Early Modern Germany (1999)* and *Reformation Europe* (2004). She also edited a volume entitled *Gender in Early Modern Germany* (2002) and *A Concise Companion to History* (2011). Her latest monograph, *Dressing Up: Cultural Identity in Renaissance Europe* (2010), received the Roland H. Bainton Prize.

Philipp Sarasin is Professor of Modern History at the History Department of the University of Zurich, Switzerland, and director of the Centre "History of Knowledge" (Zurich University and the Federal Institute of Technology, Zurich). His recent books are *Anthrax: Bioterror as Fact and Fantasy* (Cambridge: Harvard UP 2006) and *Michel Foucault zur Einführung* (Hamburg: Junius 2005). He has published on the history of the body and sexuality, on bourgeois culture in late nineteenth century, and on the theory of historiography. His current research on the history of popular science in the late twentieth century focuses on the impact of biology and sociobiology on European culture during the Cold War.

Jeffrey Schneider is Associate Professor of German Studies at Vassar College, where he also teaches women's studies and queer studies. He is currently completing a book manuscript entitled *Uniform Fantasies: The Militarization of Masculinity and Male Desire in Imperial Germany.*

Scott Spector is Professor in the Department of History and Professor and Chair of Germanic Languages and Literatures at the University of Michigan, Ann Arbor. His book *Prague Territories: National Conflict and Cultural Innovation in Franz Kafka's Fin de Siècle* won the DAAD/GSA Prize for best history book in German studies in the years 1999–2000. His forthcoming book, entitled *Violent Sensations: Sexuality, Crime, and Utopia in Vienna and Berlin, 1860–1914*, concerns sexual and criminal identities and concomitant cultural fantasies of violence in modern German-speaking central Europe.

Robert Deam Tobin holds the Henry J. Leir Chair in Foreign Cultures at Clark University, where he researches German literature and its relationship to medicine, sexuality, gender, and the body. He is the author of two books: *Warm Brothers: Queer Theory and the Age of Goethe* (2000) and *Doctor's Orders: Goethe and Enlightenment Thought* (2001). He has also co-edited *A Song for Europe: Popular Music and Politics in the Eurovision Song Contest* (2007). Currently, he is completing a book on the emergence of modern vocabularies of sexuality in nineteenth- and early twentieth-century German-speaking central Europe.

Merry Wiesner-Hanks is a Distinguished Professor and Chair of the History Department at the University of Wisconsin-Milwaukee. Her recent publications include *Early Modern Europe, 1450–1789* (Cambridge History of Europe, vol. 2, 2006), *Gender in History: Global Perspectives* (2nd ed. 2001), and *Christianity and Sexuality in the Early Modern World: Regulating Desire, Reforming Practice* (2nd ed. 2010). She is the Senior Editor of *The Sixteenth Century Journal*, one of the editors of *Journal of Global History*, and the editor-in-chief of the forthcoming *Cambridge History of the World*.

~: INDEX :~

Enlightenment, 80, 81, 82, 84, 86
Erotik und Altruismus (Stöcker), 190,
192–93
eugenics, 193, 216–17, 220, 223, 227,
232, 234
European Court of Human Rights, 283
"euthanasia," 218
Essentialism, 4, 22
experience, 52, 53–54, 57, 59

Federal Republic of Germany, 222, 224,
226, 260
female genital cutting, 284
femininity, 35, 44, 45, 47, 48, 49, 50,
51–52, 56, 58
feminism
of 1910s–1920s, 187–93, 232
of 1960s–1970s, 183, 269–73,
275–77, 285
of 2000s, 284
Fliess, Wilhelm, 191
Flexner, Abraham, 117
Foucauldianism, 6–7, 12
Foucault, Michel, 110–111, 120, 140–41,
146, 152, 159, 166, 184, 285–86
and biopolitics, 241, 251
and chronology, 15, 31, 32, 37, 43,
50, 58, 78
and critique of liberationist
rhetoric, 285
and deployment of sexuality,
63–66, 78
and disciplinary mechanisms, 185,
198
and ethics, 195, 197
and heterotopia, 249, 278
and imbrication of power and
knowledge, 226–27
and imbrication of power and
speech, 250, 285–86
and "polysexuality," 278
and subjecthood, 45, 185–86, 197,
285
and the construction of "sex" as
something desirable, 282, 285
and "the repressive hypothesis,"
213, 285–86
as historian, 15

as orientation for historical
scholarship, 240–41
invoked as moral authority by
critics of "sexualization," 183,
275
on homosexuals, 18, 24–25, 27,
86–87n1
Fragen und Antworten (Neubert), 235
Frankfurt am Main, 139, 140, 150–51
Frankfurt Broads' Council (Frankfurter
Weiberrat), 269–70
Frankfurt School, 240
Freundin, Die, 156–157, 160
Freccero, Carla, 20, 23, 32
Freud, Sigmund, 184, 191–92, 194–95,
203, 237, 248, 252, 286
Frevert, Ute, 125, 133–34
friendship, 17, 26–28, 85, 168n27, 299

Galenic medicine, 49
Garçonne, 156, 161
gay rights movement, 103, 270, 282
Geis, Rudolf, 204–205
gender inversion, 84
genealogies, 2, 5
German Democratic Republic, 4, 216–27,
231–42, 283
German History, 6
German League for the Reform of
Criminal Justice (Deutscher Bund für
Strafreform), 147
German National People's Party
(Deutschnationale Volkspartei), 144
German Society for Sexual Research
(Deutsche Gesellschaft für
Sexualforschung), 223
German Studies Association, 6
Geßner, Heinrich, 80
Giessen, 208
Gilligan, Carol, 54–55
Glarus, 78
Gleixner, Ulrike, 51
Goethe, Johann Wolfgang von, 89n41
Goldberg, Jonathan, 23, 24
Goldstone, Jack, 33
Gottfried von Straßburg, 72
Götz, Franziska, 219
Grandvilliers, Jean de, 79

www.ingramcontent.com/pod-product-compliance
Lightning Source LLC
Chambersburg PA
CBHW060027030426
42334CB00019B/2209